D0081294

Courtyards, Markets, City Streets

Urban Women in Africa

edited by

KATHLEEN SHELDON

WestviewPress
A Division of HarperCollinsPublishers

HQ
1787
. C68
1996

BRADFORD COLLEGE

NOV 7 1997

EBC   23170

LIBRARY

All rights reserved. Printed in the United States of America. No part of this publication may be reproduced or transmitted in any form or by any means, electronic or mechanical, including photocopy, recording, or any information storage and retrieval system, without permission in writing from the publisher.

Copyright © 1996 by Westview Press, A Division of HarperCollins Publishers, Inc.

Published in 1996 in the United States of America by Westview Press, 5500 Central Avenue, Boulder, Colorado 80301-2877, and in the United Kingdom by Westview Press, 12 Hid's Copse Road, Cumnor Hill, Oxford OX2 9JJ

A CIP catalog record for this book is available from the Library of Congress.
ISBN 0-8133-8685-3—0-8133-8686-1 (pbk.)

This book was typeset by Letra Libre, 1705 Fourteenth Street, Suite 391, Boulder, Colorado 80302.

The paper used in this publication meets the requirements of the American National Standard for Permanence of Paper for Printed Library Materials Z39.48-1984.

10   9   8   7   6   5   4   3   2   1

ENDICOTT
COLLEGE

LIBRARY

Beverly, Massachusetts

Courtyards,
Markets,
City Streets

Contents

Preface

In 1982 I arrived in Beira, Mozambique, ready to begin research on the history of Mozambican women. Although women were nearly invisible in published materials on Beira, I was determined to learn how they had contributed to that city's history. As I focused on women and work, I began to recognize that an understanding of women's employment patterns offered a new interpretation of urban development in the city as a whole. Those urban Mozambican women who shared their stories with me in the midst of war and hunger are the instigators of this project.

The collection of essays presented here began to take shape when I organized a panel on urban women and work at the U.S. African Studies Association (ASA) meeting in 1989 and subsequently arranged for a second ASA panel on women in the urban environment in 1991. It became clear that researchers were already pursuing this issue even though there was no coherent guide to the topic. Karen Tranberg Hansen, Jeanne Nanitelamio, Claire Robertson, and Aili Mari Tripp, all contributors to this volume, participated on those panels. Panel members Gracia Clark, Jane Parpart, and Christine Sylvester encouraged me as well. I have particularly enjoyed continuing support from Barbara Ellington, our editor at Westview Press, an advocate of this endeavor from the beginning. Many other colleagues shared ideas about the content and suggested possible contributors.

In June 1994 I received funding to travel to Nairobi for an International Seminar on Gender, Urbanization and Environment. The meeting was sponsored by the International Sociological Association, the Mazingira Institute, and the United Nations section on Habitat (UNCHS). Seminar organizer Diana Lee-Smith and other participants were enthusiastic about this volume and gave me constructive feedback on Chapter 1, which I presented there.

Chapter 1 was further improved by critiques from Dorothy Mc-Cormick, Claire Robertson, Brooke Grundfest Schoepf, Steve Tarzynski,

Aili Mari Tripp, and, especially, Karen Tranberg Hansen and the outside reader. Collectively, they saved me from misstatements and overgeneralizations, though as usual, those faults that remain are my responsibility.

The Ford Foundation supported this book with an individual grant for the editorial expenses that resulted from coordinating the work of contributors located in many corners of the world. This funding enabled me to engage Laura Mitchell to translate the French chapters and Chase Langford to design the map. Kelvin Kao at the University of California, Los Angeles, who was working on the Marcus Garvey Papers Project, provided essential last-minute technical assistance. I have also appreciated being a research scholar at UCLA's Center for the Study of Women, which facilitated access to many of UCLA's resources.

I hope that this collection will prove useful to all of those who helped it come into existence and that scholars, planners, and women in Africa will recognize the essential role urban women have played in developing African cities.

Kathleen Sheldon

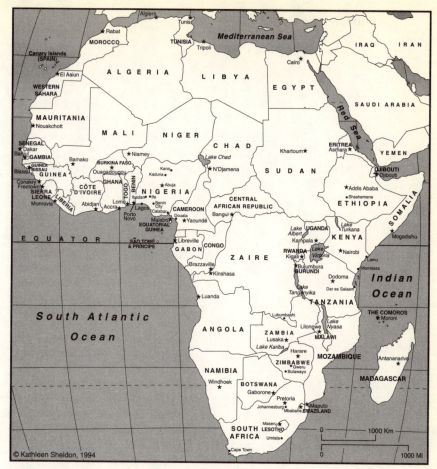

African national capitals and cities germane to the text.

© Kathleen Sheldon, 1994

Part One

Introduction

1 ☙

Urban African Women: Courtyards, Markets, City Streets

KATHLEEN SHELDON

Women have resided in African cities for as long as cities have existed. They have engaged in a wide variety of livelihoods to support themselves and their families. Whether living with men, married to them, or living alone, women have usually borne the primary responsibility for raising children. They have established households that showed continuity as well as change from rural family formations. In addition, they have participated in politics, religious organizations, and other community activities, contributing to the development of distinctively African cities. Women's urban experiences have varied over time and across geographic space, but they have always been an integral component and sometimes the dynamizing factor in African urban life. The contributors to this volume demonstrate how cities and the process of urbanization have been influenced by women's presence; how urban living has affected women's family life, work, and community efforts; and what great variety there has been in these influences and efforts. The contributors also help us move toward a new understanding of the processes of urbanization in Africa: Neither cities nor women remained unchanged once women settled in urban areas.

The tempo of urbanization has accelerated markedly in the last few decades of the twentieth century, and Africa is now the world area with the fastest rate of urbanization. This is evident not only in capital cities and sprawling urban settlements such as Nairobi, Kenya, and Lagos, Nigeria, but also in secondary cities that increasingly provide a regional urban focus. About 30 to 35 percent of all Africans (including North Africans) lived in cities in 1980, an increase from 13 percent in 1950, and this figure was expected to reach 50 percent by 1990 (Gilbert and Gugler 1992:8, Rondinelli 1988). Zambia, one of the most urbanized African countries, already counts nearly 50 percent of its population as residing in cities (Munachonga 1988:173). Yet Africa is still the world's least urbanized region; Lagos was the only sub-Saharan city to appear in the top twenty megacities in the world (United Nations statistics, cited in Linden 1993). Africa's urban population jumped from under 30 million in 1950 to well over 125 million in 1984 (Mabogunje 1990:121). Much of that growth is now a result of urban births, as migration from rural to urban areas has slowed during recent economically difficult times. Although statistics on urban growth are scarce after 1984, it is clear that cities have continued to expand, often beyond the capacity of their infrastructure or governments to manage with ease.

The contributors to this book take a gendered approach to the process of urbanization. Urbanization for African women has meant both new opportunities not available in the rural areas and continued limitations based on sex and class. The diverse contributions from historians, political scientists, demographers, geographers, and anthropologists found in this volume underline the variety as well as the commonalities of African urban experience, the possibilities as well as the restrictions.

Although the development of African urban research has been thoroughly discussed elsewhere (Coquery-Vidrovitch 1991; Magobunje 1990), women and gender have rarely held center stage in accounts of urban analytic issues. If referred to, women and gender relations have been discussed mainly as "add-ons." Earlier studies were especially prone to categorize women in the circumscribed terms of their attachment to men (a noted example of this approach was Little 1973). Even recent overviews in African urban studies include scanty information on women, thus reinforcing the traditionally dominant view that women have been marginal to African urban studies, if not to the cities themselves (Becker, Hamer, and Morrison 1994; Wekwete 1992). This volume has been conceived to present all areas of women's lives as central to an understanding of urban Africa and to suggest how the concerns of women can be integrated into African urban studies.

In an early discussion of African urbanism, Akin Mabogunje argued that "cities are essentially the points of articulation of an economic system" (Mabogunje 1968:22). Three economic characteristics marked the development of African cities in particular, and though Mabogunje did not emphasize women's participation, the characteristics he delineated clearly demonstrate that women were at the center of the process of urbanization. The three fundamental features of urbanization were (1) a surplus of agricultural production to support an urban class of specialists, (2) a group in power to control the distribution of that surplus, and (3) a class of traders to transmit food and other supplies to those who needed them (Mabogunje 1968:35). As women have long played central roles as farmers and traders in Africa, their contributions lie at the root of African urbanization despite their exclusion from centers of power. This is especially clear in the history of West African cities, where women traders were an essential force in urban development, but the pattern holds true in other regions as well. Because women cultivated the food that sustained the urban community and actively marketed that food as well as other supplies, cities could grow quickly and urban communities could exhibit the vitality that marks them today.

Cities offer new opportunities for success for some people, but they only transform the difficulties of others. The presence of gender, ethnic, and class hierarchies have limited women's options in countless ways. Women in some areas were restricted from migrating to the cities, and in most cities they faced obstacles to working for a wage, so the development of an urban waged working class was primarily a male experience. Women worked in cities but not in ways that fit into existing ideas about workers and developing classes. The key to determining their class position has thus sometimes eluded analysts. Some of the important factors in developing a realistic gendered approach to class position include assessing women's access to critical resources such as education, land, and labor; illuminating the complexity of their dependency on men; and interpreting the ways that women have organized along gender lines (Robertson and Berger 1986). In the urban setting, these guidelines shift the focus from male waged work as the essential form of urban labor to the wide range of female and male economic activities.

The intersection of rural African ideologies with Western beliefs has been most dramatic in the urban areas. Some of the women who came to the cities hoped to create new lives for themselves, free from rural patriarchy. Others based their urban practices on their rural skills as farmers, traders, and preparers of food. That the urban reality contained its own forms of restrictive patriarchy did not detract from women's hopes for a better life or from their efforts to survive in the city. Urban women developed alternative family configurations, established new areas of work and employment, and expanded their political and religious involvement. Urban areas, with their ongoing struggles, offered women new possibilities for work, family, and community that rural areas could not.

Migration and Urbanization

The history of urban migration from the women's point of view is complex and barely uncovered. Cities have often been presented as male domains that were dangerous for women or as the abode of women who were themselves dangerous. This interpretation was based in part on demographic evidence. In Africa, some urban populations were primarily, and sometimes overwhelmingly, male throughout the colonial era, though West African cities have long had a large female population. Whereas urban centers established under European colonialism tended to be predominantly male (for example, Nairobi; Harare, Zimbabwe; and Windhoek, Namibia), old cities with long-established populations had nearly equal numbers of resident men and women (Accra, Ghana; Dakar, Senegal; Lomé, Togo; and Porto-Novo, Benin, among others). Since independence, it appears that the numbers of men and women in African cities have been approaching parity across the continent (Gugler 1989:349).

In the first decades of the twentieth century, a policy of excluding women was consciously enforced by the colonialists in southern and eastern Africa, who assumed that low male wages would be supplemented by women's rural agricultural production and who "repatriated" urban women to rural areas on a regular basis. The establishment of new urban centers in settler societies was founded on the idea of the city as a European settlement, with the Africans, both men and women, present as temporary laborers. This idea also meant that proper African female behavior included rural residence; African women in town were considered a threat to the evolving patriarchal order and were therefore subject to severe restrictions.

Despite these obstacles, women began moving to urban areas during the early years of colonialism. Their options were determined in part by the local geography, as they chose to move to a major urban center or to a smaller regional city. The relative poverty of a woman's rural home region also affected her decision to migrate; women from impoverished rural districts were more likely to settle in the urban areas. Women often saw migration to a city as a way to improve their own situation and take control of their own future.

In Chapter 2, Sean Redding presents the experience of women in Umtata, South Africa. Rather than the larger cities of Johannesburg or Pretoria, Umtata, a small city in the Transkeian region, was a focal point for women leaving the rural areas. It was easier for these women to move to a smaller city closer to their home regions and make a more gradual transition to urban living. The forces that affected women's decisions to migrate included increased poverty in the rural areas and the perception of expanded opportunities in Umtata, but the precipitating event that led women to migrate was frequently a personal difficulty or family conflict. Thus, the intersection of various social and economic conditions was key to these women's migration histories.

Claire C. Robertson, in Chapter 3, analyzes Kikuyu women's movement into Nairobi, where many worked as street and market traders and confronted attempts by the colonial government to control them and their work. Robertson shows how the effort to control female Kikuyu traders shifted from a focus on women themselves to a class-based desire to control itinerant street vendors, whether male or female. In the course of this discussion, Robertson highlights the changing relationship between African men and colonial men. African men sometimes concurred with European colonial officials' efforts to control women's freedom of movement; at times, African and colonial men worked together to maintain African male authority over women. At other times, there were conflicts as African men observed their control over women being eroded by colonial state actions. Officials in colonial Nairobi permitted women to settle permanently, but some rural African male elders insisted that *they*, not colonial officials, should issue travel permits for women. Robertson provides us with a nuanced understanding of the issues of control over women, their entrance into urban areas, and their ability to support themselves in colonial settler cities.

The experience in West Africa was markedly different, as that region contained many centuries-old cities where women had long been resident and active in trade and other pursuits. Even newer cities drew on that history of female urban activity as they developed. In Chapter 4, Catherine M. Coles discusses Hausa women in Kaduna, Nigeria, within the context of a family history. Hajiya, the oldest woman whose history is presented, came to Kaduna from Kano with her husband as part of a large group of settlers. Her story as a family leader and midwife in the community illustrates women's involvement in the development of a new city. Hajiya's daughter and granddaughter actively sought less traditional types of work and family organization, including a reduced adherence to seclusion that reflected the increasingly urban focus of their lives. Coles demonstrates how women's experiences changed over time and over generations. As the city of Kaduna developed, the common urban experience of increased options for work, community involvement, and family life is clearly shown through the lives of Hajiya and her descendants.

It was most common for women to move to a nearby urban area in the country of their birth. With this pattern, it remained easy to visit relatives in rural areas, to cultivate land held outside the city, or to return to one's home village for important social rituals such as births, marriages, and funerals. With the absence of industrialization in most of Africa, cities remained solidly part of a primarily rural economy and society, and women played a central role in developing ties between rural and urban areas. In one example, the high proportion of young women in some West African towns has been attributed to the migration of women into the city to marry and their return to the adjacent agricultural villages as they age (Watts 1983).

Women also traveled to neighboring countries when improved economic opportunities arose. Women from Mozambique were known as beer brewers at the mines in South Africa, many of the prostitutes in Nairobi were from Tanzania, and women from Zaire traveled to Zambia to seek work. Female migration also varied along ethnic lines. For example, prostitutes in Dar es Salaam, Tanzania, were predominantly Haya, which reflected Haya women's inability to inherit land and the resulting difficulties they had in supporting themselves in the rural areas. In Ethiopia, Amharic women were found to be much more active than other groups, both as migrants to the city of Shashemene and in the economic life of the city after they arrived. This reflected the tendency for more literate and higher social status Amharic women to migrate to the urban areas in the 1960s and 1970s when the research was conducted (Bjerén 1985).

Although many women moved to urban areas with a husband or other kin, this was not true of all women. In Nigeria, one-half of the women interviewed in Benin City in 1980 came with a husband, and one-fifth accompanied their parents. A further one-fifth came primarily for a job or for further education (Okojie 1984). An overview of the reasons for urban migration across the continent in the early 1980s indicated that about one-half of African women came to the city for economic reasons (including schooling), whereas just over one-third came for family reasons (primarily for marriage or with their husbands) (Findley 1989). In an interesting variation, statistics from Nigeria indicated a growing trend for older people, especially mothers, to move to the city to join their adult children who were urban residents (Peil, Ekpenyong, and Oyeneye 1988).

A less common but still potent rural difficulty that encouraged women as well as men to migrate to urban areas was political unrest. The Nigerian civil war in the late 1960s, the independence struggle in Zimbabwe in the 1970s, and the postindependence war in Mozambique during the 1980s drastically increased the numbers of urban dwellers. Although men and entire families also came to the city under these conditions, men were more likely to join the fighting, leaving women to make their own way to the cities.

Much is still unknown about such salient issues as the distances traveled, patterns of migration to smaller and larger cities, and the reasons for women joining husbands or female kin such as sisters or aunts. In the 1980s, urban migrants have included increasing numbers of women who were unmarried, had no children, had attended school, and were in their twenties. Thus, younger single women currently dominate the population of urban migrants. Whatever their motives, women who have migrated to urban centers have had a deep impact on urbanization, a process that has depended on women's contributions and abilities.

Courtyards: Marriage, Family, and Housing

Urban African women and their families found a wide range of options available in the cities, choices that were in some cases unthinkable in the rural areas. Although most women still married and raised children within that marriage and many of the migrant women arrived in the city with their husbands and families, city life included new arrangements of various kinds. For women who lived in female-headed households or lived on their own, these choices could be the result of ongoing struggles. Married women also faced new structures of authority and situations that required sharing decisionmaking with their husbands, which at times produced conflict when men refused to accept relationships based on equality desired by women. Women's needs and desires shaped urban family life in ways that are still contested.

The families and households in which urban women lived vividly demonstrated some of the differences between rural and urban living. In many African countries, a marrying couple could choose between customary marriage and statutory marriage, a monogamous legal form of marriage introduced under colonialism and often associated with Christianity. Colonial education emphasized women's responsibility for domestic chores and was intended to impart European values about motherhood, marriage, and family to educated African women. Elite African women were more affected by this; while some women were cooking at kitchen stoves under European colonial supervision and approval, others were barely managing to survive by selling sex and domestic services along the margins of urban society. Yet no matter which marital form was followed or how Western their household, women found themselves negotiating to protect and improve their position.

Karen Tranberg Hansen, in Chapter 5, describes the way in which conjugal conflict was presented in urban courts in Zambia, where judges tried to accommodate both established expectations about marriage and the modern reality of poverty-stricken urban living. The language used in court and the decisions that were rendered there dramatically illustrate the continuing redefinition of family life and marriage in the city.

This constant struggle over proper behavior and responsibilities in urban marriages has been reflected in a number of earlier studies. One report on families in Accra in 1967–1968 indicated that women who had education or income in the same range as their husbands or who were close in age to their husbands were likely to have a greater say in family decisionmaking (Oppong 1970). Urban middle-class families in Nairobi in 1979 usually pooled their money when both husband and wife earned incomes, though husbands were more likely to keep a larger portion of their income for their personal use. Decisionmaking, especially regarding financial issues, was male-dominated, and women had primary responsibility for household chores. Although there was a greater tendency for urban than for rural couples to practice a pattern of shared decisionmaking, urban women had fewer areas in which they made unilateral decisions affecting the household (Stichter 1988). Similarly, educated urban Ijo women in Nigeria in monogamous, nuclear families faced an erosion of domestic power when compared with rural Ijo women (Hollos 1991).

Changes in marriage practices, male and female work, and household responsibilities forced couples to develop strategies for household support. Patterns of behavior in Lusaka, Zambia, mirrored other cities in the postcolonial era as women had greater responsibility for providing food for the family, though their work was rarely as remunerative as men's. Because men were not willing to let their wives control family budgets, there was continual negotiation between men and women to determine how best to support household needs, with much greater fluidity than in the rural areas. Keeping husbands' and wives' incomes separate was an ideal in Western-style marriages where women had formal-sector employment as well as in poorer households where wives wanted to keep control over part of the family budget (Munachonga 1988; Tripp 1989). In 1974 in Côte d'Ivoire, both women and men with high incomes claimed to spend more than their spouses on family needs, while accusing the other of spending less. In this potentially acrimonious situation, women were sometimes known to hide their income from their husbands (Lewis 1977).

Some marital practices apparently based in rural social and economic structures have persisted in urban areas. In Chapter 6, Philippe Antoine and Jeanne Nanitelamio address the widespread continuation of polygyny in urban areas. They present extensive demographic evidence and experiences from Dakar to illustrate the various reasons that men and women choose to marry polygynously. For men, these reasons include a demonstration of actual or desired wealth; a return to traditional cultural practices, especially among urban Muslims; and instances where parents have "given" a second wife to their son. Some women voiced a preference for polygynous relationships because they liked sharing domestic tasks, felt a large extended family was beneficial for raising children, and thought polygyny was an accepted part of Muslim identity and practice.

In southern Africa, the exchange of bridewealth upon marriage (usually a transfer of goods or services from the family of the groom to his new in-laws) persisted in urban areas where couples valued bridewealth as a way of legitimating marriage. Bridewealth still acted to transfer child custody to the husband's family, but in the urban context, it was also expected to stabilize the marriage, repay the woman's relatives for their expenses in educating her (thus higher bridewealth is expected for educated women), cover wedding expenses, and act as a symbol of African cultural identity, among other attributes (Brandel 1958).

One area that marks a dramatic change from rural norms is the increase in single women in urban areas. It is not always easy to determine actual marriage rates, and official figures regarding marital rates need to be used carefully. Because government officials had a history of harassing and trying to control unmarried urban women, falsifying one's marital status for officials was a deliberate survival measure. One researcher found that in the early 1970s only 20 percent of the women in Mathare Valley, Nairobi, were really married, whereas the official census claimed that 60 percent of the women in that neighborhood were married (Nelson 1978–1979:86). Many women prefered to rely on their own income-earning capabilities without the demands of a semiemployed or unemployed husband. Another study, conducted in 1974–1975, suggested that rural Ghanaian norms contained many negative stereotypes about unmarried women, yet the situation in urban areas indicated a remarkable change. Cultural expectations still anticipated marriage for all adults, but many young urban professional women avoided what they saw as a "highly inequitable marriage bargain" (Dinan 1983:349). These women often wished to marry in an egalitarian relationship but were unable to find a man who was committed to that kind of marriage.

The apparent increase in the numbers of urban single women has a variety of causes and motivations. Some women continue to search for a husband despite obstacles from their family, who may reject men from different ethnic groups, and despite the difficulties in establishing new households when confronted with housing and job shortages. Others have accepted their unmarried status and have even welcomed their independence from men. Although higher levels of education have been related to later age at marriage, statistics gathered in the 1980s indicate that regardless of education level, young women have been marrying later than their mothers and aunts. In Muslim towns, families have kept tight control over their daughters, whereas in non-Muslim towns such as Brazzaville, Congo, unmarried women living on their own have been more visible (Antoine and Nanitelamio 1992).

Some women have developed female-centered households, which might include grandmothers and adult sisters as well as women and their children, all of whom live together and support each other through shared income-earning and household and child-care responsibilities. In South Africa, female-headed households were often created in response to the historic control of the workforce and urban residence. Positioning themselves as household head was not a choice women made, but rather a result of extensive and long-term male migration for work in the mines and cities of southern Africa. Social survival depended on women's working to maintain their families and households in a situation where men were unwillingly absent and families were forced to live in separate housing.

Urban women's experiences with sexuality and fertility are also different from rural women's. Sadly, studies of African sexuality have expanded recently only in response to the spread of AIDS. As Brooke Grundfest Schoepf discusses in Chapter 7, all women are vulnerable due to their dependent position vis-à-vis men in their societies. As Schoepf's case studies indicate, even privileged women cannot control their husbands' sexual behavior and are susceptible to venereal diseases and AIDS despite their efforts to avoid exposure. Poor women who have no option but to turn to some form of prostitution face elevated possibilities of disease and death as a result of their struggle to survive. The use of condoms both for protection from disease and as a birth control method is not widespread, and there are many cultural prohibitions that make condom use difficult for men and women.

Urban women's fertility rates have not always fallen, as some demographers have expected, especially as the use of contraceptives is correlated to education and employment, all of which are generally higher in urban areas. A study in Calabar, Nigeria, found that there was little reason to expect urban fertility rates to decrease, in part because the cultural value of children was much greater than the desire for increased living space. Thus, the problem of high-density living did not mean that families would decide to reduce the number of children through birth control or other fertility control measures (Uyanga 1978).

Nonetheless, it appears that urban woman do use contraceptives more than rural women. In the 1980s about 25 percent of the urban market traders in Ibadan, Nigeria, were using birth control, as compared with a countrywide rate of only 6 percent (Iyun and Oke 1993). But as another study indicated, urban women's motivations for bearing children and using contraceptives varied. Adolescent girls in urban South Africa were choosing to become mothers for a number of reasons, including lack of information about birth control and a desire to exhibit adult behavior (Preston-Whyte and Zondi 1989).

The continued strength of rural practices in urban areas is illustrated in urban Benin, where women have struggled to accommodate rural beliefs regarding childbirth and maternity with urban expectations of reliance on modern medicine. As a result, they have tended to avoid government medical centers and to give birth unattended in order to satisfy cultural demands for stoicism and control over reproduction (Sargent 1989).

The outcome of women's fertility and childbirth is, of course, the presence of children. Women's options for child care sometimes became more restricted in urban areas, where conditions were difficult, housing in short supply, and relatives unavailable. To overcome these problems, children were sometimes sent to the rural homes of grandparents or other kin.

At the same time, rural families sometimes sent children to live with urban relatives. A young girl might move in with relatives living in an urban area with the expectation that she would perform household chores in exchange for access to urban schooling, to modern lifestyles, and to expanded job opportunities as she grew older. Some urban women chose to foster rural kin in order to have a dependent with obligations to themselves rather than to their husbands (Etienne 1979).

As women's families have changed, they have had to search for suitable living quarters. In Chapter 8 on Gweru, Zimbabwe, Miriam Grant describes how women struggle continually to arrange for decent housing. The type of housing required changes throughout their lives, as they marry and divorce, have children who live with them or not, and attempt different ways of earning an income. The intervention of the government in providing access to housing at a reasonable cost is an essential element in improving women's daily lives. Without such support, women face a parade of small temporary rooms and rental situations, accommodations that usually lack sufficient space for their children and basic amenities such as running water.

Women have been at a disadvantage in getting access to legal housing and have borne the brunt of government attempts to control illegal settlements. They have often suffered an enforced dependence on men for access to urban housing because they have lacked the education, employment, or a recognized marital situation entitling them to housing in their own right. This is a legacy of colonial housing policies that assumed urban male workers did not have wives and children with them; in line with these policies, which ignored polygyny and extended family arrangements, single-family homes were constructed. However, women's urban work brewing beer or preparing food for sale required that they have a house where they could do that work.

African cities, especially in southern and eastern Africa, are often marked by a clear division between "cement cities" and squatter neighborhoods. This division was a racial one in colonial times, but it has persisted as a class division in the decades since independence. Women's class position was determined by such factors as whether plumbing was located inside the house, in the courtyard, or down the street; whether the area allocated for cooking was a modern kitchen or a wood fire in the yard; whether there was space for a small garden in the side yard; and whether the sleeping area included beds or floor mats for family members.

Housing as an indicator of class was not only evident in eastern and southern Africa. In Kano, polygynous men demonstrated their wealth by building compounds with separate quarters for their wives arranged around a central courtyard. Other West African residential patterns favored women. Studies of women in Accra and of Yoruba women in Nigeria indicate that women's autonomy was related in part to cultural practices that favored separate housing for women and men. Women's access to independent housing has several implications. For Yoruba women and other West Africans, the relationship between physical space and social space was an important feature of urban society. The existence of separate quarters for women and men allowed women to live with female kin and facilitated the organization of the work women shared, such as market trading.

The great variety of family and household arrangements for urban African women is the feature that most differentiates urban experiences from rural ones. Choices about whether or not to marry, increased opportunity for deciding when to have children and how many to have, and possibilities for developing networks of female kin are options that are more available in the urban areas and are sometimes inducements for women to come to the city. Although rural ideals and connections often have an impact on urban behaviors, urban women confront new family opportunities and make decisions from a different reality. Women's struggles for urban family life have shaped the experiences of all city dwellers.

Markets: Work and Survival

Women's search for work in the city has helped define the structure of employment for women and men. Numerous case studies on women's urban work have emphasized the informal sector, from which the majority of women derive an income. Although their work as market vendors and in microenterprises has been the most visible, women have also taken professional and clerical jobs, worked in factories, and engaged in paid domestic service. Much attention has also focused on women working as prostitutes, a primarily urban work category. Although a few women have become wealthy by developing new urban opportunities for income generation, most women work long, hard hours for a meager income.

Women have been affected by extensive job segregation. Especially when compared with men, women have many fewer options due to their lower level of education, the expectation by husbands that their wives will not work for a wage, and the responsibilities associated with motherhood. That women on the average earn less than men has been a result of job segregation rather than pay discrimination alone (Cohen and House 1993). But job segregation is intimately related to women's reduced education. In Dar es Salaam, women made up one-half of the urban working-age population in 1971, but their lack of education meant that they were nearly absent from the formal waged sector of the economy (Shields 1980:5).

Women's possibilities for improving their situations are also limited, though some women have been able to save money from market trading or prostitution and then develop small shops or other more capital-intensive activities. The importance of women's class position is shown in Dorothy McCormick's Chapter 9 on women garment industry entrepreneurs in Nairobi. McCormick compares male and female opportunities to own and expand small-scale garment factories. Although the study revealed some differences in their experiences, statistically the male- and female-owned businesses were equally profitable. Both men and women had middle-class backgrounds that gave them the necessary skills and access to obtain start-up financing and other forms of support.

A series of studies conducted between 1968 and 1976 compared women in Ghana, Nigeria, and The Gambia and found that women's marital situation, education, and religion affected women's work opportunities. Although most women worked as market traders, women's long-term residence in urban centers and increasing education for girls meant that many women held professional jobs as teachers, nurses, and office workers. Only a very small number of women worked as prostitutes. Islam was a central factor mitigating against employment outside the home, although women of all backgrounds commonly stopped work for a time early in their marriages when they had small children. Women who had obtained a secondary school education were more likely to be employed (Peil 1979).

The intersection of marriage, employment, and class position was shown in a comparison of women's work and family situation in two neighborhoods in Douala, Cameroon. In a middle-class neighborhood where 95 percent of the women were married, over one-half did not work outside the home. In a poorer neighborhood, 40 percent of the women were unmarried, and 85 percent of them earned an income, many as waged workers in a business or office (Mainet 1985).

Street or market vending of food is a central aspect of both women's work and of food distribution in the urban areas. Selling snacks or even full meals not only is an important source of income for women but provides a reliable source of food for urban wage earners. Although women in all regions of Africa are involved in market trading, those in West Africa are recognized as being exceptionally well organized. Contrary to popular images of women selling a limited number of homegrown vegetables or easily prepared foods, Yoruba women in Ile-Ife, for example, have been observed selling over three hundred different types of food to the public, at sites ranging from curbsides to formal markets. The work is full time, though sometimes seasonal, and many women have continued to work as market traders for years. The efforts made by these women for a meager financial return have contributed to the development of the urban community of Ile-Ife through providing needed services at low cost and underwriting the social cost of reproducing the workforce (Pearce, Kujore, and Agboh-Bankole 1988). A comparison of female and male traders in Mali in the mid-1980s found that whereas women predominated in trading agricultural and food products, men controlled most of the trade in manufactured goods such as textiles, shoes, and metal pots. Although these goods required the vendors to make a greater investment to purchase them, the items were not perishable and the vendors could realize a greater profit (Harts-Broekhuis and Verkoren 1987).

Although some researchers have described a prevailing ideology of individualism in the markets, others have shown how market traders' business and personal networks comprise the overlapping categories of kin, friend, and customer (Clark 1991; Lewis 1976; Trager 1981). The shrewd business sense of West African market women is evident in their ability to conduct complex financial transactions, though they are illiterate, and to alter their marketing strategies when necessary. In Nigeria, for instance, they shifted from selling yams to distributing beer when customer demand changed, and in another case, women in Ghana adapted to the advent of motorized transport and changing fashions (Robertson 1975/1976; Trager 1985). In a third case, Hausa women in Nigeria continued to trade from seclusion by relying on children to act as go-betweens (Schildkrout 1983).

The historic roots of women's extensive trading experience have also been well illustrated in Sierra Leone and other parts of West Africa. Although market women in eastern and southern Africa do not usually have the same long history in trade as West African women do, recent research from the 1980s and 1990s discussing traders in Zimbabwe, Kenya, and Swaziland has demonstrated their resourcefulness as well as the importance of such work to urban life and the national economy (Horn 1994; Mitullah 1991; Sandee and Weijland 1988). A review of household budgets in Kinshasa, Zaire, in 1987 revealed that the income from women's trade supported the family in a time of economic crisis. Under national structural adjustment programs, when professional salaries often did not cover even one-half of a household's monthly food expenditures, the money earned from trade and other so-called informal ventures was vital to survival (Schoepf and Engundu 1991). In a study conducted in Sudan, 80 percent of market vendors were found to be the sole or the major source of support for their families (Salih 1986:37).

In many cities, street vendors have been subject to official wrath, with problems of sanitation frequently serving as an excuse for harassment. Sometimes, officials have believed that women traders were a wealthy elite and thus a legitimate target of government restrictions in economic hard times. In reality, the vast majority of female traders work on such extremely slim profit margins that illness or other temporary hardship can bring ruin. The constraints imposed by authorities were part of an overall strategy to control women, urban workers, and the process of urbanization—all interests that continue to preoccupy postcolonial governments.

Some women have entered and left the market-trading sector throughout their lives. In studies in Lusaka in the 1970s and 1980s, where women's street vending is a vital part of family support, young women who were newly married and had very young children did not engage in trade. But when children reached school age or as women grew older and were divorced or widowed, they commonly turned to street marketing as a means to earn money needed to feed and clothe the children. Older Hausa women in Kaduna also practiced a wider range of activities once their children were grown. Older women sometimes have the security of position and wealth that allows them to participate more actively in economic and political affairs as well as to exert greater control over family and kin. Some types of work, such as midwifery, are primarily the occupations of older women (Coles 1990).

Women have developed new areas of endeavor in the informal sector, sometimes based on skills that were introduced in a strictly gender-based idea of appropriate work for women. In Chapter 10, Mary Johnson Osirim documents the intensive labor of women in Zimbabwe as they sew or crochet clothing for sale. The sale of such items as baby clothes and lace tablecloths can be a source of income for women who learned this skill in school or from friends. Their working conditions are very difficult, as they often sit in open lots with no protection from the weather or access to sanitation. They hope to sell the items they have created to passersby, and they are dependent on tourist shoppers in the case of the more intricate and expensive items. Other microenterprises such as hairdressing are also gendered.

Paulette Beat Songue presents some recent information in Chapter 11 on prostitution in Cameroon. Her research findings were that many women turned to prostitution in times of economic crisis. Although this provided these women with a source of income, they did not become wealthy, nor did they gain greater control or authority in their lives. African prostitutes are not under the control of pimps or madams. But women involved in prostitution have always been dependent on men for their economic well-being, and now with the spread of AIDS, they are also dependent on male clients for their health and survival.

In colonial Nairobi, prostitution was but one employment option among several; however, the profession changed over time as the Kenyan economy became incorporated into the international colonial and capitalist system (White 1990). The exchange between a prostitute and a customer often included domestic work, such as providing bathwater and cooking breakfast, in addition to engaging in sexual intercourse. Such domestic support was a necessity when colonial regulations made it difficult for male urban workers to settle with their families. Studies of prostitution in Lubumbashi, Zaire, and Addis Ababa, Ethiopia, after independence have highlighted the variety of styles of prostitution, the class nature of the work, and the lack of stigma attached to women working as prostitutes (Bujitu 1979; Dirasse 1978).

A small number of women have been able to gain the education required to obtain work as nurses or teachers, or in other professional occupations, though typically men held these jobs in African cities in the colonial era. Professional women were discriminated against because of their sex and were subjected to sexual harassment and abuse by male superiors when they either tried to secure a job or tried to be promoted. The results of a study show that both male and female professionals in Lagos felt that women should work outside the home, but many expressed concern over the timing of that work. A common expectation of both men and women was that women would postpone work until children were grown (Karanja 1981). Although a popular view holds that urban professional women have lost touch with their kin, a Kenyan research project conducted in the 1980s found that women in demanding careers in Nairobi had extensive contacts with their families, both giving assistance and receiving help from family members (McAdoo and Were 1989).

African women have had extremely limited access to factory jobs, especially when compared to the experience of young women in other world areas. When they have found industrial labor, it has generally been in food processing (cashews, fish, fruit, vegetables, and baked goods) or in the textile and garment industries. In South Africa, women have had unusual access to factory work, though still primarily in the sectors of textiles and food processing. White women first found positions sewing clothing in wartime; later, black women joined them there and in the food processing factories. South African women developed a strong tradition of organizing unions to protect their interests as workers and as women. These unions were occasionally successful in transcending racial boundaries as well (Berger 1992).

Balancing the demands of work and family became especially important when women working for a wage faced limited options for child care. Women in urban areas sometimes lost access to the extended family that could watch small children in rural communities. In most African cities, families arrange for their own individual caregiver, who may be a young relative or someone hired to live with the family. With the exception of South Africa, domestic servants in Africa have more often been men, yet girls and women were frequently hired as child-care workers within the home. The establishment of child-care centers has not been common, despite women's expressed desire for such institutions. The continuing emphasis that is given to motherhood as an attribute of female adulthood in many parts of Africa and the assumption that women should be responsible for child care have been important factors limiting women's work opportunities.

The frequent necessity for more than one income has been an important aspect of urban work in recent decades. Urban families have faced increased economic difficulties since the implementation of structural adjustment programs in the 1980s, forcing women to seek new sources of income as female poverty increased. Women with office jobs, for instance, may develop a small market trade or cultivate an urban garden as additional economic security. These gardens can range from small plots of vegetables in the yard designed to supplement purchased food to relatively extensive plots where maize or rice is grown, with the surplus sometimes being sold in local markets. In the current economic crisis, urban working women have turned increasingly to agriculture as an additional mechanism to avert hunger. Urban farming has formed an essential part of urban family diets and requires a substantial outlay of time and energy by the women who pursue it.

Urban women have a much wider variety of occupations open to them than women do in the rural areas, but they still confront a series of obstacles to attaining equal opportunity with men. Their relative lack of education, their family and child-care responsibilities, and the attitudes of employers intersect, so that women are most frequently found in the least profitable sectors of the urban economy. Yet within those constraints, their innovative efforts have shaped the way urban dwellers work and have improved the possibilities of survival for urban families.

City Streets: Politics and Community

Women's contributions to African politics at the local level have been myriad, though not always acknowledged. Although women have been underrepresented in formal political structures, their contributions to community organizations have been critical to developing urban neighborhoods and networks. Women have made fundamental contributions to the development of nationalism, to urban organizations, and to religious associations. They at times formed the core of resistance movements.

As John Nauright demonstrates in Chapter 12 on Alexandra Township, South Africa, women became leaders in organizing bus boycotts to protest fare hikes because of their own economic difficulties. Their resistance to this increase in their daily expenses began with a little-known action in 1918 and developed into more visible protests in the 1930s and 1940s, as women called on the networks they had developed in their neighborhoods and through their work brewing beer. Their actions were part of a stream of antiapartheid struggles throughout this century in South Africa.

Women have been acknowledged leaders in anticolonial resistance movements. In one of the most famous events, the 1929 Aba women's war, women in Nigeria demonstrated to protect their position in the markets when their palm oil sales were threatened through taxation. In Tanzania, standard nationalist histories had placed Westernized educated Christian men at the forefront of the liberation movement led by the Tanganyika African National Union (TANU), but it is now clear that TANU's success grew from the organizing abilities of semiliterate and illiterate Muslim women who mobilized dance societies and other traditional associations in Dar es Salaam (Geiger 1987). These actions drew on traditional women's solidarity associations as well as on urban political and community networks.

The current climate of expanded democratic rights and increased multiparty political systems in Africa might seem to offer new opportunities for women, but Aili Mari Tripp argues that this is not the case. In Chapter 13, Tripp discusses the way urban women's history of organizing confronts a more general political history of female exclusion from acknowledged centers of power. The result in Africa has been widespread disillusionment with political parties, though women have continued to form nonparty organizations to bring their issues to public notice.

African women have formed a wide array of community groups and political organizations that have depended on women's support. The issues they have dealt with include improving educational opportunities for girls, trade union organizing, and protecting women's market rights. They have organized purchasing clubs, revolving credit associations, burial clubs,

Christian prayer groups, and local branches of the YWCA (Young Women's Christian Association). Most of these associations have engaged in important business and financial activities, while also providing a space for women to socialize.

Women's associations have also played a vital role in linking rural and urban women and in providing a source of support for women dealing with adaptation to urban life. For example, in the 1980s in Mozambique, urban women farmers organized a cooperative with a membership that was 90 percent female. Among other issues, the organization advocated protecting women's access to land (Gentili 1985). Urban concerns for the environment have also given rise to activism. In one such environmental group, a struggle to protect agricultural zones on Nairobi's periphery gained international attention for the movement's leader, Wangari Maathai.

Religious membership and activism have also involved women in Christian prayer groups, indigenous religious societies, Islamic guilds, and other groups. The Ahmadi community in Abidjan, Côte d'Ivoire, has offered education, training, and support for Muslim women new to the city. In assisting these women to find urban work and in helping them adjust to life away from their home regions while providing some religious continuity between the old and new lifestyles, the organization Ahmadiyya has played an important stabilizing role for poor immigrant women (Yacoob 1987). In *zaar* spirit possession groups in Khartoum, Sudan, women of varied ethnic backgrounds have come together in a shared religious activity (Constaninides 1979). Because urban living has introduced new stresses into these women's lives, the religious associations have taken on a particularly urban character to help women cope.

Urban women's dance societies have also been an important site of congregation for new immigrants and long-term residents of varying ethnicities. In Mombasa, Kenya, these associations have contributed to the development of an urban community by providing entertainment and social assistance through networks of women. These women later drew on the connections and organizing skills gained in the dance societies to establish advocacy groups for women's education and other issues (Strobel 1976).

Women have also formed other, less formal networks based on their work and residence connections, and these have also helped women become integrated into city life. Kenyan beer brewers in Nairobi's Mathare Valley neighborhood, for instance, have relied on good relations with other women to secure their own economic survival. These affiliations have transformed the potentially alienating city into a cohesive community for women (Nelson 1979). Women in a Bamako neighborhood in

Mali have formed complex interrelationships based on reciprocal gift giving, both voluntary and obligatory. Individual women commonly give more than one gift a day, most often food. These gifts are often a matter of survival, with contributions providing support to new arrivals in the city, to younger kin who are less established, and to others living in relatively more precarious conditions (Vaa, Findley, and Diallo 1989).

Women have made contributions as well to the cultural and artistic life of African cities, writing and producing material for television, theater, and radio, writing fiction, working as journalists, and so on. The audience for these productions and publications has included women, but little has been published that analyzes gender in this important part of the urban experience. Some of the best fiction on city life has been written by women writers. Miriam Tlali's novel about a young working woman in South Africa, Buchi Emecheta's fiction portraying Nigerian women's difficult choices, and Ama Ata Aidoo's stories about urban professional women in Ghana have all enriched African and world culture and have brought attention to the situation of women in African cities (Aidoo 1969; Emecheta 1983; Tlali 1979). In contrast to male writers, who often portray fictional urban women as prostitutes, female writers such as these describe a wide variety of women facing new choices in work, family, and political life (Davies 1993).

Urban public life as manifested in political and religious organizations, cultural production, and the development of neighborhood networks has benefited from and sometimes pivoted on African women's contributions. The development of urban communities in African cities has depended on women's contributions in central ways—through their political involvement, religious activism, and economic organization. Women's daily efforts to enhance their own communities have been a major force in creating particularly African cities.

Conclusion

Women's contributions to African urbanization have been immense. Women's work in agriculture and trade helped build the cities. African cities have evolved into their contemporary form as a result of women's active development of urban work, family life, and community. Yet city life can be contradictory for women. Although urban living can offer new opportunities for economic independence, at the same time, women face more obstacles than urban men do. More choices in structuring family life have at times provoked marital or familial conflict. New forms of connecting with neighbors and community have not extended to bringing women into the central structures of political power.

Women's marriage and family choices, their work in markets and businesses, their involvement in religious and political organizations, and their artistic endeavors all contribute to shape cities to meet women's needs as well as men's. Although women's desires for remunerative work, contented families, and fulfilling community involvement have not been entirely met, their actions demonstrate their ongoing commitment to improving urban life. The essays collected here restore women to the center of the African urban experience: living in family courtyards, selling in the markets, and organizing in the city streets.

References

Aidoo, Ama Ata. 1969. *No Sweetness Here.* New York: Doubleday.

Antoine, Philippe, and Jeanne Nanitelamio. 1992. "More Single Women in African Cities: Pikine, Abidjan and Brazzaville." *Population. English Selection* 3:149–169.

Becker, Charles M., Andrew M. Hamer, and Andrew R. Morrison. 1994. *Beyond Urban Bias in Africa: Urbanization in an Era of Structural Adjustment.* Portsmouth, N.H.: Heinemann.

Berger, Iris. 1992. *Threads of Solidarity: Women in South African Industry, 1900–1980.* Bloomington: Indiana University Press.

Bjerén, Gunilla. 1985. *Migration to Shashemene: Ethnicity, Gender, and Occupation in Urban Ethiopia.* Uppsala: Scandinavian Institute of African Studies.

Brandel, Mia. 1958. "Urban Lobolo Attitudes: A Preliminary Report." *African Studies* 17, 1:34–51.

Bujitu, Tshibanda Wamuela. 1979. *Femmes libres, femmes enchainées: La prostitution au Zaire.* Lubumbashi: Editions Saint Paul.

Clark, Gracia. 1991. "Colleagues and Customers in Unstable Market Conditions: Kumasi, Ghana." *Ethnology* 30, 1:31–48.

Cohen, Barney, and William J. House. 1993. "Women's Urban Labour Market Status in Developing Countries: How Well Do They Fare in Khartoum, Sudan?" *Journal of Development Studies* 29, 3:461–483.

Coles, Catherine. 1990. "The Older Woman in Hausa Society: Power and Authority in Urban Nigeria." In *The Cultural Context of Aging: Worldwide Perspectives,* ed. Jay Sokolovsky, 57–81. New York: Bergin and Garvey.

Constaninides, Pamela. 1979. "Women's Spirit Possession and Urban Adaptation in the Muslim Northern Sudan." In *Women United, Women Divided: Comparative Studies of Ten Contemporary Cultures,* ed. Patricia Caplan and Janet M. Bujra, 185–205. Bloomington: Indiana University Press.

Coquery-Vidrovitch, Catherine. 1991. "The Process of Urbanization in Africa (From the Origins to the Beginning of Independence)." *African Studies Review* 34, 1:1–98.

Davies, Carole Boyce. 1993. "Epilogue: Representations of Urban Life in African Women's Literature." In *Women's Lives and Public Policy: The International Experience,* ed. Meredeth Turshen and Briavel Holcomb, 171–181. Westport, Conn.: Greenwood.

Dinan, Carmel. 1983. "Sugar Daddies and Gold-Diggers: The White-Collar Single Women in Accra." In *Female and Male in West Africa,* ed. Christine Oppong, 344–366. London: George Allen and Unwin.

Dirasse, Laketch. 1978. *The Socio-economic Position of Women in Addis Ababa: The Case of Prostitution.* Ph.D. diss., Boston University.

Emecheta, Buchi. 1983. *Double Yoke.* New York: George Braziller.

Etienne, Mona. 1979. "The Case for Social Maternity: Adoption of Children by Urban Baule Women." *Dialectical Anthropology* 4, 3:237–242.

Findley, Sally E. 1989. "Les migrations feminines dans les villes africaines: Une revue de leurs motivations et experiences." In *L'insertion urbaine des migrants en Afrique,* ed. Philippe Antoine and Sidiki Coulibaly, 55–70. Paris: Editions l'ORSTOM.

Geiger, Susan. 1987. "Women in Nationalist Struggle: TANU Activists in Dar es Salaam." *International Journal of African Historical Studies* 20, 1:1–26.

Gentili, Anna Maria. 1985. "Da Lourenço Marques a Maputo: La trasformazione delle aree agricole suburbane." *Africa* (Rome) 40, 2:183–219.

Gilbert, Alan, and Josef Gugler. 1992. *Cities, Poverty and Development: Urbanization in the Third World.* 2d ed. Oxford: Oxford University Press.

Gugler, Josef. 1989. "Women Stay on the Farm No More: Changing Patterns of Rural-Urban Migration in Sub-Saharan Africa." *Journal of Modern African Studies* 27, 2:347–352.

Harts-Broekhuis, E.J.A., and O. Verkoren. 1987. "Gender Differentiation Among Market-Traders in Central Mali," *Tijdschrift voor economische en sociale geografie* 78, 3:214–221.

Hollos, Marida. 1991. "Migration, Education, and the Status of Women in Southern Nigeria." *American Anthropologist* 93, 4:852–870.

Horn, Nancy. 1994. *Cultivating Customers: Market Women in Harare, Zimbabwe.* Boulder: Lynne Rienner.

Iyun, B. Folasade, and E. A. Oke. 1993. "The Impact of Contraceptive Use Among Urban Traders in Nigeria: Ibadan Traders and Modernisation." In *Different Places, Different Voices: Gender and Development in Africa, Asia, and Latin America,* ed. Janet Henshall Momsen and Vivian Kinnaird, 63–73. London and New York: Routledge.

Karanja, Wambui Wa. 1981. "Women and Work: A Study of Female and Male Attitudes in the Modern Sector of an African Metropolis." In *Women, Education, and Modernization of the Family in West Africa,* ed. Helen Ware, 42–66. Canberra: Australian National University.

Lewis, Barbara C. 1976. "The Limitations of Group Action Among Entrepreneurs: The Market Women of Abidjan, Ivory Coast." In *Women in Africa: Studies in Social and Economic Change,* ed. Nancy J. Hafkin and Edna G. Bay, 135–156. Stanford: Stanford University Press.

———. 1977. "Economic Activity and Marriage Among Ivoirian Urban Women." In *Sexual Stratification: A Cross-Cultural View,* ed. Alice Schlegel, 161–191. New York: Columbia University Press.

Linden, Eugene. 1993. "Megacities." *Time,* January 11, 28–38.

Little, Kenneth. 1973. *African Women in Towns: An Aspect of Africa's Social Revolution.* Cambridge: Cambridge University Press.

Mabogunje, Akin L. 1968. *Urbanization in Nigeria.* New York: Africana Publishing.

——. 1990. "Urban Planning and the Post-Colonial State in Africa: A Research Overview." *African Studies Review* 33, 2:121–203.

Mainet, Guy. 1985. "Le rôle de la femme dans l'économie urbaine à Douala: Exemples du quartier Akwa et de la 'Zone Nylon.'" In *Femmes du Cameroun: Mères pacifiques, femmes rebelles,* ed. Jean-Claude Barbier, 369–383. Paris: Karthala-ORSTOM.

McAdoo, Harriette, and Miriam Were. 1989. "Extended Family Involvement of Urban Kenyan Professional Women." In *Women in Africa and the African Diaspora,* ed. Rosalyn Terborg-Penn, Sharon Harley, and Andrea Benton Rushing, 133–164. Washington, D.C.: Howard University Press.

Mitullah, Winnie. 1991. "Hawking as a Survival Strategy for the Urban Poor in Nairobi: The Case of Women." *Environment and Urbanization* 3, 2:13–22.

Munachonga, Monica. 1988. "Income Allocation and Marriage Options in Urban Zambia." In *A Home Divided: Women and Income in the Third World,* ed. Daisy Dwyer and Judith Bruce, 173–194. Stanford: Stanford University Press.

Nelson, Nici. 1978–1979. "Female-Centered Families: Changing Patterns of Marriage and Family Among Buzaa Brewers of Mathare Valley." *African Urban Studies* 3 (new series):85–103.

——. 1979. "'Women Must Help Each Other': The Operation of Personal Networks Among Buzaa Beer Brewers in Mathare Valley, Kenya." In *Women United, Women Divided: Comparative Studies of Ten Contemporary Cultures,* ed. Patricia Caplan and Janet M. Bujra, 77–98. Bloomington: Indiana University Press.

Okojie, Christiana E. E. 1984. "Female Migrants in the Urban Labour Market: Benin City, Nigeria." *Canadian Journal of African Studies* 18, 3:547–562.

Oppong, Christine. 1970. "Conjugal Power and Resources: An Urban African Example." *Journal of Marriage and the Family* 32, 4:676–680.

Pearce, Tola Olu, Olugemi O. Kujore, and V. Aina Agboh-Bankole. 1988. "Generating an Income in the Urban Environment: The Experience of Street Food Vendors in Ile-Ife, Nigeria." *Africa* 58, 4:385–400.

Peil, Margaret. 1979. "Urban Women in the Labor Force." *Sociology of Work and Occupations* 6, 4:482–501.

Peil, Margaret, Stephen K. Ekpenyong, and Olotunji Y. Oyeneye. 1988. "Going Home: Migration Careers of Southern Nigerians." *International Migration Review* 22, 4:563–585.

Preston-Whyte, Eleanor, and Maria Zondi. 1989. "To Control Their Own Reproduction: The Agenda of Black Teenage Mothers in Durban." *Agenda* 4:47–68.

Robertson, Claire. 1975/1976. "Ga Women and Change in Marketing Conditions in the Accra Area." *Rural Africana* 29:157–171.

Robertson, Claire, and Iris Berger. 1986. "Introduction: Analyzing Class and Gender—African Perspectives." In *Women and Class in Africa,* ed. Claire Robertson and Iris Berger, 3–24. New York: Africana Publishing.

Rondinelli, Dennis A. 1988. "Giant and Secondary City Growth in Africa." In *The Metropolis Era.* Vol. 1, *A World of Giant Cities,* ed. Mattei Dogan and John D. Kasarda, 291–321. Beverly Hills, Calif.: Sage.

Salih, Alawiya Osman M. 1986. "Women in Trade: Vendors in Khartoum Area Markets." *Ahfad Journal* 3, 2:37–40.

Sandee, Henry, and Hermine Weijland. 1988. "Dual Production and Marketing of Vegetables in Swaziland: A Case of Marginalization of Female Traders." In *Scenes of Change: Visions on Developments in Swaziland*, ed. Henk J. Tieleman, 150–162. Research Report no. 33. Leiden: African Studies Center.

Sargent, Carolyn Fishel. 1989. *Maternity, Medicine, and Power: Reproductive Decisions in Urban Benin*. Berkeley and Los Angeles: University of California Press.

Schildkrout, Enid. 1983. "Dependence and Autonomy: The Economic Activities of Secluded Hausa Women in Kano." In *Female and Male in West Africa*, ed. Christine Oppong, 107–126. London: George Allen and Unwin.

Schoepf, Brooke Grundfest, and Walu Engundu. 1991. "Women's Trade and Contributions to Household Budgets in Kinshasa." In *The Real Economy of Zaire: The Contribution of Smuggling and Other Unofficial Activities to National Wealth*, ed. Janet MacGaffey, 124–151. Philadelphia: University of Pennsylvania Press.

Shields, Nwanganga. 1980. *Women in the Urban Labor Markets of Africa: The Case of Tanzania*. Staff Working Paper no. 380. Washington, D.C.: World Bank.

Stichter, Sharon B. 1988. "The Middle-Class Family in Kenya: Changes in Gender Relations." In *Patriarchy and Class: African Women in the Home and the Workforce*, ed. Sharon B. Stichter and Jane L. Parpart, 177–203. Boulder: Westview Press.

Strobel, Margaret. 1976. "From Lelemama to Lobbying: Women's Associations in Mombasa, Kenya." In *Women in Africa: Studies in Social and Economic Change*, ed. Nancy J. Hafkin and Edna G. Bay, 183–211. Stanford: Stanford University Press.

Tlali, Miriam. 1979. *Muriel at Metropolitan*. London: Longman.

Trager, Lillian. 1981. "Customers and Creditors: Variations in Economic Personalism in a Nigerian Marketing System." *Ethnology* 20, 2:133–146.

———. 1985. "From Yams to Beer in a Nigerian City: Expansion and Change in Informal Sector Trade Activity." In *Markets and Marketing*, ed. Stuart Plattner, 259–285. Lanham, Md.: University Press of America.

Tripp, Aili Mari. 1989. "Women and the Changing Urban Household Economy in Tanzania." *Journal of Modern African Studies* 27, 4:601–623.

Uyanga, Joseph. 1978. "Fertility Behavior in Crowded Urban Living." *African Urban Studies* 2 (new series):49–59.

Vaa, Mariken, Sally E. Findley, and Assitan Diallo. 1989. "The Gift Economy: A Study of Women Migrants' Survival Strategies in a Low-Income Bamako Neighborhood." *Labour, Capital and Society* 22, 2:234–260.

Watts, Susan J. 1983. "Marriage Migration, a Neglected Form of Long-Term Mobility: A Case Study from Ilorin, Nigeria." *International Migration Review* 17, 4:682–698.

Wekwete, K. H. 1992. "Africa." In *Sustainable Cities: Urbanization, and the Environment in International Perspective*, ed. Richard Stren, Rodney White, and Joseph Whitney, 105–140. Boulder: Westview Press.

White, Luise. 1990. *The Comforts of Home: Prostitution in Colonial Nairobi.* Chicago: University of Chicago Press.

Yacoob, May. 1987. "Ahmadiyya and Urbanization: Easing the Integration of Rural Women in Abidjan." In *Rural and Urban Islam in West Africa,* ed. Nehemia Levtzion and Humphrey J. Fisher, 119–134. Boulder: Lynne Rienner.

Part Two

Migration and Urbanization

2

South African Women and Migration in Umtata, Transkei, 1880–1935

SEAN REDDING

The history of migration of African women in South Africa is central to our understanding of the history of both Africans in South Africa and women in Africa generally. In South Africa, African women have frequently borne the burden of holding African society together, despite their relatively low status in the hierarchy of industrial wage labor. In Africa generally, South African women provide an extreme example of the effects of a gender-stratified workforce in a period of rapid industrialization and social change. The study of women's migration opens a window on African social and family life, on the decline of agriculture, and on the impact of the state on individuals. From studying women's movements, we can also develop an understanding of the complex circumstances that affected individual decisions to migrate.

In this chapter, I discuss the migration of African women in the Umtata District in the Transkeian region of South Africa over the period 1880 to 1935. The Umtata District encompasses both rural areas and the small town of Umtata. It is important to look at the migration of African women within the rural areas and to observe their movement to the smaller urban centers as well in this early period for two reasons.

First, because most of the literature has focused on female migration mainly to the large urban area of Johannesburg (and to a lesser extent, to

Cape Town), research has fallen prey to certain statistics. It is true that the migration of women to Johannesburg surged from the 1930s onward, but authors have frequently studied this surge to the exclusion of studying earlier and continuing migration elsewhere in the country (Hellmann 1934, 1949; Wilson 1961:434; Reader 1961:36–52; van der Horst 1964; Southall 1983:74–78). Scholars have rarely looked at the rural and small towns to which women had already been migrating for some time (Simkins 1986; Bozzoli 1983). A study of Umtata may give us some insight into the migration of women prior to the 1930s, which may in turn enrich the accounts of post-1930s migration.

Second, some scholars have concentrated on the economic motivations for women's migration. For example, researchers have largely emphasized the higher wages offered in the cities as a "pull" factor that drew women out of the countryside. Although one should not discount these economic factors, by focusing on them exclusively, a lot of nuances have been lost. In fact, there were often other, pressing reasons that drove women away from their rural homes. Although these "push" factors may have had economic roots, they had some noneconomic ones as well. Social conditions, marital unhappiness, and a lack of social services were all factors that entered into some women's decisions to move to town (Bozzoli 1991).

Because the Umtata District in the Transkeian region of South Africa contains both the rural departure areas and an urban destination, it may supply us with the details of the larger picture of female migration. This movement of African women prior to the 1930s has to be set against the background of four important forces: the ongoing history of female migration even before the development of male labor migration; the decline of agricultural productivity, particularly after 1910; the onset of *male* labor migration that surged after 1906; and the changing legal and economic relationship of people to the land that resulted from administrative changes and policies emanating from the Cape's Native Affairs Department in the early 1920s.

Migration Resulting from Marital Tension

Long before the onset of widespread male migrant labor from the district in 1906, women were already migrating for many reasons within the rural areas. Parents occasionally sent girls to be brought up by relatives. Women, both single and married, frequently went visiting, and these visits could last several months or even years. Women eloped with or were carried off by young men. And wives left their husbands' homes under two different customs, *ukuketa* and *ukuteleka,* even after *lobola,* or full bridewealth, had been paid by the woman's parents. One Transkeian lawyer, A. Qunta, described *ukuketa* in detail for the 1930–1932 Native Economic Commission (NEC K26 15, "Transkei Statements"):

> Ukuketa custom. Where the woman leaves the husband's kraal [homestead] without any reason, the husband makes attempts to fetch her back. If she refuses to go back to her husband's kraal, then the husband demands back the dowry [bridewealth][1] he paid for her from her father. If the woman has had children by him, the father deducts a beast [a cow] for each child out of the dowry paid for her. A deduction is also made (a Beast) for wedding outfit if the father supplied it on the occasion of marriage.

The *ukuketa* custom had been upheld in local magistrates' courts since the beginning of colonial rule in the region. In one case in 1897, a husband, Bushulu, sued his wife's brother for the return of his *lobola* cattle (eleven head) or their monetary worth, £27 10s. Bushulu testified (1/UTA 2/1/1/27, Case 133):

> I married defdt's [defendant's] sister Nomantyi three years before the Tembu-Gcaleka war (1872). I paid eleven cattle as dowry. My wife left me at the time of Umfanta's war [1878]. She had one child by me a daughter . . . [the daughter] was given in marriage by defdt and he has the dowry for her . . . I have never entered any action anywhere before for the recovery of my wife.

Clearly, this was not a simple case about the dissolution of a marriage. Bushulu was officially trying to reclaim the bridewealth he had paid for his wife, but in his testimony he was making a secondary claim for the bridewealth that had been paid for his daughter. The brother-in-law attempted to rebut Bushulu's claim: "Pltf [plaintiff] married my sister and paid seven cattle as dowry. His wife returned to us in 1877 said she had been smelt out [accused of witchcraft]. Pltf has never come himself or sent for his wife until last spring."

If indeed the wife had been driven away by a witchcraft accusation, then the *ukuketa* custom would not hold, and because witchcraft allegations were illegal and therefore not justifiable grounds for driving a woman out, her family would have had the right to retain the bridewealth. The woman, unsurprisingly, corroborated her brother's testimony:

> I am sister of defdt, pltf is my husband. I left him because I was smelt out. My children died in infancy and pltf after the death of the last born at his kraal went to a doctor [probably a priest-diviner] and on his return said I had been smelt out as causing the death of my own and other children— told me to go . . . and I left. He has made no effort to recover me until this autumn.

The magistrate chose not to believe the witchcraft-allegation story and issued a judgment that shows the complexity of these cases. He found for the plaintiff in his secondary claim for his daughter's bridewealth, less three head of cattle to reimburse the wife's family for the daughter's maintenance over the years and for her *intonjane* (initiation rites) and wedding expenses. In addition, he found for the plaintiff in his original claim for return of the *lobola* cattle of eleven head, less seven head to reimburse the wife's family for her living expenses over twenty years (1877–1897). It should be noted that this case came to trial in May 1897, *before* the rinderpest cattle disease hit the district and killed 95 percent of the cattle, as is discussed later in the chapter. Ironically, most of the cattle that changed hands in this lawsuit were probably dead within the year.

The second custom, *ukuteleka*, differed from ukuketa in that, according to lawyer Qunta, it was the parents who took the woman away from her husband:

> Ukuteleka custom. Where a man has paid part of the dowry [bridewealth] and the woman returns to her people, she is detained by her people for further dowry. When the husband goes to her people to fetch her, he is told the woman is detained or impounded for further dowry. In order to release her he must pay a beast [a cow] (which is regarded as part of the dowry) to the father of the woman. Then the woman is released and she goes back to her husband's kraal. In the event of her returning to her people she is again telekaed [detained] until the dowry required by the father is satisfied.

Of course, a woman also migrated to her husband's (or her parents-in-law's) homestead when she married and sometimes returned to her own father's home when her husband died. Thus, there was actually a great deal of largely undocumented movement of women within the rural areas, and it continued beyond 1935.

The only way the historian gets a glimpse of this movement is through the civil and criminal cases that sometimes resulted. The usual civil cases involved *lobola* when a husband sued his father-in-law in the resident magistrate's court for the return of either his *lobola* or his wife (CMT 1/146, CMT to Native Laws Commission, 27 Sept. 1881; SANAC 3, evidence of E. E. Dower; Wilson 1961:203–205). Umtata's resident magistrate kept a record for the five years 1898–1902 of the number of cases brought to his court for the return of bridewealth resulting from the wives' desertion (Table 2.1).

The Umtata District's total population hovered around 44,000, and of this number, the magistrate estimated (in 1892) that married women numbered 6,603, so these cases represented only a small fraction of the population (CMT 3/169, Letter 286). But the cases do indicate tendencies and patterns that existed prior to the exodus of male labor migrants.

TABLE 2.1   Civil Cases for the Return of Bridewealth Tried by
                        Umtata Magistrate

Year	Cases Heard	Cases Decided in Husband's Favor
1898	21	16
1899	44	35
1900	52	36
1901	24	16
1902	31	25

Source: Chief Magistrate of Transkei Records 3/172, Letter 280, Acting Resident Magistrate of Umtala Edwin Gilfillan to Chief Magistrate, 23 March 1903.[2]

Women could also be driven away from their husbands' homesteads by allegations of witchcraft, and since the colonial state had made such allegations illegal, these cases could end up in court. Nor was it uncommon for a woman to become pregnant by a man who was not her husband and have this result in her leaving home. In addition, daughters who objected to marriages arranged by their parents occasionally absconded, as a Ciskei magistrate noted in 1903 (SANAC 3, evidence of R. J. Dick):

> If a man marries another man's daughter, and she refuses to live with him, or if she has escaped and run away from him, he is first of all compelled by Native custom to try and ascertain her whereabouts. If he succeeds in finding her and she refuses to return to him, he goes back and says to the father of the girl, "Your girl is living in such and such a district with so and so; go and bring her to me." If the girl declines to obey her father, the husband goes to the court, and if it is found that the girl has left him because they could not live happily together, the marriage is annulled, and the husband gets a certain portion of his dowry [bridewealth] back.

Economic Causes of Migration

The second "push" factor behind female migration was economic: a decline in rural agricultural production. When the Umtata District and most of the Transkei had enjoyed a modest economic boom in the 1880s and early 1890s, most people invested whatever they could in livestock, especially in cattle and sheep (CMT 1/83, Annual Report for 1888; CMT 1/37, Letter 250; CMT 3/170, Letter 952; Redding 1987, chap. 2). Unfortunately, in 1897 the rinderpest disease killed 95 percent (approximately 190,000 out of 200,000) of Umtata's cattle population, and other districts experienced similar losses (CMT 3/170, Letter 952; Ballard 1986; van Onselen

1972). To forestall starvation, many people slaughtered and bartered away sheep and goats and thus saw all of their stored wealth disappear within a few months. This devastation of the local economy set the stage for the development of greater labor migration of both men and women. In killing cattle, rinderpest simultaneously destroyed a source of food, wealth, income, and credit for Africans. It also destroyed the common currency of bridewealth payments. Although agriculture rebounded for a short time early in the twentieth century, few African households were able to reestablish their independence from wage labor (Redding 1987, chap. 2).

The loss of cattle and the consequent agricultural decline had other direct effects on marriage and migration. Cattle had been the principal currency for the payment of *lobola*. After rinderpest, people did substitute sheep, goats, horses, and cash, but some cattle still figured into the final deal. The cattle shortage meant that people had to postpone marriage or pay *lobola* over a number of years. Both of these situations increased the possibility of migration by men and women—by men to earn money to buy cattle and by women to increase family earnings prior to marriage.

The dearth of cattle and the resulting impoverishment also brought about an increase in marital desertions. In the 1898–1902 period, as is apparent in Table 2.1, there was an increase in cases brought by husbands for the return of *lobola*. There was also an increase in cases of men assaulting their wives in the first two years after the rinderpest epidemic (see Table 2.2). Although many other factors may have been involved, there was a strong temporal coincidence between the devastation of the rinderpest epidemic and an increase in marital disputes that ended in the magistrate's court. (It is equally possible, however, that marital tensions had always existed but that economic distress simply made them worse.)

The agricultural decline that began in 1897 continued up to and beyond 1935. There were severe droughts in 1911–1912 and again in 1919–1922. The cattle diseases called East Coast fever, red water, and lung sickness destroyed many of the cattle that people had worked so hard to acquire after rinderpest struck. In addition, veterinary quarantines resulting from these epidemics depressed the market in cattle and hides. As African farmers turned increasingly to sheep raising, wool prices plummeted after the end of World War I and did not recover until the beginning of World War II. By the early 1930s, many rural families routinely had difficulties in covering their expenses (Mears 1947:117–118; Southall 1983:81; Redding 1992; NTS 1771, File 64/276/4, Annual Report for 1929).

Unable to sustain themselves in the rural areas, both men and women migrated to seek wage-earning employment. For men, job seeking often took the form of traveling to the gold mines or to the larger urban areas of the Cape Colony; for women, Umtata initially provided a closer alterna-

TABLE 2.2   Criminal Cases of Husbands Assaulting Their Wives

Year	Cases Heard	Convictions	Discharges
1898	3	3	—
1899	16	14	2
1900	4	3	1
1901	6	5	1
1902	6	4	2

Source: Chief Magistrate of Transkei Records 3/172, Letter 280, Acting Resident Magistrate of Umtata Edwin Gilfillan to Chief Magistrate, 23 March 1903.

tive that allowed for short-term employment and permitted continued contact with rural kin.

The Effects of Male Labor Migration

The onset of large-scale male labor migration after 1906 was the third force behind female migration. There were several crucial, if indirect, effects of male labor migration. The loneliness that both marriage partners experienced often contributed to infidelity that destabilized marriages. Husbands sometimes stopped sending money back home or stopped sending enough to sustain their rural families. Unforeseen circumstances sometimes prevented the man from returning home on the date originally promised. And the brutal character of life in the mines occasionally caused men to abuse their wives after their return. These circumstances affected the quality of the marriages and often influenced women's decisions about whether to leave their husbands.

From court cases, one can find examples of these unfortunate marital consequences of men leaving to find wage labor. One African woman in 1913 explained to the magistrate's court why she had left her husband. He was suing for the return of his *lobola* of eight cattle or for their value of £40. The point of contention was whether or not he had mistreated her, for if he had, she was legally justified in leaving him, and he could not win the case. The wife testified (1/UTA 2/1/1/81, Case 169): "I was once married to Plaintiff according to Christian rites and I deserted him on account of ill-treatment. He used to beat me with a stick and his fist and sometimes kicked me . . . I brought a criminal charge against plaintiff for assault and he was fined £8." The woman emphasized the fact that his violence toward her had only begun once he returned from working in the Johannesburg gold mines: "Even before Plaintiff went to the mines we quarrelled. . . . Plaintiff did not strike me before he came back from the mines but swore at me. . . . Plaintiff was away a year." Her father corroborated her testimony: "I am the father of Martha. . . . I have never seen an assault like this before especially amongst Christian natives. Pltf [plaintiff] has forfeited his dowry [bridewealth] owing to cruelty." The woman had left her husband because of this violence and had returned to her people. The resident magistrate, however, evidently felt the woman was not completely justified in leaving her husband and ruled partially in the husband's favor: He ordered her father to return one-fourth of the bridewealth, that is, two cattle, or £10, and to pay court costs.

In a case in 1922, a man living in a rural region explained how his wife had left him while he was a labor migrant. Unlike the husband in the previous case, he was not suing for the return of his *lobola*, but instead was suing the man who had made his wife pregnant for damages amounting to £25 or five cattle. He gave the background to the case (1/UTA 2/1/1/107, Case 343):

> I went to the Mines in January 1920. I first worked on the New Comet and then transferred to the City Deep where I commenced work in August 1921 and discharged in January 1922. When I came back home I found my wife in an advanced stage of pregnancy. The child was born early in March. . . . I received information in November [1921] from one Peter Petelo that my wife was pregnant. . . . My wife had left my kraal and I had to go to her people to inquire about the pregnancy. My wife told me at her father's kraal . . . [that] it was an Umtata policeman [who was the father of the child].

The wife had left her husband while he was a labor migrant and had herself migrated to the town of Umtata. Despite the fact that the policeman denied all of the charges, the magistrate ruled in the husband's favor and additionally ordered the woman to return home.

The same kinds of indirect effects on marriages continued after 1935, of course. In another case, a husband sued his father-in-law for the return of bridewealth paid (four cattle or £12) or for the return of his wife. Once again, to defend successfully against the case the wife had to prove that she had been the victim of cruel treatment at the hands of her husband. The wife, Nosayini Komanisi, explained in court how her husband had expelled her from his homestead after he returned from the mines in 1936 (1/UTA 2/1/1/145, Case 401): "I married him about thirteen years ago [1924] and have had three children by him. They are all dead. I left plaintiff's kraal during scoffling season 1936 [scoffling season was in late spring, at which time people weeded their fields]. I left because I was driven away by my husband." The reason behind her husband's driving her away, she stated, was the death of their children, for which he held her responsible: "I asked him to take me to the doctor but he said he would not do so as I was killing my children myself. He was imputing witchcraft to me. He threw my belongings outside and told me to clear out as he did not want me." The wife recounted that until her husband returned from the mines, she had remained at his homestead and tended his land; in other words, she claimed that she had not deserted and thus was not at fault for the disintegration of the marriage:

Up to this time I have always lived at Plaintiff's kraal. I ploughed his land last ploughing season and I reaped his land in 1936. . . . My husband returned from the mines last winter. . . . After I was driven away I was given a necklace of a horse's tail by my husband's people and I took this necklace to [Headman] Johnson. The necklace was a reproach to me, i.e., that they were driving me away. . . . My husband was away about three years. . . . My husband said that he could not live with a woman who could not rear children. . . . I wanted to be taken to a European doctor because my children were dying.

The husband denied all of his wife's charges, probably for two reasons: First, he undoubtedly wished to win the case; and second, it was a criminal offense to accuse anyone of practicing witchcraft. His denials were apparently persuasive, since the magistrate ruled in the husband's favor. The magistrate ordered the wife to return to her husband within three weeks or else her family had to return the lobola.

These are very poignant descriptions of women trapped by the migrant labor system. Violence to the wife in the first case and loneliness in the second case threatened to destroy the marriages. In the third case, Nosayini Komanisi's children died while her husband was away, possibly as a result of malnutrition or in one of several measles or influenza epidemics, and then she was herself blamed for the deaths (Redding 1987, chap. 5). In the second case, the woman had moved at least once between the countryside and the town of Umtata; in the other two cases, the women's migrations were within the rural areas.

Aside from economic problems and marital tension, another important indirect effect of male migration was its influence on the status and psychological position of women within the family. Left in the countryside, women often had to take more control of family affairs that had formerly been the domain of men. When men returned, some women were reluctant to surrender that control and ended up leaving the marriage. In addition, daughters continued to escape their fathers' authority by migrating to the urban centers, where they could lead a relatively anonymous life (Mayer 1971:233–251). The desire for independence was often a strong motivation for migration.

Women's Migration to Umtata

The final factor influencing women's migration was the changing economic and legal relationship of people to the land. Before 1921 in the Umtata District, rural wives were extremely important to male migrants for legal reasons, if for no others: A man could not legally be assigned an arable plot of four to six morgen (roughly three to five hectares) unless he was married. In addition, in the years before 1921 a man still received an additional plot for each additional wife. The only stipulation to these requirements was that the wife and family had to be in continuous occupation of the land. Thus, if the man had any hope at all of establishing himself as a farmer independent of wage labor, he had to have a wife. This requirement put a great deal of pressure on husbands to keep marriages together so that they could retain their land and on fathers to keep control over their daughters so that they would receive a high bridewealth. It is not surprising, then, that it was in this period that African men began to express greater concern to government officials over the migration of women.

But circumstances began to change around 1920. Between 1919 and 1921 the arable allotments in the Umtata District were surveyed under the terms of the Glen Grey Act of 1894. One result of the survey was that after 1921 there was a finite number of arable allotments and use rights to them were inherited by the oldest son of the father's first wife (unless the father had multiple allotments under the pre-1919 arrangements). The sudden limitation in the number of plots available decreased the economic value of rural wives for those men who did not already hold an allotment. The shortage of plots simultaneously increased the economic necessity for single women and women whose husbands did not have allotments to become migrants themselves. Land scarcity had abruptly become acute. People without arable land had no option but to migrate in search of wage labor.

Some of these migrants ended up in the nearby town of Umtata. After its founding in 1880, Umtata provided an alternative for women who were either dissatisfied with their rural life or who were unable to continue living in the country. It afforded a new environment with the possibility of economic self-sufficiency, removed from the daily demands of the rural family. The town remained a destination over the years as women continued to leave marriages, families, or poverty in the countryside (Redding 1987, chap. 5).

The statistics for the African population of the town of Umtata are not very trustworthy, but they do give at least an approximate idea of the trends. In 1903, the combined African population (both men and women) of the town was approximately 650 (as compared to a white population of

2,075). By 1921, the combined African population of the town as a whole had risen to 1,614, of which 920, or 57 percent, were women; the white population was 1,813. In 1938, the total African population had increased to 2,300, of which 799, or 34.7 percent, were women; the white population numbered approximately 2,348 (Redding 1987).

The relatively high percentage of African women in town in 1921 may have been partly a function of different destinations for migrating men and women. More migrating men at that time chose to go to Johannesburg than to Umtata, whereas for women the choice of destinations was reversed. Obviously, by 1938 that differential pattern had changed (although again, the figures are not reliable). The change may have resulted from several different trends. Increasing numbers of women were going to Johannesburg and elsewhere as new industrial employment options opened up for them. Additionally, Umtata's share of state bureaucracy was growing, and it employed more African men as clerks and translators.

One other possible cause behind the declining percentage of women in the African urban population was the partial success of the municipal government's attempt since the early 1930s to restrict the rights of African women to live in town. The town council had for years tried to implement locally the 1923 Natives (Urban) Areas Act. Under that act, the municipality would have had the right both to evict all "surplus" Africans, meaning unemployed Africans, and to prevent employed African men from bringing their wives to live with them in town. The purpose of the act, on a nationwide scale, was to halt the development of a permanent urban African population as a way of keeping Africans from meeting the criteria for claiming political rights equal to those held by whites. Essential to this purpose was the notion that African families had to be kept intact (even if not all family members resided at home) and families had to be kept in the rural areas (Davenport 1970). The Umtata Municipal Council could not proclaim the act locally until 1943, however, largely because there was not enough segregated housing available for the "legitimate" (under the terms of the act) African population. Yet the council followed the spirit of the act, which resulted in aggressive, if spasmodic, campaigns to throw single women who were not legally employed out of town. These campaigns occurred throughout the late 1920s and 1930s, and although officials did not succeed in ridding Umtata of single African women, they did manage to label and treat most single women as criminals (Redding 1987, 1992).

For women living outside of a family setting, employment in town was tenuous at best and paid very poorly. For example, in 1920, laundry women earned 5 shillings per month; female domestics earned 10 to 17 shillings per month; male gardeners earned 10 to 15 shillings per month;

butchers' workers earned £1 to £2 per month; government messengers earned £3.5 to £4.5 per month; and clerks and interpreters earned £4 to £5 per month (3/UTA 18, File 48A, letter, Umtata Native Association to town clerk, 24 June 1920). Independent women had to supplement (or replace) wages through various activities. Agriculture was the most widely practiced supplementary activity, as most women living in the "Native Location" and elsewhere in town tended small (approximately one acre, or one-half hectare) gardens of maize, pumpkins (squash), and other vegetables for personal (and in the case of married women, family) consumption. A handful of women over the years owned or controlled some of the larger "garden lots" (four to eight hectares) in town, where they raised produce for sale at Umtata's weekly market (1/UTA 6/1/2, vol. 2, File 2/14/4, letters, T. M. Makiwane to resident magistrate, Umtata, 4 August and 19 October 1942). Livestock also supplemented household incomes. Women commonly kept chickens and goats, and by the 1920s, a few women had become owners of substantial numbers of cattle (four head or more).

Some women engaged in nonfarming activities to augment meager incomes. These included the brewing and sale of beer, the keeping of lodgers, hawking food with or without a license, and prostitution. Beer selling and prostitution were illegal, and criminal fines were part of the cost of doing business; prostitution was also unhealthy and thus inflicted heavy individual and social costs of its own. Illegal activities brought the women more directly into contact with the municipal government that tried to police them; but beer selling and prostitution also changed the relations between black men and women from those of intimate mutual dependence in the rural areas to less personal market interactions in town (Redding 1987:203–212, 245–254).

When single black women came to the town to work or to make their own livings, many looked for unskilled or agricultural labor. From the 1880s to the turn of the century, the urban settlement of white single men and families created a market for domestic workers, and they usually preferred to hire women for these positions (Cock 1979). In addition, white-owned farms surrounding the town created a demand for both domestics and farm laborers. As white families became more numerous after 1900, they hired more black women as nursemaids and as general domestics who took care of entire households. Black men and women also occasionally hired their own servants to cook meals, take care of children or livestock, or keep house. As African middle-class households began to increase in number in Umtata after 1908, they began to hire more domestic servants. Existing as a separate subset of female servants through the 1940s were the very poorly paid casual laborers who were washerwomen or who did needlework or ironing. Most domestic servants in Umtata were women, the exceptions being gardeners, herdsmen, and cooks in the three major (white-owned) hotels.

This urban division of labor meant that African women were consistently relegated to the lowest paying jobs. In 1938, 51 percent of all African women (excluding children) in Umtata were domestics. Officially, only 9 percent of the adult female population was unemployed, although this may have been a substantial undercount (3/UTA 66, File 48H, letter, town clerk to Native Affairs Committee of Umtata Municipal Council, 26 October 1938). The other 40 percent of women was made up of wives (who were not counted as "unemployed" as long as they lived with their husbands) and a small number of business owners, teachers, and nurses.

In addition to facing economic hardships in town, single African women had to deal with social disapproval. This disapproval came not only from the white population and state officials but also from African men and women who frequently assumed that any woman living outside of a family was immoral. Rural African society had a word for an independent, adult woman—*idikazi*. The word had both positive and negative connotations, however, as Monica Wilson, in her 1936 study of the ama-Mpondo, noted (Wilson 1961:207):

> The position of an *idikazi* is difficult to estimate justly. Any woman is flattered if you greet her as *idikazi*. "That is the name we like best." But a wife living temporarily at [her father's] home will explain indignantly that she is not the sort who frequents *iitimiti* [in this context, beer-drinking gatherings or parties]. It seems that, as with Europeans, many would deny being "fast women," but would infinitely prefer being called "fast" rather than "slow."

In fact, in the urban setting, the word *idikazi* more often connoted the negative image of a "fast" or "loose" woman, whose presence in town was simply one more temptation for married men (1/UTA 1/1/1/29, Case 170, 7 March 1901). Educated Africans frequently considered these women as "spoiled"—that is, their families could not expect to get any bridewealth for them even if they did eventually marry—and as "spoilers," in the sense that by occasionally engaging in prostitution, they threatened the institution of African marriage (Mayer 1971:275–282). In Umtata in 1931, the Native Location Advisory Board, staffed by six middle-class African men, recommended the following motion to the all-white Municipal Council: "That any native entering the Location bringing with him his wife must bring a letter from the Magistrate or headman of his district, certifying that she is his lawful wife according to Christian rights or by native law" (3/UTA 18, File 48E, letter, location superintendent to town clerk, 21 May 1931). This motion was a clear attempt to limit the presence of single African women in the interest of preserving both rural and urban marriages.[3] By the mid-1930s, many educated Africans felt that the migration of single women to town had reached crisis proportions.[4] In fact, they often seemed to confuse the symptom with the disease—a crumbling of rural economic and social life that left some women with little to look forward to.

The position of single women in town seems to have changed little between 1880 and 1935. Wages remained roughly the same in real terms, and the nature of the jobs available varied little. The major changes occurred instead in the kind of forces that drove women out of the rural areas and in the lengths to which the municipal and national governments were willing to go to keep single women out of the urban areas. By the mid-1930s, a single African woman, simply by moving to town, had become a criminal in the eyes of the Umtata Municipal Council and a social problem in the eyes of many Africans.

Conclusion

African women were more mobile at an earlier date and for a more complicated set of reasons than the standard historical accounts usually recognize. By focusing on the women who ended up in large urban centers and by concentrating on economic gains from migration, such accounts miss the important push factors that drove many women to relocate. Frequently, early women migrants chose to move to small towns, places that afforded them access to wage-earning jobs and greater independence without cutting them off entirely from their rural networks. In addition, there was a long-standing history of relocation in the rural areas for social, cultural, and personal reasons that predated the development of migrant labor altogether.

Finally, I would suggest that by looking at both the migration of women prior to the 1930s and the noneconomic reasons for migration throughout the 1880 to 1950 period, we might achieve a greater understanding of the dramatic increase of female migrants to the major cities in the post-1935 period. The usual explanation is to see this population increase in terms of economic push and pull factors. That it certainly was. But one can speculate that if women had not already established the practice of migrating within the rural areas and to small towns, they would not so readily have shoved off for the major cities in the 1930s. Without that history, there might also have been less willingness among women to migrate alone, an action that frequently defied the desires of both their relatives (who feared they would be "spoiled") and the South African state (which feared they would form the nucleus of a permanent urban African population). By the 1930s, women already knew how to migrate and how to fend for themselves.

Notes

The research for this paper was conducted largely in 1984, 1987, and 1990 and was funded by a Fulbright-Hays Training Grant and by an Amherst College Faculty Research Award. An earlier version of this paper was presented at the workshop on "Migration and Its Effects on Family Life in Africa," convened by the Program on International Cooperation in Africa, Northwestern University, Evanston, in January 1991. I am indebted to the workshop participants for all of the comments I received. In addition, Peter Siegelman provided valuable criticisms of previous drafts.

1. Although A. Qunta uses the term "dowry" in this document, he is referring to bridewealth. Dowry is the property a woman herself brings to her husband upon marriage, and bridewealth, which was the custom in much of Africa, is a transfer of goods from the bride's parents to the groom's family, which sometimes extended over a period of time before the marriage was finalized.

2. Magistrates in other districts reported similar percentages for husbands winning *lobola* cases in this five-year period. See chief magistrate of Transkei Records (CMT) 3/131, letter, Resident Magistrate (RM) Mt. Frere (Leary) to CMT, 27 February 1903; CMT 3/92, letter, RM Engcobo (King) to CMT, 23 February 1903; CMT 3/55, letter, Acting RM Bizana (Cotterell) to CMT, 4 March 1903; and CMT 3/161, "Conjugal Condition of Natives in the Native Transkeian Territories District Tsolo," dated 13 March 1903, Acting RM Tsolo (Vlok) to CMT.

3. In 1984 I interviewed Mrs. Virginia Makiwane, wife of T. M. Makiwane, one of the members of this Advisory Board, and herself a trained social worker. She stated that in the 1930s and 1940s, most educated Africans felt that the presence of single African women in town was the foremost social problem requiring immediate attention. Interview, 24 September 1984, at Ncambedlana (a suburb of Umtata). See also Redding 1987:165.

4. Testimony of Africans before the Native Economic Commission of 1930–1932 is replete with images of young girls leaving homes and straying into lives of immorality. For examples, see File K26 12, "Records of Johannesburg Statements," statement of Walter Nogqoyi, president, African Residential Association, Benoni, and File K26 15, "Records of Statements from the Transkei," evidence of Thomas Poswayo at Umtata, 1930.

References

Ballard, C. 1986. "The Repercussions of Rinderpest: Cattle Plague and Peasant Decline in Colonial Natal." *International Journal of African Historical Studies* 19:421–450.

Bozzoli, B. 1983. "Marxism, Feminism, and South African Studies." *Journal of Southern African Studies* 9:139–171.

———. 1991. *Women of Phokeng: Consciousness, Life Strategy, and Migrancy in South Africa, 1900–1983.* Portsmouth, N.H.: Heinemann.

Chief Magistrate of Transkei Records (CMT). Various dates. Cape Province Archives Depot. Cape Town, South Africa.

Cock, J. 1979. *Maids and Madams: A Study in the Politics of Exploitation.* Johannesburg: Ravan Press.

Davenport, T.R.H. 1970. "The Triumph of Colonel Stallard: The Transformation of the Natives (Urban) Areas Act Between 1923 and 1937." *South African Historical Journal* 2:77–96.

Hellmann, E. 1934. *Rooiyard: A Sociological Survey of an Urban Native Slum Yard.* Cape Town: Oxford University Press.

———. ed. 1949. *Handbook on Race Relations in South Africa.* Cape Town: Oxford University Press.

Mayer, P. 1971. *Townsmen or Tribesmen? Conservatism and the Process of Urbanization in a South African City.* 2d ed. Cape Town: Oxford University Press.

Mears, W.J.G. 1947. "A Study in Native Administration: The Transkeian Territories, 1894–1943." D.Litt. diss., University of South Africa.

Native Affairs Department Records, Union of South Africa (NTS). Various years. Central Archives Depot. Pretoria, South Africa.

Native Economic Commission Records (NEC). 1930–1932. Minutes of Evidence. Central Archives Depot. Pretoria, South Africa.

Reader, D. H. 1961. *The Black Man's Portion: History, Demography and Living Conditions.* Cape Town: Oxford University Press.

Redding, S. 1987. "The Making of a South African Town: Social and Economic Change in Umtata, 1870–1950." Ph.D. diss., Yale University.

———. 1992. "South African Blacks in a Small Town Setting: The Ironies of Control in Umtata, 1878–1955." *Canadian Journal of African Studies* 26:70–90.

Simkins, C. 1986. "Fertility, Mortality, Migration and Assimilation in the Cape Colony: Evidence from the 1891 and 1904 Censuses." Paper presented to the Southern African Research Program Workshop, Yale University.

South African Native Affairs Commission Records (SANAC). 1903–1905. Minutes of Evidence. Central Archives Depot. Pretoria, South Africa.

Southall, R. 1983. *South Africa's Transkei: The Political Economy of an "Independent" Bantustan.* New York: Monthly Review Press.

Umtata District, Transkei, Records of the Resident Magistrate (1/UTA). Various dates. Cape Province Archives Depot. Cape Town, South Africa.

Umtata Municipality, Transkei, Records of the Town Clerk and Municipal Council (3/UTA). Various dates. Cape Province Archives Depot. Cape Town, South Africa.

van der Horst, S. 1964. *African Workers in Town.* Cape Town: Oxford University Press.

van Onselen, C. 1972. "Reactions to Rinderpest in Southern Africa, 1896–97." *Journal of African History* 13:473–488.

Wilson, M. 1961. *Reaction to Conquest: Effects of Contact with Europeans on the Pondo of South Africa.* 2d ed. London: Oxford University Press.

3

Transitions in Kenyan Patriarchy: Attempts to Control Nairobi Area Traders, 1920–1963

CLAIRE C. ROBERTSON

Patriarchy is often said to be more important than class among structures of dominance affecting women. This, of course, is too vast a generalization and leads to futile arguments in which both phenomena are assumed to be mutually exclusive. But patriarchy, or male dominance, to be more accurate, is not a fixed phenomenon, is historically situated, and changes along with the society that encodes it; it may change from being a primary method of ascribing socioeconomic status to being embedded within a larger class matrix. In this chapter I argue that in the Nairobi area, male dominance, which was firmly embedded in Kikuyu socioeconomic structure and British colonialist thinking and practice, was transformed from a specific ethnically based effort to control women traders to a more diffuse class-based repression of an urban underclass. In this process, gender relations became enmeshed in a web of conflicts—between older and younger Kikuyu men, between British-appointed Kikuyu authorities and anticolonial Kikuyu factions, and ultimately between the poor and the better off. The case of Nairobi area traders is an interesting one that illustrates how, when economic and political interests coincide, colonialist and colonized men may cooper-

ate in the attempt to control women. That these efforts moved from a
specific gender-linked context to a more general class-based struggle is
symptomatic of rapid changes in central Kenya from decentralized relatively egalitarian societies to a highly stratified urban complex—
Nairobi. The women pioneers who helped to form the Nairobi informal
sector, many of them traders, were in the early years the only African
women in the area who experienced the maximum effects of urbanization and who cushioned those effects through various strategies, including migration.

This chapter focuses on attempts to control women's trading activities
in Nairobi and Kiambu, the dominantly Kikuyu area immediately ad-
joining Nairobi to the north and northwest.[1] Kikuyu women's trade
stretches well back into the nineteenth century but was transformed by
colonialism as new opportunities and imperatives encouraging trade
presented themselves. I concentrate here on the period between 1920
and 1963, during which the scope of the women's trade increased, as
did the intensity of their involvement. With this increase, Kikuyu men
perceived more need to control such women's activities, particularly
their movements.

The attempts to control the activities of women traders in the Nairobi
area moved through two phases. The first phase represents the more
particularistic efforts initiated mainly by Kikuyu men. It began after
World War I in the 1920s when there was a large increase in the number
of women going to Nairobi to trade or to practice prostitution, or both.
A strong protest against women's trading activities came from Kikuyu
men. This protest was part of a crisis that also included complaints
about the growing impact of mission education, which condemned
polygyny and clitoridectomy (part of girls' initiation ceremonies), and
resulted in the independent schools movement. Local efforts in Kiambu
by male elders and younger male militants to stop this trade failed because of British colonial opposition. The second phase signaled a shift
from rural to urban concentration and more generalized attempts to
control population movement, initiated mainly by the British administration. The ethnically based efforts of Nairobi-based associations diminished and seem to have disappeared. The second phase began in
the 1940s with measures undertaken to control the African population
and extended through the Emergency of the 1950s, which entailed extreme control measures. This phase ended with a hawker war in the
early 1960s, which showed the incapability of the policy of hawker
eradication to deal with the urban underclass. The chapter ends at the
point when male dominance expressed in control efforts had changed
from an ethnically based particularistic effort to a more diffuse class-
based campaign.

Historical Background

In Africa, "loss of economic control over traders is equated with loss of sexual control over women" (Clark 1988:8), and control over labor, specifically women's agricultural labor, determined the wealth a man could accumulate. We need therefore to look at the background of male attempts to control women's behavior in general as well as to observe governmental attempts to control hawking behavior in general. What mechanisms existed in Kikuyu culture before colonialism that limited, or provided for expansion of, women's actions, especially actions that would facilitate women trading? Were there elements in Kikuyu culture that contributed to the equation of economic and sexual control?

Before the British arrived in the course of building the East African railroad and founded Nairobi in 1899, the area was sparsely populated by Maasai, Kikuyu, and Kamba peoples and was the site of a considerable late nineteenth-century trade between ecological zones as well as a supply source for caravans buying foodstuffs. In Kiambu, the mixture of Maasai and Kikuyu was promoted by raiding for cattle and women and by a long tradition of women leading trade expeditions to Maasailand. Up to one hundred women might go on an expedition which, according to L.S.B. Leakey, was protected by a well-respected market peace rule (Leakey 1956:172–173; Thomson 1887:177). Thus, ethnicity was a fluid concept in the area later rigidified by the British imposition of physical boundaries separating "tribes."

Certain mechanisms both hindered and facilitated the trading activities of Kikuyu women, as well as determined their living situation. The Kikuyu were and are predominantly patrilineal and patrilocal, with women joining their husbands on the husband's father's land. Women had no right to own land, only to use land allocated to them by their husbands, or rarely, by their fathers or brothers. The lack of independent land rights for women put pressure on them to stay in marriages; divorce seems to have been extremely rare before 1930 (Robertson forthcoming). Marriages were usually arranged by the male elders in consultation with the prospective groom or at his request; the prospective bride was sometimes consulted, sometimes not. Paradoxically, one method of circumventing this arrangement, ritual kidnapping of the bride, was sometimes a means for a woman to have a say in her choice of partner by arranging ahead of time for her preferred suitor to abduct her. A woman was supposed to obey her husband and his parents, especially his mother, for whom she worked. Men had the right to beat their wives, but persistent or severe abuse was inhibited by a woman's male relatives, if they chose to protect her. Polygyny was common but not intensive (few men had more than two wives).

There were, then, two elements substantially affecting women's trading activities. Women were sent out of their natal families to join the husband's lineage, thus diminishing opportunities for trading partnerships with sisters, daughters, or mothers, and trading partnerships with co-wives were inhibited by lack of trust and rivalries. Co-wives might walk to the market and sit together to trade, but they did not share stock or profits (A Wangige, interview by author, 9 June 1988).[2] According to Jomo Kenyatta ([1938] 1959:62–63), having a surplus to trade was a matter of pride and competition among wives. There is no evidence of trade partnerships among mothers, daughters, or sisters, which were still rare in the 1980s, although sometimes daughters-in-law helped mothers-in-law by taking over cultivation of farms, freeing the mother-in-law to trade to town.

The coercion sometimes present in pawning and marriage arrangements also diminished women's freedom of action. Pawning arrangements usually involved girls, who, if not redeemed, as often happened, became in effect unfree labor (Ambler 1988:61–62). In the 1890s, there was widespread pawning of Maasai and Kamba women to Kikuyu as a result of the *Ulaya* (Kiswahili for "European") famine accompanying the arrival of the first permanent European settlement at Machakos in Ukambani and at Nairobi. In early Nairobi, this trade in women translated itself into a "regular trade in girls between Maasai villages and railway officials" (White 1990:32, 35). The development of commercial agriculture to serve trade in the area between 1890 and 1900 pushed Kikuyu men to establish more control over women's labor—either by demanding more labor from women or by acquiring more women from the flood of refugees from the famine. Some women were sold as slaves. Parents married off daughters at a young age to get bridewealth or returned daughters-in-law to their parents to secure return of bridewealth in the famine-induced crisis, while pawning increased rapidly (Ambler 1988:115–118, 126–133). In any crisis, those who are most vulnerable because of lack of rights or poverty suffer the most. Women had neither independent land rights nor the right to unquestioned freedom of action, both of which would have inhibited capital accumulation in trade and economic autonomy. Moreover, because of their labor value in agriculture, Kikuyu women were not only vulnerable but valuable assets for men, and they suffered accordingly.

However, there is also countervailing evidence that older women could achieve a certain authority, although some of that was based on their control of junior women's labor. The *ndundu ya atomia*, the women's council, had authority over women and children but was not consulted by male elders (Maas 1986:56). Kikuyu women also practiced the ritual cursing or insulting of men who had transgressed in their behavior toward women in the same way as West African women did—by throwing off their clothes and calling out verbal abuse (Likimani 1985:71). Women had certain limited rights to dispose of their own crops, which in Africa is the usual basis of women's trading activities. But proceeds (which until the twentieth century were normally in kind rather than cash because of barter) were to be used for family needs, not personal luxuries, although a husband could assert his right to the profits since the crops were grown on his land (Leakey 1956:169; A Wangige, interview by author, 9 June 1988). On one occasion at least, a Kikuyu woman in Murang'a, Wangu wa Makeri, an ally of the British-appointed chief, Karuri wa Hinga, was appointed chief in her own right by the British in 1902 and managed to secure her son's succession (Kamau 1984:9; Kenya National Archives Staff n.d.:1). It can be seen here that even such "rights" as women had were either based on their control of younger women or were granted by explicit male permission. Nothing could be assumed.

It is not surprising, then, that the advent of colonialism brought attempts by some women to use the situation to escape control. These were often unhappy wives or widows fleeing levirate marriages (McVicar 1969:8). Before World War I, this took the form of going to Nairobi to trade or to practice prostitution, or both. At the Indian Bazaar, Nairobi's first commercial center, some women rented rooms in the back for prostitution (White 1990:41–42). In 1907–1909 there was an attempt to "clean up" Nairobi by arresting and repatriating some three hundred prostitutes (among a total urban population of about twelve thousand). Repatriating women to the rural areas reflected the idea that women did not belong in the urban areas (Stichter 1977:10).[3] Prostitution and female drunkenness were not acceptable behavior in the culture but also were clearly becoming uncontrollable before World War I.[4] Prostitutes were valuable assets for town inhabitants, who were overwhelmingly male, because they provided domestic services of all kinds. In addition, the provisioning of fresh food to Nairobi was largely in the hands of itinerant women traders. Coercion of women did not disappear in town, however, since violence against women early on became an established fact of life. Some women sought protection with missionaries instead.[5] Early on, both elders and younger Kikuyu men took advantage of British authority to assert control over women. Forest guards robbed women gathering firewood of axes and cords and, if the women were beautiful, insisted upon submission to sexual intercourse (Beech 1912). This, then, is the setting for the first phase in the attempt to control women traders that began after World War I in the 1920s.

"Modesty Like Firewood": Women's
Resistance and Male Reaction, 1920–1939

Both local and long-distance trade was well established as a women's activity in Kikuyu culture by the 1920s. It was in the urban context, however, that Kikuyu men found it objectionable. Older men felt they were losing control over young men and women; young men did not want women claiming the same freedom that they themselves obtained from wage work, freedom that allowed them to pay their own bridewealth and choose their own brides (Beech 1912). As women moved into urban trade, Kikuyu men had greater difficulty in controlling their women's sexual activities, activities that were likely to occur with strangers. Moreover, some women staying permanently in town were able to accumulate wealth, freeing them completely from male economic control.

For their part, British officials were not overly concerned about women hawkers coming to Nairobi at this time—they supplied food to the town, they usually went home at night to Kiambu, and they were not troublesome. Prostitutes were considered to be undesirable, however, and were periodically cleared out by the police.[6] Traders were not specifically enumerated as undesirable in the pass law of 1922, although as early as 1903 there was an East African ordinance that forbade hawking without a license (KNA Nairobi Administrative District AR 1926:55; Wood 1974:39). There is evidence of illegal hawking of foodstuffs by Africans in the World War I era but no evidence of systematic arrests. Whereas those selling their own produce did not need licenses in the 1920s, those who could afford licenses, market stalls, and legality were more likely to be men (Onstad 1988; East African Protectorate, *Official Gazette*, 1 June 1904, 5 October 1921).

Meanwhile, Kikuyu men had ample reason to worry about keeping their authority intact. In 1923 a census of Nairobi prostitutes showed over one-half of them to be Kikuyu. Some rural women were using trade as an excuse to go to Nairobi for prostitution, but others saw prostitution as a supplementary source of income to their trade. Amina Hali, a longtime Nairobi resident, described picking beans by the river in Nairobi as a routine excuse used by women who derived income from prostitution: "She would take a [gunny sack] which . . . she would use . . . as a blanket . . . When they saw a woman lying on [it] they would take out their money, and she would motion for him to lie down with her. They paid us and sometimes they gave us babies, so we were rich, we had money and babies that way." Crowded housing conditions, a highly uneven sex ratio, the lack of wage-earning opportunities for women, and the vagrancy laws that subjected women alone on the street to arrest, extortion, and sexual harassment were all factors promoting prostitution (White 1990:71, 41, 75).

In Kiambu, trade in market-garden produce was growing rapidly, with English potatoes becoming a staple in the trade to Nairobi, as well as a popular food. Women sometimes went to Nairobi and never returned, or they came back in bad shape from hard living and sexual abuse (B Wangige, interview by author, 22 July 1988). Young politically conscious men involved in the Kikuyu Central Association (founded in 1924) took up the cause of stopping the women's Nairobi trade with nationalistic fervor, securing the backing of the Local Native Council (LNC) and the chief, Kinyanjui wa Gathirimu. The subsequent struggle is documented in *Muigwithania* (Kikuyu for the *Unifier*, hereinafter referred to as *Muig.*), a Kikuyu newspaper edited by the young Jomo Kenyatta (Barnett and Njama 1966:37). The grievances expressed in 1928 were consistently vehement on the subject of loss of control over both married and unmarried women. Xenophobia was evident in some protests; control over women was seen as one determinant of a nation's greatness. One correspondent from Kahuhia stated that the chiefs should

> look after the matter of those Kikuyu women who live amongst the Foreigners, in the towns of the Foreigners. Because this custom is one which causes the Kikuyu nation to decrease, for these women bear children among the foreigners and are taken to other nations and, further, these women have given for them not even a bean . . . to be eaten by the Kikuyu . . . [no bridewealth]. If we allow our nation to become scattered in this way, how shall the seed of the Kikuyu be made to increase? Will it not just become stunted? (*Muig.* 1, 7, November 1928)[7]

Kenyatta in response asserted that the strength of nations is symbolized by their maintenance of control over women.

> Raise your eyes and see how the powerful nations and those who are most famous—how they have exalted their women and girls and made prohibitions concerning them. . . . Guard against dropping your child (or daughter or wife) like a millet stalk by the wayside, lest you make yourself despicable, while all the time you look upon it as a joke. (*Muig.* 1, 7, November 1928:2)

He was clearly not fooled by the gilt on British middle- and upper-class women's cages.

Another correspondent said that people in Nairobi were impugning Kikuyu manhood because of Kikuyu women's immodesty, while Kenyatta went on to say that it was women's trading that was leading them to corruption (*Muig.* 1, 7, November 1928). Perhaps the most purple prose was in an article by George Ndegwa and Dishon Waihenya entitled "The Trading of Girls and Women in Potatoes and Other Things in Nairobi— This Is the Cause of the Beginning of Insubordination."

The trading . . . is a danger to the girls and newly married women, being produce not from their own gardens . . . frequently it is the road to the beginning
of Prostitution, although the woman did not desire it. . . . When they are selling they . . . are spoken to by people of many nations and shameless things
are said to them. . . . We are being exterminated at a blow. . . . Oh you Bride
of Kabete, you have done wrong without knowing it: would you deceive
your husband by saying that you are going to sell potatoes [but] when noon
arrives you are sitting at a table [drinking is implied]? . . . These days, on account of trade and other things pertaining to profit-making they have all
burned their Modesty like Firewood, for even any stranger whatsoever can
stop a Kikuyu girl or woman on the road to talk to her. If it were the old days
the childless thousands who are now prostitutes . . . would be in Kikuyuland
with their fathers and husbands, and would have children as numerous as
they. . . . Are We to Die Thus Without Protest?" (*Muig.* 1, 8, December
1928–January 1929)

"Insubordination" more than immorality was disturbing to the authors.[8]
Clearly, the men were also worried about perpetuating their own lin-
eages, while women like Amina Hali liked having their own money and
their own children not claimed by the fathers.

But most of the protest centered on women going to Nairobi and becom-
Prostitution was also becoming a rural problem in men's view, for
which there is corroborative evidence.[9] An anonymous contributor signified his outrage at overhearing two girls at Maragua Market in southern
Murang'a plotting to deceive their parents. He said many young girls
came to sell around 6:00 P.M.; he heard some discussing the deception the
next morning. One said, "I shall deceive my mother by telling her that
when one goes to sell maize she should spend the night at Maragua so as
to get a good price for it! . . . Should I want to come often there is no one
to stop me!" The author implied that these were schoolgirls (*Muig.* 1, 7,
November 1928).

But most of the protest centered on women going to Nairobi and becoming what one contributor called "*njara-ruhi*" (Kikuyu for stretchers-out-of-
the-palm, or beggars), wicked city women who rejected the authority of
their fathers and husbands and exploited men by taking their bodies and
their possessions. K. Kirobi, a work seeker in Nairobi, wrote to the newspaper to express his outrage that a Kikuyu man in Pangani was *murdered*
by a woman. He went on to say that such women made bad wives (!) since
they would not settle down; after all, they had left their homes for bad reasons such as disobedience to their menfolk, not wanting to repay
bridewealth, and so on (*Muig.* 1, 8, December 1928–January 1929:14).

Women's trading was a dominant issue, in fact, in the protest over un-
controlled women, which also included ire over girls going to European-
run schools. Going to school was associated with a whole range of evil
consequences. Girls ran away to missions and were put in schools to be-

come Christians. Not only were they out of the control of Kikuyu men, but also their reproductive powers had been given to foreigners and they were forsaking their own culture. The missionaries raised objections to polygyny and clitoridectomy, both of which many Kikuyu felt were central to the fabric of their society (Kenyatta [1938] 1959:132–133). There was, then, a whole complex of issues pressured by the intensifying impact of the colonial presence in the late 1920s, and this came to a head with one of the loci being control of women's trading activities. The fact that some prostitutes in Nairobi were becoming independently wealthy must have only added fuel to the fire (White 1990:124–125; Stichter 1977:11).

One reaction by both the elders and the younger politicos was to try to stop women from going to Nairobi to trade. In his youth, Chief Kinyanjui had been promiscuous and had made many girls pregnant without marrying them, causing his family to disown him. In his older years he was consistent in his negative view of women, forbidding his daughters to go to school and, under pressure from the LNC, forbidding women to trade in Nairobi (Kinyanjui 1975:22, 42). This prohibition was preceded by a host of Kiambu LNC resolutions aimed at controlling women's chastity: forbidding young men and women to bathe together at the river lest it lead to "indecent assault," forbidding certain dances held at midnight "for the purpose of violating virgins," asking that women's lodgings on settler farms be isolated from men's camps and men be forbidden entry (a request attributable to the frequently reported sexual abuse of young girls) (Ross [1927] 1968:111–113). On 22–23 November 1928, they discussed prohibiting women from going to Nairobi to sell produce, "as it leads to prostitution and disease." But the district commissioner (DC) said that it was a "domestic affair" and that legislation was "incapable of controlling women's morals." Whereas in 1927 it had been acknowledged that one of the contributing factors to prostitution was men taking and discarding mistresses, the attitude in 1928 was generally condemnatory of women.[10]

Although without the DC's support, the Kiambu and Dagoretti LNCs passed resolutions forbidding women to go to Nairobi to trade, securing Kinyanjui's help in setting his police to turn them back (*Muig.* 1, 7, November 1928:11). Kinyanjui's effort was his last act as chief. Before setting off on a trip to Maasailand he confirmed the prohibition despite the lack of support from the DC. When he returned with a tetanus infection that was to be fatal, he was told that the DC had arrested and fined his men set to stop the women and had said, "Anyone again picketing the woman or preventing a woman from passing and going to trade, I will imprison him for six months without a trial [hearing]." Nevertheless, Kinyanjui insisted that the prohibition should remain. He was then taken to Dr. Arthur's

Mission Hospital, where he died; Canon Leakey presided at his funeral (since both Arthur and Leakey were strong opponents of clitoridectomy, this was surely an irony of fate) (obituary for Kinyanjui wa Gathirimu, *Muig*. 1, 10, February-March 1929:3–4).

Nonetheless, the patrols stopped and this incident marked the failure of Kikuyu men's efforts at that time to stop women from trading in Nairobi, efforts that were predominantly based in rural areas. The DC's actions were surely not concerned with protecting women's rights, given that he shared Kikuyu men's negative opinion regarding women's morals. The 1928 Kiambu *Annual Report* stated (p. 12), "There is a strong movement in the Reserve to forbid women and young girls going to Nairobi to sell produce owing to the laxity in morals of such women and the well founded risk of their becoming prostitutes; the establishment of markets on the borders of the Reserves and the Nairobi district is being considered." The DC was more concerned about the necessary services and produce supplied by women to the predominantly male Nairobi population. Alternative supplies of fresh food were difficult to come by, and a cheap urban food supply was a cornerstone of the British administrative policy to promote a cheap labor supply (Onstad 1990, chap. l). If Kikuyu elders and intelligentsia objected to women trading, there were surely other men involved in market gardening who needed the women's help in realizing cash for their produce (Kitching 1980:67).

In the 1930s, the effort to stop women's trade in Nairobi was renewed, the Nairobi Native Advisory Council (NNAC) going so far as to ask that pass laws be extended to women for this purpose. The fact that African men but not women at this time were restricted by pass laws must have caused considerable resentment and heightened concern over women escaping men's control. Again the men got no support, this time from the Municipal Native Affairs Officer.[11] The growth rate of Nairobi slowed due to the depression—it went from having an African population of approximately 28,000 in 1930 to 41,000 in 1939 (Onstad 1990:48–49). Nevertheless, women, impelled by economic and social necessity, continued to go to Nairobi in large numbers. A Kamba woman who arrived in Nairobi in the 1930s said, "Trouble is what showed me Pumwani [an African neighborhood in Nairobi], problems make you find anywhere to stay." Women continued to flee forced marriages or sought support for themselves and their families when widowed or divorced (White 1990:84). The Kiambu and Dagoretti Local Native Tribunals dealt with a steady stream of cases in which men sued other men for enticing away their wives or daughters, which appeared in the Nairobi court records as adultery cases. In August 1932 the Kiambu DC commented, "This enticing away of women causes great resentment and in many cases the men who do it are without property, and the girl is returned with great trouble and difficulty and is by this time 'soiled goods.'"[12] Clearly, the diminishing control over women by the propertied was used by the landless to secure women (a phenomenon also evident in some marriages in my 1987–1988 sample of fifty-six women). The DC left the adultery cases to the Local Native Tribunal but rape and indecent assault were viewed as criminal offenses to be tried under British law and not subject to Kikuyu customs that treated women as property and compensated men for property damage or loss.[13]

In Nairobi, undesirables continued to be deported to the Reserves and a Local Native Tribunal was established in 1930 to advise the Municipal Native Affairs Officer, a position that had been established in 1928 (Onstad 1990:104). Neither prostitutes nor traders were greatly harassed in the 1930s. A ninety-four-year-old Kamba woman interviewed in 1987, who began hawking in Nairobi in the 1930s, said that she was not bothered by European officials; most regarded her as a beggar, gave her bits of cash, and told her, "Here, go eat something" (77 Ngara, interview by author, 11 November 1987). In 1934 the municipal trade licenses inspector claimed that he and his two African assistants were unable to control hawking. Produce hawkers in the 1930s paid only 1 shilling per month for a license, a sum that the Kikuyu Central Association appealed on behalf of vegetable hawkers in 1931 (Onstad 1990:11, 52, 105). In Kiambu, the number of trade licenses granted declined because of staff shortages, and enforcement was nil.[14] In 1939 only one person was arrested for hawking without a license, compared to hundreds arrested for remaining in the municipality without work for over thirty-six hours and for breaking the 10:00 P.M. curfew.[15]

Prostitution was apparently spreading to small towns such as Limuru and Fort Hall. But it remained more of an urban preoccupation of men. Chief Muhoho of the Kikuyu complained that young men were coming out from Nairobi on Sundays and inducing girls to return with them to Nairobi "where they become prostitutes."[16] In 1938 the Nairobi Municipal Native Affairs Officer, Eric Davies, said that *malaya* prostitution (involving domestic services in addition to sex) was a necessary part of African urban life and saved the cost of housing families, while making it unnecessary to pay men enough to support a family. Nonetheless, there were occasional campaigns to deport "undesirable females" from Nairobi.[17] According to one observer, most court cases in the 1930s concerned property rights in women and cattle. Women left their husbands because they were maltreated or the bridewealth had not been paid (Desmond O'Hagan, DC Nairobi 1944–1945, interview by author, 8 November 1988). In 1939 Davies noted that the 8:1 male: female sex ratio in Nairobi created a huge demand for prostitutes and encouraged young women to leave home.[18] The combination of unpleasantness, constraint, and poverty at home and the prospect of mobility and independence in Nairobi, whether as traders or prostitutes, must have been irresistible to some women.

"Nefarious Happenings": The Exigencies of War at Home and Abroad, 1940–1964

In the second phase of men's efforts to control women traders, the focus shifted from controlling women's bodies—their sexuality—to stopping their movement and business activities. This phase is marked by several wars—World War II, the civil war of the Emergency (between the British, Kikuyu loyalists, and Kikuyu freedom fighters), and the first hawker war (the second began in the 1980s). All three wars had the effect of spurring efforts to tighten controls over population movement, especially that of traders; the first of the hawker wars began because of attempts to tighten controls after a temporary relaxation. These tightened controls also made illegal much of the activity in what is now known as the informal sector. If the groundwork was laid earlier with pass and vagrancy laws and hawker regulations, in Kenya the first serious attempt to enforce those laws efficiently was provoked by the wars, and the resentment caused by that enforcement also helped to cause the rebellion called Mau Mau by the British; the guerrilla fighters called themselves the Land and Freedom Army (LFA).

In this period, gender was only episodically salient when it was used by the British and the loyalists in their attempt to consolidate their control. Thus, if in the 1920s and 1930s colonial officials often did not abet elders' attempts to control women, in the 1940s and 1950s the emphasis on controlling population movement and helping local collaborators with the regime changed the picture considerably. The alliance of young and old Kikuyu men against women broke down with the young militants joining the Land and Freedom Army. As independence approached in the early 1960s, efforts to maintain male dominance were becoming embedded in class struggles and therefore were no longer focused narrowly on gender issues alone but expanded to a wider arena.

Class divisions became apparent early in the 1940s when African shopkeepers, a small but growing element, objected to competition from hawkers and joined in the effort to control them. In April 1942, the East Africa Traders Association wrote to the Nairobi Acting Town Clerk, urging tighter restrictions on the granting of hawkers' licenses and saying, "The majority of hawkers obtain licences to cloak various nefarious happenings."[19] Such class differentiation among traders was regarded as desirable by policymakers, who wished to create a more prosperous type of male trader; gendered class formation was a conscious aim of British administration. The Nairobi Municipal Native Affairs Officer stated in the 1941 *Annual Report*:

> The aim is to evolve a class which will, with a little capital, be able to supply more people at lower prices . . . the native hawker is usually a Kikuyu from sixty to seventy miles away taking advantage of temporary booms. . . . He usually lives in the most overcrowded parts of Pumwani and rarely has his wife or family with him. What is desirable is a more stable figure living at a higher level of subsistence and more knowledgeable in his trade.

Why did such people come to Nairobi? The answer is that the pay from hawking was better than either rural or urban laborers' pay, and the war had caused a jump in the prosperity of the town.[20] The African population of Nairobi went from 41,000 in 1939 to 70,000 in 1941 (Onstad 1990:49). Thus, encouraging those men who could afford fixed selling places or licenses was approved, but itinerant unlicensed traders were undesirable. Women were invisible in this thinking.

But the most important shift in government policy in the early 1940s was the agreement that trading licenses "which were at present only a revenue producing measure should be a *control* measure."[21] This decision meshed with a pass law aimed particularly at prostitutes, whereby all Africans permanently resident in Nairobi had to carry passes or risk repatriation to the Reserves, and the number of hawkers' licenses was reduced from five hundred to three hundred in 1941.[22] Nairobi women had to carry passes, whether hawking or not. While the NMC (Nairobi Municipal Council) was not willing to forbid hawking altogether, it adopted the policy of gradually widening the number of commodities requiring licenses to sell. Nonetheless, in 1945 those selling fish, poultry, vegetables, eggs, fruit, milk, prepared food, firewood, newspapers, and handicrafts did not require licenses.[23] Under a 1942 Nairobi "spiv" law (a spiv being a person regarded as making a living from shady dealings), two hundred persons a month were picked up and deported to the Reserves as vagrants in 1949 (Onstad 1990:89).[24]

What was happening regarding women traders in particular? Prostitution, venereal disease, and women escaping husbands were of increased concern to the Kiambu LNC and the NNAC, as well as to the Kikuyu Houseboys Association.[25] The colonial administration cooperated to an extent unknown in the first phase. The Kiambu District Officer fined men for taking young girls to Nairobi for European-type dances; compulsory medical examinations for prostitutes were introduced. A woman could not obtain urban employment as a maid or child minder without "it first being established that she was not a runaway girl or wife." Wives living in overcrowded conditions did not get their passes renewed, probably as much from the fear of prostitution as from desire to reduce population density. Prostitution itself was changing, becoming more limited to merely sexual encounters, which made it less useful to British administrators concerned about labor stability (White 1990). Women were forbidden to enter African eating houses.[26] Neither the Kiambu nor the Nairobi African councils had a woman member.

In 1945 the Municipal African Affairs Officer came up with a plan to reformulate the administration of African affairs along the lines of indirect rule through "native associations" in a move designed to prevent "the drift to the towns of women and girls" who became prostitutes or traders.[27] Because the commercial infrastructure of Nairobi was better developed in the 1940s than the 1920s, it was not so dependent on itinerant traders, but women were still flocking to Nairobi, with the heightened demand of the military presence offering opportunities. Meanwhile, rural conditions involving unwanted marriages, abusive husbands, hard labor, and landlessness through widowhood or divorce still exerted pressure. The 1942 Nairobi Municipal Native Administrative District *Annual Report* said that it was more due to difficulties at home than to the attractions of town that women ran away, adding that "Kikuyu girls require less excuse and now predominate amongst the young girls who have run away to town for its attractions . . . it is not easy to make a girl stay home who has once enjoyed the idle life of town."[28] The situation in the Reserves was not good economically and the position of women in the household division of labor had been undermined. Kiambu was becoming a bedroom community for Nairobi, with men leaving their wives there to do more of the agricultural labor than previously, while socioeconomic differentiation proceeded apace (Throup 1988:77, 89).

Without the diversion of World War II, the growing internal socioeconomic crisis became more evident—and acute. The African population of Nairobi was no longer as amenable to control. The authorities responded with ever more stringent efforts. A February 1946 ordinance allowed any authority to remove any African from the municipality for any reason without warrant or appeal (Aaronovitch and Aaronovitch 1947:121). The trade licensing officer said that without more help he could not control increased trading activities involving more than two thousand unlicensed traders (Throup 1988:172). The Kikuyu General Union (KGU) rounded up wayward girls for trial and repatriation to rural homes.[29]

Markets were becoming sites of protest; on 30 July 1947, a squad of plainclothes police involved in "mopping up spivs" was stoned in a market and had to fight its way out of the crowd.[30] The result of these conditions was another rash of laws in 1949 attempting to control both traders and "voluntarily unemployed persons."[31] One observer of the scene in 1950 commented,

If one of the happier pictures of colonial Africa is that of the District Officer and local chief proudly surveying a cotton crop or a new village well, the most gloomy is that of the police of East Africa harrying the vegetable sellers, usually women, on a periodic roundup of unauthorized markets in an urban estate. (Werlin 1974:56–57).

In concert with the British authorities, the African councils renewed their push to ban women from trading, associating it as always with prostitution. Again, younger activists supported controlling women; the Kenya General Union carried out campaigns to force uninitiated girls to be excised. Nairobi women traders were prohibited from having trade licenses by government order. This 1945 ruling was canceled, however, due to a protest from "porige sellers" and the hardship imposed on urban women. The NNAC agreed that the restriction was only to apply to women coming from the Reserves and made so many exceptions for porridge sellers, who were supplying most African workers with their meals, that the prohibition became meaningless.[32] By the late 1940s, the legal restrictions on both marketing of foodstuffs and movement of traders were such that most urban Africans were dependent on an underground economy, chiefly produce hawked by women from Kiambu and Thika (White 1990:153; Throup 1988:188). At the same time, the first African businessman was appointed to an important trade advisory committee, a harbinger of the entry of a new element into hawker control efforts.[33]

It has long been recognized that the 1950s Emergency was a complex conflict, both a reaction to rural landlessness and an urban revolt in which the role of traders was evident (Furedi 1977:237). It was no accident that Tom Mbotela, a Nairobi African Council member and popularly considered to be an archcollaborator, was assassinated on 27 November 1952 in Burma Market. The stall holders of Burma Market were immediately arrested, and the market was destroyed by fire the same night (*East African News Review*, 5 February 1948; Onstad 1990:84). The struggle for land and freedom was also explicitly gendered; women entered into it as freedom fighters, as farmers supplying food, and as traders (Kanogo 1987, 1988:143ff.). The issue of social and economic control of women was prominent among freedom fighters, as well as among loyalists. The difference was that among freedom fighters in the forest, traditional gender roles were eventually challenged and overthrown in some cases, whereas among the loyalists, the pressure remained on women to conform (White 1988:15).

In Nairobi, "petty traders were natural recruits for [the LFA]: most of them had a strong impetus to fight the colonial government while their livelihood gave them a perfect cover for subversive activities" (Onstad 1990:110). But male traders seem to have been more likely to support the revolt than females because the activists carried out considerable sexual harassment against women. Veronica Wanjiru, a trader who came to Nairobi in the early 1950s to peddle vegetables and fruit, said, "I could see that the Mau Mau harassed the beautiful girls, the ones who were older than myself. The Mau Mau, they would like to 'marry' the girls by force" (Onstad 1990:115). Women were sometimes kidnapped by forest fighters. But then, loyalists also harassed women. Among the sample of fifty-six Nairobi area traders interviewed in 1988, two were Kikuyu women interned as young teenagers in the 1950s and forced to "marry" loyalists in Kiambu, no bridewealth being paid and no consent asked from their parents. One of them commented, "Going to bed with him was a nightmare. But I persevered as it was a time of problems. If one was not in a secure place there was the danger of being killed by Mau Mau" (112 Ngara, interview by author, 23 November 1987). Rape by loyalist home guards was common (Likimani 1985:76). Many women may have had more interest in avoiding any political involvement as too risky. Muthoni Likimani (1985:92) has described one common Kikuyu reaction to the Emergency political situation as *komerera* (Kikuyu for "lie low, keep out of trouble"), which was also the term for the buses that secretly transported traders back and forth to Nairobi during the Emergency.

Before the declaration of Emergency in 1952, ethnic associations still expected to be able to control women. In 1950 the Kikuyu General Union said that four groups of women should be allowed to stay in town: those who were legally married and living with their husbands, registered domestic servants, householders, and "old prostitutes who have lived this way for a long time and cannot find alternative means of employment." Also, taxi drivers carrying prostitutes and prostitutes' customers were to be punished. In practice, however, the prostitutes themselves were the chief victims of the harassment when salaried female informers interrogated runaways, who had to show proof of marriage and explain why they had left their husbands or parents. Both the KGU and the Kalenjin Union asked that unsatisfactory maids be reported to them (White 1990:192–193).

However, by the end of the 1950s, the chief loci of efforts to control African women were British laws and authorities, as demonstrated in a decline in the efforts by loyalist African authorities to control women. Court records, as shown in detail elsewhere (Robertson forthcoming), indicate clearly the decline in expectations of sexual control of women by the African tribunals and an increase in rowdy behavior by women in both Kiambu and Nairobi, especially the latter.[34] Adultery cases declined as a proportion of cases, but liquor- and pass-related offenses by women in Nairobi increased. Nairobi's growth made control of women ever more difficult, while men's expectations that such control was possible declined, submerged in the political crisis preceding independence.

Meanwhile, efforts by local authorities to control unlicensed trade were being heightened. In 1952 in Kiambu, there was only one trade-related case against a woman (0.8 percent of the 123 cases), whereas 2.6 percent of the 1,463 cases brought against men fell into this category. The underground economy, in which many participated, flourished largely unmolested. By 1960 in Kiambu, the situation had only changed a bit; 1.8 percent of the cases brought against women were related to trade, versus 3.4 percent of those charged against men. In Nairobi in 1951, very few cases were trade related and none were brought against women, but in 1960, 7 percent of the cases brought against women and 5.8 percent of those against men involved hawking without a license.[35]

During the Emergency the colonial administration turned its attention to controlling hawking in Nairobi by drastically reducing the number of licenses granted. A good indicator regarding the position of women traders in Nairobi is the number of *uji* (gruel) licenses granted, since women sold it. From 1952 to 1957, the number of *uji* licenses stood at 105, but the total number of hawkers' licenses fell from 667 to 185. From 1953 to 1954 alone, the number dropped from 804 to 391 (Onstad 1990:63; Dickerman 1978:37–39). The chief argument for maintaining the number of *uji* licenses was the need to provision workers cheaply, so it was not affected by the removal of 37,000 Kikuyu, Embu, and Meru (called KEM in documents) from Nairobi in Operation Anvil in April 1954 (Hake 1977:61). But KEM tea hawkers, who were usually among the more prosperous male traders, were forbidden to sell completely in 1953 because they were thought to be witnesses or accomplices to Mau Mau crimes who refused to inform the police (Ross 1975:20). In May 1953, the police raided and destroyed some 600 temporary market stalls at the rear of Kariakor Market, arrested the occupants, and also tore down illegal stalls later at Shauri Moyo.[36] Shops of presumed activists were confiscated and redistributed to non-KEM, while fences were built around African locations and curfews were enforced. Spot raids were conducted to catch violators of the many restrictions, and squatter villages like Kariobangi were destroyed (Dickerman 1978:12, 18–19, 20, 38, 41). Plans were made to limit Kikuyu to no more than 25 percent of Nairobi's population.[37]

After the most violent part of the Emergency died down, the authorities decided to crack down further on hawking regardless of the commodity sold; in 1958, only 80 *uji* licenses were given and in 1959, only 60.[38] When a group of widows appealed the reduction, the chief municipal inspector of markets gave them short shrift, saying, "all unlicensed hawking must stop and the offenders will be relentlessly prosecuted until that end is achieved. It is therefore necessary for the widows you mention to take up some form of livelihood that is lawful." Former licensees got nowhere upon appeal.[39] At the same time, the General Secretary of the

Nairobi People's Convention Party complained to the Town Clerk about the arrests of women hawkers, who were fined 50 shillings or got two months in prison.[40] Other protests concerned the initiation of the policy that itinerant hawkers could only sell in their own "racial area."[41] Of course, for most women traders, licenses and infrastructure were in any case unaffordable, nor were they granted licenses in rural areas when the few who could afford it applied to the African District Council. Most women could also probably not afford the bribes necessary to obtain licenses both in urban and in rural areas.[42]

The articulated concerns of government, however, did not mention gender when justifying the attempt to obliterate the hawker population. The focus was rather on the security risk (with particular attention paid to the fact that most traders were Kikuyu), the presumed unsanitary methods of operation for cooked foods, general dirtiness, traffic congestion, the nuisance of traders' importunities to European housewives, and their assumed involvement in crimes more serious than the elementary one of illegal hawking. Another argument involved their posing unfair competition for shopkeepers (Werlin 1981:199–200). According to Likimani (1985:65), Europeans perceived women traders during the Emergency as being "dirty Mau Mau savages." Walter Elkan, T.C.I. Ryan, and J. T. Mukui (1982:249) aptly described the cosmetic concerns in the Kenyan government's attitude: "If there was poverty in Nairobi, the way to deal with it was to sweep it out of sight so that it would not offend the sight of those who so proudly proclaimed Nairobi the most modern city in tropical Africa." There was also a strain of concern about poverty and its possible dangerous political consequences. The 1954 Kenya government *Report on Destitution* said (p. 5):

> The tendency to reduce the numbers of open-air traders may make a contribution to the number of indigents. Questions of hygiene, traffic problems and no doubt many other factors induce the desire in those responsible to impose severe limitations on the numbers of African petty traders, but we would nevertheless urge that the opportunity of a modest livelihood that these activities afford should be provided whenever possible.

As we have seen, this recommendation was ignored whenever possible.

The Emergency policies probably harmed women more than men because women were legally more vulnerable. Even the more prosperous women suffered. Because a married woman's right to live in Nairobi was contingent upon her husband's status, she was automatically removed along with her husband. A glimpse of the kind of thing that could happen comes from a letter from a woman shopkeeper to the Nairobi DC (28 April 1956). Wangui was watching her husband Chege's shop for him after he was repatriated, a tactic some employed so as not to lose their en-

tire investment. She complained that the Ngara chief Owiso was harassing her, claiming that she had no right to sell, but that she always paid the
rent, had a legal pass, and four children to support.

> Whilst I maintain my loyalty to her Majesty's Government I feel extremely
> injustified by Chief Owiso's action against me. Had I been a woman without
> proper standings and left to roam in the town then his actions would be jus-
> tified and fair, however he is on the contrary and has no mercey upon my fu-
> ture being together with my children.
>
> It is not the intention of the Government to make the women poor and I
> believe the Government is doing the best it could to see that the African
> women are advanced, but with [this] action it is to reverse our progress and
> stir hatred or bad feelings by misusing the Government Policy to the loyal
> citizens.
>
> I lay my trust on nobody but the British Government and I pray that Chief
> Owiso be stopped from his merciless actions on me.

On 12 May 1956, the Nairobi DC told the Municipal African Affairs Officer that he was not going to reply to her as she had already been repatriated and was supposed to have gone with her husband in the first place.[43]
Several informants stopped going to Nairobi to trade at that time because
they could not get passes from the loyalist chief, whether they were Mau
Mau supporters or not, or because "they were beaten so hard" (667
Kangemi, interview by author, 25 July 1988; 561 Kawangware, interview
by author, 23 June 1988).

The hawker war of the early 1960s was directly precipitated by the late
Emergency measures to get rid of hawking and by the subsequent lifting
of the Emergency restrictions on movement that allowed thousands of
hawkers to go to Nairobi. This influx only grew because of the increasing
landlessness provoked by land consolidation entailed in the Swynnerton
Plan of 1954, which furthered the considerable privatization of ownership
already present in 1941 in Kiambu (Throup 1988:78). The pressure on
Nairobi was such that an immediate increase in the number of licenses
was precipitated. But there were two key political factors influencing that
shift. First, the hawkers themselves, primarily the men, were getting organized to defend their interests. Second, the British government's reluctant recognition of the inevitability of independence, fostered by their
problems with keeping control, led to the Africanization and politiciza-
tion of the hawker struggle in Nairobi, as African politicians sought to secure hawker support. In July 1960, the NMC decided to issue over four
hundred trading licenses; in November, that was raised to over eight hundred. The African mayor of Nairobi made granting more hawkers' licenses a priority in 1962, despite the fact that fifteen hundred had already
been issued in August.[44] Nevertheless, illegal hawkers still predomi-

nated—by 1963 there were over two thousand of them (Werlin 1981:200–201). Most of the unlicensed traders were selling prepared foods, and many were women.[45]

By mid-1961, the authorities felt that things were out of control. Three major hawkers' organizations were formed between 1960 and 1962 and fought to obtain the right to establish their own permanent or itinerant selling space. Their agenda included not only the right to secure selling spaces of their choice but also an increased number of licenses, relaxed regulations to allow permanence and expansion of businesses and capital accumulation, and the cessation of police harassment.[46]

The boycotts of designated trading locations, protest marches, and the constant street fights in which bystanders came to the aid of hawkers whom the police were trying to arrest were as effective as the written petitions and protests. The Crime and Incident Reports for 1960 are full of incidents of hawkers resisting arrest. A typical one occurred on 8 July 1960, when police constables from Shauri Moyo were attempting to arrest illegal hawkers at Machakos Country Bus Stop, still a center for illegal trading. The police were stoned by the crowd, only succeeded in arresting one juvenile, and sent for reinforcements to extract themselves from the imbroglio. There were three incidents on 16 November 1960 at Shauri Moyo Market, including one in which a large crowd prevented two plain-clothes officers from making an arrest by pushing them out of the market, one officer having been bitten on the finger, and two in which police were stoned by the crowd.[47] By the end of 1962, the Nairobi City Council (NCC) had given up on trying to stop hawking altogether and was hoping instead to be able to control it somewhat. In the 1963 scramble for new bylaws aimed at controlling hawkers (the old ones were invalidated by the court in 1962 as not applicable to itinerant hawkers and too general), the old ones were repealed inadvertently with no new ones yet passed, and governmental disarray was complete.[48] Although the bylaws were reinstated, this situation stands as a symbol of the inadequacy of colonial hawker policy under the onslaught of postcolonial conditions.

Conclusion

From 1940 to 1963, Nairobi African markets had become a locus of political and economic protest that was not segregated by gender. Both women and men took part in the escalating level of street violence in and around markets—fighting the police, hiding miscreants, and generally refusing to accept the dictates of authority where their livelihoods were concerned. It is clear that both the nature and the role of gender concerns in the struggle over hawking had changed irrevocably by 1963. More particularistic concerns about controlling women's sexuality, which were so prominent in earlier attempts to stop their hawking, had by 1963 been supplanted by class-based efforts to maintain law and order, which further criminalized many of the activities of the informal sector. Although prostitutes were still being persecuted on moral grounds, traders were being attacked primarily on economic grounds. For women, the shift was from controlling traders to controlling trade, where women's disabilities derived more from discrimination in access to capital and trading sites than from their sexuality.

This transformation was the symbol of the increasing dominance among the upper classes of concerns over controlling the lower classes rather than over ethnic or gender conflicts. Class conflict has since widened in Kenya, requiring escalating levels of force from the government. The state as the arm of the bourgeoisie is very evident here. Gavin Kitching (1980:453) has called Kenya's "state bourgeoisie" its most exploitative class. It is clear that before independence, the colonial government, both in the heat of Mau Mau and in the cooler venues of hawker policy, succeeded in encouraging and promulgating class distinctions. After independence, these distinctions were promoted with enthusiasm by Kenyan merchants and rulers, whose accession to power and influence was rooted securely in the events of the 1950s. Later attempts to control women traders are the subject of another essay (Robertson 1993), but the history of petty traders in Nairobi—their burgeoning numbers and militance, along with the failed attempts to control them—lends urban illustration to Christopher Leo's image of a government powerless to control an expanding peasant sector (1984:186–187). Events under colonialism help to explain how women who were a permanent migratory urban trading population derived from the peasantry have now become an increasingly militant urban underclass. Whatever the attempts to control their activities, they are most often landless and must support their families; they will not go away.

Notes

1. Data for this study were gathered in 1987–1988 under a Fulbright fellowship; their compilation has been partially supported by grants from Ohio State University. They consist of extensive primary and secondary archival materials gathered in five Nairobi libraries and two U.S. libraries, as well as three surveys of traders in the Nairobi area, the largest being a census of approximately 6,000 traders in 17 markets. Most traders are Kikuyu, but there is also substantial Kamba representation. Archival research was conducted in the Kenya National Archives (KNA), whose staff was uniformly pleasant and helpful. Archival references given here indicate KNA files; NCC indicates a Nairobi City Council/Commission file. AR indicates an Annual Report, at various government levels.

2. Traders who were interviewed were assigned a letter or number and the name of the location where the interview was conducted to protect their identity, necessary due to their possible involvement in illegal trading activities.

3. PC/CP 4/2/1 Ukambani AR 1908–1909.

4. DC/KBU 1/5 Dagoretti AR 1913–1914:15.

5. DC/KBU/1/3 Kiambu AR 1911–1912; PC/CP 4/2/1 Nairobi AR 1909–1910:2b; DC/KBU 1/4 Kiambu AR:14.

6. PC/CP 4/1/2 Kikuyu Province AR 1924:9.

7. This newspaper was found in KNA files DC/MKS lOB/13/1. The correspondent was Gideon M. Kagika, the translation by the missionary A. R. Barlow.

8. I am indebted to John Lonsdale both for alerting me to the unlikely location of this material and for this observation (Berman and Lonsdale 1992:386).

9. PC/CP 4/1/2 Kikuyu Province AR 1924:4; PC/CENT Kiambu LNC Minutes, 19–20 March 1934.

10. PC/CENT 2/1/4 Kiambu LNC Minutes, 4 April 1927, 22–23 November 1928.

11. NCC file 27/10; Nairobi Municipal Council (NMC) Native Affairs Committee Minutes, 11 August 1932, 3 November 1932.

12. See CNC 10/45, DC Kiambu to Attorney General; CNC 10/29 more generally on adultery cases.

13. CNC 10/45, Attorney General to DC Kiambu, 18 July 1931; Solicitor General to DC Kiambu, 10 August 1931.

14. DC/KBU/1/30 Kiambu AR 1939:27.

15. LG 3/3207 Nairobi Municipal Native Affairs Department AR 1939:47.

16. Quote in PC/CENT 2/1/4 Kiambu LNC Minutes, 2–4 May 1933; see also PC/CENT 2/1/4 Kiambu LNC Minutes, 19–20 March 1934; ARC (MAA) 2/3/1/VIA Nairobi AR 1938:15.

17. ARC (MAA) 2/3/1/VIA Nairobi AR 1938.

18. Nairobi Municipal Native Affairs Department AR 1939:34.

19. LG 2/125 Doc. 2, 22 April 1942.

20. ARC (MAA) 2/3/8III:22.

21. MCI 6/881, Sixth Annual Conference of District Council Representatives, 11–12 September 1945. Trade licenses bound licensees to particular locations and commodities and were not to be reallocated by the licensee, as in subletting fixed locations. Traders were not to live in their shops or to use flimsy construction materials and were to observe sanitary regulations. Agri 4/68.

22. PC/CP 4/4/1:4.

23. LG 2/125 Doc. 27, 1942 Amendment to Hawkers Bylaws; MCI 6/881 Crown Counsel to Honorable Chief Secretary, Ministry of Commerce, 2 March 1945.

24. African Affairs Department AR 1949:57.

25. PC/CENT 2/1/13 Kiambu LNC Minutes, 3–5 July 1944:3, 11–14 December 1944:11; NNAC Minutes, 3–4 September 1945; Stichter 1982:171.

26. CNC 10/45 D.O. Kiambu to Crown Counsel 26 January 1946; PC/CP 4/4/2 NMC AR 1944:12; CS 1/14/11 NNAC Minutes, 9 May 1944, 11 July 1944:3, 19 August 1944:1.

27. MAA 7/491 memo Askwith to Chief Native Commissioner:1.

28. ARC (MAA) 2/3/8III:27.

29. LG 3/3139 NMC General Purposes Committee Minutes, 17 February 1947; MAA 8/22 Askwith to Superintendent C.I.D., 29 October 1947; MAA 8/22 Superintendent of African Locations to Superintendent C.I.D., 28 October 1947; White 1990:191.

30. PC/CP 4/4/3 Nairobi AR 1947:10.

31. NCC 2/281 Doc. 1, Verandah Trading By-laws; ARC (MAA) 2/3/36VII Central Province AR 1950:54.

32. PC/CP 2/1/13 Kiambu LNC Minutes, 13–15 March 1945:9; NCC 27/10 DC Nairobi to Town Clerk, 4 October 1945; LG 3/3140 NMC Native Affairs Committee Minutes, 6 January 1949; CS 1/14/11 Nairobi Native Affairs Committee Minutes, 15 October 1945:4, 13 November 1945:1.

33. MAA 8/22 Chief Native Commissioner to Municipal African Affairs Officer, 6 January 1948.

34. CNC 10/46, 10/30; MAA 2/24, 2/26, 2/16.

35. MAA 2/24, 2/26, 2/16.

36. LG 3/3143 NCC African Affairs Committee Minutes, 6 May 1953, Finance Committee Minutes, 18 May 1953.

37. AA 13/1/8/9 Kiambu AR 1957:1.

38. LG 3/3147 NCC African Affairs Committee Minutes, 12 October 1957; LG 3/3149 NCC General Purposes Committee Minutes, 4 September 1959.

39. Quote is in NCC 27/10 Chief Municipal Inspector to Githuka s/o Kikuyu, February 1959; see also LG 3/3149 NCC General Purposes Committee Minutes, 6 February 1959.

40. NCC 27/10, February 1959.

41. LG 3/734 Salim Faraj to Town Clerk, 17 December 1959.

42. Government of Kenya, *Commission of Inquiry Report* 1955–1956:44–45; CS 1/14/33 Kiambu ADC Trade and Markets Sub-Committee Minutes, 28–29 January 1954:1.

43. MAA 9/904.

44. NMC General Purposes Committee Minutes, 22 July 1960, 4 November 1960; Onstad 1990:160.

45. AA 13/1/8/9 Nairobi Extra-Provincial District AR 1960:17.

46. Onstad 1990:127–128, 138–142, 157; LG 3/3048 Kenya Auctioneers, Hawkers, Marketeers and Traders Union to Town Clerk, 25 October 1962; Nairobi Hawkers Traders Association to Prime Minister Kenyatta, 4 May 1964; KAHMTU and Nairobi Vegetable, Fruits, Hawkers Traders Association to Governor of Kenya, 5 January 1963.

47. LG 3/3048 Inspector General of Police to Minister of Internal Security and Defence, 16 March 1964; Crime and Incident Reports, 1960–1964.

48. AA 13/1/8/9 Nairobi Extra-Provincial District AR 1962:4; Onstad 1990:132–133.

References

Aaronovitch, S., and K. Aaronovitch. 1947. *Crisis in Kenya*. London: Lawrence and Wishart.

Ambler, Charles H. 1988. *Kenyan Communities in the Age of Imperialism: The Central Region in the Late Nineteenth Century.* New Haven: Yale University Press.

Barnett, Donald L., and Karari Njama. 1966. *Mau Mau from Within.* London: MacGibbon and Kee.

Beech, M.W.H. 1912. "The Kikuyu Point of View." Memorandum in PC/CP 1/4/2 Kikuyu District Political Record Book 2, 1912–1914.

Berman, Bruce, and John Lonsdale. 1992. *Unhappy Valley,* vol. 2. Nairobi: Heinemann.

Clark, Gracia. 1988. Introduction to *Traders Versus the State,* 1–16. Boulder: Westview.

Dickerman, Carol. 1978. "Africans in Nairobi During the Emergency: Social and Economic Changes 1952–1960." M.A. thesis, University of Wisconsin, Madison.

Elkan, Walter, T.C.I. Ryan, and J. T. Mukui. 1982. "The Economics of Shoe Shining in Nairobi." *African Affairs* 81, 323:247–256.

Furedi, Frank. 1977. "The African Crowd in Nairobi: Popular Movements and Elite Politics." In *Third World Urbanization,* ed. J. Abu-Lughod and R. Hay, Jr., 225–240. New York: Methuen.

Gordon, David. 1986. *Decolonization and the State in Kenya.* Boulder: Westview.

Hake, Andrew. 1977. *African Metropolis, Nairobi's Self-Help City.* New York: St. Martin's.

Kamau, Kiruri. 1984. "When a Woman Ruled!" *Standard* (Kenya), 8 February, 9.

Kanogo, Tabitha. 1987. "Kikuyu Women and the Politics of Protest: Mau Mau." In *Images of Women in Peace and in War: Cross-Cultural and Historical Perspectives,* ed. S. MacDonald, R. Holden, and S. Ardener, 78–99. Madison: University of Wisconsin Press.

———. 1988. *Squatters and the Roots of Mau Mau.* Nairobi: Heinemann.

Kenya National Archives Staff. N.d. "The Reign of Wangu Makeri."

Kenyatta, Jomo. [1938] 1959. *Facing Mount Kenya.* London: Secker and Warburg.

Kinyanjui, Alex R. 1975. "A Biography of Paramount Chief Kinyanjui wa Gathirimu (1865–1929)." B.A. thesis, University of Nairobi.

Kitching, Gavin. 1980. *Class and Economic Change in Kenya: The Making of an African Petite Bourgeoisie, 1905–1970.* New Haven: Yale University Press.

Leakey, L.S.B. 1956. "The Economics of Kikuyu Tribal Life." *East African Economic Review* 3, 1:165–180.

Leo, Christopher. 1984. *Land and Class in Kenya.* Toronto: University of Toronto Press.

Likimani, Muthoni. 1985. *Passbook Number F.47927: Women and Mau Mau in Kenya.* London: Macmillan Publishers.

Maas, Maria. 1986. *Women's Groups in Kiambu, Kenya.* Leiden: University of Leiden African Studies Centre Research Report no. 26.

McVicar, K. G. 1969. "Twilight of an East African Slum: Pumwani and the Evolution of African Settlement in Nairobi." Ph.D. diss., University of California, Los Angeles.

Onstad, Eric. 1988. "Age Mates: Petty Traders and Wage Laborers in Nairobi, 1899–1960." Seminar paper, University of Nairobi.

———. 1990. "Street Life." M.A. thesis, University of Nairobi.

Robertson, Claire C. 1993. "Traders and Urban Struggles: The Creation of a Militant Female Underclass in Nairobi, 1960–1990." *Journal of Women's History* 4, 3 (winter):9–42.

———. Forthcoming. *"Trouble Showed the Way": Women, Men, and Trade in the Nairobi Area, 1890–1990.*

Ross, Marc H. 1975. *Grass Roots in an African City: Political Behavior in Nairobi.* Cambridge: MIT Press.

Ross, W. McGregor. [1927] 1968. *Kenya from Within.* London: Frank Cass.

Stichter, Sharon. 1977. "Women and the Labor Force in Kenya, 1895–1964." University of Nairobi Institute for Development Studies Discussion Paper no. 258.

———. 1982. *Migrant Labour in Kenya: Capitalism and African Response, 1895–1975.* London: Longman.

Thomson, Joseph. 1887. *Through Masai Land.* London: Sampson, Low, Marston, Searle, and Remington.

Throup, David W. 1988. *Economic and Social Origins of Mau Mau.* Nairobi: Heinemann.

Werlin, Herbert H. 1974. *Governing an African City: A Study of Nairobi.* New York: Africana Publishing.

———. 1981. "The Hawkers of Nairobi: The Politics of the Informal Sector." In *Urbanization and Development Planning in Kenya,* ed. R. A. Obudho, 194–214. Nairobi: Kenya Literature Bureau.

White, Luise. 1988. "Separating the Men from the Boys: Colonial Constructions of Gender, Sexuality and Terrorism in Central Kenya, 1939–59." Paper for Wenner-Gren Foundation symposium on "Tensions of Empire: Colonial Control and Visions of Rule."

———. 1990. *The Comforts of Home: Prostitution in Colonial Nairobi.* Chicago: University of Chicago Press.

Wood, L. J. 1974. "Market Origins and Development in East Africa." Makerere University Department of Geography Occasional Paper no. 57.

4

Three Generations of Hausa Women in Kaduna, Nigeria, 1925–1985

CATHERINE M. COLES

This chapter explores urbanization and social change in twentieth-century northern Nigeria through the lens of the experiences and perceptions of three Muslim Hausa women, which are presented in the form of life histories. Personal narratives, of which life histories are but one type,[1] have gained attention in many fields of study as a means of "reconstructing reality" by illuminating the previously ignored experiences and perspectives of marginal or oppressed individuals. In anthropology, their use is part of a movement toward person-centered ethnography, with a focus on the intersection between social and cultural forces shaping an individual's experiences and that individual's own strategies and life course.

As the fundamental importance of gender in social organization and processes is better recognized and understood, personal narratives of women assume particular significance. Narratives are primary sources that illuminate gender roles, relations, and identities and illustrate the relevance of gender to inequality in relationships and systems of power (Personal Narratives Group 1989:3–7). Like any historical text, personal narratives reflect the social, cultural, and ideological contexts within which they are produced and within which both subject and researcher live. Herein lies a special problem for women's narratives: How is it possible to move beyond hegemonic patriarchal modes, with their inherent limited vision of female gender roles, to write and interpret women's biographies and autobiographies? Carolyn Heilbrun, in *Writing a Woman's Life*, describes this as a need "to make clear, evident, out in the open, those events, decisions, and relationships that have been invisible outside of women's fictions" (1988:18). Writing of personal narratives in a Western context, Heilbrun points to the factors that have led to the production of biographies portraying women as lacking in independence, ambition, and achievement: the inability of women (whether writers of their own life histories or recorders of others' narratives) to deal openly with issues of power and control in their lives; gender prescriptions that preclude the attribution of power to women; and frequently, the absence of a language, text, or narrative form through which women can express their true selves.

Heilbrun's arguments are equally relevant to life histories of non-Western women. In the case of African women's life histories, it is primarily Western scholars who are currently researching, collecting, recording (often from oral sources), and interpreting the texts, which are then published in European languages.[2] The challenge for these scholars is to cultivate a heightened awareness of how their own gender conceptions, frameworks of analysis, value systems, and perspectives affect their understanding and presentation of African women's lives in a very different context. The ultimate goal must be to overcome the limitations of one's own worldview in order to represent the worldview of others. One model for the treatment of these issues is Marjorie Shostak's biography, *Nisa: The Life and Words of a !Kung Woman* (1981). In a recent article, Shostak (1989) elaborates on her collaboration and relationship with Nisa, on her own goals, motivations, and expectations as a twenty-four-year-old American woman at the time of her research, on her hope of achieving a true friendship with Nisa, and on the implications of these factors for the final product. Shostak makes clear that a life history reflects not only the context of the subject or narrator's life but also that of the researcher-interpreter-recorder, as well as reflecting the relationship between the two individuals (see also Personal Narratives Group 1989:201–203).

Life histories of African women produced by scholars in various disciplines have been important to developing an understanding of the range of women's experiences in diverse contexts and time periods and in societies that are patriarchal in varying degrees (Geiger 1986). These scholars have documented women's vulnerable status as captives and slaves (Wright 1975, 1983; Alpers 1983; Strobel 1983; Robertson 1983) as well as the power of important female public figures (Wilks 1988; Johnson 1986; Obbo 1988). Multiple life histories have been collected within single studies to examine women in different castes (Codere 1973), systems of gender stratification (Obbo 1986), and the differential effects of changing economic conditions on women (LeVine 1979). Of particular relevance to the life histories of Hausa women presented here is the study done in the early 1970s by Sarah Mirza and Margaret Strobel (1989) on three Muslim Swahili women in Mombasa, Kenya, whose lives cover the first half of the twentieth century. Life histories of Muslim African women are rare, and many historical accounts of Islamic societies in Africa have neglected any consideration of women's involvement in public life or social change. As Strobel states in an earlier work, "To write about women on the Swahili coast is to probe the history of the inarticulate and invisible. Evidence written by women themselves is scarce. Even when the subject is women, men write" (1979:4). Thus, life histories are a valuable means of allowing the voices of Islamic women to be heard.

Muslim Hausa women have also been described as "invisible" (Pittin 1984a, 1984b), primarily because most of those living in urban centers, as well as many in rural areas, observe at least partial seclusion during their childbearing years. The seclusion of women has contributed to a lack of understanding of their life experiences and perceptions as well as to inaccurate assumptions about their activities and the power they wield. Furthermore, women's "invisibility" has been perpetuated in historical accounts focusing almost exclusively on formal political structures and events dominated by men—particularly in accounts dating from the time of the Fulani jihad (holy war) early in the nineteenth century, when Islam was strengthened considerably in Hausaland (M. G. Smith 1960, 1978). Such analyses are both inaccurate in their depiction of women's roles and provide fundamentally incomplete accounts of Hausa society as a whole (Coles and Mack 1991).

As part of a growing body of literature and the increasing focus of attention on women in Hausa society, three life histories of women in northern Nigeria have been published, each portraying women's experiences in traditional settings—in a rural village and in the old walled city of Kano. The earliest, Mary Smith's *Baba of Karo: A Woman of the Muslim Hausa* (1954), recorded the life of a rural woman who lived from 1877 to 1951. The narrative of Baba's life points out, according to historian Susan Geiger,

> the weaknesses of androcentric ethnography that fails to encompass, and therefore cannot accommodate, women's lives. This point is made within the covers of the book as the reader compares the introduction to Hausa culture written by Mary Smith's anthropologist husband, M. G. Smith, with Baba's recorded life history. Baba's narrative frequently contradicts and invalidates M. G. Smith's generalizations about Hausa society, especially on subjects central to Baba's life such as marriage, divorce, household and compound re-

lations, kinship, and, most particularly, social relationships among women. While M. G. Smith dismisses women's relationships as of little importance, Baba's narrative consistently demonstrates their power and vitality in Hausa life. In addition, because she herself is unable to achieve biological motherhood, Baba further extends her influence by adopting children, arranging many of their marriages, and meeting the obligations of and reaping benefits from these fictive kin relations (1986:341–342).

More recently, Beverly Mack (1988) presented the life story of Hajiya Ma'daki, a royal Hausa woman born in 1907 whose father and husband were emirs (rulers of the large Muslim chiefdoms known as emirates) during the colonial period. Hajiya Ma'daki had substantial influence in public affairs even though she did not hold formal office. Her life contrasts sharply with that of Hajiya Husaina Ibrahim, a "commoner of Kanuri origin" living in Kano from 1937 to 1983, as described by Enid Schildkrout (1988). In Hajiya Husaina's life history, Schildkrout emphasizes the limitations and constraints on her life, explaining them as due in large part to her lower-class position in Hausa society.

Hausa women lived in a very different context in Kaduna, a migrant Hausa community situated outside Hausaland that was home to non-Muslim, non-Hausa people from throughout Nigeria. Kaduna's origins date to 1912, when the British colonial official Lord Lugard selected a site twenty miles south of Hausaland in a sparsely settled area of the Gwari people, along the Kaduna River and the Lagos-Kano rail line. The site was chosen to be a military and administrative headquarters for the Protectorate of northern Nigeria, accessible to the thirteen Hausa-Fulani emirates that made up the protectorate, yet outside indigenous Hausa-settled areas and thus free from disruptive political influences of urban centers such as Kano or Sokoto. From its beginnings, Kaduna developed as an ethnically pluralistic, diverse city to which migrants came from throughout Nigeria. By 1985, with a population of over six hundred thousand, the city had become an industrial, commercial, and transportation center, as well as the capital of a northern state.

The complex, pluralistic nature of urban life in Kaduna shapes, and is shaped by, all who live there, including the three women whose narratives are presented here. Members of succeeding generations within a single family, these women have both experienced and contributed to the development of the city. Furthermore, in many ways their lives are changing more rapidly than are those of Hausa women in more traditional contexts. Women in Kaduna and other similar milieus, such as newer areas growing up around the old Hausa cities, may be in the forefront of social change in Hausa society, serving as role models for other women's development.

Few anthropologists have used life histories to examine social change, even though such narratives have been a component of many twentieth-century ethnographic studies (Langness and Frank 1981). Life histories have sometimes been collected as part of a focus on family groups, with several individuals within a household or kin group studied, as in Oscar Lewis's descriptions of Mexican and Puerto Rican families (1959, 1961, 1964, 1965). Two analyses that use life histories together with family studies to investigate social change in a migrant community are Dan Aronson's examination of Ijebu Yoruba in Ibadan, Nigeria (1980), and Lillian Trager's analysis of female migrants to Dagupan City in the Philippines (1988). Both researchers attempt to understand how individuals and families simultaneously experience and contribute to social and cultural forces and to change in a developing city; each author does so by bringing together the personal/particular view and the social/general view (Aronson 1980:xix). This same purpose directed my own research among Hausa women in the Nigerian city of Kaduna.

Three questions underlie the presentation and discussion of the narratives that follow. First, how did Hausa women experience and perceive life in Kaduna from 1925 to 1985? Second, to what degree, if any, did Hausa women influence the content and course of change in their community and in the city as a whole during this period? These questions are considered by viewing women's life histories within the social and cultural milieu in Kaduna and the local community. They may ultimately help to answer a third, larger question: What can be learned about urbanization in Africa in this century and about the development of Kaduna itself by focusing on the experiences and perceptions of women whose lives were intertwined with these processes?

Constructing the Life Histories

The women whose life histories follow are Hajiya Asabe, her daughter Hajiya Mero, and Hajiya Mero's daughter Binta. Ranging in age in 1985 from approximately eighty-five to thirty (none knows the exact year of her birth), they represent three successive generations and stages in the life cycle. Hajiya Asabe, an "old" woman (*tsohuwa*), came with the earliest group of Hausa migrants to Unguwan Kanawa, just outside Kaduna, in the 1920s, during the colonial period. Hajiya Asabe's daughter, a middle-aged woman (*dattijuwa*), was born in Unguwan Kanawa and grew up in an increasingly heterogeneous society, as migrants from throughout Nigeria moved into the local area to live alongside the Hausa, during the time when Nigeria moved through the colonial period to nationhood. Binta, a married woman of childbearing age (*mace*), is the second daughter of Hajiya Mero. The three life histories are among twelve collected as part of a larger research project investigating changes in Hausa women's roles in Unguwan Kanawa and Unguwan Shanu, two wards of Kaduna, conducted for two years in 1979–1981 and in a two-month return visit in 1985.[3] Data were obtained primarily through extensive interviews with local women and participant observation within the community and within the families of the women themselves.

I met Hajiya Asabe, Hajiya Mero, and Binta soon after beginning field-work. Binta's next-younger sibling, a brother named Usman, was asked by the Mai Unguwa (the local ward head) to assist in introducing me in the community—a necessary entrée for a stranger, especially a foreign woman entering the area alone. A student in an advanced teacher train-ing college and well known in the community because of his family's standing, Usman introduced me to male household heads in whose com-pounds I wished to work and to his own family, including his mother, Hajiya Mero, his sister Binta, and his grandmother Hajiya Asabe. Usman's family soon adopted me: I lived periodically in Binta's com-pound, constantly visited the homes of Usman's mother and grand-mother for work and pleasure, and became well acquainted with their en-tire network of family and friends.

Hajiya Asabe, Hajiya Mero, and Binta also rapidly became primary in-formants in my research. I sought their agreement to compile life histories because they were key individuals in the social life of the local Hausa community, possessed of personal qualities that made them leaders and innovators among other women. Hajiya Asabe is one of a small group of highly respected senior women, the best-known midwife in the area, and an herbalist whose command of ritual makes her much in demand in the community. Although younger, Hajiya Mero and Binta are also well known: as members of one of the first Hausa families to settle in the com-munity, as pious Muslim women, as wives and mothers, and as hard-working and occupationally successful women. These characteristics make them more typical Hausa women in the area than is Hajiya Asabe, because of her ritual activities.

Constructing life histories with these women was complicated by their very social nature: Each was usually at the center of family and social ac-tivities, constantly visiting or entertaining, working at her occupations, attending social events, caring for children, and doing domestic chores. Tape-recorded interviews were not feasible under these circumstances, nor would the women speak freely when recorders were used. Instead, a few formal interviews were supplemented by ongoing informal discus-sions occurring as I participated in and observed the activities of their lives. Using all available data, I wrote the life histories in the third person, checking with each woman upon completion to correct inaccuracies and to add further comments she might wish to have included.

Three Life Histories

Life History 1: Hajiya Asabe

Hajiya Asabe was born nearly eighty-five years ago in the old walled city of Kano. Her mother and father were both Kano Hausa; their large family compound was near Dalla Hill. Hajiya's father was a *mallam* (a Koranic teacher) who conducted a Koranic school in their house; her mother had read the entire Koran, was strictly secluded, and as an occupation cooked food that young girls in her household sold on the streets. Hajiya Asabe's mother had many children, of whom Hajiya was the *auta*, or the last: All the others had died. As a child, Hajiya was taught in her father's Koranic school. As the daughter of a *mallam*, she was rarely permitted outside the family compound.

At the age of twelve, Hajiya married her cousin, the son of her father's brother, in a marriage of *auren zumunci* (kin). The *sadaki* (payment for contracting the marriage) was one goat. Since it was marriage between kin, there was no payment to her family from that of her husband; from her own family, however, Hajiya received bags of noodles, rice, salt, groundnut oil and other foods, her bed, dishes and pots, and other *kayan aure* (marriage gifts). Like her father, Hajiya's first husband was also a *mallam*. Hajiya was the only wife and was strictly secluded during this marriage, yet she managed to trade and sell food from inside her compound. She gave birth to two children, both of whom died when small.

In 1926, Hajiya came with her husband to Unguwan Kanawa ("the place of Kano people"), along with the first group of Kano settlers. The emir of Kano, Abdullahi Bayero, in response to a request from Lieutenant Governor Palmer, had asked Mallam Ibrahim, father of the current Mai Unguwa of Unguwan Kanawa, to lead the group. Mallam Ibrahim, a Kanuri trader from Maiduguri who had settled north of Kaduna in 1911 to trade with the Gwari people, brought one hundred men and their families, about 170 people in all.[4] Of all those who came with Hajiya, only she and her good friend, the wife of the first Mai Unguwa, are alive today. Along with the settlers, the emir sent *mallamai* (Koranic teachers) to drive the spirits away from the wild, dense bush where they would have to live at first. When the group arrived in Unguwan Kanawa, Kawo village to the northeast and small settlements in Kaduna South and Kaduna Township were already in existence, but they were some miles away. Unguwan Shanu ("the place of cattle"), today a densely populated area next to Unguwan Kanawa, was open land where the governor's cattle grazed.

To assist the Kano settlers when they arrived in Unguwan Kanawa, the colonial government gave them money for food for the first year, which they purchased at Kano Market or the Central Market in Kaduna town. The government also built rooms for them. Soon the Kano men built their own houses and began farming. Hajiya's husband built a compound directly behind that of the Mai Unguwa, where Hajiya still lives today. Another compound next to Hajiya's was built by a man from Sokoto and his family. Some of the original settlers returned to Kano; others left trading because they could not make enough money in it. As time passed, Hausa from Kano, Katsina, Zaria, Sokoto, and Jos joined the original group; Fulani, Kanuri (Beriberi), and a few Nupe, all northern peoples familiar to the Hausa, also came in the early days; non-Hausa southern Nigerians came to settle later. Regardless of their origins, all these migrants to the area recognized the leadership of Mallam Ibrahim as Mai Unguwa and approached him to request land for houses and farming.

Once in Unguwan Kanawa, four of the women who came along with Hajiya returned to Kano with their husbands because they didn't like Kaduna. Hajiya and the other women who stayed regularly went into the bush to collect herbs for preparing medicines and had to do other work that took them outside their compounds. At first, there were not many children or older women to run errands or do this work for married women, so seclusion was not possible. Gradually the Hausa community grew in size. Some marriages for the migrants' children were arranged with kin left behind in Kano; others took place among the migrants' families in Unguwan Kanawa. Hajiya herself gave birth to two more children: Hajiya Mero and a son who lived to adulthood. Unlike many other Hausa women who returned to their family homes in Kano to give birth, Hajiya did not.

Hajiya raised her two children in Unguwan Kanawa, as it grew and changed. She recalls that between the two world wars, Unguwan Kanawa and the nearby settlements of Unguwan Shanu, Abakpa, and Kawo became small outlying villages of Kaduna. Late in the 1930s, nearby Unguwan Shanu contained only a few huts on eight or nine lanes, and a path led into Kaduna town by way of Lugard Hall. Yoruba tailors and traders came to work or sell goods but did not build homes until the late 1940s and early 1950s, when the first Ibo, Igala, and other non-Hausa settlers from the south report arriving. Soldiers living in nearby army barracks settled their families in Unguwan Shanu, and after World War II many retired there.

Early in the 1950s, Hajiya's husband became ill and died, and ownership of their compound in Unguwan Kanawa passed to her. Hajiya remained in her compound for five months following his death. When she began going out again, Hajiya was approached by a visitor from Sokoto in the compound of her neighbor. This man, a laborer who had worked at the palace of the Sardauna of Sokoto, asked Hajiya if she would marry him. Hajiya at this time was no longer bearing children, nor was she secluded. She herself made the decision to marry him and negotiated the conditions of the marriage. Since Hajiya's own father was dead, the Mai Unguwa acted as her wali, or representative, in the marriage ceremonies. Her new husband then joined Hajiya in her house. Hajiya was his only wife.

Hajiya began practising ungozomanci (midwifery) before her first husband died. As a younger woman, she became interested in learning midwifery when she was once left alone in her compound with a woman giving birth. After this experience, she decided to learn from other women in her family. Hajiya also learned to treat women and children for sicknesses, gathering herbs and making her own medicines. For a long time Hajiya was the only midwife in Unguwan Kanawa. Her work as a midwife includes the delivery of infants (she must be the first to touch a newborn child), cutting of the umbilical cord, and initial washing of the baby. She then returns to wash the infant twice daily for a week and takes part in the naming ceremony, or *suna*, for which she receives the head, skin, and legs of the ram that is slaughtered for the ceremony. She also instructs young mothers in the proper techniques for washing themselves with nearly boiling water for several weeks after the birth. Hajiya performs other ritual duties that include preparing young girls for their first marriage by participating in ceremonies lasting several days. When women or children die, Hajiya prepares the body, notifies members of the family, carries out rituals associated with the death and burial, and supervises the distribution of the estate of the deceased. She has also worked in Unguwan Kanawa with Hajiya Mai Magani (a well-known herbalist and resident in the area) and has cooperated with local hospitals in Zaria and Kaduna in programs for testing the medicinal value of local herbs and in developing other programs for prenatal care for women.

Hajiya is a wealthy woman by Unguwan Kanawa standards. She is paid for her midwifery and ritual services with money, cloth, food, and personal gifts. She also sells *lalle* (henna, used for cosmetic staining of women's hands and feet) and *goro* (kola nut), and she receives rent from lodgers in her compound. Hajiya's wealth has enabled her to make several hajj, or pilgrimages to Mecca, and to send her daughter as well. In 1985, Hajiya made her third hajj, returning ill and weak from the trip. Two days later, before she had recovered, thieves broke into her house during the night, stealing all the gifts she had brought back from Saudi Arabia. Gold jewelry, stereo tape players, leather goods, and many other items were taken. When Hajiya awoke and tried to go after the thieves, they pushed her to the ground. Hajiya believed them to have been men from Unguwan Kanawa, who would have known she had just returned from Mecca. Hajiya's kin and neighbors rallied around her after the attack, incensed at the increase in crime in the community, which they attributed to non-Hausa from the South.

Hajiya is now one of the oldest and most respected members of the local Unguwan Kanawa and Unguwan Shanu Hausa community. Her *kawaye* (close friends) are all other elderly women in the area—the mother of the present Mai Unguwa, the mother of the Mai Unguwa's first (now deceased) wife, the former co-wife of the Mai Unguwa's mother (to whom Hajiya has given a room in her compound, rent free), and two other women who live nearby and have lived in Unguwan Kanawa for over sixty years, like herself. Hajiya Asabe's company is sought often by others: She is nearly always carrying out her midwife duties, visiting other friends or residents, or being visited in her own home. She is rarely to be found alone.

Hajiya's ties to her kin in Kano remain strong. Among the many children she has fostered is the daughter of her elder brother's son from Kano. Hajiya sent her to primary school, then arranged her marriage at the age of thirteen in Unguwan Kanawa. The young woman now lives with her husband and infant in Unguwan Shanu. Hajiya travels frequently to visit members of her own family in Kano, bringing news to many in Unguwan Kanawa of their own relatives in Kano. Most of Hajiya's time is spent in Unguwan Kanawa, however, with her daughter, grandchildren, and great-grandchildren. Hajiya recently arranged the marriage for her daughter's son, Usman, in his early twenties and a teacher at a primary school in Kaduna. Hajiya and the rest of Usman's family paid for two years of secondary school education for his intended bride, as well as for the many gifts sent to her and her family. During July and August of 1985, Hajiya was supervising the building of new rooms in her compound for Usman and his wife to move into after their marriage. An elder sister of Usman was also living with Hajiya after a divorce, having lost her children to their father, and Hajiya was looking for a husband for her as well. Her younger grandchildren and their children frequently stay with Hajiya, receiving her care and keeping her from feeling lonely. Hajiya's daughter and grandchildren are devoted to her: They regularly assist her in her travels, cook and clean for her, and run errands (such as obtaining travel documents for her or doing her banking) throughout Kaduna. Hajiya calls Kaduna her home now, because her daughter and grandchildren are there.

Hajiya's experiences as a girl and young woman were similar to those of other females in the old walled cities and large villages of Hausaland at the time, experiences that even today characterize the lives of many Hausa women. As Hajiya's life illustrates, first marriage constitutes a rite of passage to adulthood, frequently taking place for girls between the ages of eleven and fourteen. Usually the marriage is arranged by parents or elder kin, with only nominal assent from the young girl. Preferred marriages are with certain cousins—the father's brother's son or the mother's sister's son—although after the first marriage such unions are less frequent. Often the groom is considerably older than his bride.

Marriages are frequently polygynous (the maximum of four wives being in accord with Muslim law), with senior wives having higher status and prestige and sometimes actually controlling the material resources within a household. Women typically marry, divorce, and remarry two to four times. Divorces may be obtained by a husband pronouncing the *talaq* (the phrase used by husbands to initiate divorce) in accord with Muslim law, but women have to go to court to initiate a divorce. Within marriage, Hausa women have primary responsibility for bearing and raising children and for domestic labor in the home. Even though many adult women are secluded, they also carry out income-earning occupations, often from within their homes, with the assistance of children, elder women, or male kin (Schildkrout 1983; Coles 1991). Women retain control over their incomes from these occupations.

Hajiya's move to Kaduna as a young woman during her first marriage profoundly changed her world, for she left a life of seclusion to experience a degree of autonomy and lack of supervision previously unknown to her. Descriptions provided by Hajiya and other women who came in this first group of Hausa from Kano suggest that few, if any, women of middle or old age were among the migrants. Seclusion was not possible in this new environment: Large family groups were not available to support the institution, older women were not present to enforce it, and women's labor was required outside their compounds. As Hausa from other locations in the North joined the Kano settlers in Unguwan Kanawa, a broader Hausa community gradually formed that may have served to reestablish cultural norms such as seclusion for women.

Aspects of Hajiya's life during middle and old age reveal the power that older Hausa women exercise. Once past childbearing age, women are no longer secluded but move about freely: They have access to more lucrative occupations, have a greater voice in choosing spouses upon remarriage than do younger females, and exert greater power and influence over others in the community, both male and female (Coles 1983, 1990; Schildkrout 1986). It was when Hajiya was older that she lost her first husband and negotiated a second marriage of her own choosing. The fact that her second husband's social position was inferior to her own in no way lowered her own established status. This new husband joined Hajiya to live in her compound, for even after marriage, Hajiya's property remained her own, completely under her control: Only she could decide who might stay there, and only she would receive income from renters; ultimately, she will pass the property on to her own kin.

It was also in middle age that Hajiya began to practice midwifery, taking on important social and ritual roles in the local Hausa community. Her age, experience, and growing expertise contributed to growing respect for her among both men and women. Assuming the role of adviser to younger females, both kinswomen and other new migrants in the area, she prepared young girls for marriage and oversaw their behavior as married women. By this time, women of childbearing age were experiencing greater seclusion in Unguwan Kanawa than earlier migrants had known there: Older women were a key to enforcing it, as were larger families that supported the institution through the availability of children and nonsecluded individuals to run errands for secluded women. Hajiya was an important figure in this group of older women that was responsible for inculcating proper values and behaviors in younger women. Hajiya's actions brought her great respect in the community, and her duties as midwife brought income sufficient for her to make several trips to Mecca and to send others in her family, thus further increasing her status.

It is primarily, though not exclusively, through her occupation that Hajiya has been able to influence and shape the course of change in the local Hausa community in Unguwan Kanawa and beyond. Clearly an innovator, she seized the opportunity that became available with the spread of Western orthodox medicine to link herself with processes of development in the health field. In the 1970s, Hajiya's skills were recognized by local Kaduna hospitals, and she was invited to work with them in testing indigenous medicines and in prenatal screening of local women who might require additional care beyond her own services when they delivered children. Through her work as a midwife and herbalist, she has been able to promote the adoption of new medical practices, encouraging women to seek medical care for themselves and their children at Western medical facilities. Hajiya has served as a role model for other Hausa women in the community—as a successful woman intensely devoted to her occupation and to her local community and also as a woman actively involved in the larger society. Hausa women in northern Nigeria could not vote until 1976, and few were active in formal politics (during the twentieth century) before that date (Mack 1988; Callaway and Schildkrout 1985; Callaway 1987). Hajiya Asabe was undoubtedly one of few women in the local area to be involved with government or political and economic institutions outside the immediate community, in her case through her work with the Kaduna hospitals.

Hajiya Asabe's Life and the Colonial City of Kaduna

Hajiya Asabe's life experiences in Unguwan Kanawa portray her own role in the development of the area; they also illuminate just how Unguwan Kanawa, and Kaduna itself, grew from a small colonial settlement to become a large, diverse economic and political center in Nigeria. Originating as a classic African colonial city set up for the administrative and commercial purposes of the British (O'Connor 1983), Kaduna's early development followed the 1917 Lugard Plan: Government Residential Areas surrounded polo grounds, a race course, and an open area that later became Lugard Hall, a parliamentary seat. Sabon Gari ("New Town") housed strangers from other parts of Nigeria or West Africa; across the railway line was the Public Works Department Labor Camp, which later grew into Tudun Wada, a Hausa settlement area. Commercial and trading areas were set up, and in Kaduna Junction (later Kaduna South) across the river, the railway station, army headquarters, Survey Department, and settlements of workers in Makera and Kakuri were located.[5] Between the two world wars, growth in government activities, services, and employment opportunities provided the major impetus for Kaduna's development. By the mid-1940s, several new areas had sprouted up: Abakpa, Unguwan Shanu, Kabala, Kurmin Mashi, Nassarawa, Tudun Nupawa, and Kawo. Many lay along the railway line, as did Unguwan Kanawa, which was located just over one mile north of what was to become the central business district of Kaduna.

When Hajiya Asabe first came to Unguwan Kanawa as a migrant from a traditional Hausa city, she moved into a setting with no established community in place, considerably more rural than the area from which she had come. The Hausa community of which she was a part in Unguwan Kanawa, as in Kaduna proper, gradually became what David Parkin (1969) and Aidan Southall (1975) describe as a "host" group for other migrants. Intermarriage within the community created new Hausa families whose primary identification was with Unguwan Kanawa, at the same time that migrants maintained ties with communities of origin throughout Hausaland. Unlike Hajiya and her cohort, later migrants to Kaduna could join or seek assistance from kin, friends, or employers already established in the community and city, and non-Hausa formed voluntary associations or unions (Gugler and Flanagan 1978; Hannerz 1980; Epstein 1958, 1964; Southall 1961).

For Hajiya, as for many of the early migrants who came with her to Unguwan Kanawa, Kano remained an affective "home" for many years. Today, Unguwan Kanawa is her home in a different sense—because her people are here and because it is a place she has helped to create and shape. Kaduna itself, the larger city, is more the home of her daughter and grandchildren.

Life History 2: Hajiya Mero

Hajiya Mero is the only living child of Hajiya Asabe. Born about fifty-two years ago in Unguwan Kanawa and raised by her mother and father in the compound where Hajiya Asabe now lives, Hajiya Mero attended Koranic school when young but did not complete the Koran. Because her father was a *mallam*, Hajiya was not permitted to move freely outside her family compound as a girl. When Hajiya was five years old, she met the man who would become her husband: Alhaji Hassan was about fifteen years older than she, and he was from Kano. When she was seven, her parents asked if she would marry him, and she "agreed"; however, the marriage did not take place until she reached the age of fourteen. Hajiya says that both she and her husband wanted to marry, so their marriage was *auren so* (a marriage of love). The *sadaki* for the contracting of the marriage was a goat, and Hajiya received *kayan aure*, her food and marriage gifts, from her own family, as well as gifts from her husband.

Hajiya Mero was secluded at first after her marriage. At the time of the marriage her husband already had one wife, but this woman died after giving birth and Hajiya raised this *riko*, the daughter of another wife. Later, Hajiya's husband married a *budurwa* (a previously unmarried girl); however, the girl soon left the marriage. Finally, the present co-wife of Hajiya entered their life: Although this junior wife has separated from Alhaji more than once, she has stayed in the marriage. Hajiya remains the *uwar gida* (first wife), with her authority recognized by all residents in the large compound.

Hajiya has given birth to eleven children. Two sons died, one soon after birth (the firstborn) and the other at the age of fifteen. Her other children range in age from about thirty-five to the youngest, about ten years old. The two eldest are females who have married and have children; all the others (both male and female) have attended, or are now attending, non-Koranic secular schools. Hajiya says that her husband refuses to allow the daughters to go beyond primary school, and all have been married when they were between twelve and fourteen. Two of the boys are now in secondary school. Her eldest son, Usman, lived at home until his marriage in 1985 and was especially helpful to her in many situations: For example, he dealt with the police after her favorite sheep got loose and roamed about the streets in search of food, only to be confiscated.

Since the beginning of their marriage, Hajiya and her husband have lived in Unguwan Kanawa. They now own and live in a large compound that in 1985 housed over sixty people, including their unmarried children. Alhaji is a builder and contractor, as well as a bonesetter and healer. An old woman who lives in their compound assists him by preparing herbs for his use in healing. Many rooms in the compound are rented. All residents are Muslims from northern Nigeria or Niger, except for an Ibo woman who married her Fulani husband when he was a soldier stationed in Biafra during the Nigerian civil war. Some residents are non-Hausa Fulani, Shuwa Arab, or Kanuri. Hajiya and Usman do much of the maintenance on the compound since Alhaji Hassan became ill around the time of the 1985 interviews.

Hajiya calls herself middle-aged and is no longer secluded. She has always been very active in occupations such as trading and preparing and selling food, but she chose not to learn the work of a midwife that her mother does. Instead, she prefers her present work: Hajiya goes daily to large markets elsewhere in Kaduna (at Kakuri or Kawo) or outside the city (to Kujama or Amana) to purchase food in bulk, returning with it to Unguwan Kanawa, where she sells it to women who prepare and cook it for sale. She buys whatever foods are seasonally available (tomatoes, peanuts, maize, peppers, green vegetables, yams, and spices), spending up to 100 naira a day. She makes her purchases from middlemen with whom she has established relationships at each market, then transports her goods back to Kaduna by taxi. Local women buy from her on credit, paying her for their supplies after they have sold food. Occasionally, Hajiya buys clothing or other items the family needs when she is at a market, and she also prepares food for sale herself. Hajiya is an active and successful trader in food, salt, oil, clothing, and other goods, supplying many younger women in the community who are unable to travel to markets because they are either secluded or have young children and must work from within their compounds.

In 1980, Hajiya Mero received severe burns when cooking oil was splashed on her body. Her recovery was slow, taking four months, and scars from the burns are still visible on her face and body. Hajiya Asabe was so thankful that her daughter had lived through such an ordeal that she sent Hajiya Mero to make the hajj to Mecca. In 1985, Hajiya Mero was regularly attending Islamic school. She lived only a five-minute walk from her mother, whom she saw nearly every day; she visited her married daughter Binta, less frequently and with greater formality. But like both of them, Hajiya Mero was constantly occupied with friends and family, with business in her compound, with her occupation, or with attending *biki* (ritual celebrations) in Unguwan Kanawa or elsewhere in Kaduna. Hajiya said that her best women friends were Hausa, but she was also on good terms with women of other ethnic backgrounds, both within her compound and within the local community.

Hajiya Mero's life and experiences represent intermediate and, in many senses, subtle changes in comparison to the contrasts evident between the lives of her mother and her daughter Binta. Hajiya Mero's was the first cohort of Hausa to be born and live continuously in Kaduna. Growing up in a community increasingly heterogeneous in ethnic and religious terms as migrants moved in from throughout Nigeria, Hajiya's contacts with non-Muslim non-Hausa individuals have probably been much more frequent than those of women in Hausaland proper.[6] Hajiya's life in a new city has created, and reflects, this expanded Hausa cultural experience.

As Hajiya passed from childhood to being a young married woman, the local Hausa community moved through a period of consolidation as Kano Hausa in Unguwan Kanawa were joined by other Hausa, who were seeking employment in the growing city. Small nuclear families of migrants grew larger as children in Hajiya Mero's generation grew older and married. Although they did not approximate the extended families present in areas from which the migrants had come, these families joined together in a combined kinship-residential network that provided the basic social groups within which life-cycle events (naming ceremonies, marriages, funerals) and Muslim holidays were celebrated and marriages were contracted. Actual kin ties were still more significant than the fictive ties that arose within this network; yet increasingly, they became part of a single system. Hajiya herself was married to a man from Kano, in a marriage arranged by her family; subsequently her husband and several of his male kin joined the Unguwan Kanawa community and remained there, establishing large families.

Within this new Hausa community, seclusion itself was reestablished, although perhaps in a somewhat new form. Whereas Hausa women in large rural villages or traditional cities are frequently secluded during their childbearing years in family compounds, in Kaduna, women are more likely to live in compounds in which rooms are rented to nonkin, changing the nature and degree of seclusion observed as well as the social relationships women have with each other and with men. Compounds in Unguwan Kanawa and Unguwan Shanu generally include a compound owner and his or her family and, frequently, distant kin or friends who pay no rent; many compound owners also rent out rooms. Usually the compounds in which Hausa families reside include only Muslims and, predominantly, northern Nigerians. Hajiya's "seclusion" during the early years of her marriage was most likely carried out in this type of setting.

In many other senses, Hajiya Mero appears to have followed the path of an ordinary Hausa woman in her life course. During her early life, secular education was largely unavailable to Muslim women in northern Nigeria (Burness 1955, 1957, 1959; Trevor 1975a, 1975b). Hajiya and most Hausa women in Unguwan Kanawa worked at many of the same occupations as did women throughout Hausaland: They traded from within seclusion, prepared and cooked food for sale, made jewelry or sewed hats; older women no longer secluded worked as midwives, herbalists, or pawnbrokers and generally engaged in more lucrative occupations and in those functions requiring the exercise of ritual power (M. G. Smith 1955; Coles 1991). A few single women practiced *karuwanci*, or prostitution. Women were largely excluded from wage labor, as these positions were reserved for men; yet even Hausa men were at a disadvantage in competing for such jobs because of their relative lack of secular education and related skills in comparison with southern Nigerians. Hajiya's occupations in trade and the preparation and sale of food are typical of those of many Hausa women throughout northern Nigeria during this century, and even in the 1990s. Similarly, her husband's work as a builder is representative of the occupations of other uneducated Hausa men in the area.

Although in many respects a typical Hausa woman, Hajiya nevertheless stands out as an influential person in Unguwan Kanawa: Her family is highly respected, and her social ties with coresidents place her at an important node in the local social network. In providing rental opportunities for migrants to Unguwan Kanawa in the large compound that she and Alhaji maintain and in her role as wife of the compound head, she helps to socialize other migrants to the local community and the larger city. As a successful trader, with an income sufficient to have assisted in educating several of her children, she presents a role model for other women. Hajiya's sons have all received secular education through secondary school or even higher institutions of learning and are moving into occupations that will bring them, and her, increased wealth and prestige. Although her elder daughters did not generally attend secular schools, they married men similar to her sons; her younger female children have attended primary school, although they have not followed their brothers to high school or any form of higher education.

Hajiya Mero's Life in a Developing Kaduna

While Hajiya Mero was growing up in Unguwan Kanawa, Kaduna itself was changing from a colonial city into a large political, commercial, and industrial center. During the 1950s, industrial development came to Kaduna, first in the form of textile industries, and Kaduna became a Capital Territory for the Northern Region of Nigeria. These developments were accompanied by large-scale migration into Kaduna from all parts of the country. Northern Nigerians have always predominated:[7] In 1965, the adult population was nearly one-third Hausa and one-fifth Ibo, with substantial numbers of Yoruba and other northern and midwestern peoples present.[8] As is typical of such cities, Kaduna's population was also young, with 36.8 percent fourteen years of age or under and 18 percent four years old or less (Max Lock and Partners 1967:127). About equal numbers of Christians and Muslims were present, with a small number of other religions represented (Population Census of Nigeria 1963).

Hajiya, like other Hausa in Unguwan Kanawa, experienced similar growth in ethnic heterogeneity in the local community. Families descended from the earliest Kano Hausa settlers in Unguwan Kanawa built their compounds close together, and members of other ethnic groups such as Ibo or Kanuri tended to cluster in specific neighborhoods, yet ethnic segregation never developed in residential or commercial areas: Even in the 1990s, Hausa compounds lie next to compounds containing mostly Yoruba or Ibo residents; a Christian church is nestled among Muslim homes. Interaction among members of different ethnic groups occurs most frequently in commercial activities and among younger residents in local schools. For example, nonsecluded Yoruba or Ibo women might sell food or wares door-to-door, freely entering secluded Hausa compounds. Community development projects occasionally draw residents of different ethnic backgrounds to participate together, but local mosque organizations carry out most of these functions among Muslims.

In spite of the mixture of ethnic groups living in the wards, Muslim Hausa-Fulani culture has always predominated in Unguwan Kanawa: It is easily visible even to a stranger, walking through the area early on a Friday afternoon, when thousands of men are making their way to prayers at the *Masallacin Jumma'a* (Friday mosque), or seeing women with faces and heads covered, streaming into a compound for the feast after a naming ceremony. The Hausa language is nearly universal: Even non-Hausa speak it sufficiently to converse with neighbors and carry out business. The Mai Unguwa of Unguwan Kanawa and ward heads of Unguwan Shanu still hold their titles and positions by virtue of their roles as indigenous Hausa-Fulani leaders in their respective areas.

Muslim Hausa-Fulani culture predominates and primary social and religious activities are carried out within networks of individuals related by kinship (actual or classificatory) or by long-term association, who are of similar ethnic and religious affiliation. Despite these strong group ties, Hajiya and her coresidents of all ethnic backgrounds openly express an identification not only with their own families and ethnic groups but also with the local, multiethnic community. The common multiethnic history of the area is shown by the knowledge longtime Hausa residents had of longtime Yoruba or Nupe residents; all remember Ibos who left Kaduna during the civil war in the 1960s, returning months and even years later to find their possessions and rooms held safely for them by Hausa or Yoruba landlords. Residents recall these events as part of their rationale for staying on in Unguwan Kanawa and Unguwan Shanu. For Hajiya Mero, this Unguwan Kanawa, together with Unguwan Shanu, is her "home"—in the affective sense that Kano still is for Hajiya Asabe—as well as being the center for the significant social and kin groups in her life. The lives of Hajiya Mero's children are more broadly grounded in the city of Kaduna, however, whereas Hajiya's existence remains centered in Unguwan Kanawa.

Life History 3: Binta

Binta, the third child of Hajiya Mero, was born about thirty years ago in Unguwan Kanawa, in the compound in which her mother continues to live. Binta attended Koranic school as a child and from the age of seven went to Muhammadiya (a more advanced Islamic school). Her closest childhood girlfriends were the eldest daughter of the present Mai Unguwan of Kanawa and the daughter of her father's elder sister's son, both of whom lived nearby. As a young girl, Binta performed *talla* for her mother, that is, she hawked food on the streets, going out to sell with her friends.

Binta was first married at the age of twelve or thirteen to a Kano man who was a tailor. Her father arranged the marriage, which was an *auren kudi*, a marriage of money, not a kin marriage or marriage of alms. After the marriage, Binta and her husband stayed together for five years, renting rooms in a compound in Unguwan Kanawa. Binta had two children during this marriage and was secluded. The marriage ended in divorce, with the husband keeping the children, as is customary for Hausa men, whereupon Binta went to stay with her grandmother, Hajiya Asabe. She completed *idda* (a mandatory period of remaining alone following divorce) and stayed in seclusion for an additional two months.

While staying with her grandmother, Binta met Kailani, a railway worker who was renting a room in the compound. In 1974, he asked Binta to marry, and she agreed. In the years since they married, Binta has been his only wife. By 1985, Binta had given birth to two girls and a boy in this marriage and was pregnant in 1985 with a fourth child. She has also fostered two children of her husband's elder brother. The oldest, a girl, hawked goods for Binta, selling small items of food, clothing, and jewelry on the streets, until she was married at the age of thirteen. Another young girl fostered by Hajiya Asabe also helped Binta by hawking.

Binta is not secluded in her present marriage, although this causes considerable tension. Her husband periodically objects to her frequent visiting and moving about outside the compound. Yet his disapproval has barely slowed Binta's work, as she continues to sell small items of clothing, jewelry, soap, and foodstuffs (such as fruits, rice, flour, and other staples) locally after purchasing the items in the Kaduna Central Market; she also works as a commission agent. At other times, she has made noodles and sweets for sale; however, these activities have ceased as she has become busier with caring for her young children. During the mornings before he goes to work, as well as on days that he can stay at home, Binta's husband helps with caring for the children, washing, dressing, and feeding them when Binta is away at school or traveling to distant areas away from Kaduna when she sells on commission.

Because she has lived in Unguwan Kanawa for her entire life, Binta knows members of the local Hausa community intimately. Hajiya Rabi, the wife of the compound head in whose compound she lives, has become her *uwar daki* (the senior woman in a client relationship). Binta visits Hajiya Mero and Hajiya Asabe several times a week and makes several trips each year to Kano to visit their relatives. Her next-youngest brother, Usman, is frequently in her compound: He and Binta are close, their tie having been formed in childhood when she "carried him on her back" as an elder sibling. He plays lovingly with her children, and Binta in turn prepares special food for him. Usman and Binta's husband are also good friends, and the three (Usman, Kailani, and Binta) spend much time helping Hajiya Asabe when she makes trips to Kano or to Mecca, and they undertake any other tasks with which she needs assistance.

Binta is much like her mother and grandmother in that she is constantly engaged with people and with various activities and is never alone. But her social contacts are frequently with individuals outside Unguwan Kanawa, throughout the city of Kaduna. Binta has a senior female patron—a wealthy Hausa woman who lives in the Government Residential Area. Binta works often at the woman's house, preparing food for special dinners or other events, and in return receives gifts and has been helped by the woman's husband to obtain lucrative work as a commission agent. In 1985, this work took her on several trips to northern towns such as Funtua, and even further. Binta has many other female friends around the entire city of Kaduna, and in the late 1970s and early 1980s, she attended *biki*, the ritual celebrations for marriages or childbirth, for them at least weekly.

Binta regrets not having attended secular school, and treats two young educated single women who live in her compound with special respect. In 1983, she began attending the new Islamic school that opened in another ward of Kaduna, before a similar school was created in Unguwan Kanawa. She continues to take several courses there, attending two hours per day. A diligent student, she makes time for at least two hours of homework a day in between caring for children, cooking, working at her occupations, and keeping up an active social life. She has begun reading in Arabic and is learning English and Hausa, with help from other women in her compound and their children. Her husband encourages her in these activities. She buys books with her earnings and says that she is firmly committed to sending her daughters, as well as her sons, to non-Koranic school.

Born late in the colonial period, as a child Binta witnessed Nigeria's independence in 1960. Her first marriage at a young age was traditional, arranged by her parents with a man from Kano. Yet this marriage ended, and after a short time as a single woman, Binta married again, choosing her own husband. The characteristics of her second husband and the nature of her marriage to him illustrate many of the social changes occurring in Unguwan Kanawa at the time and their impact on the lives of individuals. Binta's second husband, Kailani, is literate and educated;[9] he is close in age to Binta; in many ways he is a companion to her as well as a husband, agreeing to a marriage without her seclusion, encouraging her education, cooperating in child care, and making it possible for her to engage in occupations that frequently require travel. Binta and Kailani's marriage is untypical of most Hausa marriages in Unguwan Kanawa; however, it may be an example of future trends. They live in a compound headed by a retired soldier and his wife. Of the seven couples in the compound, each woman except one is the only wife in the marriage by choice of the couple; each husband is educated and works in the civil service or holds a position in commerce or industry; and all children of school age (both male and female) are attending secular school, some at university level.

Binta's disappointment in her lack of formal education has been replaced with great energy expended in her pursuit of Islamic education. Universal primary education reached northern Nigeria only in 1976; however, it took a full decade before significant numbers of Hausa girls began attending secular primary schools. Binta was an adult by that time, with children and no easy access to secular education. Beginning in 1983, local Islamic schools rapidly increased in number, bringing Islamic education to adult women in the area. This change accompanied a trend toward a stronger identification with the Islamic world and the growth of Islamic fundamentalism among Nigerian Muslims. Since education is highly valued within Islam for all individuals, many Hausa women in Unguwan Kanawa and throughout Kaduna are attending these schools with the assent of their husbands. Yet the schools themselves offer not only the opportunity to study subjects related to Islam and to gain literacy (first in Arabic, then in Hausa) but they also provide women with the freedom to leave seclusion for part of every day. In their long blue gowns that resemble chadors, women stop to visit along the way home, sell their wares to others at the school, and shop. Even educated wealthy women wear these gowns when attending school. Among Hausa women, such dress may come to serve as a form of veiling and may eventually replace seclusion as a means of maintaining women's modesty within Islam.

Binta's Life Under Changing Economic Conditions in Kaduna

Binta's life has spanned a time of dramatic economic, demographic, political, and social change in Unguwan Kanawa and Unguwan Shanu, in Kaduna, and in Nigeria as a whole. With reorganization and the abolition of the country's regions in 1967, Kaduna became a state capital. Since then, it has also become a commercial and transportation center and part of the North's "industrial triangle" (the Kano-Kaduna-Jos area), where population is concentrated (Ajaegbu 1976:53–60). During the 1970s, increased federal revenues financed development programs that expanded transportation, communications, and energy systems, stimulated industrial growth, and initiated universal primary education (Nigeria Fourth National Development Plan 1982; Watts 1987; Bienen 1985). By 1981, six textile factories in Kaduna were producing over 280 million square meters of material per year, drawing upon local cotton production and water supplies. A Peugeot assembly plant, a phosphate fertilizer plant, the Nigerian Breweries, an oil refinery and petrol production plant, and the headquarters of the National Grains Production Company, the Nigerian Agricultural Bank, and the Nigerian Livestock and Meat Authority were also located in the city. By 1985, the population of Kaduna itself exceeded six hundred thousand and was growing annually by 9 to 11 percent (Adedeji and Rowland 1973:231).[10]

This rapid growth both in Kaduna and throughout the country was uneven, however, and basic services in many areas were seriously neglected (International Labour Office 1981; Watts and Lubeck 1983). Furthermore, the 1982 international oil crisis led to a cut in Nigerian oil production and a concomitant decline in oil revenues. In Kaduna, unemployment rose sharply, wages were frozen, teachers went unpaid, rapid inflation occurred, and many basic commodities became scarce or unavailable. Urban residents with limited access to land or agricultural produce found their ability to subsist seriously threatened. All of these problems were visible in the local community where Binta and her husband lived and struggled to support their family.

By 1980, Unguwan Kanawa and Unguwan Shanu's combined population had grown from 6,500 (in 1965) to 27,440, and population density reached 384 per hectare.[11] Much of this growth resulted from immigrants joining family members already residing in Unguwan Kanawa and Unguwan Shanu (Coles 1983). The ethnic diversity of Kaduna as a whole was mirrored in Unguwan Kanawa and Unguwan Shanu, where 56.32 percent of residents were Hausa, 11.29 percent Ibo, and 11.08 percent Yoruba; the remainder were primarily other Muslim northerners and groups from the Middle Belt and the Midwest. Muslims accounted for 62.93 percent, 31.25 percent were Christian, and 5.8 percent were classed as "other" (Kaduna Polytechnic 1981).[12]

Hausa residents of Unguwan Kanawa and Unguwan Shanu include both the urban poor and an urban middle class. Most Hausa men are unskilled laborers; a small number are clerks or low-level civil servants.[13] Residents live in compounds usually constructed with a mud wall exterior, a tin or thatched roof, rooms built around a central interior open courtyard, and a separate kitchen, a latrine, and washing rooms shared among residents. Even in 1985, few compounds had pipe-borne water: Wells inside the exterior wall or public standpipes outside provided water. About two-thirds of all compounds had electricity, and wood or kerosene was used for cooking. Outside the compounds, open drains and lack of refuse collection have increased congestion on unpaved roads—problems that worsen with the heavy rains each year. These living conditions produce serious health hazards for local residents, and illness is frequent. The two wards are served by a single medical facility—a maternal and child welfare clinic at Unguwan Shanu—although it is unequipped to handle medical care for the general population. Most residents seek treatment at hospitals in the city center, and they go to herbalists, bonesetters, local midwives, and *bori* (a spirit-possession cult) practitioners.

In light of the serious economic recession that affected Nigeria after the decline in oil prices early in the 1980s, Binta's own earnings became increasingly necessary to the support of her family. She, like other Hausa women, must devote increasing amounts of her income to family subsistence (Coles 1991). Because of her lack of education and the dearth of opportunities for women in the formal sector, Binta is limited to informal sector activities for earning income. Normally, a Hausa woman of childbearing age would be secluded and limited to occupations practiced from inside her home; however, by departing from those occupations practiced traditionally by Hausa women and from the seclusion they observed, Binta has greatly increased her own and her family's income. Her husband obviously feels ambivalent about her behavior, but he is willing to countenance it given the income Binta earns through her work as a commission agent and trader.

Many other women in Binta's cohort in Unguwan Kanawa do not experience the autonomy and independence she does on a day-to-day basis: Binta is nearly unique among those her age who did not attend secular school. Yet all Hausa women in Unguwan Kanawa are now able to vote in public elections, and many, like Binta, are becoming literate by attending Islamic school. Most of their daughters attend secular schools, at least through the primary level. Binta has many friends among women who still observe seclusion, both locally and in Kano. Yet she moves freely around the city of Kaduna and ranges even further to cities throughout the North. In doing so, Binta is testing and even pushing back the normative boundaries for Hausa women's roles. And the "home" to which Binta returns, and to which she evidences affection and attachment, is not the local community of Unguwan Kanawa—it is Kaduna, the city.

Hausa Women's Lives and the Development of Kaduna

Current assumptions about Muslim Hausa women portray them as powerless, as legal minors dependent upon men, as relegated to the private or domestic realm, and as insignificant actors in public affairs. Some of these assumptions are valid for Hausa women in Kaduna: As long as the Maliki legal code and shari'ah law are in effect, women will continue to inherit half the property shares of men; males are still able to divorce a woman through a husband's pronouncement of the *talaq* without any court proceedings, whereas a wife can only obtain a divorce that she initiates through legal action in a court. Yet the life histories provided here allow us to move beyond stereotypes to examine the complexity of Hausa women's roles. We see individual women moving out of seclusion, becoming major contributors to their family's subsistence and the local economy, playing active roles in maintaining social networks in the community, and getting involved in restructuring and expanding the repertoire of female roles. It is Hausa women's innovative and entrepreneurial characteristics that propel them to take such actions. To the extent that women depart from their traditional roles and create new ones, they are engaged in social change. In the case of Muslim Hausa women in Kaduna, some of this change comes about as women move within and maintain the "spirit" of former norms—norms of modesty, deference, piety, and commitment to the family—but all the same depart from the "law." Hajiya Asabe is the best example of this as she exhorts young married women in Unguwan Kanawa to remain in seclusion and above all else to obey their husbands—while at the same time marrying her granddaughters to men who do not seek to keep their wives in seclusion and while facilitating the mobility of her granddaughter, Binta, by caring for her children when she must travel for her work.

The view of urbanization in Kaduna provided through the life histories of Hajiya Asabe, Hajiya Mero, and Binta is a personal one, chronicling each woman's own decisions and activities as she passed through the life cycle. Yet taken together, the narratives illustrate how changing social and economic conditions have provided both the constraints and the opportunities that have shaped these women's ability to make particular choices and follow specific courses of action. In the economic realm, the availability of Western medical facilities provided Hajiya Asabe with an opportunity to expand her occupational activities and to increase her prestige, power, and influence in the local community. Analogous opportunities have not been available for most uneducated Hausa women, some of whose occupations have been threatened with wider economic developments: New textile factories have replaced with machine-produced goods the local cloth that women have long woven; and the recent recession has disrupted almost all government services and local economic activities, pushing women out of trade in expensive items.

The increasingly heterogeneous social world of Kaduna, especially in ethnic and religious terms, has been experienced personally by Hajiya Mero and Binta as they have lived alongside non-Hausa women who are more highly educated and not secluded; the Hausa women are visibly benefiting from the freedom and accomplishments of their non-Hausa neighbors. At the same time, growing Islamic fundamentalism and the creation of Islamic schools offer Muslim Hausa women opportunities for personal advancement within their own cultural framework. For Hajiya Asabe, Hajiya Mero, and Binta, urbanization in Kaduna has presented the need to adapt, to maintain some cultural values while abandoning others, and to build new types of social linkages within their "home" community. In the individual strategies they develop and carry out, these women have actively contributed to the social adaptations that become necessary with urbanization.

Notes

Research for this chapter was funded in part by the University of Wisconsin and the Department of Anthropology Goodman Fund, Dartmouth College. An earlier version of this essay was presented at the International Seminar, University of New Hampshire, March 2, 1990. I thank Deborah Pellow, Karen Endicott, Susan Geiger, Beverly Mack, and Deborah Winslow for their helpful suggestions at various stages of writing.

1. Other types of personal narratives are biographies, autobiographies, and diaries or journals.

2. One notable exception is Mirza and Strobel (1989), a work that was also published in Swahili. Mirza is a Kenyan scholar who took part in editing and producing the life histories.

3. The informants for this study were all initially interviewed in 1980–1981, when they were residents of two wards in Kaduna, Unguwan Kanawa and Unguwan Shanu (N=125). The formal sample represents a network of women descended from the first Hausa families in the wards, now connected through kinship and social ties. In 1985, about two-thirds (N=79) of those in the original sample were still resident in the areas, and they were then reinterviewed. Data obtained from 34 additional women not part of the original sample are also drawn upon: All are kinswomen or close friends of women in the formal sample and are of special interest for their income-earning occupations or social activities in the local community.

Data were collected through participant observation activities, administration of an interview schedule focusing on marital and fertility histories, economic activities, education, contacts with kinswomen and other females, and collection of life histories. The author herself collected almost all the data, working primarily in Hausa, with occasional assistance in interpreting from three local Hausa women who also spoke English. One of these research assistants also conducted a small number of the standard interviews.

4. Among them, Hajiya remembers Alhaji Usman, Abdulmumuni, Sa'adu, Mallam Abu, Babban Amina, Garba Mai Ganga, Mallam Mohammadu Sokoto, Kauma, Mallam Darhu, Garba dan Kodi, Mallam Halidu, Mallam Idi, Mallam Bijinyawa, and Usman Bicha.

5. Lord Lugard was a British official instrumental in setting up colonial administrations in Nigeria and Uganda, among other colonies.

6. In fact, most Kaduna Hausa, like those who form part of the Hausa trade diaspora, live in constant daily contact with Yoruba and Ibo from the south of Nigeria (Cohen 1966, 1967, 1969, 1974; Works 1972), with Nupe, Tiv, and others from the Middle Belt region. With increasing opportunities for education, employment, and mobility and with the development of national political parties and a federal government in which Hausa have played a major role, Hausa cities and towns have attracted substantial populations of non-Hausa residents. Hausa have also found themselves employed and living in non-Hausa cities far from home. These alternatives to dominant Hausa experiences appear to be increasingly frequent given contemporary social, economic, and political changes.

7. Survey data from 1965 show that 30.6 percent of the population had been born in Kaduna; 70 percent were migrants, and 40 percent of the population had arrived within the previous five years. Of all immigrants, 66.7 percent were from the northern provinces, and Hausa predominated among residents present for twenty-five years or more (Max Lock and Partners 1967:125–130).

8. Max Lock and Partners, which conducted extensive surveys as part of town planning, gave the following figures representing ethnic identity of residents: "The Hausa were naturally the largest, counting slightly less than a third (28.0 percent) of all adults amongst their membership. The Ibo were next with just less than one fifth (19.1 percent). They were followed by a large group of people belonging to many small tribes of Northern Region origin. Almost the same size as these were the Yoruba. These two groups accounted for 15.2 percent and 14.7 percent of all adults respectively. The next set of communities were the larger minorities of Fulani, Idoma, Nupe and Tiv each having between 3 and 4 per cent of the

total. Finally came the small minorities which were, in order of size, Kanuri (2.0 percent), minor Mid-West tribes (1.6 percent), minor Eastern tribes (1.4 percent), persons from other African countries (1.0 percent), Gwari (0.9 percent), Edo (0.8 percent) and Ibibio (0.5 percent)" (1967:128).

9. Kailani attended some form of postprimary school but not university.

10. The last official federal census showed a population increase from 39,000 in 1952 to 149,000 in 1963. Adedeji and Rowland (1973:231) estimate a 1972 figure of 260,000, with the annual rate of increase at 11 percent. In personal communications with development officials, I was given population estimates of up to 750,000. The city covered an area of 117 square kilometers (although not all land was suitable for habitation), and squatter settlements had grown up beyond city boundaries in several areas (Max Lock and Partners 1967:91–99).

11. One hectare=2.47 acres, or 10,000 square meters. The two wards had expanded to their limits, covering 71.512 hectares, and were closed on all sides: To the north and west, across a stream that flows west into the River Mashi, lie the market and burial ground that serve the communities, a green belt, and the Nigerian Defense Academy; the railway and major roads lie to the south and east; on the western fringe is the village of Abakpa.

12. There were more males than females in every age group except between the years of fifteen and twenty-four, with 54.76 percent of the population being male and 45.24 percent female. This reflected the presence of young Hausa women who came into Kaduna from other parts of the north and subsequently married polygynously. Residents fourteen years old or younger made up 39.2 percent of the total population.

13. Many individuals engage in more than one occupation: For example, a clerk in a government office might also operate a small shop or engage in trading. Data on average incomes for residents in Unguwan Kanawa and Unguwan Shanu collected in the Kaduna Polytechnic survey (1981) suggest that about 42 percent of those employed earned 600 naira per year or less, and another 34 percent earned between 600 and 1800 naira (in 1985, 1 naira=$1.25). This does not include the unemployed portion of the adult population, however, nor are data available to compute average per capita incomes.

References

Adedeji, Adebayo, and L. Rowland, eds. 1973. *Management Problems of Rapid Urbanisation in Nigeria.* Ile-Ife, Nigeria: University of Ife Press.

Ajaegbu, Hyacinth I. 1976. *Urban and Rural Development in Nigeria.* London: Heinemann Educational Books.

Alpers, Edward. 1983. "The Story of Swema: A Note on Female Vulnerability in Nineteenth-Century East Africa." In *Women and Slavery in Africa,* ed. Claire C. Robertson and Martin A. Klein, 185–219. Madison: University of Wisconsin Press.

Aronson, Dan R. 1980. *The City Is Our Farm.* Cambridge, Mass.: Schenkman.

Bienen, Henry. 1985. *Political Conflict and Economic Change in Nigeria.* London: Frank Cass.

Burness, Helen Margaret. 1955. "The Position of Women in Gwandu and Yauri." *Overseas Education* 26, 4:143–152.

———. 1957. "Women in Katsina Province, Northern Nigeria." *Overseas Education* 29, 3:116–122.

———. 1959. "The War Against Ignorance." *African Women* 3, 3 (December):49–53.

Callaway, Barbara. 1987. *Muslim Hausa Women in Nigeria.* Syracuse, N.Y.: Syracuse University Press.

Callaway, Barbara, and Enid Schildkrout. 1985. "Law, Education and Social Change: Implications for Hausa Muslim Women in Nigeria." In *Women in the World,* ed. Lynne B. Iglitzin and Ruth Ross, 181–205. Santa Barbara, Calif.: Clio Press.

Codere, Helen. 1973. *The Biography of an African Society: Rwanda, 1900–1960.* Tervuren: Musée Royal de l'Afrique Centrale.

Cohen, Abner. 1966. "Politics of the Kola Trade: Some Processes of Tribal Community Formation Among Migrants in West African Towns." *Africa* 36, 1:18–36.

———. 1967. "Stranger Communities: The Hausa." In *The City of Ibadan,* ed. P. C. Lloyd, A. L. Mabogunje, and B. Awe, 117–127. London: Cambridge University Press.

———. 1969. *Custom and Politics in Urban Africa.* Berkeley: University of California Press.

———. 1974. "Introduction." In *Urban Ethnicity,* ed. Abner Cohen, ix–xxiv. London: Tavistock.

Coles, Catherine. 1983. "Muslim Women in Town: Social Change Among the Hausa of Northern Nigeria." Ph.D. diss., University of Wisconsin, Madison.

———. 1990. "The Older Woman in Hausa Society: Power and Authority in Urban Nigeria." In *The Cultural Context of Aging: World-Wide Perspectives,* ed. Jay Sokolovsky, 57–81. New York: Bergin and Garvey.

———. 1991. "Hausa Women's Work in a Declining Urban Economy: Kaduna, Nigeria, 1980–85." In *Hausa Women in the Twentieth Century,* ed. Catherine Coles and Beverly Mack, 163–191. Madison: University of Wisconsin Press.

Coles, Catherine, and Beverly Mack. 1991. "Women in Twentieth Century Hausa Society." In *Hausa Women in the Twentieth Century,* ed. Coles and Mack, 3–26. Madison: University of Wisconsin Press.

Epstein, A. L. 1958. *Politics in an Urban African Community.* Manchester: Manchester University Press.

———. 1964. "Urban Communities in Africa." In *Closed Systems and Open Minds,* ed. Max Gluckman. Edinburgh and London: Oliver and Boyd.

Geiger, Susan N. G. 1986. "Women's Life Histories: Method and Content." *Signs* 11, 2:334–351.

Gugler, Josef, and William G. Flanagan. 1978. *Urbanization and Social Change in West Africa.* New York: Cambridge University Press.

Hannerz, Ulf. 1980. *Exploring the City.* New York: Columbia University Press.

Heilbrun, Carolyn G. 1988. *Writing a Woman's Life.* New York and London: Norton.

International Labour Office. 1981. *Nigeria: First Things First.* Addis Ababa: ILO.

Johnson, Cheryl. 1986. "Class and Gender: A Consideration of Yoruba Women During the Colonial Period." In *Women and Class in Africa,* ed. Claire Robertson and Iris Berger, 237–254. New York and London: Africana.

Kaduna Polytechnic. 1981. *Department of Town Planning.* Urban Renewal Study. Kaduna, Nigeria.

Langness, L. L., and Gelya Frank. 1981. *Lives: An Anthropological Approach to Biography.* California: Chandler and Sharp.

LeVine, Sarah. 1979. *Mothers and Wives: Gusii Women of East Africa.* Chicago: University of Chicago Press.

Lewis, Oscar. 1959. *Five Families: Mexican Case Studies in the Culture of Poverty.* New York: Basic Books.

———. 1961. *The Children of Sanchez: Autobiography of a Mexican Family.* New York: Random House.

———. 1964. *Pedro Martineza: A Mexican Peasant and His Family.* New York: Random House.

———. 1965. *La Vida: A Puerto Rican Family in the Culture of Poverty: San Juan and New York.* New York: Vintage Books.

Mack, Beverly. 1988. "Hajiya Ma'daki: A Royal Hausa Woman." In *Life Histories of African Women,* ed. Patricia Romero, 47–77. London and Atlantic Highlands, N.J.: Ashfield.

Max Lock and Partners. 1967. *Kaduna 1917–1967–2017: A Survey and Plan of the Capital Territory for the Government of Northern Nigeria.* London: Faber.

Mirza, Sarah, and Margaret Strobel, eds. and trans. 1989. *Three Swahili Women: Life Histories from Mombasa, Kenya.* Bloomington and Indianapolis: Indiana University Press.

Nigeria. 1982. *Fourth National Development Plan, 1981–85* (revised). Lagos: Federal Ministry of Economic Planning.

Obbo, Christine. 1986. "Stratification and the Lives of Women in Uganda." In *Women and Class in Africa,* ed. Claire Robertson and Iris Berger, 178–194. New York and London: Africana.

———. 1988. "Bitu: Facilitator of Women's Educational Opportunities." In *Life Histories of African Women,* ed. Patricia W. Romero, 99–112. London and Atlantic Highlands, N.J.: Ashfield.

O'Connor, Anthony. 1983. *The African City.* New York: Africana.

Parkin, David. 1969. *Neighbours and Nationals in an African City Ward.* London: Routledge and Kegan Paul.

Personal Narratives Group. 1989. *Interpreting Women's Lives. Feminist Theory and Personal Narratives.* Bloomington: Indiana University Press.

Pittin, Renée. 1979. "Marriage and Alternative Strategies: Career Patterns of Hausa Women in Katsina City." D.Phil. diss., University of London, School of Oriental and African Studies.

———. 1984a. "Migration of Women in Nigeria: The Hausa Case." *International Migration Review* 18, 4:1293–1314.

———. 1984b. "Documentation and Analysis of the Invisible Work of Invisible Women: A Nigerian Case-Study." *International Labour Review* 123, 4:473–490.

Population Census of Nigeria. 1983. Lagos: Federal Office of Statistics.

Robertson, Claire C. 1983. "Post-Proclamation Slavery in Accra: A Female Affair?" In *Women and Slavery in Africa,* ed. Claire C. Robertson and Martin A. Klein, 220–245. Madison: University of Wisconsin Press.

Schildkrout, Enid. 1983. "Dependence and Autonomy: The Economic Activities of Secluded Hausa Women in Kano." In *Female and Male in West Africa*, ed. Christine Oppong, 107–126. London: George Allen and Unwin.

———. 1986. "Widows in Hausa Society: Ritual Phase or Social Status?" In *Widows in African Societies*, ed. Betty Potash, 131–152. Stanford: Stanford University Press.

———. 1988. "Hajiya Husaina: Notes on the Life History of a Hausa Woman." In *Life Histories of African Women*, ed. Patricia Romero, 78–98. London and Atlantic Highlands, N.J.: Ashfield.

Shostak, Marjorie. 1981. *Nisa: The Life and Words of a !Kung Woman*. Cambridge: Harvard University Press.

———. 1989. "'What the Wind Won't Take Away': The Genesis of *Nisa: The Life and Words of a !Kung Woman*." In Personal Narratives Group, *Interpreting Women's Lives: Feminist Theory and Personal Narratives*, 228–240. Bloomington: Indiana University Press.

Smith, Mary. 1954. *Baba of Karo: A Woman of the Muslim Hausa*. London: Faber and Faber.

Smith, M. G. 1954. Introduction and notes in Mary Smith, *Baba of Karo: A Woman of the Muslim Hausa*. London: Faber and Faber.

———. 1955. *The Economy of Hausa Communities of Zaria*. Colonial Research Studies no. 16. London: HMSO.

———. 1960. *Government in Zazzau*. London: Oxford University Press.

———. 1978. *The Affairs of Daura*. Berkeley: University of California Press.

Southall, Aidan. 1961. *Social Change in Modern Africa*. London: Oxford University Press.

———. 1975. "Forms of Ethnic Linkage Between Town and Country." In *Migration and Urbanization*, ed. Brian M. Du Toit and Helen I. Safa, 273–283. The Hague: Mouton.

Strobel, Margaret. 1979. *Muslim Women in Mombasa, 1890–1975*. New Haven: Yale University Press.

———. 1983. "Slavery and Reproductive Labor in Mombasa." In *Women and Slavery in Africa*, eds. Claire C. Robertson and Martin A. Klein, 111–129. Madison: University of Wisconsin Press.

Trager, Lillian. 1988. *The City Connection: Migration and Family Interdependence in the Philippines*. Ann Arbor: University of Michigan Press.

Trevor, Jean. 1975a. "Family Change in Sokoto, a Traditional Moslem Fulani/Hausa City." In *Population Growth and Socioeconomic Change in West Africa*, ed. John Caldwell, 236–253. New York: Columbia University.

———. 1975b. "Western Education and Muslim Fulani/Hausa Women in Sokoto, Northern Nigeria." In *Conflict and Harmony in Tropical Africa*, ed. G. Brown and M. Hiskett, 247–270. London: Allen and Unwin.

UNDP (United Nations Development Program). 1979. Kano-Kaduna Sewerage Drainage and Refuse Disposal, Appropriate Sanitation Technologies Pilot and Demonstration Projects. Dr. G. Holfelder (Frieburg) and G.K.W. (Mannheim), Germany.

Watts, Michael. 1987. *State, Oil, and Agriculture in Nigeria*. Berkeley: Institute of International Studies, University of California.

Watts, Michael, and Paul Lubeck. 1983. "The Popular Classes and the Oil Boom: A Political Economy of Rural and Urban Poverty." In *The Political Economy of Nigeria*, ed. William I. Zartman, 105–144. New York: Praeger.

Wilks, Ivor. 1988. "She Who Blazed a Trail: Akyaawa Yikwan of Asante." In *Life Histories of African Women*, ed. Patricia W. Romero, 113–139. London and Atlantic Highlands, N.J.: Ashfield.

Works, John. 1972. *Pilgrims in a Strange Land*. New York: Columbia University Press.

Wright, Marcia. 1975. "Women in Peril: A Commentary on the Life Stories of Captives in Nineteenth-Century East-central Africa." *African Social Research* 20:800–819.

———. 1983. "Bwanikwa: Consciousness and Protest Among Slave Women in Central Africa, 1886–1911." In *Women and Slavery in Africa*, eds. Claire C. Robertson and Martin A. Klein, 246–267. Madison: University of Wisconsin Press.

Part Three

Courtyards: Marriage, Family, and Housing

5

Washing Dirty Laundry in Public: Local Courts, Custom, and Gender Relations in Postcolonial Lusaka

KAREN TRANBERG HANSEN

In the course of my long-term fieldwork on household dynamics and on the struggle to make a living in Mtendere Township in Zambia's capital, Lusaka, I decided in 1988 to spend some of my research time in the Local Court at Chelston to which Mtendere residents took their civil cases. As the postcolonial successors of the Urban Native Courts, Urban Local Courts continue to adjudicate disputes that fall within "customary law." I was particularly intrigued by Mtendere women's insistence that "one shouldn't wash one's dirty laundry in public," when in fact they brought cases concerning conjugal disputes and personal insult/defamation of character to court much more readily than men. In this chapter I explore why women consider the Local Court a strategic place to settle such disputes, and I focus on two issues: how gender relations are negotiated in Local Court and what this tells us about the relationship between "custom" and society.

The codification of customary law in colonial Central Africa was shaped both by European notions about Africans and by the concerns of Africans, especially chiefs and male elders (Chanock 1985). As such, customary law is a dynamic historical formation that "at once shapes and is shaped by economic, political, and social processes" (Roberts and Mann 1991:8). Whereas the customary law of the colonial era often supported ruling-class (European) and African elite (male) interests, both the Urban Native Courts of the past and the Local Courts of today were, and still are, flexible in their arbitration and judgment of dispute cases, reckoning with the political and economic circumstances in the wider society. Thus, there are both constraining and enabling aspects of African customary law (Starr and Collier 1989:12). As I demonstrate with material drawn from Local Court cases, certain aspects of customary law appear to persist, but on closer scrutiny, these legal features are far from "customary." Rather, they represent reconstituted notions of custom that urban justices invoke in their arbitration. What is more, these same justices are creating "custom" out of practices that were not recognized as such in the "traditional past." In short, this chapter presents a discussion of the ongoing creation of custom and of the court as a resource that urban women use in struggles over poverty, work, autonomy, and, above all, identity in postcolonial Lusaka.

The case method of legal presentation that A. L. Epstein pioneered in his work on the Copperbelt in the 1950s offers a compelling framework for analyzing situations that produce conflict as well as for exploring the place of legal bodies in the broader structure of power in a particular society (1953:4). In describing a number of cases pertaining to the two seemingly disparate categories of conjugal problems and personal insult/defamation of character, I seek to identify some core issues that are central to both. These issues expose questions about what kinds of people women and men want to be, in contrast to the sort of people the wider society supposes them to be.

Beginning in Mtendere, I first briefly describe how the population I studied reacted to ongoing socioeconomic changes and characterize the dominant gender relations that structure women's and men's opportunities on unequal terms. Then I follow some residents to the Local Court, summarizing court procedures and presenting cases that fit the two categories of conjugal problems and personal insult/defamation. In the subsequent section, I tease out a body of shared ideas from these two categories of cases. And I identify some of the criteria the Local Court follows in issuing judgments. My concluding comments concern the powers of custom and court to redefine female and male against a backdrop of socioeconomic change.

The Setting

Mtendere was established as a site-and-service scheme of self-built housing in 1967. By the late 1980s, its population was close to forty thousand.

The majority of its residents originate from many different ethnic groups in Zambia's eastern province. Although Mtendere is a low-income settlement, the range of occupational groups represented there includes teachers, clerks, and nurses. By far the largest part of the male population performs semiskilled and manual labor, and an ever-growing proportion of women and men seek to make a living from informal sector activity. As a residential community, Mtendere has a population of private house owners and a growing proportion of tenants.

The proliferation of informal sector work and tenancy that I observed in Mtendere over the years has occurred in the wake of the deterioration of the country's economy from the mid-1970s and onward, when copper export revenues went on a downward slide, oil prices rose, and little industrial diversification or agricultural improvement took place. Massive external borrowing provided temporary and very costly remedies. The low-income group, in particular, experienced the effects of skyrocketing inflation, shortages of basic commodities, and the deterioration of essential services such as those provided by schools and hospitals. There were, and continue to be, high pressures on wage employment and housing. Some Mtendere home owners added to shrinking incomes by subdividing their houses or building on extensions for rental. More and more people who had lost their jobs turned to the informal sector. Previously home-bound women joined them in order to be able to feed and clothe their children. And some people who still held on to their wage labor jobs began working "on the side."

These processes were reflected in the experiences of members of the sample of one hundred households whose activities I have followed from the early 1970s through the 1990s. Their effects differ significantly by gender. The economic deterioration in society at large plays a part in this, but so does something that might be described as "custom," which, when invoked, often privileges men over women. The households that remained in Mtendere throughout the period of my observations seemed to have weathered the deterioration of the overall economy in part because of women's work. But this assessment masks a number of issues because it interprets women's activities merely as responses to a depressed economic situation.

My ongoing research in Mtendere showed that these women's troubles in making ends meet were not exclusively economic. In effect, their income-oriented activities had evolved as a response both to economic hardships *and* to dynamics that characterized the cultural domain of gender relations within their own households (Hansen 1989). Women's specific responses to Zambia's depressed economy depended on their age and on their changing relationship to husbands over the course of the household development cycle. My work, and that of others in Lusaka, shows that women who trade and market are neither young girls just arrived from the countryside nor newly married wives (Todd and Shaw 1980). Rather, they tend to be middle-aged women who are close to or beyond their childbearing years. Increasingly so, they also include single heads of households with dependents to care for.[1]

These observations must be explained in the context of the unfolding household development cycle and the changing expectations spouses have about each other. A wife expects her husband to "keep" her and her children—providing them with shelter, clothing, and a household allowance—yet cultural norms do not obligate him to do so. A husband's earnings are not household income in the sense of a common purse to which the wife has equal access. The urban wife has no assurance of her husband's support, no security for daily needs, and no provision for her children's education.

Over the course of the household development cycle, women and men hold different and changing views about who should work and about how to spend earnings. They use money and networks for different ends. In their concern to benefit in their own right from economic activity, some Mtendere women who were close to or beyond their childbearing years devised ways of concealing part of their earnings. As I discuss further on, such economic negotiations in everyday life are influenced by cultural norms and expectations about gender relations in society at large.

Gender relations in Zambia have much in common with those elsewhere in Africa: Cultural norms and assumptions support male authority and power, regardless of whether descent is traced patrilineally or matrilineally (as in most societies in Zambia). A woman's access to productive resources is mediated through a man: her father, husband, uncle, or brother. On a husband's death, property devolves on his descendants, not his wife. A critical issue in Zambia in this regard is the dissolution of property in matrilineal descent systems. When a husband dies, his matrilineal relatives may descend on the urban household, grabbing all it contains and sometimes claiming the house, thus ignoring the fact that household property is a product of the work of both spouses. In spite of the introduction of the new Intestate Succession Act in 1989 (Coldham 1989),[2] allowing widows and children some access to resources, there is sufficient evidence to show that prevailing ideology often makes the new act ineffective in practice.[3] The fact that such practices continue to occur reminds the urban wife that she should not expect security for her old age.

In addition to the possibility of a spouse's death, there is the prospect of divorce. Women ought not expect to receive property or maintenance for themselves and their children once a marriage has been dissolved, because customary divorce law, which persists unreformed, imposes no such obligations on husbands. Even while women are married, the constancy of men's attentions is uncertain. Only a portion of a man's disposable means reaches his own household; some of it might be spent on entertainment, including "a wife on the side" and drinking. As in the past, the conjugal domain is fraught with tensions, in part due to the persistence of marriage practices permitting polygyny and to the existence of a sexual double standard that permits men's extramarital relations while blaming women for sexual promiscuity (Epstein 1981, Powdermaker 1962).

Hierarchical power relations in interpersonal gender relations extend beyond the household to reinforce gender inequality in society at large. For instance, housing and housing allowances are allotted to men; wives get access to housing through husbands; and single heads of households cannot claim housing in their own right (Hansen 1992). Similar observations hold for land, credit, and building materials.[4] Above all, formal jobs are few and far between, and men, not women, tend to get them. The construction of gender that results from such practices is based on assumptions that women should be dependent on men.

Although women need men, they also know that they cannot rely on them. Women's reaction is double edged: While seeking to retain men's attentions, some Mtendere women become increasingly concerned to create an income source in their own right as they age. Thus, there are built-in tensions both in gender relationships and in women's and men's individual efforts at defining themselves (Hansen 1984). The problems these tensions produce are difficult to contain in Lusaka's depressed economy. They are fought over by women and men in households and between women in neighborhoods. When such problems become persistent, they may end up in court.

Dispute Mediation and Local Court

When Mtendere residents take problems to court, they do so because of *mavuto* (of which the singular form is *vuto*), which in Nyanja, the most frequently spoken language in Lusaka, means "persistent trouble." Not all disputes turn into *mavuto*, and third-party resolution through court is considered a last resort (Himonga 1985:200–201). As the case material I present here illustrates, before reaching court, attempts to handle the problems might have been made in informal family forums. If one or more of the parties to a dispute is an active church member, problems might have been brought before church elders or, depending on the issue at stake, before an employer or social welfare officers (of the Ministry of Labor and Social Services); or the police might have been called on. Above all, the bureaucracy of the local township administration might have been consulted in a process through which disputes move from the section to the branch chairman. When problems persist unresolved in spite of such mediation efforts, they become *mavuto*. In such instances, the party chairman will encourage the complaining party to issue a court summons against the offender(s).

Local Courts are the lowest judicial bodies in Zambia's legal hierarchy. Their jurisdiction pertains to civil disputes under customary law, including such issues as marital and property claims. Appeals lie with subordinate courts, whence they may be advanced to the High Court, and then on to the Supreme Court (Himonga 1987:58). Local Courts are supervised by a presiding justice, who in some courts sits with a number of court justices. Justices are not trained lawyers, and their chief qualification seems to be their knowledge of customary law (Himonga 1985:226–227). During my observations at the Chelston Local Court, one of five such institutions in Lusaka, the presiding justice worked alone, assisted by a court clerk.

The procedures at this urban Local Court had much in common with those Epstein described on the Copperbelt in the 1950s: The facts of the issue are presented to the court by way of statement, each party—plaintiff (PL) and defendant (DF)—first speaking without interruption from the presiding justice (PJ) (1953:7–8). The justice in turn questions and probes in an attempt to discover the cause of the problem.[5] He sometimes cross-examines the parties, which can include codefendants (CO-DF), and occasionally he calls witnesses (WI). Then the justice sums up the matter and issues a judgment.

There were four broad categories of disputes among the wide range of matters Mtendere residents took to their Local Court after other mediation efforts had proved futile.[6] Almost one-half of the cases revolved around conjugal problems (e.g., marital disputes; divorce; chasing from home, desertion, or neglect and cruelty; adultery; and premarital pregnancy). The second-largest category consisted of complaints about defamation of character, insult, and witchcraft accusation (and combinations of these). I deal with these two largest categories in the sections that follow. Complaints about debt and theft constituted the third-largest category, followed by a miscellany of disputes involving, for instance, tearing of clothes; refusal to return borrowed items; retention of blue book, national registration card, or land record card; outstanding rent payment; and contempt of court.

Conjugal Cases

Striking gender distinctions are evident in the broad category of cases involving conjugal problems. By and large, women took men to court for marital problems, for chasing them away from home, and for divorce.

Men took women to court for deserting the home, and they took other men to court for committing adultery with their partners. As the following cases demonstrate, the outcome depends to a large extent on the status of the conjugal union, which in the judgment of the presiding justice hinges on whether bridewealth was transferred. In the records of the court clerk at the Chelston Local Court, bridewealth is rendered as dowry. I have retained this usage in order to indicate the reworking of a "traditional" concept. The term *lobola* occurs occasionally, as do other vernacular terms for specific transactions.

In *Zulu v. Mbewe* (No. 754 of 1987), Mrs. Zulu sought a divorce from her husband, Mr. Mbewe, to whom she had been married with a dowry of K 130 since 1982;[7] they had one child. The plaintiff (PL), Mrs. Zulu, recounts:

> The defendant (DF) married me in 1982. That same month, September 1982, he chased me [away from home] saying I am barren. After a few days I was sent back to him. In October 1982 he chased me again but the church elders advised him to talk to me and he agreed.
>
> I stayed with him for a few months and I conceived from him. Later after giving birth, he again chased me when the baby was one month old. I was sent back to him but he said he doesn't want me and he sent me to . . . where his parents are. He was giving me mealie meal [maize or corn meal] in a newspaper [i.e., in a scrap of paper, not a standard bag], and he was not buying me clothes.
>
> On 7/17/85 I went to my parents in Mtendere compound. He came and produced money as a sign of divorce. In April 1987 again he chased me but he was advised by church elders to take me back. He refused and sent me to his relatives at . . . but I was sent back to him but still he refused and I went to my relatives. Then I decided to cut [issue] him a [court] summons.

The Presiding Justice (PJ) then engaged the parties in a discussion:

DF. How many times have I taken you to church elders for reconciliation?

PL. Six times.

DF. Were you cooking and washing for me?

PL. Yes.

PJ. Did DF start to chase you [away from home] a long time ago?

PL. Yes.

PJ. Why are you forcing youself to go back to his house?

PL. It is because I am pregnant.

DF. I deny to reconciliate with the PL because she does not follow my instructions in the house. She does not wash for me and she does not cook. I have taken her before church elders six times but she would not change for the better. I then gave her K 10 as a token of divorce.

PL. Do you think I am a liar?

DF. Yes.

PL. Do you want me to give birth to children without keeping them?

DF. No.

PL. Who sleeps with me?

DF. It is me.

PL. Why don't you want me?

DF. It is because you don't want to listen to my instructions.

PJ. Is the pregnancy yours?

DF. It is mine.

PJ. Why can't you keep her till she gives birth?

DF. It is because one [i.e., the child] may die in the future.

PJ. In accordance to your custom, is it lawful to divorce a pregnant woman?

DF. Yes.

A witness (WI) from Mtendere enters in support of the plaintiff.

WI. The plaintiff is my sister. I suppose the marriage has come to an end. Since they married, troubles have not ceased. The same year he married PL, he started chasing her. The church elders have tried their level best to reconcile the couple but [with] no change.

On 11/17/85 we held a discussion with DF's mother and in her presence DF vowed to say he has lost love for PL. On 8/4/86 DF proscribed K 2 [a payment DF was asked to pay?] in presence of church elders was furnished. Later he produced K 10 and gave it to PL and told her to go to the law.

This case demonstrates the failure both of church elders and relatives to mediate in a difficult marriage situation. In summarizing it, the presiding justice argued that since the defendant had already agreed to divorce his pregnant wife, he had to compensate her with K 400 to assist her in preparing for the child's birth.

Aside from the special issue surrounding a wife's pregnancy in this case, court instructions for men to pay compensation to estranged wives were also common in other divorce cases, provided that the spouses had been married "with dowry." Just how the court defines marriage is at issue in several of the following cases.

The *Banda v. Mutale* (No. 770 of 1987) case was brought to court by Mrs. Banda, who wanted to divorce Mr. Mutale because he "chased her [drove her from home] constantly." They had been married since 1976, without dowry, and they had four children. Mrs. Banda explained:

PL. DF chased me from the house on 7/11/87. This was not his first time to chase me. He has chased me thrice since we married. At one time when he chased me he followed me and asked me to rejoin him. My parents told me to join him.

One day during his absence about four people came to demand their monies. I refunded the whole money totaling K 300 when he was out at Lundazi. Later he went to Mansa and told me I should be keeping K 100 each month. So when he came back in June he found me with K 600, which he demanded me to give him and I did. Due to our troubles I reported at DF's place of work and his boss advised me to sue him.

The PJ seeks to identify the problem:

PJ. Where do you come from?

PL. Petauke.

PJ. Is there no dowry?

PL. It is not marriage.

DF. I started the friendship with PL in 1979 and asked her whether she has relatives in Mtendere; she told me she doesn't have. But she told me that she had an uncle in Mandevu [a low-income township in Lusaka] and that she will one day take me there. One day a certain relative of PL came to the house, and since I did not know her I was shocked. When I came from Mansa it is true I found PL has kept K 650 and I asked her to give me so that I can go and shop for the children at home. In June 1987 when I came asking PL to stop the child from sucking milk because the child has grown up. But my wife refused. She was even refusing me to have sexual intercourse with her. I have accepted the marriage to end because she does not listen to my advice.

PL. Was I not merely following by saying that I don't want to produce?

DF. It was not a joke.

PL. Do I refuse you in bed?

DF. Yes.

PJ. Do you accept to divorce even now?

DF. Yes.

PL. I want DF to give me property for the services I have rendered for him. DF also took my children.

DF. This time I took the children and I want my money which she refused.

The justice, in trying to ascertain the status of this union, elicited information about whether relevant relatives had acknowledged the relationship as a marriage. He summed up as follows: "This court dissolves the friendship because no dowry was paid to make the marriage legal. In this regard, no divorce certificate will be issued. In addition, PL cannot claim property which she bought before DF proposed to her and DF cannot take the children because no custom was followed in the sense that no dowry was paid."

The critical issue of childbearing in relation to marriage from men's perspective is also evident in the next case. In *Mushanga v. Phiri* (No. 631 of 1987), Mr. Mushanga took his wife to court to request divorce, claiming that she caused "a lot of dispute in the house." The court record describes them as married in 1982, with no dowry and no children. The presiding justice probed into the matter and learned that a damage fee (and not dowry) of K 15 had been paid at the beginning of the relationship.[8]

PL. In 1982 the DF became my girlfriend and I was told I had [im]pregnated her. But it was not true and I was charged K 60 out of which K 15 was paid. We looked for medicines but all in vain. This is why I don't want her because we have no children.

PJ. How long have you been in friendship?

PL. Since 1982 up to date.

DF. My brother asked PL how many witch doctors we have gone to. The PL told him and my brother decided that we should stop looking for medicines.

PJ. Is this a proper marriage?

DF. It is just friendship.

A witness for the defendant next argued that "the parties should separate because they were not properly married." Asked by the presiding justice whether he agreed that "this was a mere friendship," the defendant's witness answered in the affirmative. The presiding justice then issued the judgment that the friendship should be dissolved because "no dowry was paid."

In this and in several other "divorce cases," the compensations paid to women depended on the status of the union: whether the parties had been properly married, that is, whether dowry had been given. This meaning of "proper marriage" also entered into the court's decisions concerning compensation after adultery, as the following case illustrates.

In *Chirwa v. Poloti* (No. 378 of 1987), Mr. Chirwa claimed that Mr. Poloti had abducted his wife. Mr. Chirwa had been married to his wife since 1963, with no dowry, and they had several children.

PL. I sued DF because he committed adultery with CO-DF [codefendant]. She had missed from the house and when I looked for her, I found her in the house of the DF. The DF threatened to hit me with a hammer.

PJ. Is CO-DF your wife?

PL. She is my wife.

PJ. Did you pay dowry?

PL. No.

PJ. Is she your proper wife then?

PL. She is just a friend.

DF. When I met CO-DF she told me that she was not married. So I took her to my house.

PJ. Did she tell you that she was not married?

DF. That is what she told me.

PJ. (to DF) Is CO-DF your wife?

DF. She is my wife.

PJ. Did you pay dowry?

DF. No.

PJ. Is CO-DF your wife then?

DF. She is my girlfriend.

CO-DF. The reason I gave in to DF is that the PL doesn't support me. The PL doesn't stay at home.

PJ. Did DF pay dowry?

CO-DF. No.

This case was dismissed by the presiding justice "due to the fact that PL and DF are just boyfriends to CO-DF. No dowry was paid from either side." It contrasts to other adultery cases where husbands were awarded compensation from men who had engaged in sex with their "properly married wives."

In relationships between women and men, marriage—that is, being properly married with dowry—rather than friendship, is increasingly difficult in today's strained economy, as the *Mbewe v. Phiri* case (No. 694 of 1987) illustrates. Mrs. Mbewe took Mr. Phiri to court because he had deserted their home; she wanted reconciliation. They were married in 1963, had four children, and only part of the agreed-upon dowry had been paid.

PL. I married DF in 1963 and he has four children with me. When we went home we stayed on the farm. He left me in 1985 at the farm, but he came [to Lusaka] for good. So I came to sue the DF for reconciliation.

DF. In August 1985, the PL went home to see her parents but when she arrived at home her grandmother wrote to say that PL will not come back until I pay *lobola*. So I came home and I was charged to pay four heads

of cattle. I told them I would pay in money but they wanted the animals. So I came here [to Lusaka] in March to work so that I can raise
money to buy animals to pay.

Asked by the presiding justice about why he had not paid yet, the defendant explained that he was still looking for money to buy cattle. When
cross-examined by the presiding justice, the defendant explained:

DF. I am prepared to get her but the problem is accommodation because I
     am occupying a one-roomed house. At present I am not working, so I
     cannot promise [her accommodation]. I still want my wife, but the prob-
     lem is that her parents who charged me animals will think that I have
     disobeyed their order.
PL. I am going home so when he finds a house he will write me.

In this case, the presiding justice argued that the plaintiff "did not
desert her but her parents said he should take her after paying four animals *lobola*." And the presiding justice advised: "The court cannot force
them to marry, but DF should show love to his wife by making sure that
he finds accommodation for her."

The case just presented indicates that the Local Court does reckon with
some of the difficulties hard economic times pose for "observing custom." This court also, as the next case shows, makes distinctions between
rich and poor. *Mwila v. Sinyinda* (No. 171 of 1988) is just one of the many
cases involving partners who in the court's view are not properly married. As discussed earlier, in most such cases, women do not get compensation from husbands once their marriages are dissolved. But Mr.
Sinyinda was a chief accountant for a well-known firm and therefore
much better able than most urban men to compensate his estranged
wife. They had been married since 1969 and there was one child. As Mrs.
Mwila explained:

PL. I married DF in 1969 after divorcing my first husband. I also told him
     that I was once married and I had one child. He accepted to keep me
     and my child. He paid K 4 dowry to my brother because I was once
     married . . . The cause of breakage of marriage is because DF sent me
     home and maintained another woman. Later he was accusing me of try-
     ing to [be]witch him . . . and he wrote me a separation letter. Since 1980
     the DF never bothered to support me and my child.

Seeking to ascertain the facts, the presiding justice asked about the
chief reason for termination of the marriage.

DF. No support.

PJ. Since when has he not been supporting you?

PL. Since 1980.

PL. I have built a house at Kaunda Square [a low-income township in Lusaka], which he promised that he would build for me. But since he has not built me a house, I would be glad if the same house could be surrendered to me.

In the judgment of the presiding justice, Mr. Sinyinda was charged to pay compensation of K 1,500 to his wife for the house he was expected to build but for whose construction she had been responsible.

Insult/Defamation of Character and Witchcraft Accusations

As mentioned at the outset, these cases predominantly involve women. They all revolve around issues that women consider crucial to their definition of themselves. The insult case of *Zulu v. Sakala* (No. 426 of 1987) was brought to court by Mrs. Zulu (PL) who wanted compensation from Mrs. Sakala (DF).

PL. In April 1987 the DF came to my house and accused me of committing adultery with her husband. She started insulting me.

PJ. Is this true?

DF. It is very true.

PJ. Did DF find you with her husband?

PL. No.

DF. When I came home from work, I used to meet my husband with PL. When I complained to my husband, he gave me a nasty answer. This annoyed me and I went to insult PL.

PJ. Were you right to go and insult PL?

DF. I was wrong.

WI-PL [witness for plaintiff]. The PL is my neighbour and whenever DF sees me with PL, she (DF) suspects me of being a boyfriend to PL.

In the view of the presiding justice, the defendant had admitted that she insulted the plaintiff, and he charged her to pay K 180 compensation to the plaintiff.

In *Mbewe v. Metson* (No. 237 of 1988), Mrs. Mbewe argued that Mr. Metson falsely accused her (PL) of telling that his (DF) wife "bitches" about with other men. Mrs. Mbewe wanted compensation.

PL. It was one day when DF came to ask for money from me. I told him I
    had no money but when leaving he banged the door. I then went to tell
    his wife that her husband came to ask for money. Later . . . I saw the DF
    and when he asked me, I told him. But when I bent down to pick up a
    stick he threw a bottle at me. When I asked him why he did that, he
    started shouting at me that I am a bitch. When I heard those words I
    left. The following day I went to his house . . . and he apologized. But
    another day he accused me of having told him to say that his wife
    moves about with other men and that he has frequently been beating
    his wife.

The defendant then asked the plaintiff: "So did you say you beat your
wife because I told that your wife bitches a lot. I did not tell you such
words. I did say that if you are mad, then I will take you to Chainama [the
nearby state mental hospital]."

DF. It was early February 1988 one day [when] I was coming from work. I
    met PL by her home and I asked her whether *munkoyo* [a lightly fer-
    mented homemade beverage] was there and she told me it was there.
    Then she added words saying that my wife bitches about with other
    men. So I waited for my wife until she came home. I asked her where
    she was and she said at church. On 2/21/88 again PL was calling her
    bitch . . . She shouted at me, saying, "Have you divorced your wife be-
    cause of me?" When I heard such words I told her that I wanted to wait
    for her husband so that we can solve the matter. Then the other day I
    sent for PL to come to my house for a discussion. When she came, in-
    stead of listening to what she was called for, she uttered words directed
    to me that "if you are mad then I should take a wheelbarrow and take
    you to Chainama."

After some cross-examination and hearing of witnesses, the presiding
justice concluded: "DF has failed to produce proof as to whether it is true
that PL told him to say that his wife bitches with other men. This proves
to this court that by merely defaming PL's character as such he (DF) must
compensate PL the sum of K 80."

"Bitching" and "moving about" are serious issues, as demonstrated in
the *Nfonse v. Sitali* case (No. 204 of 1988), which involved witchcraft allegations as well. Ms. Nfonse explained how Mrs. Sitali had invoked witchcraft against her and that she had called her a "bitch" in a letter.

PL. On 2/18/88 I received a letter from her labeling me a bitch and that I am
    an AIDS carrier. She also bewitched me. Lastly she threatened that she
    will do bad whenever she will meet me.

DF. I wrote PL an insults letter because whenever she went to Kabwe and came back she used to convey greetings from Kabwe to me. PL is my friend, but to my surprise when I went to Kabwe, I caught a letter which PL wrote to the girlfriend of my husband and addressed it as Mrs. Sitali. So I got angry and wrote PL an insulting letter.

The court record contained the letter exhibit:

Stupid Beatrice,
. . . You were just fooling me coming to my house when you know the secret of Sitali, he is married to your friend . . . You are the one making me suffering. Why can't you look for your own husbands who are not married so that you also experience how it pains when you hear that your husband is moving with another woman . . . *ma hule imwe* [you bitch], you even wanted to beat another woman because of your friends' husbands. You AIDS carrier, you even came saying Sitali wanted money from the bank when you know it was going to your fellow bitch. You idiots, why *mukonda ku sokweza ma nyumba banzanu* [why do you like to break your friends' houses]?

Strong allegations, to be sure. In the judgment of the presiding justice, the defendant was reprimanded that she was wrong to insult the plaintiff in such a way. She was instructed to compensate the plaintiff K 120 for the insults.

Mavuto: Persistent Trouble

Raising touchy questions about gender relations and sexuality, the complaints in these cases expose complicated issues concerning power, autonomy, and gender identity in postcolonial Zambia. These cases also prompt questions to which I return shortly about the Local Court as a forum for negotiating such matters and about whether, and if so, how, the court is able to effect changes in gender relations.

The two categories of cases described above touch on thorny problems in Zambia's strained economy. Specifically, these cases expose charged issues that arise over tensions both between male authority and female dependence in private households and between women in the wider social arena. As the *Zulu v. Mbewe*, *Banda v. Mutale*, and *Mushanga v. Phiri* cases demonstrate, men expect women to follow their instructions to provide unpaid domestic services: to cook, clean, and supply sex on demand. In their turn, women expect men to "keep" them and their children. Mrs. Zulu conveys her husband's utter lack of concern when she explains his tardiness with household money by describing his bringing her "mealie meal in a newspaper" and "not buying her clothes."

Having sex and having children are central to men's identity as the household head and person in control, as is illustrated in both the *Banda v. Mutale* and the *Mushanga v. Phiri* cases. Women also need children to legitimate their part in the conjugal relationship, and women occasionally sue men for divorce because they do not allow them to seek "traditional" advice and remedies to facilitate conception. Some of these women fear that they might lose their partners' attention and support or that their partners might take second wives or girlfriends.

Husbands take men to court for committing adultery with their wives, but wives do not take husbands to court for committing adultery with other women. Chuma Himonga relates the incident of a wife who complained of her husband's affairs to an informal forum of elders only to be told that she could not stop a man from going out with other women if he wanted to and that that was "the nature of men" (1985:204). In cases not included here, where husbands took wives to court for deserting the home, the language of accusation often turned such wives into "bitches." As noted earlier, customary law approves polygyny, and society at large does not object to men's extramarital relations. But wives do, as we have seen. It is not surprising that when women bring charges of lack of support to court, the figure of the other woman or girlfriends often looms in the background, as exemplified by the *Mwila v. Sinyinda* case. By suing men in such cases, women are drawing public attention to men's failure as household heads.

The insult/defamation cases illustrate vividly how suspicious women are of other women. The emphatic way they define themselves as their husbands' wives through categorical statements about other women who "move about," "move with," or "bitch" displays their anxiety about maintaining their own status as married wives. The troubled voice of Mrs. Sitali in *Nfonse v. Sitali* speaks with an immediacy and directness when she tells "how it pains to hear that [one's] husband is moving with another woman."

If the conjugal relationship is so tense, why then do women such as those in the insult/defamation cases so vehemently demonstrate their status as wives? In airing their anger in public over what appear to be petty interpersonal squabbles, such women show concern over the potential for sexual misconduct. In some of these cases, the amount of compensation the defendants were asked to pay indicates that the charges were considered to be very grave ones. The issues, I suggest, are about personal identity, that is, they are about what it means to be a woman and a man in conjugal relations and about what sorts of people women and men are supposed to be in the wider Zambian setting. The two, of course, are intertwined, and the cases I have discussed reveal striking information about economic and social relations in urban Zambia that put strain on friendship, both between wives and husbands and between neighbors. Thus, many of these cases have to do with publicly asserting that the plaintiff is someone's wife, for being married is a more respectful status for an adult woman in Zambia than being single. A single lifestyle easily translates into "bitching," as we saw in Mrs. Sitali's allegations against Ms. Nfonse. But beyond that, the sexual slurs with which women charge other women barely mask the insidious battle that men and tight economic circumstances help to provoke between women.

No Dowry, No Custom

The judgments issued at this Local Court in Chelston are informed by notions of gender that define women and men as different vis-à-vis the law: Men have authority and thus have rights and can make claims, whereas women are merely dependent. This difference is well expressed in the words of a twenty-seven-year-old daughter in one of the Mtendere households I have followed over the years. Having experienced too many troubles with her husband, she finally took him to court for divorce. "I hope they [the court] will grant me freedom," she said, "[but] I don't think I stand any chance because according to our Zambian law a woman should not say, 'I don't want marriage,' but a man has got all the right to say, 'I don't want my wife'" (Personal communication, 1985).

In the court's application of customary law, marriage has been redefined, transformed from being a series of processes involving a variety of transfers of wealth (Richards 1940) into one event that hinges on whether or not bridewealth was paid; or as this court renders it, marriage is defined according to whether the parties were "married with dowry." Epstein made similar observations in the 1950s when he argued that "in insisting on bridewealth as a criterion of a valid marriage, the Urban Courts were following, as much as creating, Copperbelt practice" (1981:279). In the divorce cases that Mtendere women brought to Local Court, judgments tended to favor men if they did not agree to divorce women they had married with dowry. Having paid dowry, "men own women," according to popular male sentiments ("Leave Lobola Alone" 1992; "Excessive Lobola Puts Off Marriages" 1992). But if men agree to divorce and dowry has been given, the presiding justice in this and other Local Courts tends to obligate men to pay some support to women and their children

(Himonga 1987:66). In the view of this Local Court, such women had been properly married, that is, with dowry. This contrasts to divorce cases in which the parties were not married with dowry. As the cases I have presented illustrate, the court does not consider such unions to be legitimate marriages but "mere friendships." In spite of the length of some of these unions and the number of children born, the court views such wives as girlfriends.[9] Save under exceptional circumstances, such as in the *Mwila v. Sinyinda* case, the female party receives nothing from the male on the dissolution of the union. And in cases of adultery, men receive compensation from men who have had intercourse with their wives only if they were married with dowry.

In short, there are certain advantages for both women and men, though for different reasons, in having married properly. Perhaps women's knowledge that the court may judge in their favor and award compensation, provided they were properly married and the husband agrees to the divorce, explains why, when troubles (*mavuto*) with husbands have become persistent, women decide to wash their dirty laundry in public and bring divorce cases to court much more frequently than men. Judgments in women's favor are more likely to be issued in Local Courts than in informal family forums and in the Superior Courts (Himonga 1985:249, 286). In *Zulu v. Mbewe*, Mrs. Zulu sued her husband for divorce in the hope of getting maintenance even *after* her mother and church elders had accepted the divorce. And perhaps the fact that divorce settlements in women's favor are indeed made encourages the many women who are not "properly married" to go to court, hoping to be granted support or maintenance. The *Banda v. Mutale* case shows Mrs. Banda, who had been married for twelve years without dowry and had four children by her husband, demanding to "obtain property for the services [she had] rendered." Her claim to property was not approved, yet she kept the children. This case demonstrates Mrs. Banda's attempt both to define a conjugal relationship and to contest it.

Pressures on both the job and housing markets make it increasingly difficult to become properly married with dowry in Lusaka's strained economy. In the *Mbewe v. Phiri* case, Mrs. Mbewe's rural relatives would not allow her to join her husband, Mr. Phiri, in Lusaka until he had paid up in cattle. But Mr. Phiri had a hard time finding a job and he lived in a one-room dwelling, so how could he at once accommodate his wife and four children and buy four head of cattle? A large number of cases of divorce, marital problems, chasing from home, and neglect involved women and men who had lived together and had children, who described themselves as married, though in the view of the court they were categorized as living "in friendship." Here, as in some other parts of southern Africa (Comaroff 1980), the gender politics of everyday life give rise to considerably more ambiguity than does the Local Court over the meaning of marriage.

The gender-divergent tensions that are inherent in women's and men's aspirations for proper marriage and individual autonomy are difficult to contain in Zambia's strained economy. I noted earlier that women's own designs on life become increasingly evident as they grow older. As is illustrated in the case of the twenty-seven-year-old woman I quoted at the beginning of this section, one aspect of this design is gaining freedom from unsupportive or philandering husbands. The cases discussed here show that although this Local Court seeks to uphold a notion of what a proper marriage is, it is simultaneously revising the definition in women's favor along lines that are more congruent with economic needs. Upholding a notion of reconstituted custom, the Local Court also exercises some freedom in the way it adjudicates disputes that contemporary socioeconomic difficulties aggravate. In effect, the Local Court is an arena where changes may be expressed, negotiated, and at times, legitimated (Comaroff and Roberts 1977:122). This is so in divorce cases where estranged but "properly married" wives have no customary claim to support from husbands but often are granted such support by the court. Although the overall emphasis in the court's decisions is biased in favor of men, the evidence presented here indicates that this bias contains space for contests that may be resolved to women's benefit.

Custom, Court, and Gender Politics

When Mtendere residents explain their own behavior and attitudes regarding marriage in the courtroom, a concept such as descent begins to lose its jural meanings. Responding to queries from the presiding justice, women and men from Mtendere talk about lack of support and loss of love in terms that resonate with their experiences of hard economic times and troubles in the conjugal domain. Their language of kinship draws its everyday meaning from ongoing social interaction that makes distinctions between in-laws and one's own relatives and makes available to women and men differently constituted resource networks.

The court's usage of kinship language includes fragments of rights and claims distinctions that are informed by reconstructed "customs." The two most important terms in relationship to the cases described here are "dowry" and "support," the application of neither of which is "traditional." As I have shown, dowry refers to a reconstructed marriage practice in which the transfer of bridewealth has been transformed from a process into an event. And support applies to divorce cases in which "properly married" men are charged with noncustomary obligations.

In sum, the court's administration of customary law is flexible. Its decisions concerning proper marriages with dowry, which tend to privilege men's rights over women's, also encompass judgments that in divorce cases may work to women's benefit. The Local Court is thus much more than a mere instrument for upholding the status quo. It is also a forum in which women and men are both contesting and redefining conjugal arrangements and a place where "properly married" women who attempt to redraw restricting gender lines are getting a small measure of court approval in divorce settlements. Although social interactional practices still leave much to be desired from the women's perspective, this legal flexibility opens up the opportunity for Zambians to further redefine gender relations in terms of rights and claims rather than according to male authority and female dependence. A case in point is the 1989 enactment of the Intestate Succession Act, which stipulates the rights of widows and children to specified parts of a deceased's estate, although property grabbing has not ceased entirely.[10] Perhaps Local Court practices and women's own contests inside and outside of court may also become instrumental in enacting reforms of Zambia's customary divorce laws, legalizing women's rights to compensation for long-rendered services.[11]

Notes

Some of my follow-up work in Mtendere was undertaken while pursuing other research interests in Lusaka. My research in Lusaka during the summers of 1988 and 1989 was supported by grants from the Social Science Research Council (U.S.) and the University Research Grants Committee of Northwestern University. I returned to Lusaka during summer 1992 with funding from Northwestern University to explore a new project. The discussion of recent events in this chapter also draws on observations from that trip. Permission to attend sessions and analyze records in the Chelston Local Court was granted by the High Court of Zambia in 1988. I am grateful to the Institute for African Studies, University of Zambia, for continuing to provide institutional affiliation and facilitating my research, to Presiding Justice Nathan Kubikisha and his court clerk for their insights and patience, and to Elizabeth Colson and John L. Comaroff for their constructive comments on an earlier version of this essay. This chapter draws on, but is different from, a contribution written for a Festschrift for A. L. Epstein, currently in preparation.

1. Between 1990 and 1991, Elisabeth Weinberger, a German Ph.D. student, followed up my work in Mtendere. See Weinberger 1992.

2. A protracted discussion involving a legal commission and debates in Parliament and in the news media preceded the passing of this law. See Coldham 1983 and Longwe 1990.

3. For background on the new law and an assessment of problems in its implementation, see Mwanza 1990.

4. These practices continue to shape urban gender inequality, as the statutory rules introduced after independence in 1964 do not rule them out specifically.

5. This practice appears to differ from that observed by Elizabeth Colson in the Tonga-speaking Local Courts in the Southern Province in the early 1970s. She reports that justices interrupted litigants, telling them "to stick to facts, not to digress, and that only the issues cited in the summons might be raised" (1976:26–27).

6. I sat in on court proceedings and studied an entire year's court records (April 1987–May 1988), making a list of all cases brought in by Mtendere residents and taking notes on particular disputes. The court records for this period contained approximately 600 cases, out of which I took notes concerning 100 that involved Mtendere residents. The actual court proceedings are conducted in the vernacular, in this court, in the Nyanja language. Translation is provided if one of the parties involved does not speak Nyanja. For example, one case I observed was accompanied by translation into Tonga. The court clerk writes the record of cases in English that often contains Zambian-English colloquialisms. I have retained the court clerk's renditions of cases, adding occasional clarifications. The court records do not indicate ethnicity, but they do list place of birth, such as Lusaka or the village and chief's area, for the parties. The majority of names that appear in the cases in this discussion are common in the Eastern Province among such groups as Nsenga, Chewa, Tumbuka, and Ngoni. Among the personal names appearing in this chapter that are used in other regions are Mutale and Mwila (Bemba); Poloti (Lamba or Kaonde); Sitali (Lozi); Sinyinda (Tonga or Lozi); the derivation of Nfonse is uncertain.

7. In 1987, 1 U.S. dollar was worth approximately 8 kwacha (K).

8. Damages are fines paid for impregnating a young woman.

9. Bonnie Keller's research in the Mazabuka Local Court in the mid-1970s offers striking parallels to this attitude. Her specific concern was with "marriage by elopement," a nontraditional method for establishing a potential marital union that had become common in the Gwembe Valley since the 1950s and was exceedingly frequent at the time of Keller's research. She describes marriage by elopement as a Tonga way of marrying, about which non-Tonga are generally contemptuous (1979:581). The Local Court practice in Mazabuka of awarding compensation to the father or guardian of an eloped woman was not carried out in the Chelston Local Court during the period of concern in my research. But the practice of calling such unions "mere friendships" and describing the women as "girlfriends" in spite of the length of such unions was evident in both courts. In both instances, the women were assigned a status—girlfriends—that would attract little respect from others, given the thin line between girlfriends and prostitutes in the popular view. In turn, such women's ability to fulfill themselves and gain respect from others as "properly married" wives was probably reduced.

10. One recent case that attracted dramatic attention involved widows of the Zambia National Football Team who perished in an air disaster in Gabon in 1993. In a march to State House, widows complained of greedy relatives seizing their belongings. This practice, they argued, was "a sordid reminder that the nation is still bogged down in a primitive culture which condones harassment of widows and children" (*Times of Zambia*, July 31, 1993).

11. Information campaigns and lobbying activity in both rural areas and towns were carried out by women's groups prior to the passing of the new act, especially by the Zambia Association for Research and Development (ZARD). See, for example, Longwe and Clarke 1990.

References

Chanock, Martin. 1985. *Law, Custom and Social Order: The Colonial Experience in Malawi and Zambia.* Cambridge: Cambridge University Press.

Coldham, Simon. 1983. "The Law of Succession in Zambia: Recent Proposals for Reform." *Journal of African Law* 27, 2:162–168.

———. 1989. "The Wills and Administration of Estates Act 1989 and the Intestate Succession Act 1989 of Zambia." *Journal of African Law* 33, 1:128–132.

Colson, Elizabeth. 1976. "From Chief's Court to Local Court." In *Freedom and Constraint: A Memorial Tribute to Max Gluckman,* ed. M. J. Aronoff, 15–29. Assen: Van Gorcum.

Comaroff, John L. 1980. "Bridewealth and the Control of Ambiguity in a Tswana Chiefdom." In *The Meaning of Marriage Payments,* ed. J. Comaroff, 161–196. New York: Academic Press.

Comaroff, John L., and Simon Roberts. 1977. "Marital and Extra-Marital Sexuality: The Dialectics of Legal Change Among the Kgatla." *Journal of African Law* 21, 1:97–123.

Epstein, Arnold L. 1953. "The Role of African Courts in Urban Communities of the Northern Rhodesia Copperbelt." *Rhodes-Livingstone Journal* 13:1–17.

———. 1981. *Urbanization and Kinship: The Domestic Domain on the Copperbelt of Zambia 1950–1956.* New York: Academic Press.

"Excessive Lobola Puts off Marriages." 1992. *Times of Zambia,* July 1, 6.

Hansen, Karen T. 1984. "Negotiating Sex and Gender in Urban Zambia." *Journal of Southern African Studies* 10, 2:119–138.

———. 1989. "The Black Market and Women Traders in Lusaka, Zambia." In *Women and the State in Africa,* ed. J. Parpart and K. Staudt, 143–159. Boulder: Lynne Rienner.

———. 1992. "Gender and Housing: The Case of Domestic Service in Lusaka, Zambia." *Africa* 62, 2:248–265.

Himonga, Chuma N. 1985. "Family Property Disputes: The Predicament of Women and Children in a Zambian Urban Community." Ph.D. diss., London School of Economics and Political Science.

———. 1987. "Property Disputes in Law and Practice: Dissolution of Marriage in Zambia." In *Women and Law in Southern Africa,* ed. A. Armstrong, 56–84. Harare: Zimbabwe Publishing House.

Keller, Bonnie. 1979. "Marriage by Elopement." *African Social Research* 27:565–585.

"Leave Lobola Alone." 1992. *Times of Zambia,* June 19, 3.

Longwe, Sara H. 1990. "Lessons from the Struggle to Give Women Equality Under the Law: Reforming the Law on Inheritance in Zambia." Paper presented at the Women, Law, and Development Conference on "Networking for Empowerment in Africa," Harare, Zimbabwe.

Longwe, Sara H., and R. Clarke. 1990. "Research Strategies for Promoting Law Reform: Lessons from Changing the Law on Inheritance in Zambia." Paper presented at seminar on research methodology organized by the Women and Law in Southern Africa Research Project, Harare, Zimbabwe.

Mwanza, Iris C. 1990. "'Give Me a Little Peace of Mind': The Law of Succession and the Intestate Succession Act, 1989." LL.B. degree paper, School of Law, University of Zambia.

Personal communication. 1985. Letter from Mtendere resident to author, 25 November.

Powdermaker, Hortense. 1962. *Copper Town: Changing Africa. The Human Condition on the Rhodesian Copperbelt.* New York: Harper and Row.

Richards, Audrey. 1940. *Bemba Marriage and Modern Economic Conditions,* Rhodes-Livingstone Paper no. 4. Livingstone, Northern Rhodesia: Rhodes-Livingstone Institute.

Roberts, Richard, and Kristin Mann. 1991. "Law in Colonial Africa." In *Law in Colonial Africa,* ed. K. Mann and R. Roberts, 3–58. Portsmouth, N.H.: Heinemann.

Starr, June, and Jane F. Collier. 1989. "Introduction: Dialogues in Legal Anthropology." In *History and Power in the Study of Law: New Directions in the Study of Law,* ed. J. Starr and J. F. Collier, 1–28. Ithaca, N.Y.: Cornell University Press.

Todd, David, and Chris Shaw. 1980. "The Informal Sector and Zambia's Employment Crisis." *Journal of Modern African Studies* 18, 3:411–425.

Weinberger, Elisabeth. 1992. "Frauen as Kleinstunternehmer in Lusaka, Zambia." Report, Koblenz University, Germany.

6

Can Polygyny Be Avoided in Dakar?

PHILIPPE ANTOINE AND
JEANNE NANITELAMIO
Translated by Laura Mitchell

Polygyny is one of the main features of sub-Saharan African marriage systems. The frequency of polygyny is much lower in other parts of the world. Polygyny refers to the practice of men marrying multiple wives and is a more specific term than polygamy (the word usually used in French), which literally means "many spouses of either sex." If the agricultural mode of production in large part justified polygyny in rural areas (Boserup 1970), then according to a number of authors, urbanization and Westernization should have led to a progressive erosion of polygyny in the urban milieu. The organization of space, better education, the mode of production, and the diffusion of new ideas and ways of living should also have restrained the practice. But the expected disappearance of polygyny in the city has not occurred yet (Clignet 1987; Kaufmann, Lesthaeghe, and Meekers 1989; Marcoux 1991).

As early as 1960, Paul Mercier stated that in Senegalese cities such as Dakar and Thiès, urban life did not result in a rapid decrease in either the level of polygyny or in the proportion of polygynous marriages. Based on his observations in large cities in Zaire, I. Ngondo a Pitshandenge (1992) states that polygyny increases in urban settings. He emphasizes that the intrusion of polygyny can be considered revolutionary since it occurs despite the hostile structure of the urban environment, which includes housing difficulties, legal discrimination, respectability associated with monogamy, and the interdiction of Judeo-Christian religions.

The practice of polygyny in Senegal is embedded in a different context than that of Central Africa, but there is a higher incidence of this type of union than in the predominantly Islamic Sahelian countries. In this chapter, we begin with those contemporary aspects of polygyny that exist in Dakar, the capital of Senegal. The urban context is complex, since different social categories and diverse expectations coexist there. More and more women are educated and subject to new influences. As a result, they are hoping to develop new ways of living and new relations with men—in the household as well as in society. At the same time, social and religious norms continue to locate women's destiny in marriage and motherhood. To be unmarried is still considered a secondary choice, and few people remain so. These social transformations, however, operate in a context of economic crisis and the deterioration of the standard of living, and such conditions prompt certain questions: What has become of polygyny in the current context, and what are its new configurations? What role is played by gender relations that maintain or reject this form of marriage? To answer these questions, we present the results of an IFAN-ORSTOM study on the residential and marriage histories of professionals, carried out in Dakar in 1989 and 1990.[1] We have published one part of this quantitative research, which is based on 1,557 biographies of men and women (Antoine, Bocquier, Fall, and Guisse 1992). The other part of the research was carried out with almost fifty people taken from that sample in the course of the following year (Nanitelamio 1995). This chapter follows up those results with an analysis of the two different studies.

Polygyny in Africa

Most explanations of polygyny are based on a perception of the "ruralism" of African societies in the grip of a particular mode of production: a weakly mechanized subsistence economy in which the role of women as producers of food for daily existence is important. Polygyny in this context is perceived as being a bit "expensive" and an "investment for the man" (Boserup 1970). The economic argument is contested by Jack Goody (1973), who emphasizes that the level of polygyny is highest in West Africa, and yet it is in East Africa that women engage more in agriculture. Goody perceives the causes of polygyny as sexual and reproductive rather than economic and productive. He cites the practice of postpartum abstinence as the principal factor that promotes polygyny.

Other authors advance more political explanations that emphasize the internal coherence of the marriage system and of social organizations where power is in the hands of the elders (Meillassoux 1975). Here, polygyny is perceived as a means of preserving the elders' power over the young men in societies where access to women is controlled by elders.

A. B. Diop (1981) suggests several factors that favor polygyny. It permits the alliance of various groups and confers a social and political advantage. It represents an economic contribution, because women by their work or personal farming contribute to the maintenance of the household. The "production" of children allows the increase of labor, and it is expected that the children will support the mother as she ages. Polygyny is also an element of ostentation and prestige for privileged people.

The social rules regulating marriage in certain African countries that have a high birth rate and elevated mortality rate are conducted in a demographic regime favorable to polygyny. The principal factors promoting polygyny in such societies are a relatively young marriage age for women, a significant age difference between spouses, the near absence of absolute celibacy regardless of sex, and rapid remarriage (Pilon 1991; Pison 1986; Goldman and Pebley 1989).

As men marry women from a much younger and larger group in these societies, one consequence is the appearance of a greater number of "available" women on the marriage market. This fact is accentuated by the rapid remarriage of widows and divorced women. In societies where marriage remains a necessity, the competition to marry among women is accentuated by their relatively larger numbers. If some women delay marriage, they risk remaining single or accepting marriage with an already married man.

Although polygyny remains important in Africa, it is statistically difficult to retrace the evolution of its frequency. However, we do know that according to the research results recently reported by DHS (*Demographic and Health Surveys: Final Reports* 1992), the level of polygyny differs little between urban and rural milieus (Table 6.1) particularly in West Africa. In certain cases, for example, in Niger, where the level of polygyny is even higher in urban areas,[2] polygynous marriage is characteristic of affluent members of society. This reversal of tendencies is also seen in Zaire, and Ngondo a Pitshandenge (1992) shows that contrary to all expectations, the practice of polygyny in Zaire is making real inroads in urban settings. He suggests that there is a ruralization of behaviors in Zairian urban areas.

In most African countries, Islam lends polygyny a sacred context. In traditional polygyny, the number of wives is not limited, and this system is one marriage option among others. Certain social practices, such as the levirate or sororate, conform to the system of polygyny. Islam, however,

TABLE 6.1   Percentage of Married Women Currently in a Polygynous Union

Country	Rural Areas	Urban Areas
Zimbabwe (1988)	19.6	9.4
Sudan (1990)	22.6	16.0
Burundi (1987)	11.5	16.2
Kenya (1989)	24.4	17.7
Ghana (1988)	34.5	28.3
Liberia (1986)	42.6	30.2
Uganda (1989)	33.3	31.0
Cameroon (1991)	42.7	32.0
Nigeria (1990)	42.9	33.6
Niger (1992)	35.5	40.5
Senegal (1986)	49.0	41.4
Guinea (1992)	50.6	46.4
Togo (1988)	54.4	47.1

Source: *Demographic and Health Surveys,* National Reports of DHS (Columbia, Md.: Institute for Resource Development/Westinghouse, 1992).

limits the number of wives to four: "If you are anxious about unjust hardships for orphans, marry only a few women; two, three or four among those who have pleased you." However, the following verse is little cited by polygynists: "If you are still anxious about injustice, marry only one woman or one slave. This conduct will more easily aid you to be just" (Koran 4, 3).

Contrary to common opinion, the practice of polygyny is rare in the Arab countries and the Maghreb. In Algeria in 1966, less than 2 percent of married men were polygynists (Tabutin 1974), whereas 3 percent were polygynous in Egypt (Fargues 1987); and the frequency of the practice was decreasing in both countries. In Tunisia, polygyny was abolished. Given the higher levels of polygyny in countries with few Muslims, such as Zaire and Togo, and the weak level of polygyny in Islamic countries, notably in North Africa, we must question the real impact of Islam on polygynous behavior in Africa. For men who wish to marry polygynously, Islam provides an excuse and a support; for women who would prefer monogamy, Islam allows them to be resigned to their polygynous marriages. In sub-Saharan Africa, Islam seems to "regularize" older traditional practices.

If religion is only a pretext for polygynous behavior, then where can we find an explanation for it? Whatever its justifications, polygyny often has a legal status that underlines its legitimacy as a marriage system with the same privileges as monogamy. Polygyny was abolished in Guinea (1962) and in Côte d'Ivoire (1964), yet in other countries such as Mali, Senegal, and Togo, legislation allows a choice of systems. But even in the same states where it has been abolished, the proportion of polygynous marriages remains high, at 24 percent in Côte d'Ivoire, for example (Klissou 1992).

Polygyny is widespread in West Africa and present in both the cities and the countryside, whatever the law. The case of Senegal is particularly interesting, as it is a country that is relatively urbanized and strongly Islamic, where the proportion of polygynous marriages in urban areas is among the highest in Africa (Table 6.1). The greater Dakar region therefore offers the researcher a rich source for observing the changes in sociodemographic behaviors. Dakar, one of the largest African cities, was the old capital of French West Africa and became the capital of independent Senegal in 1960. At 40,000 residents in 1926, the population rose to 132,000 by 1945. The greater Dakar region counted 1,310,000 residents in 1988, about 50 percent of whom lived in the suburb of Pikine. This concentrated area accounted for 19 percent of the total population of the country and nearly 50 percent of the urban population of Senegal. Economic activities such as administration, services, and industry are also concentrated in this area, which poses a number of problems. Housing, urban infrastructure, and jobs have not followed the increasing demographic pattern. Over one-half of those who are economically active work in the informal sector, and the level of unemployment was estimated at 18.6 percent of the active population in 1989. For a sociological study, Dakar's diversity of marital practices, despite significant local nuances, parallels the situation in many African capitals (Antoine and Nanitelamio 1991).

Marriage and Polygyny in Senegal

Polygyny is recognized in modern legislation, with the Senegalese family code offering three matrimonial options: monogamy, limited polygyny, and a form of polygyny in which the man cannot marry more than four wives. The option of limited polygyny restrains the number of wives that a husband can have simultaneously. If the man fails to subscribe to one of these options, the marriage is categorized as polygynous. The equality of co-wives is emphasized in the code, which stipulates "that in the case of polygyny, each wife should expect equal treatment with the others" (Senegalese Family Code 1972).

The family code is a compromise reflecting tension between customs, Islamic law, and the effort to respond to demands for better protection of women's rights. But the compromise does not fulfill all of these objectives; even though the code has been in operation for twenty years (it was instituted in 1972), it continues to be subject to debates and demands for revisions. Islamists claim that the code does not reflect the concerns of Muslims, whereas feminists believe that it obstructs progress, supports the domination of women by men, and privileges polygyny to the detriment of monogamy.

Marriage is nearly universal in Senegal; according to DHS (1988), there are scarcely any single women over age thirty-five. Most are married, and the proportion of divorced women and widows remains relatively low. Thus, for women from ages forty to forty-four, 91 percent are married, 4.3 percent are widows, and 4.7 percent are divorced. Women, however, are marrying later than their mothers did, though they still marry at a relatively young age (the legal minimum age is sixteen years for women). A comparison of the results of two studies done in 1978 (L'Enquête Sénégalaise sur la Fécondité [ESF]) and 1986 (DHS) shows that in 1978 nearly 60 percent of women fifteen to nineteen years old were already married, whereas in 1986 the proportion was 43.5 percent for the same age group. An analysis of the median age at first marriage confirms these results: It rose from 15.9 years for the generation of 1937 to 1941 to 17.2 years for the generation of 1962 to 1966.[3]

The variation between urban and rural experience is increasing. Thus, for the generation of 1937 to 1941, whether these women lived in rural or urban areas, the median age at first marriage was 15.9 years. However, for the generation of 1962 to 1966 the median age at first marriage was 16 years in the rural areas and 18.8 years in the urban centers (DHS 1988). The elevation of the age at first marriage primarily concerns women living in urban areas, who in the space of twenty-five years saw that age rise nearly three years.

The current data come from a survey conducted in the late 1970s by ESF and suggest a low frequency of divorce. Yet the divorce rate was not insignificant. The probability of still being married after fifteen years was 71 percent, which signified that nearly one-third of all women had been divorced. The propensity to divorce was even larger among women who had married after age twenty, with urban, educated women being most likely to divorce (Lo Ndiaye 1985). Remarriage was frequent, thus 95 percent of widows and 89 percent of divorced women remarried within five years following the end of their marriage (Mboup 1992).

Early marriage and rapid remarriage after divorce or widowhood combine to bring about an elevated level of polygyny. Between 1978 and 1986, the level scarcely changed for all of Senegal. Sixty percent of women over thirty were in a polygynous marriage, with only a slight decline in the frequency of polygyny among women under thirty during the same period.

TABLE 6.2   Proportion of Women in a Polygynous Marriage According to
Socio-economic Factors

	Percent of Women Under 30		Percent of Women over 30	
Socioeconomic Factors	*1978*	*1986*	*1978*	*1986*
Residence				
Urban	33	28	59	54
Rural	40	38	61	63
Education				
None	37	37	65	62
Primary	29	28	53	50
Secondary or higher	21	18	40	37

Source: G. Mboup, "Etude des déterminants socio-économique et culturels de la fécondité au Sénégal et partir de l'enquête démographique et de santé" (Ph.D. diss., University of Montreal, 1992).

However, the decline was more marked in the urban areas, especially among women over thirty years of age. Fewer women with a higher level of education were in polygynous marriages (37 percent of women over thirty in a polygynous marriage), and the decrease in polygynists between 1978 and 1986 declined proportionately with the rise in the level of education (Table 6.2).

Let us look more closely at the evolution of marriage and polygyny in Dakar. Although there are few relevant demographic statistics, according to Benoît Ferry (1977), in 1973 the mean age at first marriage was between 17 and 17.5 years. The author noted a steady delay in the age of first marriage, even though all women over 35 were married. The age difference between husband and wife was significant and increased with the age of the husband, especially in the case of polygyny. Thus, among women aged 20 to 24, the average age difference from their husbands was twelve years. Other studies confirm a progressive delay in the age at first marriage (Antoine and Nanitelamio 1991) and show different marriage patterns that vary according to residential districts. Marriage may be delayed more often, but it is not avoided. A recent study on male marriage experience shows that the consequences of economic crisis, including a lack of housing and unemployment, have deferred men's entrance into marriage (Djire 1993). This modification in the male marriage calendar accentuates the rising age of women upon their first marriage.

Remarriage for women is frequent. In 1955, women aged 50 to 54 had, on average, been in 1.71 marriages, a figure that decreased only slightly by 1989 (IFAN-ORSTOM study 1989–1990), when women had been in 1.63 marriages. According to the data from our study, 47 percent of women in Dakar aged 50 to 54 currently lived in a polygynous union. The proportion was highest in this age group and decreased if the women were widowed. Among men aged 55 to 59, the proportion of polygynists was about 30 percent in the 1955 census and 40 percent in the 1976 census, and it had reached 45 percent in 1989. In 1955, men of age 60 had been in an average of 2.6 marriages, a number that decreased to 2.2 in 1989. In 1955, men of that age had on average 1.45 wives. In 1989, the number increased slightly to 1.70. These figures show us that polygyny continues to remain intense in Dakar.

After we had situated polygyny in its proper context, we set out to investigate the dynamics of this phenomenon, collecting data on the marriage lives of both men and women in Dakar. Marital status there is not stable, and individuals can alternate between periods of monogamy, polygyny, divorce, or widowhood (Clignet 1987). Most analysts collect information only on the marriage in effect at the time of inquiry, but only a biographical approach can take into account the variety of lived experiences.

The Cycle of Life and Polygyny in Dakar: The Treatment of Data

Our statistical analysis draws on a detailed collection of data regarding residential, professional, and marital histories, which we supplemented with biographical questionnaires (Antoine, Bocquier, Fall, and Guisse 1992). Concerning marital life, the analysis of biographies divulged information on the entrance into first marriage and on divorce and polygyny. These data meant we could develop an overview of the dynamics of polygyny among men, since we had information on the succession of marriages and the date of their eventual dissolution. We could thus follow the progress of marital events. We also collected a marital biography for women, but that was less useful in the analysis of polygyny. In the case of a woman, even if we had information on each of her marriages and the marital situation of her husband at the time of the marriage, we still could not determine the outcome of the husband's marital situation, for instance, whether he went on to marry another wife or had divorced a previous one. It was difficult for a wife to know and date precisely the marital history of her husband. However, we could indirectly describe the dynamic of polygyny that concerns women in the course of tracing men's marriages.

The methods of analyzing the biographies included survey tables and regression analysis. The most appropriate model for this purpose is the semiparametric model developed by David Cox, which permits the inclusion of a time dimension in the analysis of causality. The model measures transition, understood as the instantaneous recognized risk that an individual takes when passing from one matrimonial state to another. The risk is analyzed as a function of different independent variables, both fixed and fluctuating in time. One can thus disengage the modalities that accelerate or slow the passage from one status to another. In this type of model, one positive or negative coefficient signifies that the occurrence is more or less rapid according to the category of reference. The results are presented for each modality with "all things being equal" (Cox 1972; Courgeau and Lelièvre 1989; Blossfeld, Hamerle, and Mayer 1989; Bocquier 1992).

The analysis therefore considers the time elapsed between a point of reference common to all the research subjects and the date that observation began or ended. We present two models here: The first concerns the beginning of a polygynous marriage and the second deals with the end of a first marriage by divorce, because we feel a relationship exists between these two events.

In the first model we examine the transition between the date of the first marriage and the entrance into a polygynous union upon the arrival of a second wife. The population studied consisted of men in their first marriage who lived in Dakar until the date of the marriage to the second wife. However, according to the rules of the model, the observation ended if the first wife died or if the couple divorced. If the individual remained in Dakar and was always monogamous (and was therefore still a potential polygynist), the period of observation ended with the end of the survey. This method of treating dissolved unions allowed us to take into consideration all the biographies, even those of younger generations who were observed until the end of the study, and contributed to the calculation of the regression coefficients.

To study the transition from first marriage to divorce among men living in Dakar, the target population consisted of monogamous men. The elapsed time is measured from the date of the first marriage until the date of divorce. In cases where a spouse died, the period of observation ended at the death of a spouse or, for currently married people, with the end of the survey. The arrival of a second spouse is recorded from the date of the second marriage. This method avoids transversal analysis and takes into consideration the different situations encountered by an individual during his residential, professional, and matrimonial histories. The results are different from a classic analysis that only presents the static aspect of polygyny and reveals such information as the age at which a certain proportion of men are polygynous. Using Cox's model, in contrast, allows measurement of the time elapsed before becoming polygynous and opens the prospect of evaluating the discrete influence of different characteristics that will accelerate or slow the transition to polygyny. The Cox model does not produce the proportion of risk; instead, it reveals the probability of risk.

The dependent variables in our regressions are, for the first model, the immediate risk of entering into polygyny, and in the second model, divorcing the first wife. To simplify the presentation, we have combined the results from the two models (Table 6.3). Several other analyses were carried out. They are not presented here, although occasional reference is made to them.

Men: Potential Polygynists

Analysis of our data shows that few of the variables concerning men influence the possibility of becoming polygynous. In the section that follows, we examine these results in more detail with reference to the statistics presented in Table 6.3. A first series of independent variables deals with the characteristics that do not change over time.

The first retained independent variable concerns groups of generations, or birth cohorts, established by the date of birth. We concentrated on three generations of individuals: those born between 1930 and 1944, between 1945 and 1954, and between 1955 and 1964. Each generation faced different economic circumstances that pertained to matrimonial status. The younger generations appeared to enter later into polygynous relationships, but the coefficient is only significant for men born between 1945 and 1954. In any case, we can conclude that polygyny will decrease among younger generations and that polygyny generally affects men older than age forty. Furthermore, our results indicate a decrease in the rate of polygyny among young men.

Two series of modalities translate the timetable of the first union: the age of the man at the first marriage and the difference in age between spouses. These variables allow for modulations of generational analysis, while taking the variation of marriage age into account. We wanted to establish whether polygyny or divorce varied as a function of later marriages or as a function of a small difference in ages between the spouses. The results indicate that a later marriage age, all other factors being equal, slows the entry to polygyny. Moreover, if the difference between the ages of the couple is small, it is less likely the marriage will become polygynous.

TABLE 6.3   Coefficients of Cox's Parametric Model: The Likelihood of Men Marrying Polygynously and Divorcing

Variable[a]	Category	Polygyny	Divorce
Generation (1930–1944)	1945–1954	.67*	1.22
	1955–1964	.56	1.00
Husband's age at 1st marriage (25–29 years old)	younger than 25	1.09	.98
	0–34	.53**	1.09
	35 and older	.36**	1.17
Difference between spouses' ages (10 or more years)	less than 3 years	.82	1.61
	3–5 years	.86	1.31
	6–9 years	.64*	1.32
Divorced father (no)	yes	n/a	1.09
Polygynous father (no)	yes	1.50	n/a
Related to first wife (no)	yes	1.42*	.54***
Religion (Muslim)	Christian	.18***	.38
Ethnicity of husband (Wolof)	Pulaar	1.04	1.68
	Serer	1.48	1.59
	other	1.52	.93
Ethnicity of 1st wife (Wolof)	Pulaar	.86	.55
	Serer	1.38	.75
	other	1.21	.80
Age at arrival in Dakar (born in Dakar)	younger than 12	.97	.65
	12–17	.93	1.02
	18–24	.75	1.28
	25 and older	.79	.56
Education of spouses (both husband and first wife w/o schooling)	H: no school, wife: any level	1.36	.90
	H: primary, wife: higher ed.	1.48*	1.43
	H: secondary, wife: no school	1.20	3.12***
	H: secondary, wife: any level	1.04	1.63
Child outside the first marriage (no)	yes	2.37***	1.04
Number of children from the first marriage (none)	varies with the number of children	n/a	.66***
No children in first marriage (no)	yes	.80	n/a
Employment status (unskilled work)	skilled work	1.19	.58
	unemployment	.46	2.70***
	retired	.68	.58

(continues)

TABLE 6.3   *(continued)*

Variable[a]	Category	Polygyny	Divorce
Housing status (renter or owner)	w/ parents	.71	1.46
	w/ immediate family	1.28	.94
	w/ extended family	.89	2.01**
Housing location (in the city)	suburbs	1.65***	1.18
Became polygynous (no)	yes	n/a	3.50***

Notes: a. The reference or baseline category is indicated in parentheses. *Significant to .01 percent. **Significant to .05 percent. ***Significant to .10 percent. n/a: not applicable.
Source: Authors' own survey, 1989–1990.

We also examined family history in order to determine what effect it had on marriage patterns of subsequent generations. The son of a polygynous father is 1.5 times more likely than the son of a monogamous father to become polygynous himself. Thus, there is a reproduction of family models that also surfaces in the interviews with the men themselves.[4]

The presence of a preexisting family connection between the spouses, if it slows the dissolution of a first marriage, can lead more easily to polygyny. However, the difference is barely significant.

As for religion, we only made a distinction between Muslims, whatever the brotherhood, and Christians. In principle, Christian churches forbid polygynous unions, and the Catholic Church is opposed to divorce. Thus, it is not surprising to note that Christianity constitutes a major impediment to polygyny in Dakar, reducing entry into polygynous marriages by 82 percent.

In order to observe the influence of cultural factors, we retained ethnicity as a variable, distinguishing between the dominant Wolof ethnic group and two other major groups, Pulaar and Serer, thereafter grouping other ethnicities together. These distinctions applied equally to men and women. According to the 1986 DHS results, the largest proportion of women, countrywide, live in polygynous unions. The ratio is 50 percent among Wolof, 45 percent among Pulaar, and 38 percent among Serer. However, we did not find any discernible effect of ethnicity in Dákar.

The age of arrival in Dakar sheds light on migration patterns and allows a distinction to be made between men born in the capital and different types of migrants. We did not note a distinctive type of polygynous behavior among migrants. We also examined the difference among natives of Dakar, those with other urban roots, and those with rural backgrounds and once again did not find any significant differences.

As a measure of education, we used the last school year completed by individuals. We chose to examine the level of education of the husband

and the first wife. We distinguished five modalities: a husband and wife without education (baseline category); a husband without education and an educated wife; a husband with a primary education, regardless of the wife's education; a husband with a secondary or higher education and an uneducated first wife; and a husband with a secondary or higher education and a wife with a primary, secondary, or higher education. A frequently advanced hypothesis suggests that a higher level of education is the principal factor in decreasing the rate of polygyny. In Dakar, highly educated men have the same rates of polygyny as illiterate men. However, men with a primary education have a higher rate of polygyny than men without any schooling.

The IFAN-ORSTOM survey of 1989–1990 produced a fairly exhaustive collection of matrimonial, residential, and professional biographies. This collection allowed us to examine economic activity, professional occupation, housing, the number of children, polygynous marriages, and divorce as independent variables that change over time.

We distinguished between children born after the first marriage (but outside of that union) and children of the first marriage. Polygyny is often associated with the sterility of the first wife. Contrary to frequently offered hypotheses, the absence of children in the first marriage does not, in Dakar, accelerate the arrival of a second spouse. However, the fact of having children out of wedlock did increase marriage to a second wife twofold. The same phenomenon is noted in Benin, where F. Donadje's 1992 survey indicates that one married man in two would marry a woman "accidentally" made pregnant (Klissou 1992).

We categorized the following types of economic activity: bureaucrats and employees with particular qualifications, workers without qualifications, the unemployed, and those not active due to illness or retirement. We chose the type of lodging to serve as an approximation of the economic independence of a given individual, classifying according to whether a person was housed by a parent or other immediate family member, was living with an extended family member, was renting on his own, or was the owner of his own house. But the results show that polygynous behavior does not vary according to these social categories.

Two modalities were retained to characterize the place of residence: the city of Dakar and the suburb of Pikine, where housing is generally less expensive and often larger than that in the city itself. Living in Pikine favored the arrival of a new wife. In this case, the effect of the location variable is clear, as other variables such as religion, economic activity, and level of education were controlled for.

Factors such as migration patterns, ethnicity, economic activity, the type of housing, and even the absence of children with the first wife do not seem to play a role as predictors of polygyny. So few characteristics are decisive that one could suppose that, in Dakar, all men are potential polygynists. Similar results have surfaced elsewhere. Education, economic activity in the modern sector, and even ethnicity do not seem to affect the practice of polygyny in African cities (Clignet 1975, 1987). We completed our statistical investigation with a series of in-depth interviews that permitted us to capture the diversity of polygyny as well as the perceptions of this situation by each sex.

Men: Largely in Favor of Polygyny

During the course of the interviews, men in general declared themselves to be in favor of polygyny, regardless of their level of education. They have, according to the remarks of an interviewer, the mentality of a polygynist and want to marry as many women as desired, since society and the Islamic religion support them in these attitudes. Men continue to perceive polygyny as one of their "privileges." Occasionally, they advance social justifications such as the belief that polygyny discourages prostitution or that it allows all women to be "settled."

Polygyny remains a social statement, a proof of success, an ambition to satisfy as soon as one has the means. It is, for some men, a method of control and subordination, especially in light of the strong competition polygyny can engender among co-wives. As a result of the interviews, we can distinguish the following four types of polygyny:

- imposed polygyny, in which the parents "give" the husband another wife;
- the polygyny of poverty, which characterizes the behavior of men who do not have the means to take in another wife but who marry a women who has a remunerative activity, thereby acquiring the social prestige without having to assume the responsibilities of her economic well-being;
- the ostentatious polygyny of the nouveau riche, a visible manifestation of social success; this is generally the most comfortable form of urban polygyny, in which the husband has the means to guarantee separate lodging and an easy material life for each wife;
- the "return" to polygyny seen among intellectuals; they acquiesce to monogamy early in their marriage but later turn to polygyny for various reasons, including a more devout practice of Islam, with polygyny justified as a return to religious values and monogamy rejected as an external imposition not adapted to "African realities."

All the same, one finds an awareness among certain men of tensions and problems encountered in a polygynous household, particularly among those who had difficult childhoods in a polygynous family and who do not want to make their children relive the experience. They are particularly sensitive to the consequences of polygyny for the education of the children and regarding issues such as inheritance. As one interviewee, a forty-year-old married man commented,

> My father separated from my mother when I was young. I lived in a polygynous family, which meant I lived with my father's wives. This is not at all appealing. With monogamy one is more tranquil, and I want to have unity among my children. . . . You don't have time to bring up the children. You see, for example, children who loiter in the streets in front of the cinema. If you ask to see their father, they say he is at the other house.

Polygyny is strongly established for many reasons that are simultaneously religious, psychological, and economic. Currently, no one is immune from the situation; men are potential polygynists and women are subjected to a latent risk. In fact, polygyny is sometimes involuntary, according to the men. One forty-year-old man explained,

> I had a wife at home, we got along very well. She had problems with my sisters all the time, up until the day my mother intervened. So she preferred to return to her home because she did not want an argument with my mother. I told her I could not live outside my own home and if she left it would be for the best. She left and we didn't see each other for three months. After that, I met another woman who had character and charm, and we got along. She worked and did not have material wants. But if my wife had not abandoned our conjugal hearth, I would not have gotten involved with her. Her brother [the second woman's] came to see me, to ask if I wanted her as a wife. I said yes. Her mother also intervened, and I told her yes as well. Since the other had left, I took her as a wife. This all happened very quickly, but the other went to see the *imam* [religious authority] of the neighborhood, and he is close to my father. The woman told the *imam* that she still loved me. We finally resolved the problem, and I found myself polygynous. But I was always against polygyny.

Women: Marry Above All Else

Women's attitudes concerning their own matrimony stem from their dependent status in society. The socialization of women leads them to privilege marriage. Their upbringing leads them to overvalue the status of wife and the importance of a husband to support them, protect them, and validate their social status. They fear solitude and social judgment,

TABLE 6.4   Women's Marriage and Husband's Matrimonial Status

		Husband's Status		
	Single	Already Married	Divorced or Widowed	Total
Woman's first marriage	68%	24%	8%	100%
Woman's second marriage	31%	55%	14%	100%
Woman's third marriage	10%	72%	18%	100%

Source: Authors' own survey, 1990.

which is little tolerant of single women, even in the city. Yet in the current economic crisis, there are an increasing number of women assuming the primary responsibility of supporting a household (Bocquier and Nanitelamio 1994); except in the case of a small minority, this change in responsibility is not producing a challenge to the notion of female dependence.

Social pressure for marriage is such that some unmarried women are prepared to enter into a polygynous union. According to our survey, among women who marry between twenty-one and twenty-four years old, 21 percent arrive as second wives and 9 percent as third or subsequent wives. When marriage or remarriage takes place after age thirty, 41 percent take the rank of second wife and 44 percent accept the role of third or subsequent wife. Even for the first marriage the proportion remains high; if marriage takes place after age thirty, 70 percent of women enter a polygynous union.

One implicit criticism of polygyny from the female point of view depends on a specific situation—when the husband takes a young girl as a second wife. Other configurations exist, notably for women who seek to remarry and who can enter a second, polygynous marriage when still relatively young. In the case of remarriage, women join a polygynous household in 55 percent of second marriages and in 72 percent of third marriages (Table 6.4).

The difference in age between spouses gradually diminishes in successive marriages. In a woman's first marriage, the difference in age is nominally ten years in a monogamous marriage and twenty years in a polygynous one. In the case of remarriage, the age difference decreases to five years for monogamous marriages and to ten years for polygynous unions. For a third marriage, the union is likely to be polygynous, with the age difference at fourteen years.

Life as a single person is experienced and perceived as a period of wait-ing, which women hope will be as short as possible; the indispensable prospect of marriage is held up before them by religion, family, and social pressure, as are the material advantages attributed to marriage (Antoine and Nanitelamio 1991). This urgency of marriage for women means that prolonged waiting is anguished and often brings a downward revision of marriage ambitions, since certain single women would rather be in a polygynous household than remain unmarried. A twenty-three-year-old single woman in Dakar said, "Monogamy or polygyny—it makes little dif-ference as long as it is a marriage. Everything that follows is good." For the majority of single women, unmarried life brings only inconvenience and has few advantages. Certainly the necessity of marriage is also valid for men; however, this urgency is not felt in the same way. Being unmarried is a more serene state for men, who do not feel "rushed." They wait to have the material and financial means necessary to support a household.

Women married to polygynists justify their preference by citing the benefits of mutual aid in reducing their numerous domestic chores and social obligations and by the possibility of having a large family in which the children can flourish. For example, one respondent said, "I like polyg-yny. I get along well with my co-wife; we help each other with the house-work" (thirty-three-year-old migrant woman in a polygynous house-hold). Another commented, "One woman in the house is not enough. Between two it is better, since you share the daily work. I come from a big family, I have half brothers and our mothers get along well. We don't dif-ferentiate between our mothers" (twenty-five-year-old migrant woman in a polygynous household). The sharing of tasks between co-wives gives women free time to devote to remunerative activities such as trading. However, the results of our survey do not indicate a different level of eco-nomic activity among women according to matrimonial status. Forty-two percent of monogamous wives between forty and forty-nine years old work outside the home, as do 40 percent of wives from polygynous households. The acceptance of polygyny is facilitated, above all else, by the approval of Islam.

Among certain divorcées—women with regular income and their own housing—the necessity of marriage is less pressing. It is important above all for form, religion, society, and the children, who would benefit from being raised under the "authority" of a father. The urgency of marriage also diminishes for women over forty who have grown children who can provide for them. For some divorced women, the approbation of polyg-yny benefits their marital experiences and their current situation. Given their age and the number of children from previous marriages, they have fewer reasons than others to insist on monogamy. Some of them previ-ously lived in monogamous marriages, others did not. The fact that they divorced gives them greater tolerance of polygyny, the only possibility if they are to remarry: "You can have a co-wife and get along with her. You can also not have a co-wife and not get along with your husband; anything can happen" (thirty-five-year-old unmarried woman in Dakar).

The arguments for permitting polygyny also contain the weight of a certain religious discourse that, ironically, legitimates a matrimonial regime that exists in other, non-Islamic African societies:

> Everyone should opt for polygyny, at least I would not personally refuse polygyny. We must realize we are Muslims and the religion permits men to have as many as four wives. We must accept it. There are women who say, "I will not join anyone with her husband, it's not normal." All women who think like that should not get married. If you find a husband, thank God and content yourself with what comes afterward. The important thing is to have a good household. (Thirty-five-year-old unmarried woman in Dakar)

Women in monogamous marriages who fear the arrival of a second spouse have the most unfavorable opinions of polygyny. They justify their choice by the greater "tranquillity" offered in a monogamous marriage, and they invoke fear of quarrels as a negative element of polygyny. In fact, quarrels between co-wives can take a dramatic turn, and they fill the "general interest" columns in the press.

> I chose monogamy because there are good and bad women. When you share your husband with these bad women, they will create all sorts of problems: They can stab you with a knife, they can embroil you in all kinds of scenes. I had a half sister who was burned like that, she was the first wife. When the second one came, she didn't want to see the first wife, and didn't tolerate her. She waited until the husband went to work. She heated the oil until it was hot and she poured it on the first wife. She was healed, but her arm no longer straightens. The husband kept both wives; he didn't divorce either one. (Twenty-five-year-old monogamously married woman in Dakar)

The other advantage claimed for monogamy is economic. Too many domestic expenses arise from the fact that the husband must treat his spouses equally. "If you are with your husband and your children, you don't have a heavy burden. In contrast [from a husband's point of view] if you have two or three wives and you want to do your duty as husband in each house, you must satisfy them. With the current situation that's not possible" (thirty-seven-year-old monogamously married migrant woman). Finally, there is widespread confirmation of a refusal to "share a husband."

There are even accommodations of polygyny within radical intellectual discourse. Some women have reappraised the institution that permits them to have a husband and a validated social status at the same time that it allows them a certain autonomy. They say they have negotiated the material conditions of the polygynous contract in their favor.

Polygyny: A Factor in Divorce

The statistical analysis of divorce biographies gives results with starker contrasts (Table 6.3). Two factors slow the separation from a first spouse: family connections and the number of children. Preferential marriages break up with difficulty, which favors polygyny. Also, having children impedes the dissolution of a first marriage. In contrast, precarious economic circumstances favor divorce. Thus, unemployment increases the risk of divorce by 2.7 times. The fact of living with extended family members, such as an uncle, doubles the likelihood of divorce. In theory, the husband must assume financial responsibility for the upkeep of the household, but when economic circumstances deteriorate, the marriage often proves fragile. Default on the husband's financial obligations is often cited as a cause of divorce.

Furthermore, a great difference in the spouses' level of education accentuates the possibility of divorce. When the husband has at least a secondary education and the wife has no schooling, the risk of divorce is three times higher than among couples without any formal education. However, there is no difference among other levels of education.

In our study on divorce, we took into account periods of polygyny in order to verify the hypothesis that the arrival of a second wife accelerates the departure of the first. The creation of a polygynous union markedly increases the risk of divorce for the first wife. The model only considers the unfolding of events as related by the individual interview subjects. However, our method of analysis is close to lived experiences, since it is becoming more common for the first wife to be presented with a fait accompli.[5] Sometimes she is not even informed until the second wedding has already taken place. Following this transition to polygyny, divorce results after a phase of observation and conflict. The amplified coefficient (the potential for divorce increases by 3.5 times) shows that polygyny often engenders a reaction and a reply from the first wife, as our interviews confirmed.

> The existence of a co-wife brought me to divorce. My husband married a second wife without letting me know. He finished his army duty. I told him that with what little money he had he should open a boutique; with the money he would make we could meet our expenses. He went to rent a boutique in Tilène [a market in Dakar]. He stayed at the boutique and married another woman. One day I went to see the shop and I was told he was no longer there, so I went to see one of his friends. The wife of that friend told me,

"Your husband married another woman, but he is not happy with her." That is how I learned he had another wife. I left him a note to say he should come home because our child was sick. When he arrived, I told him, "I wanted you to succeed, but you don't want to. I made sacrifices and suggested that you open a boutique so that we could benefit from the profits. Since you prefer another wife to success, give me a divorce. I will go work." That was the reason for my second divorce. I took custody of the children. (Forty-nine-year-old divorced woman)

Polygyny can be perceived as betrayal not only by the first wife: "When my husband died, I married another man. I was the third wife. I found two other co-wives. Soon after he married a fourth. I divorced him because he took a fourth wife" (fifty-year-old widow).

Polygyny, Divorce, and the Status of Women

Women, generally not in favor of polygyny, have ambivalent attitudes and behaviors that nevertheless reinforce the institution. They submit to polygyny for reasons of status and justify their behavior by relying on arguments that only underline their dependence on men: "If you sign up for monogamy, your husband takes many mistresses and you don't see him. But in polygyny, he marries another woman, you know her, you are at ease, and you are calm" (thirty-eight-year-old divorced woman).

The urgency to marry felt by many women adds to the strong pressures of family and society, which present the female "destiny" as one of marriage and motherhood. In Dakar, there are other types of relationships; however, those that are outside of marriage remain clandestine, which contrasts with other African capitals where such behavior is tolerated.

The reasons for accepting polygyny are clear, even though the problems it engenders are recognized. Polygyny meets individual needs, since it is better to be part of a polygynous marriage than not to be married at all. It conforms to religious convictions, since both marriage and polygyny are seen as religious duties.

In this context, what other alternatives are open to women? An uncomfortable single status perceived as less desirable than a polygynous marriage? A monogamous marriage perceived as provisional, awaiting the menace of a second wife? It is difficult to live as an unmarried woman in Dakar, just as it is difficult to resist polygyny.

Despite the weight of social and religious convictions, the city allows women a certain autonomy. The rate of divorce is relatively high in Dakar, but a divorce is generally followed by a rapid remarriage. The desire for independence is more often manifested in divorce than by women remaining single. Women play an active role in divorce, which is often used as a response to an imposed marriage, a husband's infidelity, polygyny, inadequate financial support, verbal and physical abuse, or meddling in-laws.

> Men are not frank, which causes many divorces. He marries a first wife and they have many children. He goes to look for a second wife, and she benefits at the expense of the first, which was my case. When he brought home the second wife, he went two years without spending the night with me. During those two years I did not get any attention, he was always with his second wife. Always. The woman let me know that I was nothing in the house, that she was the beloved wife of our husband. She and I always fought, and he was always on her side. I cooked when it was my turn, but he spent every night with his other wife. Despite all this I resigned myself to my fate. There were always fights. When the children fought the mothers also took it up, each on the side of her child, and our husband on the side of the second wife. Finally he sold the furniture from my living room, but that did not keep me from staying. . . . But when he sold my bed, then I knew we no longer had a marriage. Not even God likes that type of marriage, so I told him to give me a divorce. He refused. I took him to court, where they gave me custody of the children and I received Fr 54,000 three times each year.[6] I don't know what he did after that, but next I received only Fr 12,000 in each payment. Twelve thousand francs for seven children. That's not much, but I am tired of him and I won't even bother to return to court. I thought it would be better for me just to find work. Now I have temporary work, I'm the head of a team, but I would like to be taken on permanently. (Thirty-seven-year-old divorced woman in Dakar)

Adherence to traditional norms concerning the social position of women is firmly anchored in Dakar. There is, however, a dichotomy between the discourse of women regarding their status and the reality of their behavior. In Dakar, divorce, more than other manifestations of change, reveals new attitudes. It demonstrates the creation of a status for women detached from the ideology of dependence. However, for strategic reasons, social diplomacy, or simply in the name of older norms, the solid core of the pedestal that upholds the models of womanhood is little shaken. Still, the changes currently taking place nibble away at certain aspects of status. These aspects are located in specific areas and are couched in terms of individual aspirations: the choice of husband, divorce, attitudes toward polygyny, and a greater participation in managing household affairs.

Conclusion

Few socioeconomic factors stand out in our analysis to explain differential male behavior regarding polygyny. Only certain demographic features—such as marriage age, the age difference between spouses, and the conception of children out of wedlock—seem to play a role. Women have diverse attitudes toward polygyny, ranging from resignation through realism to hostility. Women's reactions, however, are rooted in a latent opposition to the institution. The analysis of divorce shows a higher probability of a first marriage breaking up after the arrival of a second wife.

As paradoxical as it may seem, there is evidence of diversification of polygynous situations in Dakar. The link between the city and polygyny is not as "negative" as generally believed. It is not surprising that polygyny is maintained in Dakar, in an environment where that institution is supported. Polygyny benefits from official, religious, and social legitimation. It plays a social and demographic regulatory function. It enjoys a popularity and normality that make the existence of the institution seem banal, especially to men. For men, polygyny remains a privilege they may grant themselves, an ambition that allows them to advertise their social success, and a means of controlling and dominating women. The meaning of polygyny is found in the process of redefining relations between men and women.

The psychological form assumed by the modification of women's status is specific to each context. It depends on apparent compromise, on discretion, and also on the acceptance of masculine preeminence. In the face of polygyny, women's strategies range from resignation to contestation. But the autonomous will of women in Dakar struggles against the resistance of men, for whom polygyny remains the bastion of their domination.

Notes

1. This research was conducted jointly by IFAN (Institut Fondamental d'Afrique Noire) and ORSTOM (French Institute of Scientific Research for Development in Cooperation) and was funded by the French Ministry of Research. The research team was composed of P. Antoine, P. Bocquier, A. S. Fall, Y. M. Guisse, and J. Nanitelamio.

2. The results of DHS Niger confirm those of the 1988 census (Klissou 1992).

3. The median age at first marriage is the age at which 50 percent of women were already married.

4. The reference, or baseline, category is indicated in parentheses.

5. In an extreme case, a front-page story in the Senegalese newspaper Le Soleil reported the death of a woman who suffered cardiac arrest when her husband announced his plan to marry a second wife (4 October 1993).

6. The currency is CFA francs. In 1989, $1 was worth approximately CFA francs 300.

References

Antoine, P., and J. Nanitelamio. 1991. "More Single Women in African Cities: Pikine, Abidjan and Brazzaville." Population. English Selection 3:149–169.

Antoine, P., P. Bocquier, A. S. Fall, and Y. M. Guisse. 1992. "Etude de l'insertion des migrants à Dakar: Presentation de la méthodologie d'enquête." In *La ville en mouvement: Habitat et habitants,* ed. E. Lelièvre and C. Levy-Vroelant, 247–257. Paris: L'Harmattan.

Blossfeld, H., A. Hamerle, and K. U. Mayer. 1989. *Event History Analysis: Statistical Theory and Application in the Social Sciences.* Hillsdale, N.J.: Lawrence Erlbaum Associates.

Bocquier, P. 1992. "L'insertion et la mobilité professionnelles à Dakar." Doctoral diss., University of Paris V.

Bocquier, P., and J. Nanitelamio. 1994. "Family Determinants of Women's Professional Activity in Dakar, Senegal." Presentation to Union Internationale pour L'Etude Scientifique de la Population seminar on women and demographic change in sub-Saharan Africa, Dakar.

Boserup, E. 1970. *Women's Role in Economic Development.* London: George Allen and Unwin.

Clignet, R. 1975. "Distribution et fonctions de la polygamie en milieu africain: Ses effets sur les rôles familiaux." *Psychopathologie africaine* 11, 2:157–177.

———. 1987. "On sait que la polygamie est morte: Vive la polygamie." In *Transformations of African Marriage,* ed. D. Parkin and D. Nyamwaya, 199–209. Manchester: Manchester University Press.

Courgeau, D., and E. Lelièvre. 1989. *Analyse démographique de biographies.* Paris: Editions de l'INED.

Cox, D. R. 1972. "Regression Models and Life Tables." *Journal of the Royal Statistical Society* 34:187–220.

Demographic and Health Surveys: Final Reports. 1992. Columbia, Md.: Institute for Resource Development/Westinghouse.

DHS-Sénégal. 1988. "Enquête démographique et de santé au Sénégal 1986." Direction de la Statistique.

Diop, A. B. 1981. *La société wolof: Tradition et changement.* Paris: Karthala.

Djire, M. 1993. "Un aspect de la dynamique de la nuptialité en milieu urbain: L'entrée des hommes en premier union à Dakar." M.Sc., University of Montreal.

Donadje, F. 1992. "Nuptialité et fécondité des hommes au sud-Bénin: Pour une approche des stratégies de reproduction au Bénin." Demographic Institute, Catholic University of Louvain.

Fargues, P. 1987. "La démographie du mariage arabo-musulman: Tradition et changement." *Maghreb Machrek* 116:59–73.

Ferry, B. 1977. *Etude de la fécondité à Dakar (Sénégal): Objectifs, méthodologie, résultats.* Dakar: ORSTOM.

Goldman, N., and A. Pebley. 1989. "The Demography of Polygyny in Sub-Saharan Africa." In *Reproduction and Social Organization in Sub-Saharan Africa,* ed. R. Lesthaeghe, 213–237. Berkeley: University of California Press.

Goody, J. 1973. "Polygyny, Economy and the Role of Women." In *The Character of Kinship,* ed. J. Goody, 175–190. Cambridge: Cambridge University Press.

Kaufmann, G., R. Lesthaeghe, and D. Meekers. 1988. "Les caractéristiques et tendances du mariage." In *Population et sociétés en Afrique au sud du Sahara,* ed. D. Tabutin, 217–247. Paris: L'Harmattan.

Klissou, P. 1992. *La polygamie au Bénin et dans la sous-région ouest-Africaine.* Institute of Demography Working Paper no. 169, Catholic University of Louvain.

Lo Ndiaye, K. 1985. "Entrée en union et divorce." In *Nuptualité et fécondité au Sénégal,* ed. Y. Charbit, L. Gueye, and S. Ndiaye, 37–58. INED No. 112. Paris: Presses Universitaire de France.

Marcoux, R. 1991. "Nuptualité, activité des femmes et maintien de la polygamie en milieu urbain au Mali." In Conference *Femme, famille et population* 1:350–368. Ouagadougou: UEPA.

Mboup, G. 1992. "Etude des déterminants socio-économiques et culturels de la fécondité au Sénégal à partir de l'enquête démographique et de santé." Ph.D. diss., University of Montreal.

Meillassoux, C. 1975. *Femmes, greniers, et capitaux.* Paris: Maspero.

Mercier, P. 1960. "Etude du mariage et enquête urbaine." *Cahiers d'études africaines* 1:28–43.

Nanitelamio, J. 1995. "Insertion urbaine et représentations des statuts féminins." In *La ville à guichets fermés? Itinéraires, résaux, et insertion urbaine,* ed. P. Antoine and A. B. Diop, 277–288. Dakar: IFAN-ORSTOM.

Ngondo a Pitshandenge, I. 1992. "Nuptualité et structures familiales en Afrique au sud du Sahara." In *The Structure and Dynamics of Family Formation in Africa,* 28–45. Dakar: UEPA, Troisième Conférence de la Population Africaine.

Pilon, M. 1991. "Contribution à l'analyse de la polygamie." *Etude de la population* 5:1–17. Dakar: UEPA.

Pison, G. 1986. "La démographie et la polygamie." *Population* 1:93–122.

———. 1988. "Polygamie, fécondité et structures familiales." In *Population et sociétés en Afrique au sud du Sahara,* ed. D. Tabutin, 249–278. Paris: L'Harmattan.

Tabutin, D. 1974. "La polygamie en Algérie." *Population* 2:313–325.

7

Health, Gender Relations, and Poverty in the AIDS Era

BROOKE GRUNDFEST SCHOEPF

This chapter examines AIDS in Kinshasa, Zaire, a large city of 4 million inhabitants, where many sexually active people are at risk. Two case studies of women in Kinshasa are used to show how HIV/AIDS is related to both socioeconomic conditions and to other health issues. Women are especially at risk because of their poverty, their relative powerlessness in the overall organization of Zairian society, and their subordinate position with respect to men. These factors circumscribe their options so that few are able to practice safer sex. Some do not feel able to open dialogue with sexual partners on the subject. Others who have attempted to do so have experienced rejection and retaliation. Those who have reduced their risk most are women with negotiating strengths based on their capacity to support themselves and their dependents without resort to sex within or outside of marriage. Although the poor are at highest risk, the experience of married women dependent on wealthy husbands shows how ephemeral and transitory women's class position can be. Linking macrolevel political economy to microlevel ethnography demonstrates that although gender relations are sometimes subject to negotiation, women's struggles to improve their condition take place in circumstances not of their own making. These factors shape the ways in which women live, work, give birth, and care for children, elders, and men—that is, do the work of "social reproduction."

The HIV virus that causes AIDS is now pandemic. The World Health Organization (WHO) estimates that throughout the world some 20 million people have been infected and about 12 million of those are in Africa (WHO/GPA 1995). By the year 2000, the number will reach 40 to 110 million globally, and as many as 20 to 34 million Africans will have been infected. Most of those who die will be adults, many of whom will leave behind orphaned children and elders.

AIDS is unique in several respects. Interrelated biological and sociocultural factors make it difficult to prevent by means of vaccine development or education. Spread mainly through sexual intercourse, HIV is the most damaging virus that attacks the human immune system. In the process of reproducing itself, the virus destroys the body's capacity to fight off other infections. The virus makes genetic errors at a great rate during reproduction, causing new strains to arise and complicating the search for a vaccine.[1] Drug resistance emerges rapidly as well. Although it is not known if all those infected will go on to develop AIDS, until now the course of full-blown AIDS has invariably been fatal. Thus, behavior change directed at reducing the risk of infection is the only feasible way to stop the spread of HIV.

AIDS is the leading cause of death among young adults in a number of African countries. Most become infected through sexual relations unprotected by condoms. In Africa, as elsewhere, AIDS is freighted with extraordinary symbolic power because sex is invested with cosmological significance, is strongly valued as the essence of life, and is crucial to the survival of individuals, families, and communities. The multiple meanings with which AIDS is invested, the social and economic contexts of transmission, and cultural constructions of contagion and disease create constraints to understanding and acting upon information about prevention. All these factors contribute to denial of risk, to stigmatization of the afflicted and their families, and to withdrawal of social support.

The variable and lengthy period between infection and disease—three to ten years on average—makes it difficult for laypeople to come to terms with the fact that healthy-looking people can transmit HIV infection throughout their lives. Confusion is compounded by the fact that in high HIV–prevalence areas many common diseases seen today have invisible immune system damage as their underlying cause. In any event, fatal illness is often ascribed to social and supernatural rather than biological ("natural") causes. Since people have alternative explanations ready at hand, these ideas may be more powerful than prevention messages emanating from biomedical sources. The AIDS epidemic may be more damaging to society than other fatal afflictions that are also often attributed to sorcery—a potent metaphor for human relations gone awry.

In addition to cultural obstacles to the assimilation of biomedical knowledge, HIV/AIDS prevention encounters several other sets of obstacles residing in social inequalities of class, gender, and international relations. These factors bring urgency to the search for cultural change and self-sustainable development that would ensure that sexual risk is reduced and necessary resources are provided to affected families and communities.

HIV risk in Africa is not confined to any special "risk group" or category of persons. AIDS is not only a disease of poor women engaged in commercial sex work ("prostitutes") and long-distance truck drivers. Although men and women in these occupations are at extremely high risk, they do not form bounded groups. In the cities, their social networks extend into virtually every social milieu, spreading out along the international trade routes and via secondary roads and markets to all but the most remote villages. In a continent where 5 to 30 percent of sexually active adults and adolescents are already infected, prevention involves convincing the general population to alter highly valued behaviors that are widely considered to be normal and "natural." To date, prevention strategies targeting only groups perceived as high risk have not been able to stop the spread of HIV infection.

In 1989, a World Bank team estimated that new infections in Kinshasa could be reduced by 75 percent by "eliminating prostitution." These men did not indicate how "prostitutes" were to be defined and identified. They were not concerned with other multiple-partner relationships, such as "sexual networking" by wealthy men, that are also likely to lead to chains of HIV transmission.

AIDS is a disease freighted with emotionally charged issues of sex, blood, and death. With Africa designated as the source of the virus that causes AIDS, some Westerners believed that African sexuality was more "promiscuous" and "different" from that of people elsewhere and that exotic customs were responsible for passage of the virus from monkeys to humans. In reality, cross-species transfers are probably not recent and may have occurred simply as a result of butchering monkeys and chimpanzees for consumption.

Such racist constructions of African culture provoked defensive responses from African leaders and peoples. That racism retarded efforts to halt the spread of infection, as politicians, professionals, and the public experienced the need to defend African cultures and personhood. The disease has also become a stigmatizing condition within Africa. As in the United States, stigma and anxiety have sometimes led to social distancing, to "othering," of both the afflicted and those associated with them.

Consequently, many people are afraid to make their condition known, and some families hesitate to care for the sick for fear that neighbors will ostracize them.

The sexual culture of any urban community is pluralistic. Kinshasa includes an unknown proportion of mutually monogamous couples and celibate single people who live according to traditional or Christian tenets. Their numbers have undoubtedly increased, since some people report that they have changed their lifestyles in response to the risk of AIDS. Those who have chosen premarital celibacy and mutual monogamy may attend prayer groups that help to support their resolve.

Nevertheless, casual sex continues. Furthermore, polygyny is widespread and many other types of multiple-partner relationships, with varying degrees of social recognition and legitimacy, exist among people of all social classes and ethnic origins. Even socially recognized relationships may be of relatively brief duration, leading, as in the West, to what has been termed "serial polygamy." In Zaire, President Mobutu's government ideology of African "authenticity," promulgated partly to undermine the influence of the Catholic Church, made polygyny respectable. Access to numerous women is a symbol of male power and wealth in the late twentieth century, just as it was in the slaving period in the nineteenth century and earlier and during the violent years of colonial penetration that followed.

The Zairian economy has met with ever-deepening crises since 1974 when world market prices for copper, its major export, plummeted. Massive theft of public resources by Zaire's leaders was justified by a pervasive counterculture of corruption. Government control was bolstered by patronage networks, arbitrary arrest, and political violence. Incomes have fallen far behind the pace of hyperinflation, which has driven up the cost of essentials, including food, rent, charcoal, clothing, health care, education, and transport. Many urban families that were just scraping by in 1987 have since fallen destitute. Young people without steady employment are unable to establish stable families. Zaire is now so far in arrears on its debt payments that the International Monetary Fund (IMF) was reported to be considering suspending further disbursements. The national debt of some $5 billion is exceeded by the personal fortune of President Mobutu, who was widely reputed to have amassed more than that amount through systematic looting of public resources. Although no statistics exist, research observations from CONNAISSIDA suggest that multiple-partner situations, particularly those involving various forms of sexual patron-client relationships, have increased as a result of the deepening economic and political crisis.

About 15 percent of sexually active adults and adolescents in Kinshasa were estimated to be infected with HIV/AIDS in 1993.[2] People with multiple partners or those whose partners currently or previously had more than one partner during the past ten years were able to obtain considerable protection through regular condom use. Although condoms had not been popular in the past, fear of AIDS and a skillful campaign by a U.S. Agency for International Development–funded social marketing project raised condom sales to 18 million nationwide by mid-1991. Although that amounted to only one condom for every sexually active person, it represented an enormous increase over the three hundred thousand sold monthly in 1987. Condoms were used mainly by young men in casual encounters. Issues of trust between steady partners and others who are emotionally attached continued to make condom use and acknowledgment of risk extremely difficult.

Rioting by the military in 1990 and 1991 destroyed the formal economic sector and led foreign-supported assistance projects to withdraw from Zaire. Since then, health services have suffered from an even greater dearth of medicines, supplies, transport, and staff salaries than before. Lapses in condom distribution have resulted in shortages of quality condoms.

The case studies that follow highlight some interrelated obstacles that an effective prevention program must address[3] and suggest possibilities for change. Understanding these obstacles will be useful when it becomes politically feasible to refocus on HIV/AIDS prevention under a popularly elected government accountable to the citizenry, with leaders who are not afraid of community mobilization and social change.

Nsanga's Story

In 1987, Nsanga was twenty-six years old and very poor. She had a five-year-old daughter and a son starting primary school. Until recently, she had been contributing to the support of a younger brother in secondary school. A younger sister also lived with Nsanga in her single room, which was part of a corrugated-roofed block surrounding an open courtyard. The yard contained a shared water tap, a roofless bathing stall, and a latrine, but no electricity. In good weather Nsanga and her neighbors moved their charcoal stoves outdoors to cook. In the courtyard, they also washed dishes and clothes and prepared vegetables for the pot. Wastewater ran out to an open ditch outside. Like the yard, the street was unpaved, deeply rutted, muddy in the rainy season, and dusty in the dry months. Mosquitoes were ubiquitous in the neighborhood, and malaria and diarrheal diseases were common causes of death in young children. Many families ate only one meal per day and children were especially undernourished. Many people had deep, hacking coughs that suggested pulmonary tuberculosis.[4]

Nsanga wasn't always the head of her household. She was raised in a village where she lived until her marriage to a schoolteacher in 1980. They managed to subsist—somehow—on his skimpy salary, despite galloping inflation of nearly 100 percent each year. Beginning in 1983, the IMF instituted a series of structural adjustment measures designed to bring about an "economic recovery." These reforms reduced government expenditures for already inadequate public services and imposed user fees for access to health and other services. One objective was to enable Third World leaders, who had borrowed heavily in the 1970s, to make payments on international debts. More than eighty thousand Zairian teachers and health workers were fired during this *"assainisse-ment"* in 1984.[5]

Many of those government workers who were fired were women who found it difficult to obtain other employment despite having some secondary education. Nsanga's husband was one of the men who lost his job at that time. As he lacked a powerful patron to intercede for him, he joined the ranks of the unemployed. Forty to 60 percent of men were without waged employment in 1984. That figure has climbed since, reaching nearly 90 percent in the mid-1990s, as many large and small firms have closed their doors. After six fruitless months of waiting in offices, Nsanga's husband began to drink heavily. He sold off the household appliances to pay for beer and, when the price of beer rose, *lutuku*—a cheap, strong, home-distilled alcohol. Their relationship deteriorated. Nsanga harangued him about wasting money. Sometimes when he got drunk he beat her, and Nsanga locked him out of the house.

Meanwhile, Nsanga tried many things to earn money. Like most poor women in Kinshasa, she received only a few years of primary schooling, and like her husband, she had no powerful friends or relatives. Nsanga was unable to find waged employment. Only 4 percent of women held regular paid jobs with social benefits in 1984. Since the colonial period, low levels of education have combined with preferential hiring of men to confine most women to the "informal sector" of petty trade and production. Nsanga cooked food for neighborhood men, and she sold uncooked rice and dried fish in small quantities when she could obtain supplies cheaply. These efforts brought in only pennies at a time. She tried growing vegetables in a vacant lot, but soldiers stole her crops before she could harvest them.

In 1986, Nsanga's husband vanished. The children ate up her food stocks. With nothing left to sell, Nsanga went into debt for the rent. She asked an older brother for a loan, but he refused, pleading poverty. Although he had a steady job as a laborer on the docks, he had two wives and nine children. His monthly salary was just above the minimum wage and, by 1989, no longer bought even a fifty-kilogram bag of manioc flour.

Business failures in the informal sector were common, as large numbers of people tried to make a living from this "penny capitalism." Since Nsanga could not obtain new start-up capital, exchanging sex for subsistence seemed the obvious solution. Nsanga became a *"deuxième bureau"* (second office), "occupied" by a married lover who paid her rent and gave her regular support. She also had a few "spare tires" to help out when her children were sick and she needed cash for medicine. But after a year she got pregnant and the "occupant" left. His salary couldn't stretch that far, he told her. So Nsanga had to take on more partners—a fairly typical downward slide. The neighborhood rate was equivalent to U.S. fifty cents per brief encounter in 1987, and Nsanga said that with luck she might get two or three partners per working day, for a total of thirty dollars a month (at most). At the time, this was equal to the wage of a nurse at a private hospital and was more than five times what Nsanga had earned in petty trade. Clients became scarcer over the years, however. In 1989, Nsanga said, "Many men now avoid pickups because the mass media have identified 'prostitutes' as a source of AIDS infection. Most of my 'husbands' are men I know, not clients I meet in bars or clients off the street." Indeed, men often consider women they know as "old friends" to present less risk because these women do not fit their idea of prostitutes.

In 1983, Nsanga had an ectopic pregnancy and needed a blood transfusion. Her last baby, born in 1987, was sickly and failed to thrive. It died before its second birthday, following prolonged fever, diarrhea, and skin eruptions. Nsanga believes it was because semen from so many men spoiled her milk. Like most young children who die in this neighborhood, Nsanga's baby was not tested for HIV. Women with greater access to health care often learn of their own HIV infection when a sick infant is diagnosed.

Sexually transmitted diseases (STDs) can impair reproductive health and increase the risk of HIV transmission. Many people are quite casual about gonorrhea. In the 1970s, Zairian university students called it "the college cold" (*le rheume académique*). Women may not know they are infected because they have no discernible symptoms. For others, vaginal discharge is so common that they consider it to be "normal." Nsanga reported that she has had a few bouts of vaginal discharge and burning. About a year earlier, she had terrible abdominal pains for several months but had no money to consult a doctor. She took some tetracycline pills on advice from a medicine shop clerk. Self-treatment of STD symptoms with antibiotics purchased at shops and markets is popular. As a result of incomplete treatment, penicillin-resistant gonorrhea became wide-spread (50 to 75 percent of cases analyzed) in Central and East Africa in the 1970s.

Nsanga and her neighbors pointed to the need for free diagnosis and treatment of STDs. They want a health care setting that respects their need for privacy and dignity. Nsanga says that the European nuns at the dispensary in her neighborhood do not treat such "dirty" diseases. Laboratory diagnosis for STDs is available at the nearby university clinic, but in 1987 its cost equaled the income earned from thirty sexual encounters, so none of the women Nsanga knows could afford it.

What about prevention? In 1987, Nsanga said that she had heard of condoms but had never actually seen one and commented that "men use them to prevent disease when they have sex with prostitutes. If a lover were to propose using a condom, I would be angry! It would mean that he doesn't trust me."

Nsanga rejected the morally stigmatizing label of prostitute: In her own eyes, she is not a prostitute because she is not a "bad woman." On the contrary, as a mother who has fallen on hard times through no fault of her own, she is trying her best, "breaking stones" (kobeta libanga), to meet her family obligations. Abandonment, divorce, and widowhood force many women who are without other resources into commercial sex work. In the presence of HIV, however, this survival strategy has been transformed into a death strategy. Because neither they nor their male partners define them as "prostitutes," narrowly targeted prevention information does not reach them.

Women voice other objections to condoms. For example, Nsanga believes that condoms are harmful. She has heard that semen contains nourishing "vitamins" needed to keep women mentally healthy, fertile, and physically attractive. Moreover, she has been warned by older women that condoms can break and remain inside the body where they cause infection and even death. In any case, since condoms don't offer 100-percent-sure protection from HIV infection, Nsanga's clients have said: "Why bother? We might as well enjoy life while we can."

Whether virginity is an issue or not (precolonial cultures varied considerably), adolescent women today are not supposed to be "ready for sex," and early pubertal physical development may be stigmatized as a sign of "precocious" sexual activity. Misinformation, denial, and notions of propriety combine with gender inequality to increase young women's vulnerability to unplanned pregnancies, STDs, and HIV. In 1987, one of Nsanga's neighbors commented about the risk to women and girls: "Even if they know about les Prudences [this brand name became a popular term for condoms], what's the use? Men won't use the things and the girls can't make them. Anyway, a young girl would be ashamed to ask her friend to use a condom. He would think she was a prostitute! It's the same as with birth control pills."

Girls are still socialized for subservience. Although at least one-half of the adolescents in Kinshasa are sexually active by age seventeen, many adults—fathers, particularly—do not consider their daughters' desires legitimate and avoid the subject. Mothers may be more realistic. Many fear for their daughters because so many older men now seek out young girls, believing that they are free of HIV infection. Having sex with a virgin is sometimes considered a way for a man to rid himself of STD. Rape and other forms of sexual coercion are common, as it is often difficult or even dangerous for young women to say "no." Men of means may pay compensation to angry fathers. A popular song in Kinshasa advises a well-known politician "to leave the girls alone" ("Tika Bana"). Abusive or not, sex with older men, combined with anatomical and physiological immaturity, explains why HIV is spreading especially rapidly in adolescent women throughout Africa.

By 1989, Nsanga's attitude toward condoms had become more favorable. Nevertheless, she said: "I can't afford to insist on men using condoms. If I did, they might go to women who don't insist." By this time, Nsanga had become very thin and suffered from fevers and a persistent cough. Neighbors whispered about her condition. Nsanga said: "They suspect that I have AIDS. But people say this about everyone who loses weight, even when it is just from hunger and worry. All these people who are dying nowadays, are they really all dying from AIDS?"

Obviously, they are not. Tuberculosis, malaria, and other diseases that cause weight loss and fever are common in Kinshasa. Nevertheless, 50 to 70 percent of patients on adult medical wards are HIV-infected. AIDS-related conditions are the leading cause of death among adults twenty to forty-nine years old.

Nsanga's defensiveness is shared by numerous women in similar circumstances, for whom denial is a stratagem for coping with a situation they cannot change. We do not know if Nsanga was HIV-positive or, if she was, how she might have acquired the infection. She had not been tested. Slipping in and out of denial, Nsanga considered testing a needless expense: "What's the use? If they told me I am infected, I would worry so much that I would just bring on the disease!" Many people share her belief that mental and somatic illnesses are interwoven, and some reject opportunities to learn their HIV status on this basis.

If infected, Nsanga might have gotten HIV from one of her numerous clients since late 1986. Or she might have been infected earlier by her husband. Her ectopic pregnancy suggests that he may have transmitted a "classic" STD, thereby increasing the risk of HIV infection. Husbands often fail to inform wives of their infections, since this blatant evidence of their infidelity can trigger recriminations and demands for compensation by the wife's family. Nsanga's husband was a teacher, and male teachers are known to demand sex from their pupils as a condition of obtaining good grades. Some state that sex is a perquisite of their poorly paid profession.

Or Nsanga might have gotten infected through a blood transfusion in 1983. Complications of pregnancy are a common indication for transfusion, especially since many poor women have low hemoglobin levels due to malaria and to manioc-based diets deficient in iron. Although her neighbors whisper about "the wages of sin" and "divine retribution for fornication," if Nsanga *is* infected, her sex work seems the *least* likely transmission scenario, considering the lengthy period between HIV infection and signs of disease. In any event, Nsanga, her male partners, and other women in their sexual networks are at high risk. The government's narrowly targeted campaign reinforced the moral stigma of prostitution. The more realistic social marketing campaign quickly made condom use trendy among more educated young men. In 1989, the campaign message had just begun reaching working-class and unemployed people.

Mbeya's Story

The second case study describes a woman in very different circumstances from Nsanga. Mbeya is the cousin of someone I have known since 1975. In 1987, she was a stylish, carefully groomed woman in her late forties who wore heavy gold jewelry, three-piece ensembles of imported Dutch wax-print fabric, expensive handbags, and matching shoes. Mbeya often drove the family's second car, a vintage Mercedes. A chauffeur ran errands and drove her youngest child to school. Two older children were studying in Europe and another one, in the United States.

Mbeya's husband was an important figure in the ruling party's inner circle. For such men, the company of stylish young women is a perquisite of the job, a routine part of the socializing integral to politics. Mistresses are also part of the private intelligence-gathering networks that men in high politics find necessary for political survival.

Mbeya accepted her situation as a co-wife:

> I was not too jealous because my husband always respected me as the first wife, mother of his children (*Mama ya Bana*), and kept his other women away from the house. He never brought home dirty diseases, either. There was plenty of money, and I never felt done out of my rights. I have been very lucky, unlike many of my friends whose husbands also are unfaithful.

Mbeya's friend, Anita, couldn't abide her own husband's outside wives and lovers. More than once Anita accused her husband of bringing home a sexually transmitted disease. Mbeya said:

> Anita harangued him about this so much that finally he left her. She divorced him, but he retaliated for [Anita's] insulting him publicly like that. He forbade their children to visit their mother when they came home from school in Europe. I am sure that her asthma [from which she died] was aggravated by her chagrin. Everyone wonders why *that* man hasn't succumbed to AIDS!

Members of Anita's family had related her situation to me earlier. Whereas her nieces took her side, a male cousin blamed Anita for not accepting her husband's philandering.

Confusion results from the fact that some notorious *coureurs* ("womanizers") have remained healthy and that some people get sick while their spouses do not. AIDS' apparent arbitrariness reinforces beliefs that implicate fate, luck, ancestral spirits, and sorcery in disease causation, and all of this contributes to denial of sexual risk. A story that made the rounds in Kinshasa in 1992 shows how this confusion is elaborated in cultural politics. President Mobutu was asked by foreign journalists to comment on the AIDS situation, said to be out of control in Zaire.

Mobutu replied, "Let me make a few phone calls." He dialed the telephone. "Hello, A. How are you? Still among the living? Good." He hung up and dialed another number. "Hello, B. How are you? Well and in great form? Good." He hung up and dialed "C," with the same result. Turning to the journalists, Mobutu said, "If these notorious *coureurs*, A, B, and C, are alive and still moving about, then AIDS can't be as big a threat as foreigners make out."[6]

Anita's former husband was the first man called in this story. When he died later that year, it was widely assumed that his "long and painful illness" was due to AIDS. The complex symbolic terrain interweaves international politics, gender struggles, and competing moral discourses.

Mbeya told another story in 1987. A wealthy physician-businessman living on her street and two of his wives were said to have died from AIDS. Neighbors blamed the first wife because she traded on her own account, traveling to Nigeria to purchase household appliances on commission for friends and acquaintances. Mbeya reflected: "It could just as well have been the husband who gave *her* AIDS! Who knows what younger wives do when their husband is away? And did he only sleep with his wives? After all, a doctor has many opportunities! Men are always quick to blame women, especially when women earn their own money!"

Mbeya and her friends wonder where AIDS came from. They rejected the hypothesis that the virus jumped to humans from the monkey's blood

used in love magic: "This is just one more Western racist invention."
Many "traditional" healers have claimed that AIDS is an old disease that
has become epidemic because women no longer observe the traditional
customs that required purification by ritual baths after marital sex, adultery, miscarriage, and other incidents. Mbeya's cousin, recalling discus-
sions with me when she was a university student ten years earlier,
laughed: "This is yet another tradition invented to control women!" Prior
to colonization, high-status women in Mbeya's ethnic group controlled
their own sexuality.

Some clergymen claim that AIDS is a divine punishment and that sin-
ners will be struck down while the innocent remain safe. They apply the
term "sinner" to women who fail to conform to their prescriptions of
morality: premarital chastity and marital fidelity. Mbeya and her friends
reject this moralistic construction in favor of a biomedical explanation.
They point out that "innocent, monogamous wives can be infected by
their husbands." They also say that many women cannot remain with
only one partner throughout their lifetime. They wonder if it is true that,
as they have heard, the virus came to Africa from America.

Women in Mbeya's circle were dubious about the value of the government's AIDS-prevention messages. In addition to advising men to "avoid
prostitutes" and "stick to one partner," information campaigns urged
people to avoid blood transfusions and to use disposable injection syringes. Zairian health services seldom have sufficient sterilizable sets; au-
toclaves have long since broken down and fuel for lengthy boiling is
costly. Hygiene in dispensaries and clinics is often abominable. Instru-
ments generally stand in a token pink soup of Dettol disinfectant that is
renewed infrequently. Kinshasa University Hospital required patients to
bring their own disposable needles. Health workers told of cleaners collecting disposable syringes from trash pits and repackaging them in plas-
tic to sell as "new."

Knowing these risks, Mbeya and her friends have purchased disposables for their families for more than a decade in order to protect
against hepatitis B, staphylococcus, and other infections potentially acquired in the hospital or clinic. They are aware, however, that the chief
risk is from sexual transmission. The first Zairians diagnosed with
AIDS in Europe in 1983 and 1984 were people like themselves: wealthy
men and their female partners—wives and mistresses—whose health
care access was far above average. When asked if they have changed
their behavior since the coming of AIDS, most people who responded
affirmatively reported buying disposables as the only change. Mbeya
and many other elite women have not been confused by what, in the
face of denial of sexual risk, amounts to little more than a token dis-
placement activity.

Even among elite women, awareness is frequently not matched by the power to act. In May 1987, Mbeya's husband brought home an official notice about AIDS that was distributed to high officials. He left it on her bedside table. Mbeya laughed: "He just left it there, without saying anything." Although concerned, she said that she was afraid to broach the subject with him: "I can't ask him to stop [having sex with other women], but I wish he would use condoms. Use condoms with the other women, with me, whatever. But I just don't feel I can introduce the subject. It wouldn't do any good. My husband would get angry and tell me to mind my own business."

In 1988, Mbeya became aware that her husband was sick and not getting any better. Although he had not shared his diagnosis with her, she began to suspect that it might be AIDS and told him that she wanted to use condoms. Her husband flatly refused because, he said, condoms would reduce his pleasure. Then, Mbeya wanted them to stop having sexual relations. He refused this, too, and his family was outraged at the idea. They threatened to throw her out and keep her youngest daughter. Many families are able to exert strong influence on couples' reproductive health decisions.

Mbeya acquiesced to their pressure. When her husband died, her in-laws accused her of having infected him, despite the logic of the situation. Mbeya protested that she had married as a young virgin straight from a convent school and that she was a faithful wife. Her cousin assured me that this was undoubtedly true. Lourdes Cottingham points out that the stigma and uncertainty surrounding AIDS prevent many women whose husbands have multiple partners or are sick with AIDS from summoning the support of their natal kin in favor of marital abstinence or condom use (Personal communication, 27 February 1994).

Widowed, Mbeya was obliged to leave her husband's luxurious villa and give up all the furnishings. These now belong to the husband's family, which also took possession of the cars, businesses, and rental properties her husband had acquired. Formerly, her husband's younger brother might have allowed her to live in the house, even if he did not become her actual husband. In the past, the custom of "widow inheritance" protected women in family systems that did not acknowledge joint conjugal property. My field notes from Lubumbashi record cases of widow inheritance by professional men in the late 1970s. More frequently, however, a surviving brother took charge of his deceased sibling's property and children, while the widow went her separate way.

Decline of widow inheritance is often proposed as a way of limiting HIV spread. Men, particularly, fail to reflect critically on the implications of their male relatives' multiple partners. They simply assume that widows are infected—one more example of blaming women. Mbeya believes that her affines' accusations are motivated by their self-interest: "The property is too valuable!" The house was to be sold and the money shared among her husband's brothers. Turned out of her home, bereaved, and fearing that she was infected, Mbeya went to live at the home of her brother where—after having been a respected, "take-charge" woman—she became a dependent. Law and reinvented "custom" combine to infantilize women even when they are not rendered destitute.

Mbeya's story illustrates the ephemeral nature of women's class position when it is based upon a husband's ownership of resources. As the manager of an extended family household with twenty-two people to feed, clothe, and care for, in 1987 Mbeya felt that she had no time or energy to start a business for herself. In 1989, in her altered circumstances, Mbeya said: "I envy women who trade on their own account and earn money they can keep. I never dreamt I would need to do that myself!"

Conclusion

Case studies such as Nsanga's and Mbeya's lend texture to epidemiological data. They confirm the fact that the HIV virus is spreading not because of exotic cultural practices but because of many people's normal responses to situations of everyday life. Poor sex workers are at extremely high risk because risk increases with the number of partners. However, as most of the women interviewed in the CONNAISSIDA AIDS education project were aware, the majority of those at risk are not engaged in commercial sex work.

Primary prevention of AIDS cannot be effected simply by targeting sex workers and truck drivers. It is the fact of unprotected sex with multiple partners, rather than the ways that relationships are socially categorized and labeled, that puts people at risk. Like Nsanga, many women who have multiple partners do not think of themselves as prostitutes. They are not professionals sharing a career, an identity, and a mutually supportive organization. Struggling to support their families in a period of economic crisis, they resort to sexual "survival strategies" at a time when these have turned into the opposite, leading to death.

Studies made throughout the world show that mass media and other information campaigns increase knowledge of AIDS but seldom lead to significant change in risk behaviors. Nor can education change the situations that place people at risk. For these reasons, CONNAISSIDA emphasized the search for culturally appropriate, interactive, community-based change strategies. These included experiments with a variety of risk-reduction workshops organized at the invitation of community groups. Using ethnography and participatory experiential learning methods, we presented AIDS prevention more as a *political* choice for social and cultural survival and less as a problem of *individual* behaviors.

The workshops enabled people—including some women—in various social milieus to make informed decisions about behavior changes leading to reduced risk of HIV. They also confirmed the many obstacles faced even by well-informed women. The action-research workshop method provides a learning context that empowers people to address wider issues related to health, household economics, gender, and sexual relationships. Although this does not alter power relationships that are determined by the structure of social relations in the wider society, it enables some men to understand their personal stake in changing gender relations (Walu 1991; Schoepf 1988, 1993, 1994).

Like many other pandemics, the spread of HIV infection is facilitated by socioeconomic and political conditions. The virus is a biological event the effects of which have been magnified by the conditions of urbanization in Africa. These include distorted economies dependent on a few export commodities with declining terms of trade in world markets and rapid class formation with growing inequality and mass poverty, exacerbated by the current world crisis. The obstacles to risk reduction are economic, social, emotional, and material.

AIDS prevention involves much more than the adoption of condoms or reduction in partner numbers. Rather, it involves redefinition of the gendered social roles and change in the socioeconomic conditions that have contributed to the rapid spread of HIV in Africa. Its rapid spread through heterosexual transmission in other regions of the world confirms this hypothesis. Success in the quest for AIDS prevention mandates the use of social empowerment strategies and demands changes in development goals to put people—rather than production, profit, and professional advancement—first.

Notes

This chapter draws upon research conducted with colleagues in Projet CONNAISSIDA in Zaire, 1985–1990. Grateful acknowledgment is made to Mme. Veronique Engundu Walu, Dr. wa Nkera Rukarangira, Prof. Ntsomo Payanzo, and Claude Schoepf, as well as to Mme. Lourdes de Oliveira Cottingham. I alone am responsible for the data and interpretations presented here.

1. According to Dr. M. Essex, mutations occur at about 100 times the rate in influenza viruses, which require a new vaccine every four years (lecture, Harvard University, February 1994).

2. L. Cottingham, interviews in Kinshasa, January 1994.

3. Comparison of 1985–1990 data with a recent rapid assessment made by L. Cottingham in December 1993–January 1994 indicates that these obstacles persist.

4. Immune system depletion caused by HIV infection causes latent tuberculosis to become active. Cases of extrapulmonary tuberculosis are now common and difficult to treat.

5. The term *assainissement* is unintentionally ironic; it means "to clean up" and, by extension, to make healthy. Bringing health to the budget, this housecleaning has brought malnutrition and ill health to hundreds of thousands, including low-paid government employees, their families, and those whom they formerly served. Many Zairians no longer have access to even minimal health care or education.

6. This incident took place on Zaire's national television (L. Cottingham, personal communication, 24 February 1994).

References

Schoepf, Brooke Grundfest. 1988. "Women, AIDS, and Economic Crisis in Central Africa." *Canadian Journal of African Studies* 22, 3:625–644.

———. 1993. "AIDS Action-Research with Women in Kinshasa." *Social Science and Medicine* 37, 11:1401–1413.

———. 1994. "Action-Research and Empowerment in Africa." In *Women as the Key: Feminist Perspectives on the AIDS Epidemic,* ed. Nancy Stoller and Beth Schneider. Philadelphia: Temple University Press.

Walu, Engundu. 1991. "Women's Survival Strategies in Kinshasa." M.A. thesis, Institute for Social Studies, The Hague.

World Health Organization/Global Programme on AIDS (WHO/GPA). 1995. "Cumulative Infections Approach 20 Million." *Global AIDS News* 1:5.

8

Moving and Coping: Women Tenants in Gweru, Zimbabwe

MIRIAM GRANT

This chapter highlights the struggles of urban women tenants and articulates their coping strategies in the face of growing marginalization in a fast-growing African city, Gweru, Zimbabwe. The life experience of women in Gweru is traced through individual histories that illustrate the routes by which migration brings women to the city; the way certain life events eventually set them apart from the linked household; how work cycles turn them into impermanent, insecure members of the informal labor market; and how these dislocations constantly strain their capacity to provide adequate housing. In short, the chapter outlines the contours of vulnerability for single women in the city. These conditions of vulnerability are then shown to be the outgrowth of forces operating in the city of Gweru as a whole—forces that are still at work in the nation.

The marginalization of female household heads within Zimbabwean society has been a result of the disadvantaged position of women with respect to society, law, education, employment, and household. Although the distribution of female household heads ranged from 43 to 48 percent within Zimbabwean provinces (ILO/Jaspa 1986:38) in the early 1980s, their position has continued to be tenuous. The condition of these women to a large extent has been the product of the colonial and white minority regimes and policies.

Colonial urban areas represented both a form of escape and a new form of confinement for African women. Initially, African women moved to urban areas to escape the control of male elders, fathers, guardians, or husbands. However, once customary law was codified through a male-dominated process, women became permanent minors whose mobility and sexuality were controlled by colonial officials and male elders (Schmidt 1992). By moving to town, women were attempting to defy their prescribed subordinate position in society and their spatial confinement to reserves. Nevertheless, African women's position in the capitalist economy of urban areas proved to be marginal right from the beginning. Although some women entered the male-dominated sphere of domestic service, most survived in the informal sector as beer brewers, vegetable hawkers, and prostitutes (Schmidt 1992:162). Without access to decent education or training, women were forced to assume an urban subsistence role.

Despite concerted efforts after 1980 by the postindependence Zimbabwean government to promote equal rights and to eliminate discrimination, everyday change has been elusive. For example, enrollment figures for women in education and training institutions increased over the 1981 to 1985 period, but the ratio between men and women remained constant (Batezat and Mwalo 1989:28). Further, women's participation in formal employment has not significantly increased since 1981, and they still make up less than 10 percent of factory workers (Batezat and Mwalo 1989:35–36; Sylvester 1991:151). In addition, the flight of wealthy white families and the introduction of minimum wage legislation resulted in a major drop—from one-half to one-fifth of all waged women—in the number of women employed in domestic service (Drakakis-Smith 1992:106). Not only were women left out of the better-paying formal sector, but they were subjected to a sexual division of labor within the informal sector: Single women, who had no husband to support them, were relegated to low-skill activities such as sewing, knitting, and selling vegetables (Batezat and Mwalo 1989:35–36). Further, "for many these activities are not simply a convenient means to useful household subsidies, they are a matter of life or death for families where the husband provides little or no income. Urban women who come under the 'divorced, separated, deserted and widowed' categories are particularly vulnerable in this regard" (UNICEF 1985:80). Whereas a privately funded women's bureau, along with international voluntary groups, was attempting to address the situation by offering courses for women in income-generating projects and formal cooperatives, local women's clubs continued to reinforce colonial homemaker status by offering training in cooking and sewing (Sylvester 1991:151).

Economic vulnerability extends to shelter, or residential, vulnerability. Single women tenants in cities encounter particular difficulties in securing urban shelter. First, there is an acute shortage of affordable, low-income rental shelter. Circumstances lead to household fragmentation or force tenants to search for new lodgings. Second, these women struggle to cope with their particular socioeconomic and household demands. The underlying theme for many women is to seek out the right combination of social, economic, and household characteristics that just might allow the household not only to survive intact within the city but also to progress in the urban acculturation process.

The Conditions of Vulnerability in Gweru

Gweru is a medium-sized Zimbabwean city, with a 1990 population of 110,000. It is the fourth-largest city, ranking after Harare, Bulawayo, and Chitungwiza. A staggering growth rate of 4.9 percent from 1982 to 1990 indicates much movement in and out of the city, along with natural increase.

The housing history and policies for Gweru[1] during the colonial and Unilateral Declaration of Independence[2] periods clearly reflected those of other cities in Rhodesia (renamed Zimbabwe upon independence). Urban shelter for Africans, which was tied directly to employment, was one of many tools used by colonial authorities to control rural-urban migration. In a system that depended upon circular labor migration, Africans needed passes to enter urban areas, were segregated in compounds and high-density townships, and were forced to forfeit their housing and return to rural labor reserves upon completion of their contracts or the loss of employment. Restrictive legislation such as the Land Apportionment Act (LAA) of 1931 and the Native Urban Areas Accommodation and Registration Act (NUAARA) of 1946 prohibited Africans from owning land (and thus housing) in urban areas, and allowed close control of influx by authorities. Thus, all formal market housing for Africans was rental and was supplied by employers of domestic servants, companies, municipalities (in municipal townships), and the government (in government townships). In Gweru, municipal townships (run by Gweru City Council [GCC]) included Monomatapa, Mambo, and Ascot, as well as the outlying government townships of Senka and Mkoba (which were transferred to GCC in 1966–1967) (see map).

African women and their families faced extreme difficulties in the urban arena from the very beginning. Harassment by the authorities for any presence in town without a pass was compounded by a severe shortage of married housing in a supply system geared toward hostels and

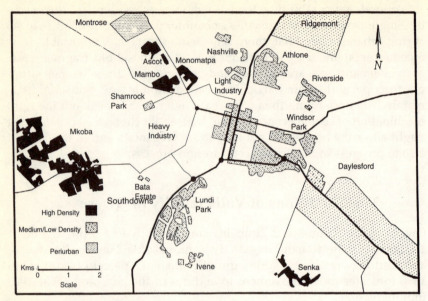

City of Gweru, Zimbabwe

shared quarters for "single" males. Many males were forced to house their wives illegally in quarters in town, in shacks in a squatter settlement, or by renting space in periurban locations (generally, a one- to two-hour walk from town) such as farms (Phimister 1988). Women were further peripheralized since, under the NUAARA, only married males were eligible for married accommodation. This forced female household heads to become tenants and precluded them from registering their children for school.

Despite the redirection of the government's priority toward family migration and a more stable labor force from the early 1950s onward, provision of married housing, particularly low-income accommodations, was woefully inadequate. For example, the Mapondera (1975) and Mangami (1978) Reports on housing and facilities in Gweru's Monomatapa Township revealed extreme overcrowding, with three families sharing one room, married couples forced to cohabit with singles, and totally inadequate facilities. These conditions engendered high rates of crime and disease, insecurity, and an impossible environment for any semblance of family life (GCC Archives: Mapondera Report 1975; Mangami Report 1978).

Independence in 1980 brought with it a clear evolution in housing policy. All new houses were to be under home ownership (privately owned), and city councils were instructed to convert most existing municipal shelter to home ownership. Existing housing was offered for sale to the sitting tenants, with a discount for every year of occupation and no deposit required, provided their names were on the waiting list. Although this process was still ongoing in Gweru in 1990, more than 8,000 houses had been converted by that time. Waiting list placement was necessary for consideration for either conversion or new home ownership and was limited to those who earned less than Z$500 (Z$1 equaled US$.44) per month. Gweru's list had exceeded 14,000 by mid-1990, and 92 percent of members could not afford even the cheapest new houses being built at Z$8,000 (US$3,524). Without access to new houses or to the limited space in municipal rental shelter, thousands of the urban poor must depend upon lodging. Within Gweru, lodging ranges from part-rooms to rooms in houses, cottages, or servants' quarters and exists in different forms in areas of varying population densities, including periurban areas.

These figures underpin the urgency of the shelter situation, especially for female household heads within this housing delivery system. Have they benefited from recent conversion policies, or has circumstance continued to limit them to shared singles' quarters and hostels or informal lodging? The "voices" of the following group of representative women tenants illustrate some of the characteristic outcomes.

The "Voices" of Key Informants

The focus here is on the particular circumstances that many tenants have experienced in their lifetime migration-housing histories. By revealing, as far as possible, the problems concerning migration and shelter from "within," these "voices" can shed light on lived experience and lived space and assist in the interpretation of motivation, priority, and action—features of the human face of sociodemographic adjustment processes.

Key informants were chosen to represent a wide spectrum of tenants: young, middle-aged, and senior; widowed, single, divorced, and married; those in lodging and municipal rental shelter. Some of these respondents were in desperate situations, whereas others could be more hopeful about the future. Their names have been changed; their voices have not.

"Dorothy": Surviving as a Widow[3]

"Dorothy" was a widow who lived in municipal hostels (single rooms, often shared with another person or household) in Monomatapa.

I was born in rural Shurugwi in 1949, number eight of ten children. My father farmed. I stayed home to help my mother because my family could only afford to send me as far as standard [grade] five in school. I married in 1968, and I stayed in the same area as my parents and had two children. When my family first moved to Gweru in 1981, the four of us had to share a room with another family in municipal hostels. We did this for three years, paying Z$7 a month for rent.

When my marriage broke up in 1983, I sent my three children to live in the rural areas and I lodged in servants' quarters in town for Z$12 a month. I found that accommodation by walking around and looking, and I stayed there for two years. To get by, I sold vegetables for around Z$60 a month. My next [fourth] move was back to Monomatapa. Through Gweru City Council I shared part of a room in a house for Z$14 rent, but I had to move after two weeks when the owner sold the house.

I then went to city council and because my name was on the housing waiting list, I was given part of a room in a municipal hostel. My rent was Z$12.63. I have now [at the time of interview] been here for five years. When I moved to the hostel, my three children came back from the rural areas to live with me so that they could attend school. Right now I am getting by through selling vegetables and handicrafts. Staying in these hostels is better than lodging, since the owners of lodging houses are sometimes a problem. I am very independent but overcrowding and dirty toilets are problems here. It's overcrowded because there is a lack of accommodation and more people are coming into the cities and staying and they are not going back [to the rural areas]. As long as my children are in school, I plan to stay. But because the cost of living in town is very high, it is almost better to go to the rural areas and do some farming there and just come into town once in a while to sell vegetables. I just don't know about my future.

"Joyce": Family Problems in a Singles' Quarters

"Joyce" was a married woman who lived in singles' quarters in Monomatapa with two of her children.

I was born in 1959 in Bulawayo, the first out of six girls and two boys. My father worked as a domestic servant in Bulawayo and we just visited him during holidays. My sisters and brothers and I stayed in rural Gweru with my mother and grandparents. We had three traditional houses, one with three bedrooms and another with two bedrooms and a kitchen. In school, I went to standard [grade] seven. I married when I was twenty, but I stayed at home for a year, until the *lobola* [bridewealth] was paid. My husband worked at the air force base in Gweru and I had one child during that year. When the *lobola* was paid, we moved in with my father-in-law at a house on the air force base. We stayed with him one year without paying rent. From there, we moved in with my brother-in-law and his wife, who were living in a singles' quarters room in Monomatapa. With our child, there were five of us in the room, but again we did not pay rent and stayed for a few months.

When our name came to the top of the city council waiting list in 1982, we were given a room to ourselves and the rent for this is now Z$24.15 [in 1990]. My two younger children live with us here, but since my daughter is grown up [thirteen years old] the room is too small for her to stay here so she lives with her grandparents and goes to school in the rural areas. My husband works out of town for the air force and returns home on week-ends. I sell knitting and tablecloths to help the family. There are many problems with singles' quarters: dirty toilets, polluted water, too many diseases for children from this, and poor building maintenance. We have been looking for a better place for five years and we would like our own house. Even now, if we could find two rooms in lodging it would be better because we wouldn't have to share [facilities] and we could bring my daughter back to stay with us.

"Mary": Vulnerability and Adaptability

"Mary" was separated, with seven children from two marriages. As a lodger in Mkoba, she had experienced fourteen moves over her lifetime.

I was the second born of six children, and I lived with my family in six huts in the rural areas of Chibi. My father worked in South Africa and he only came [back to visit] once every three years. I went to school in the rural areas up to standard [grade] four. When I was twelve years old, I went to Beit Bridge to work with my father at a supermarket. We stayed there for two years and we lived in a caravan provided by employers.

When I was fifteen, I moved to Kadoma. I heard of this job from a teacher at school and I worked as a baby minder. It was at the mission and I had one room in a six-room house. After one year, I went back to rural Chibi where I stayed with my parents and farmed for one year. When I was seventeen, I married. My husband left his job in town to farm and we stayed in three of our own huts, one kitchen and two bedrooms, for three years. During this time, I had four children [including twins]. Then my husband left me to re-marry. My children and I returned to Lower Gweru to live with my parents. There were three adults and nine children and we farmed for five years.

After my father left to return to South Africa, I moved with my mother to my brother's house in rural Shurugwi. My mother farmed and I worked in a store. There were four bedrooms altogether in the house for myself, my mother, my four children and my brother, and there was a separate hut as well.

After a year, I moved to Gweru with my two youngest children to do a dressmaking course. My three older children remained in the rural areas. In

Gweru, I stayed in Village 10, Mkoba, in part of a room with relatives. I did not pay rent, but I helped to buy food. After eight months, I finished my course but I could not get a job. At that point, I married again and lived with my husband alone in a two-room municipal house in Village 5, Mkoba. The rent was Z$16 plus Z$3 for water, and there was no electricity. We lived there from 1981 to 1984, and my two youngest children came back to be with us.

When I separated from my husband, I moved to Village 13, Mkoba, and lodged in one room for Z$30, including utilities. Four children were with me, two from my second marriage, and I was then pregnant again. Over that year, I sent one child back to the rural areas. Because I was alone, all I could do was to sell handicrafts for income. When the owner of the house returned, I moved with my four children to stay with relatives in Village 7, Mkoba. There I paid Z$45 for one room, and this included utilities.

After three months, my name came up on the housing waiting list, and I was given a two-room house for Z$30 in rent. I sent one child back to the rural areas and stayed with my other three children while selling handicrafts. After one year, I lost my municipal [rental] house when my son and I became sick, and we had to stay in Bulawayo for three months.

When I went back to Gweru, I moved in with my grandparents and three of my children. It was a one-room house in Village 6, Mkoba. Since the rent was Z$45, I had to turn to prostitution to earn some income. After four months, I found lodging by walking around and looking. I moved into this two-room house in Village 4, Mkoba, in 1986 for Z$60 rent. Now I pay Z$60 for one room and utilities and I rent out the other room for Z$45. The owners of the house had gone to prison, but they wanted someone to look after their house. I have four children now with me, the youngest at five and the oldest at eighteen years. I like the yard because it is big enough for children and for a garden. The house is not well looked after as there are too many cracks, and I had to make my own door after the old one was damaged.

Since I started to go to church, I have quit prostitution. Now I go to Botswana once a month to buy materials such as cloth and wool to bring back and sell. My monthly income is around Z$400. Out of this, my expenses include rent (Z$60), maintenance of three children in the rural areas (Z$50 per month), school fees (Z$3 per child per term), and bus fare to Botswana (Z$64), plus food. I would like to own a four-room house so that all seven of my children could live with me. I would like it to be in Village 12 because they have bigger stands and it is nearer to church—but anywhere is OK. I have been happier with my life since I started to go to church and to make a decent living.

"Alice": A Grandmother's Experience

"Alice" was a fifty-nine-year-old grandmother who lived in one room in municipal married housing in Monomatapa.

I was born here in Gweru in town in 1930 and I was the fourth of seven children. My father was a driver for the municipality. We lived in Monomatapa in four tin huts for the family. There was a bucket system for an outside toilet and the huts were very hot in the summer. I went to standard [grade] one in school. When they built some of the houses in Monomatapa, they moved families from these tin houses. When I was thirteen, the municipality moved our family to a new three-room house in Monomatapa. The rent was two shillings and six pence per month for four years, then the rent went up by one shilling and six pence every year. The house was brick, with a tin roof, a bucket system and an outside tap. It was new and very clean. I lived there with my parents and my six brothers and sisters. I worked as a housegirl [domestic servant] in town between 1944 and 1951.

In 1952, I married and moved to Mambo with my husband. We lived in a four-room house owned by the Gweru Bowling Club, where my husband worked. The rent was deducted from his wage. There was a flush toilet beside our house, which was made of brick and tin. We were not allowed to have lodgers, and lights were turned off by the municipality at a certain time every night. I had nine children and we lived there together from 1952 to 1964. I liked the house and the big garden and my family was getting on very well because we were also close to relatives and friends. During this time, I sold vegetables and chickens and I also worked as a housegirl to help the family.

In 1964, when I separated from my husband, I moved to this one-room municipal house with three of my children. The rent was only Z$2.50 then, but it is now Z$24.10, with only a light for electricity. I worked as a domestic servant until 1971. Social welfare helped to feed my children for eight years, since my husband gave no support once he left me.

Now I live here with my three grown children and five grandchildren. Two of my children work and one is at college. I sew sacks into shopping bags and I sell the small ones for Z$1 and the large ones for Z$2. Every month, I make about Z$70 to Z$100 but this is not enough for two weeks of food. I was helping my children, and the problem with my grandchildren is the fathers do not help and I don't even know some of the fathers of my grandchildren.

I hope to own this house, since it is supposed to become home ownership. If I had a larger house, I would grow vegetables and chickens in the yard and I would take in lodgers. Monomatapa is a better place because the neighbors help me when I am in trouble, but we need more women's clubs and preschools here.

"Alina": Surviving with Her Family

"Alina" headed her own household as a lodger in town.

I was born in the rural areas of Botswana in 1945. I was the first of eleven children, so I stayed home to help my mother since my stepfather refused to send me to school. When I was fifteen, I married a teacher and we lived in four huts in the same rural area. When my husband died after four years, I had one child and I was pregnant with the second. I then stayed with his parents for a few months in the same district. With my two children, I returned to my parents' home, where I farmed until 1968.

In 1968, I married a policeman. We moved to Harare while my children stayed behind in the rural areas. We lodged in one room for seven years for Z$6. When my husband quit his job, we moved to his rural home in Chilipanze. Along with our child, we lived with sisters and grandparents and grandchildren so there were many huts. We all farmed.

In 1978, my husband got a job with the National Railways of Zimbabwe (NRZ) in Zvishavane. Here we lived with three sons in a nine-room NRZ house. During this time, I fought with my husband and was stabbed and burnt. When I got out of Gweru hospital, some nurses helped me to find a room in Riverside, and I lodged there with my three sons. We stayed for two years and paid Z$40 per month in rent. Since I had gone to court, my husband was supporting us.

Then we moved to a room in a two-room house in Mkoba. There, my three sons and I stayed with the owners and their eight children and we paid Z$25 for rent. These people were trying to help me as I had no other accommodation. In 1985, I found work as a housegirl in Southdowns, where I lived with my sons in their servants' quarters. I liked this job, but it only lasted six months, since my employers moved to Botswana. After that, we lodged for one year in one room in a servants' quarters in town. I found this very expensive, since the rent was Z$60, plus Z$10 per child per month, and Z$5 for myself for water, for a total of Z$95. This was out of support payments of Z$200 a month.

I am very happy with my present lodging [the twelfth lifetime move], which I found by walking around and looking. We stay in one room in the cottage in the [rear] yard. The four of us sleep in this one bed, and I cook on a hot plate. It is quiet here and not as crowded as the last place. I pay Z$60 in rent and then the water and electricity are divided up. I still get by on maintenance. For my oldest son, I must pay Z$80 tuition a term for school, and for the younger two, it is Z$50 each per term. Mealies cost Z$10 per month, and I buy vegetables but not much meat. I try to save, but in the end, I run short of money. The lodging house has been sold, and I am worried that we will have to move again.

Within the City:
Female-Headed Households in Gweru

Themes of frustration and consistent struggle emerge from these stories. Constantly on the move, most women have had to cope with the search for affordable shelter and have had to endure family fragmentation and develop economic survival tactics. Despite these hardships, tenacity and hope for individual and family survival within the city also surfaced. In the section that follows, their experiences are framed within the macroview of all female-headed households that were part of the larger study.

Types of Shelter

The informant accounts clearly show that household composition and size were affected by the interplay of various social, economic, and spatial factors. Women who either chose to be alone or who suddenly found themselves alone assumed the dual role of socializing their children and providing for the economic survival of the household. These changing circumstances often led to household fragmentation. For example, children might be left behind in the rural areas if their mother entered into another marriage, and they might either remain there indefinitely or only until the new household was established. Similarly, they would likely stay with the rural family while their "single" mother searched for formal employment or for the means to make a living informally.

Household composition appeared to be directly related to spatial factors such as the size and design of living quarters. If the urban household was restricted to part of a room or to one or two rooms, the family might become fragmented as younger children stayed and teenagers were sent to rural areas due to lack of space or culturally unacceptable sleeping arrangements. Spatial limitations have an impact not only on immediate family cohesiveness but also on the ability to host extended family members, who can assist with domestic tasks, child minding, and household maintenance. In addition, a household's ability to earn income, either by taking in lodgers or by having access to the yard for activities such as growing vegetables to sell, is very much a function of the type of rental shelter.

High-density municipal rental shelter within the city included four designs. Dual-occupancy dwellings were newer two-room, semidetached houses with shared toilets and showers. Married quarters included older two- to four-room houses, with pit latrines located at the rear of the plots. Both married and dual-occupancy dwellings were in the process of being converted to home ownership for the sitting tenants. Singles' quarters were older blocks of six to eight rooms, each with their own entrances and with washing facilities at the end of the building; in these quarters, two to three families shared a room. Hostels, the least expensive rental shelter type in the city, consisted of small older houses, each divided into four rooms with separate entrances and neighborhood sanitation facilities. Rooms were shared with another person or family.

Four out of every five low-income female-headed households surveyed resided in municipal married housing, singles' quarters, or hostels, with rents that ranged from Z$13.25 to Z$24.10 per month. Indeed, the particular street in Monomatapa that contained most of the hostels was referred to locally as "widow row."

As noted earlier, lodging of various types extends throughout the city. Lodging can be considered informal in that the agreement between the landlord or landlady and the tenant is oral, notice required is usually less than two weeks, and there is an informal network of information on lodging, such that many tenants find lodging by word of mouth or by walking around and searching.

Lodging was the most important shelter option for middle-income, female-headed households, with nearly six out of every ten categorized as lodgers. The reason for the predominance of this type of shelter was the extreme shortage of formal rental shelter (municipal, company, private, and government), the ease of entry into informal housing, the flexibility with respect to space rented, the importance of proximity to work over quality of shelter, and the low rent that was easier on the women's limited budget for housing.

Company or private rental housing in town or in low- to medium-density suburbs is the prevalent location choice for over 70 percent of high-income female household heads. Company shelter includes housing for company management and blocks of flats for company employees; thus, the one female respondent who occupied a company flat was a widow whose husband had been in management. Other heads of high-income women-centered households in this group rented houses or flats from estate agents, with rents ranging from Z$215 to Z$365. Since the low end of this range represented more than sixteen times the rent for a shared hostel room, this elite group was the exception to most female-headed households in the city.

The one type of formal rental shelter from which female household heads were absent within this survey was government-provided and subsidized shelter for civil servants. The gender ratio within the civil service was unknown, so the noted absence must suffice.

Household Composition

Female-headed households may be differentiated according to women who lived alone (42 percent) and those who lived with either younger or older children, or both (50 percent). For the entire group, household size ranged from 1 to 13, with an average of 3.6 persons. Very few had grandchildren, other extended family members, or nonrelatives living with them and just over one-fourth supported 5 or more persons in the household.

Table 8.1 illustrates various household characteristics for each socioeconomic group. Female-headed households were distributed across the

TABLE 8.1   Demographic and Household Features of Female-headed Households by Income Group

	Income Level		
Features	Low	Middle	High
Average size of households (no. persons)	3.7	2.1	3.9
Range of household size (no. persons)	1–12	1–4	1–13
Households with young children (> 15 years) present (%)	50.0	43.0	43.0
Households with older children (< 15 years) present (%)	38.0	29.0	43.0
Households that include extended family members (%)	13.0	0.0	14.0
Females who live alone (%)	42.0	43.0	43.0
Female-headed households in each income group (%)	64.0	18.0	18.0

Source: Author's own survey, 1990.

spectrum as 64 percent in low-income and 18 percent each in the middle-income and high-income groups. Altogether, low- and high-income groups had a similar average household size (3.7, 3.9) and range (1–12, 1–13). In contrast, middle-income households were smaller on average (2.1), with a lower range (1–4). One out of every 2 low-income households had younger children resident, a figure that was slightly higher than the two other income groups. In addition, a higher proportion of low- and high-income households included older children. The incidence of solitary female household heads was consistent across the three socioeconomic classes.

Two-thirds of these women had their status thrust upon them, either through broken marriages, abandonment, or death, and many were the sole family supporters. Widows and divorcées were prevalent among both low- and high-income groups, whereas single young professionals, many of whom had chosen independence, were more clearly represented in the middle-income segment.

Only a small percentage of low- and high-income households included extended family members. For poorer families, this was usually due to the lack of space for even the nuclear family unit, whereas for higher-income tenants this might signal weakening links with rural areas. For the total group, only one low-income household sublet to lodgers. Most tenants were constrained from taking in lodgers by lack of space and, perhaps more significantly, by the illegality of this practice in municipal housing (i.e., that which had not yet been converted to home ownership), company housing, and formal (estate agent) private houses and flats. Once municipal dual-occupancy or married housing was converted to home ownership, the "new owners" would be allowed to add a room for potential lodging income. Unfortunately, since most of the poor women in this study rented shared municipal singles' quarters and hostels (both of which were excluded from this scheme), they were destined to remain tenants, without access to shelter as an investment, as a source of income, or as a base for extended family members.

The average number of rooms rented by families in each income group increased from 1.2 for low-income to 1.5 for middle-income and to 4.6 for high-income households. A higher proportion of low-income households shared part of a room with other families. More than 7 out of every 10 low- and middle-income households lived in either a room or part-room. In contrast, the high-income group enjoyed domestic space that ranged from 2 to 8 rooms. The most crowded households were those of low-income families that were confined to one-room quarters, with an average of 3.7 persons per room.

In essence, shelter and household controlled the family unit in several ways. Although high-density municipal shelter was reasonably priced, most households were forced to sacrifice privacy when they shared rooms with other individuals and families. This necessitated cooperation and full use of the yard for domestic tasks and socializing. The advantage of "free" communal water weighed against the loss of privacy in the showers and bathrooms. As mentioned earlier, the inflexibility of space can also cause the fragmentation of the family, especially as children grow.

In contrast, lodging was more flexible with respect to space, for a household might have the option of renting an extra room, if available. However, the lodging situation also usually meant the presence of the landlord or landlady or a manager, which might entail their close monitoring of the lodgers' activities and might lead to conflict, especially over noise from children. Further, many landlords illegally discriminated against single women with children, either by refusing to rent to them outright or by charging extra (usually Z$5) for each child per month on the excuse of excess water consumption. Constant surveillance of the household, as well as the ever-present threat of eviction, served to enhance the sense of vulnerability and powerlessness of women and their families.

Women alone, the majority of whom do not benefit from employer-provided shelter, faced a constant search for reasonably priced shelter with features that would allow family cohesiveness, a measure of privacy, and minimal outside interference. This accommodation also had to fulfill household-centered priorities of location and neighborhood.

Socioeconomic Characteristics

The average rent for female-headed low-income households was Z$32.18, but it was the proportion of rent to income that was significant. The most disadvantaged, therefore, were those women whose monthly incomes were below Z$40 and for whom rent represented up to 85 percent of income. More than one-half of low-income households earned Z$80 or less per month, with rent absorbing from 36 to 72 percent of income.

In the larger study, 42 percent of all high-density households were in the low-income group. In contrast, 85 percent of female-headed high-density households were low income. This emphasizes the critically disadvantaged position of poor women with respect to chances of survival in the city.

Vulnerability of low-income households was heightened by the strong predominance of units that depended on one person for support. In addition, only one out of every five earners was engaged in wage labor. The remainder survived on self-employment, chiefly by selling their own handicrafts, although some were also selling vegetables or chickens. Many traveled to Botswana to bring back goods for resale or bulk goods for making handicrafts. For this group, only one household (the largest at twelve people) received help from a relative who lived outside of the household. Furthermore, lack of any child support from ex-husbands was a common characteristic. A few women admitted having to resort to prostitution—either currently or in the past—in order to pay the rent and buy food for their families.

With average rents between Z$75 and Z$169, middle- and upper-income households paid anywhere from 36 percent to less than 10 percent of their incomes for rent. All middle-income respondents relied upon a single worker; the type of support by worker occupation was divided evenly between formal and informal employment. One out of every four middle-income families received financial help from outside the household. All high-income respondents were engaged in wage labor and received no help from outside the household. In addition, one out of every three of these households had three income earners, two in wage labor and one in informal employment.

The level of education attained changed dramatically with the three groups. Three-fourths of the low-income women had received only some primary education, 30 percent in the middle-income group had some secondary education, and 43 percent of high-income women had attended either university or college. This highlights the "double jeopardy" of low skills and low education levels faced by the majority of low-income respondents. Many women expressed the need for training programs, clubs, and community support to build skills and ease burdens.

A very small proportion (5 percent) of female-headed households within this survey were retirees, whose insecurity was usually directly linked to living in an urban setting. For example, the one retiree within the middle-income group received financial help from two externally based family members. The complete absence of retirees within the low-income group has two possible explanations. First, the cost of living in the city is so high that those who wished to retire most likely returned to rural homes. Second, for those who decided to remain in the city, usually for the sake of family, the lack of resources, pensions, or savings, along with low skill levels, meant dependence upon the informal sector for survival. This tenuous economic situation constituted a precarious life in which any drop in income or extra expense was likely to lead to immediate deprivation, especially in food consumption.

Migration Patterns and Rural Links

Almost all female household heads had a rural home. Rural links were important for all respondents in the low- and middle-income groups but diminished in significance for high-income women, where less than one-half claimed rural ties. This trend fit closely with an examination of origins, where seven to eight out of every ten low- and middle-income women family heads were born in rural areas, whereas over two-thirds of those in the high-income group came either from other countries or from other urban areas. Those with rural homes were more likely to be high-density tenants in lodging or municipal shelter. Although the women had strong rural ties, a lack of time and money kept them from visiting rural homes as often as they wanted. Two-thirds reported that they could visit their home village six or fewer times a year.

Women who headed households generally lived in the city longer than male household heads. Most of these women originally moved to Gweru for either employment or family reasons, although their moving often entailed migration following marriage or joining a spouse who had attained work. A small percentage of women were new entrants in 1990, but over 40 percent had been there for between six and fifteen years and another 40 percent had been residents for over fifteen years. Hidden in this long-term residence was the transition faced by women like Dorothy, Mary, Alice, and Alina—the change from belonging to a male-headed, nuclear family to becoming the female head of a family as a result of abandonment and, in most cases, assuming the role of the solitary support and safety mechanism for the survival of the diminished family unit. Many women, in discussing the difficulties of urban life, expressed their decision to stay in town because they perceived urban surroundings to offer better access to education and health care for their children.

The study traced three previous migration steps of respondents. The most mobile were those who had lived in Gweru for more than five years and those in low- and middle-income groups. The high mobility associated with lodging was supported here with findings that 70 percent of lodgers had executed three or more migration steps. In contrast, the same proportion of municipal tenants had moved only twice. This corresponded with the situation wherein families must meet municipal housing list requirements before securing GCC accommodation and was supported by evidence that almost one-third of moves were from lodging to municipal housing. Over one-half of private or company respondents had moved twice, reflecting the difficulty of securing this type of formal rental shelter.

The majority of moves overall were between housing types and within the same density area, whereas movement between areas was usually from periurban to high-density townships. This pattern was mirrored by migration tendencies for all households in the larger study (Grant 1995).

The principal reasons for migration included family changes (marriage, divorce, death of a spouse), crowded conditions, securing better accommodation, gaining or losing employment, and transfers by Gweru City Council. To find new lodgings, movers depended upon the municipal housing waiting list, friends and relatives, or walking around and looking. This emphasized the significance of informal support networks.

Women household heads existed on the periphery—in terms of employment, shelter, maintaining their families, and attaining a future that extended beyond the realm of daily survival. They were marginalized by circumstances, by formal processes, and by their position within society. In essence, their economic and social vulnerability was both reflected in and reinforced by their shelter vulnerability. Low levels of education and skill served to relegate women to the less productive and less remunerative lower strata of informal activities. The instability of income that is a characteristic of this type of work was exacerbated by lack of support from absent husbands and by pressures exerted on the family unit through its urban locale and the necessity of cash for food, fuel, and school and health fees. The social vulnerability of female household heads was reflected in obstacles associated with securing and retaining urban shelter—many of which impediments evolved from a combination of circumstances: poverty, the presence of children, and the absence of an adult male, both for potential income and for social acceptance and empowerment of the household unit. Obstacles ranged considerably and included severe shortage of affordable formal rental shelter, particularly municipal, and exploitation by unscrupulous landlords or landladies. Shelter vulnerability heightened economic and social vulnerability. The absence of home ownership meant lack of space and opportunity for lodging income as well as lack of space to accommodate gardens and other small potentially income-generating projects. In addition, without ownership and control of household space, the possibility of hosting extended family members who could strengthen the household unit by providing domestic and income assistance was severely curtailed. Thus, shelter vulnerability was translated into inaccessibility to economic and social conditions that would promote the well-being of urban-based female-headed households; it also entailed a tenuous and uncertain existence that mitigated against any type of economic or social security.

But were women such as Dorothy, Mary, Alice, and Alina typical of other urban female household heads? The discussion of the national arena that follows places the Gweru survey results within the broader Zimbabwean context to see whether the possibilities of national changes and policies after 1980 have in any way reduced the conditions of vulnerability for women in the city.

Within the Nation:
Female-Headed Households in Zimbabwe

In 1981, the postindependence Zimbabwean government established the Ministry of Community Development and Women's Affairs, which assumed a mandate to "remove all customary, social, economic and legal constraints" that formed barriers against full participation by women in the development process (Sylvester 1991:50). Relevant legislation passed during this period included the Customary Law and Primary Courts Act (1981), the Legal Age of Majority Act (1982), the Labour Relations Act (1985), and the Matrimonial Causes Act (1985). The Legal Age of Majority Act ended the minority status of women and allowed them to own property, to enter marriage without parental or family consent, and to become guardians of children. Under the Matrimonial Causes Act, the grounds for divorce became the same for women and men, and upon divorce, women had the right to claim part of matrimonial property (Batezat and Mwalo 1989:51). However, despite the intent of the Matrimonial Causes Act to prevent situations where widows were left destitute by the husband's relatives seizing property, Welshman Ncube (1987) has criticized the act for falling short of its intent. Wide discretion was assigned to community courts, and though a widow could choose whether she wished to be inherited by the brothers of her deceased husband or stay in the matrimonial home, many women were unaware of the change in their legal status (Schlyter 1989:33).

Within a nuclear family, the role of the wife in reproduction and family caregiving was the cornerstone of the family unit. The extent of male control was such that husbands usually decided whether their wives were allowed to work. Urban women who entered into permanent unions with men and had their children but were not legally married were at a great disadvantage. These women were usually rejected by their own families, were unable to earn a living, and became totally dependent on their men (Cormack 1983:160).

Within a female-headed household, women assumed the additional burden of earning income for sustenance while also trying to keep the family intact. With few exceptions, these women faced barriers of low skills, little education, absence of a partner's help, and lack of support from the extended family.

Women's access to urban housing was precarious due to the synthesis of factors such as official barriers, marital and socioeconomic status, and personal circumstance. Although gender discrimination with respect to shelter was not necessarily always direct, women were distinctly at a serious disadvantage. For example, even within a marriage, a husband had the right to sell their home without the wife's consent (Schlyter 1989:35). In addition, it would be difficult to measure the extent to which women who were divorced, abandoned, or widowed lost their "stake" in the marital home. This would be particularly serious where homes were owned outright or were about to be converted to ownership by the local authority. Further, women who did not have proof of divorce might have difficulty adding their names to the municipal waiting list for a plot of land on which to self-build a house. Although attaining a plot may take years, at least self-building with access to small-scale loans would allow some progress according to the financial ability of the owner.

Domestic servants usually had access to servants' quarters as part of employment. Women were subject to employers' whims as to whether they would be allowed to have children with them or whether the family would be separated in order for the woman to keep the job. Lodging was the only viable shelter alternative for thousands of single women, and this created circumstances that added stress to the household's existence.

Although women all had personal priorities, often placing their children's education before anything else, access to their own housing was a vital key to their ability to adapt and succeed as household heads, agents of family cohesion, and successful urbanites. A house of their own represented a niche in the city, a base for extended family and for local networks, a chance for privacy and unity as a family, the potential for earning income, and evidence of success in the urban acculturation process.

Women household heads have been peripheralized through time, through space, within the economy, and within the social fabric. What is needed to improve their circumstances are programs that address the role of women in education, in employment, in society, and within the household. Without a measure of security in housing and employment, these women will continue to be a "separate nation" within Zimbabwe (Muchena 1982:57). Policymakers and society as a whole must listen closely as the "voices" break the silence of marginalization.

Notes

I wish to acknowledge the generous support of both the International Development Research Centre (Canada) and the Canada Mortgage and Housing Corporation in funding the fieldwork and analysis of this research.

1. Originally known to Africans as Senka, the site of Gweru was renamed Gwelo, after the Gwelo River, and was called by that name from the time of its founding by the British in 1894 until independence in 1980.

2. In 1965, the Unilateral Declaration of Independence (UDI) was made by the minority white government, led by Prime Minister Ian Smith, and was replaced by full independence in 1980 following a civil war.

3. In some of these accounts, the reporting of time may be slightly inaccurate, as one would expect with any retelling of events.

References

Barnes, T., and E. Win. 1992. *To Live a Better Life.* Harare: Baobab Books.

Batezat, E., and M. Mwalo. 1989. *Women in Zimbabwe.* Harare: SAPES Trust.

Cormack, I. 1983. *Towards Self-Reliance: Urban Social Development in Zimbabwe.* Gweru, Zimbabwe: Mambo Press.

Drakakis-Smith, D. 1987. "Urban and Regional Development in Zimbabwe." In *The Socialist Third World,* ed. D. Forbes and N. Thrift, 194–213. New York: Basil Blackwell.

———. 1992. "Urbanization and Urban Social Change in Zimbabwe." In *Urban and Regional Change in Southern Africa,* ed. D. Drakakis-Smith, 100–120. New York: Routledge.

Grant, M. 1991. "Rental Shelter as a Coping Mechanism in Gweru, Zimbabwe." Ph.D. diss., Queen's University, Kingston, Ontario.

———. 1995. "Movement Patterns and the Medium-Sized City: Tenants on the Move in Gweru, Zimbabwe." *Habitat International* 19(3):357–369.

ILO/Jaspa. 1986. *Women's Employment Patterns: Discrimination and Promotion of Equality in Africa: The Case of Zimbabwe.* Addis Ababa: JASPA/ILO.

Muchena, O. 1982. "Institutions and Women in Southern Africa—Strategies for Change—the Role of Women's Organisations." Paper presented at the Women in Southern Africa Conference, Harare.

Ncube, W. 1987. "The Legal Age of Majority Act in Zimbabwe." In *Women and Law in Southern Africa,* ed. A. Armstrong, 193–209. Harare: Zimbabwe Publishing House.

Peil, M., and P. Sada. 1984. *African Urban Society.* New York: John Wiley and Sons.

Phimister, I. 1988. *An Economic and Social History of Zimbabwe, 1890–1948.* London: Longman.

Schlyter, A. 1989. *Women Householders and Housing Strategies: The Case of Harare, Zimbabwe.* Gävle, Sweden: National Swedish Institute for Building Research.

Schmidt, E. 1992. *Peasants, Traders, and Wives: Shona Women in the History of Zimbabwe, 1870–1939.* Portsmouth, N.H.: Heinemann.

Stoneman, C., and L. Cliffe. 1989. *Zimbabwe: Politics, Economics, and Society.* London: Pinter.

Sylvester, C. 1991. *Zimbabwe: The Terrain of Contradictory Development.* Boulder: Westview Press.

UNICEF. 1985. *Situational Analysis of Women and Children in Zimbabwe.* Harare.

Part Four

Markets:
Work and Survival

9 ❧

Women in Business: Class and Nairobi's Small and Medium-Sized Producers

DOROTHY MCCORMICK

Small enterprise studies usually ignore business owners' social class, implicitly or explicitly assuming class differences to be minimal or unimportant. Yet a study that I conducted in 1986 on small-scale manufacturing in Nairobi suggested that, for the women business owners at least, class was not irrelevant (McCormick 1988). Poor women suffered from lack of business opportunity, whereas middle-class women outperformed their petit bourgeois counterparts. A follow-up study that I conducted in 1989–1990 attempted to refine and apply the analysis to a single industry, small-scale garment manufacturing. Some measures revealed little relationship between class and business performance, but when the form of business organization was taken into account, differences between middle-class and lower-class entrepreneurs emerged. This chapter presents a comparison of the notions of class used in the two studies and raises theoretical and methodological questions essential to analyzing the implications of class for small- and medium-sized enterprises.

Class Analysis in Africa

Class analysis—defining social classes and applying the definition to concrete situations—is integral to analytic approaches that look for political and social, as well as purely economic, explanations of economic change or stagnation. Marxian class analysis is often the starting point for such approaches. Yet neither an exclusively economic basis for class determination nor Marx's portrayal of the succession of the modes of production fits Africa very well (Cowen and Kinyanjui 1977; Sklar 1979; Kitching 1980; Schatzberg 1980; Lewin 1985). In most African countries, the size and importance of government bureaucracy and the persistence of patriarchal social and productive relations make *access* to the means of production as important as their *ownership*. The spouse of a mid-level civil servant may, for example, obtain a market stall more easily than another business owner. The younger brother of a wealthy businessman can legitimately expect to receive financial assistance for his struggling business. Class appears to make a difference. Yet empirical data from the 1989–1990 garment-industry study leave many unanswered questions about the significance of class. A description of small-scale manufacturing in Nairobi provides some necessary background for a better understanding of the role of class in urban business.

Small-Scale Manufacturing in Nairobi

Nairobi's small-scale manufacturers use simple tools and production techniques to make goods for local people, tourists, and the export market. The broad study on small-scale manufacturing conducted in 1986 in the Eastlands—the large, eastern half of the city containing approximately two-thirds of Nairobi's population—encompassed the full spectrum of manufacturing activities (McCormick 1988). The second study, conducted in 1989–1990, focused on a single industry, garment production, but included firms of all sizes (McCormick 1989; McCormick and Ongile 1993; McCormick and Kinyanjui 1994). The "small-scale" producers in the 1986 study had ten or fewer regular workers. Workers included owner operators, family members, and paid employees working more or less full time in the enterprise. Of the 2,800 firms surveyed, 78 percent were engaged in textile work, metalwork, or carpentry, with the remainder involved in shoe making, basket making, wood carving, and miscellaneous manufacturing activities. Women owned 23 percent of the firms overall but owned 45 percent of the textile firms. The second study attempted to analyze the position of small-scale garment firms within the larger context of garment production in general. A census counted 2,200 firms of various sizes making garments in Nairobi. Most (97 percent) were small scale; 70 percent were owned by women. The main data for the study were collected from 1989 to 1990 and included an initial survey of 268 firms that ranged in size from one-person enterprises to large factories with over 500 workers. Follow-up interviews and subsamples were collected up to 1994 to gather data on operations and machine acquisition. The last of the subsamples, carried out in mid-1993, surveyed 40 firms with between 4 and 49 workers and was designed to identify barriers to growth in employment.

Class Makes a Difference

Class emerged as a significant—but unexpectedly so—variable in the broad 1986 study. The data confirmed others' earlier findings that poor women are virtually excluded from small-scale manufacturing and further suggested that middle-class women are more likely than others to accumulate capital.

The Intuitive Definition

In the 1986 study, class emerged unexpectedly as a significant variable. Class was loosely defined in terms of access to the means of production (Sklar 1979; Schatzberg 1980), meaning that access did not require ownership, only the ability to mobilize productive resources. The degree of access to productive resources, then, defined class position. The intuitive definition of class applied to the women in this study led to an examination of the resources women could tap for entering or operating a manufacturing business. Poor women lacked skills, education, and money or other wealth. In contrast, middle-class women were better educated, owned land, and were usually married to men employed in Nairobi. By virtue of their own or their husbands' physical or financial assets, expertise, or influence, middle-class women had an advantage in beginning and operating businesses.

The 1986 survey gathered no data on social class because it was initially assumed that there would be no class distinctions among petty producers. During the fieldwork, however, I began to observe some differences, noting in particular the prosperous appearance of several women dressmakers. Jane Kinkonda (not her real name) is typical of such women. Mrs. Kinkonda was not included among the accumulators (prospering businesses four or more years old) because her business was still new, but she had already begun to increase her capital equipment. Her husband, a manager with the Kenya railroad, took an active interest in the business. He had stopped by on his lunch hour the day of the follow-up interview and provided information about business equipment for the study. It became clear then that Mrs. Kinkonda, and perhaps other women in her social class, enjoyed class advantage in business.

Opportunity and Capital Accumulation

Most of Nairobi's female entrepreneurs are concentrated in trade and service occupations (McCormick 1992). Manufacturing accounts for less than 2 percent of the women engaged in small-scale enterprise and self-employment (Ritter and Robicheau 1988). Within manufacturing, male and female business owners tend to enter different types of activities. In the 1986 sample, almost all of the women (88.3 percent) were involved in some sort of textile work.

The concentration of women in textile work appears to be not entirely by choice; rather, it is an indication of restrictions on women's, especially poor women's, entry into small-scale manufacturing. The Kenyan educational system, by teaching girls sewing, both channels them into textile work and fails to prepare them for other trades (McCormick 1988:75–76). The occupational distribution is also due to prevailing attitudes about the appropriateness of certain types of work. For example, one-half (52.2 percent) of the male business owners who were engaged in metalwork, carpentry, and other predominantly male occupations said they would accept a woman as a trainee or an employee, yet we observed no female production workers.

Exclusion from "male" trades poses no serious economic problem for women with the training and capital to begin a textile business, but it may bar unskilled poor women from manufacturing altogether. Most poor women have not stayed in school long enough to benefit from sewing classes, nor do they have the capital to begin a textile business. As can be seen from Table 9.1, textile work generally requires more initial capital than other trades. The "typical" (median) metalworker began a business with only KSh 655, one-third of the KSh 2,000 needed to start a textile firm.[1]

Poor women without the capital to start a tailoring or dressmaking business may be forced into less remunerative and more precarious occupations like petty trade, beer brewing, or prostitution (Nelson 1979; Bujra 1979; Greenstreet 1981), whereas similarly situated men can choose metalwork, carpentry, or wood carving.

Not only do middle-class women have an occupational choice their poorer sisters lack, they also seem better able to expand the businesses they begin. Specifically, the 1986 study found that women who accumu-

TABLE 9.1   Initial Capital by Trade

		Initial Capital		
Trade	Cases	Mean (KSh)	Std Dev (KSh)	Median (KSh)
Textile work	81	6,072	8,941	2,000
Carpentry	31	5,267	9,885	1,080
Metalwork	65	3,864	6,862	655
Other	37	2,417	8,740	500

Note: Significance of F-statistic for difference in means is .1385.
Source: Author's own survey, 1986.

lated capital were more likely than nonaccumulators to be landowners, giving them stronger rural linkages than other women. An "accumulator" was defined as a business that at the time of the survey was at least four years old and had a current depreciated value of capital equipment greater than its total initial capital. The calculation of depreciation assumed a ten-year life and no salvage value. Eight out of nine (89.2 percent) accumulators owned land or expected to inherit it, whereas just over one-half (56.4 percent) of the other women had comparable claims. All but one of the female accumulators were currently married, and all but one of them lived with their husbands and children in Nairobi.

Among male accumulators, strong rural ties seemed to indicate weaker commitment to the urban enterprise and were associated with lower incidence of capital accumulation (McCormick 1988:183–187). For women, the import of stronger rural ties is less clear. For one thing, these ties could indicate unreliability of data resulting from the small number of women's firms (twenty-six) old enough to be considered as possible accumulators. However, assuming the higher rate of rural landownership by female accumulators to be genuine, these women's landownership may be a sign of personal wealth. In Kenya, land is usually owned by men (Bujra 1979; Smock 1981), and if these women own land as individuals, they are clearly not poor. Thus, the stronger rural linkage may be an important indicator of membership in a social class higher than their roles as female petty producers would normally imply. Nonetheless, in responding to the question about owning land, the women may have been referring to their rights to land by virtue of their husbands' ownership. Indigenous land tenure practices in many areas guarantee women access to a portion of their household's land and control over certain crops (Nasimiyu 1985; Davison 1988). "Ownership" in this sense is less clearly a function of class.

Social class, then, may explain women's ability to accumulate capital in small-scale manufacturing enterprises. If women business owners are, in fact, of higher class than their male counterparts, then their higher incidence of capital accumulation may be the result of their greater access to needed resources.

The educational attainment, landownership, and husband's status of female accumulators all suggest that they may bring the benefits of higher social class to their business endeavors. The data analysis reveals that both for textile workers as a group and for the entire sample, women's formal educational attainment does not differ significantly from men's. Yet Kenyan girls have consistently received fewer educational opportunities than their brothers (Kinyanjui 1988; Robertson 1986). Furthermore, Janet Bujra (1979) has found that the poor and working-class women of Pumwani had significantly less education than their male neighbors. The equality observed in the small-enterprise owners therefore suggests that these well-educated women are of a higher class than the men. The landownership noted earlier could be another indication of female accumulators' higher social class. Furthermore, 63.3 percent of the accumulators' husbands are employed. Nairobi employment patterns suggest that roughly one-half of these men work for the state. Based on Michael Cowen and Kabiru Kinyanjui's (1977) work on straddling, we can deduce that these men are probably managers and senior officials whose positions afford their wives not only enough financial support to eliminate the need for substantial withdrawals from the business but also contacts assuring availability of raw materials, good markets for finished products, continued access to a market stall, and a variety of other benefits. Such access to resources could explain these women's ability to accumulate capital.

Weakness of the Analysis

The intuitive approach used in the 1986 study was weak on several scores. First, the notion of access to the means of production was vague. Second, the failure to anticipate the importance of class meant that relevant data were not collected and class assignment depended on informal observation. Third, the particular problems of applying class analysis to women—especially the possibility of differences in class within the same household—were not recognized. Fourth, the issue of rural ties was linked too strongly to landownership. The second study focused on the garment industry in an attempt to correct these weaknesses by carefully defining the class variable in a working paper prior to fieldwork and paying particular attention to the issue of women's class (McCormick 1989).

Questioning the Relevance of Class

One of the aims of the 1989–1990 garment industry study was to test the hypothesis that women business owners differ from their male counterparts in social class and, specifically, that women entrepreneurs are more likely than men to be middle class. This necessitated a clearer definition of "class" in general and of "middle class" in particular.

Class as Access

The essence of the intuitive definition is captured in John Roemer's (1986:96) notion of class as "differential ownership of or access to the means of production." Applying the definition requires specifying both the means of production and the channels of access. Fundamental to class analysis is the assumption that the higher classes will inevitably exploit the lower.

Marxian analysis focuses on the physical assets that permit higher classes to exploit. In this view, exploitation occurs because some people own the land, buildings, or equipment necessary to produce goods for the market, whereas others have nothing of value but their labor power. Ownership of physical assets allows capitalists to exploit, that is, to appropriate some or all of the value of the surplus labor of their workers.

In socialist societies and in the bureaucratic mixed economies typical of many African countries, however, two other unequally distributed assets can be the basis of exploitation: skill/credential assets and organizational assets (Wright 1986; Roemer 1982). Skilled people (experts) are often in a position to claim remuneration in excess of their per capita share of society's assets in labor power. Thus, in the Marxian sense, they are exploiters. Likewise, those with the authority to control and coordinate the state's productive activities (managers) are rich in organization assets. They not only receive higher than average salaries but also have ready access to facilities, equipment, licenses, and other means of production controlled by the state.

Using skill/credential assets and organization assets as subordinate relations of exploitation, Erik Olin Wright (1986) offers a schematic typology of capitalist classes (see Table 9.2). The schema is divided into two parts, one for owners of the means of production and one for nonowners. Owners are classified in the usual way, as bourgeoisie, small employers, and petit bourgeoisie. Within the nonowners section, a higher class position is indicated by a higher level of both skill assets and organization assets. Thus, the proletarian in the lower right section of the table has the least and is in the lowest class position, whereas those in other categories are in higher positions along a two-dimensional grid, indicating their ac-

TABLE 9.2 Basic Typology of Exploitation and Class; Assets in the Means of Production

Owners	Nonowners (wage laborers)		
1. Bourgeoisie	4. Expert manager	7. Semicredentialed manager	10. Uncredentialed manager
2. Small employer	5. Expert supervisor	8. Semicredentialed supervisor	11. Uncredentialed supervisor
3. Petit bourgeoisie	6. Expert nonmanager	9. Semicredentialed worker	12. Proletarian
	+ $\longleftrightarrow$ –		
	Skill/Credential Assets		

Organization Assets: + $\longleftrightarrow$ –

Source: Erik Olin Wright, "What Is Middle About the Middle Class?" in Analytical Marxism, ed. John Roemer (Cambridge: Cambridge University Press, 1986), 127.

cess to both skill assets and organization assets. The expert manager thus has the most assets among nonowners. Wright argues that two distinct groups comprise the middle classes: those who have precisely the *per capita* level of the relevant asset and are thus neither exploited nor exploiting; and those who are exploited on one dimension while exploiting on another. Those simultaneously exploiting and exploited make up the "new" middle classes. In the following analysis, the middle classes include only those with above-average power to exploit some asset. Therefore, small employers and those in the three "expert" and three "manager" categories are middle class, but the petit bourgeois self-employed producer with average capital stock and the semicredentialed supervisor with ordinary organization and skill assets are not automatically included in the middle class.

Whether these or others can be described as middle class depends on their access to the means of production. Some without superior physical, skill, or organization assets may be able to draw on the assets of others. The previously mentioned spouse of a civil servant and the younger brother of a business executive fall into this category. Middle-class membership defined by access through others is less clear-cut than membership that rests only on the individual's own assets, yet it is no less real. It is undeniable that some people have improved access to productive resources by virtue of the class position of their spouse or relatives. Some might argue that this reasoning leads to an inflated membership in the middle class, since almost everyone knows someone with superior physical, organizational, or skill assets, but this view is erroneous for two reasons. First, the strong family ties in African society that require well-off persons to assist their relatives do not similarly bind them to friends and acquaintances. Thus, in judging class position for the study, only spouses and relatives are considered important. Second, middle-class or bourgeois relatives are not in themselves sufficient to guarantee membership in a particular class. To render another middle class, a person must be willing to put physical, skill, or organizational assets at the other's disposal. The middle class, therefore, includes experts, managers, small employers, and those individuals with a bourgeois or middle-class spouse or relative who is willing to assist them.

Applying the definition of class requires knowledge of the way the Kenyan social structure affects both men and women. For example, most analysts assume that women's class is the same as that of related men: husbands, fathers, or brothers. Yet African women often differ from their husbands and male relatives in ownership rights and access to resources (Robertson 1988:182). Since incomes and family financial obligations are not always pooled, women and men in the same household may occupy different class positions (Robertson 1984; Folbre 1986; MacGaffey 1988;

Stichter 1988). Judging a woman's social class, therefore, requires knowing what assets she owns or can tap. A woman who is an expert, manager, or small employer is clearly middle class. A woman with bourgeois or middle-class relations may also be, but only if she can legitimately expect these relatives to use their position for her benefit.

The foregoing discussion suggests three criteria for membership in the middle class. A business owner is middle class if any one of these criteria applies. First, business owners who are primarily managers are middle class. For the 1989–1990 study, a business owner with two or more employees whose main work was not the production of clothing is considered middle class. Forty-seven (19.8 percent) of the business owners fit this definition of middle class (see Table 9.3). Second, business owners who are experts or managers in government or other businesses are middle class. Thus, a business owner with a university degree or professional training after form 6 (secondary school) who works in a professional or managerial capacity elsewhere is considered middle class. Only three business owners met this definition of middle class. Finally, a business owner is middle class if the spouse is an expert or manager and has helped to begin or operate the business. Fourteen business owners, all women, were middle class in this sense. In four cases, business owners were middle class by two criteria. Two, both women, were primarily managers and also had expert spouses. Two others, both men, were primarily managers and were experts or managers in another business as well. Fifty-seven business owners (23.9 percent) met one or more of the conditions for middle-class membership. Contrary to our expectations,

TABLE 9.3   Middle-Class Status by Sex

	Men		Women		Total	
Criterion	N	%	N	%	N	%
Primarily managerial work	15	80.0	33	70.2	47	73.4
Expert or manager in other work	3	20.0	0	0.0	3	4.7
Expert spouse who helped	0	0.0	14	29.8	14	21.9
Total middle class	15	23.8	42	24.1	57	23.9
Total business owners	63	26.5	174	73.1	238	100.0

Note: The weighting of sample data sometimes results in fractional cases. The rounding of these amounts means that items may not always sum to the total.

Source: Author's own survey, 1989.

TABLE 9.4   Small Garment Producers by Sex of Owner, Age of Firm

	Male		Female		Business Age in Years		
Firm Size	N	%	N	%	M	F	All
1 person	20	32.2	63	36.2	9.0	4.9	5.9
2–3 person	26	41.9	75	43.1	6.8	6.2	6.3
4–6 person	13	21.0	32	18.4	9.9	7.3	8.1
7–10 person	3	4.8	4	2.3	26.2	8.6	15.3
Overall	63	100.0	174	100.0	9.1	6.0	6.8

Note: Significance of F-statistic for difference in mean business ages by sex is .003; by firm size, .002. The weighting of sample data sometimes results in fractional cases. The rounding of these amounts means that items may not always sum to the total.

Source: Author's own survey, 1989.

men and women were equally likely to be middle class, and class, as defined, had no apparent impact on business success.

Men's and Women's Businesses

The garment industry is one of the few areas of manufacturing with substantial numbers of female entrepreneurs. Table 9.4 shows the breakdown of firms by sex of the owners.[2] Women's businesses are younger than men's, especially the very small, one-person businesses and the businesses with seven to ten workers. In both categories, men's businesses include a few very old firms that significantly affect the mean for the group. This is most apparent in the seven-to-ten-person category that includes few firms. Overall, the three-year age difference between men's and women's firms, noted in the 1986 survey, has remained virtually unchanged in the second study.

The most striking feature in the search for distinguishing characteristics of women's firms in the second study is that in the most important measures—profitability and capital accumulation—they do not differ markedly from men's. Nor did women differ from male business owners in present age, age when they entered the current business, education, or training.

Although many of the women entrepreneurs conform to the popular notion of the woman as the second earner in a family, a disproportionate number were single, widowed, or divorced. Twenty-four percent of women were single, widowed, or divorced, compared with 16 percent of

TABLE 9.5   Performance of Small Garment Firms: Selected Indicators by Sex

| | | Mean Amounts | | | |
Sex of Owner	Net Income (KSh)	Total Capital (KSh)	Labor Intensity (KSh)	Profit Rate (%)	Rate of Capital Accum. (%)
Men	173,061	108,516	2.565	.4202	.64421
Women	94,815	50,923	1.672	.3458	.80871
F-statistic	2.651	5.280	3.531	1.177	.6725
Significance	.105	.022	.062	.279	.4130
N	237	236	233	236	231

Source: Author's own survey, 1989–1990.

men.[3] Although men and women averaged the same number of dependents, women counted on their business earnings less than men. On average, men derived 89 percent of the money required to support themselves and their dependents from business income, whereas women got 68 percent from the business and the rest from other sources.

Similarly, women and men differed little in their business operations. They spent roughly the same amounts of time on their various business activities. Table 9.5 shows some of the key indicators for men's and women's firms.

Women's businesses appear to be more capital intensive, but they have on average less total capital. Capital intensity, in this context, is the ratio of total capital value to labor costs. Further analysis by size of firm reveals similarities between men's and women's firms at the smaller size ranges but shows striking differences within the seven-to-ten worker range. Table 9.6 illustrates these differences.

Examination of the individual firms in the seven-to-ten-person category reveals that the means for total capital in firms owned by men are skewed by three firms having KSh 2.6 million, 1.5 million, and 1.4 million, respectively. The highest total capital for a firm owned by a woman is KSh 891,000, with the second-highest at KSh 428,000. The three large men's firms are among the oldest businesses in the sample. The first is sixty-five years old; the second, thirty-nine years old; and the third, sixty-three years old. All are located in workshops in town. Although their numbers of workers put them in the seven-to-ten category, in other respects they more resemble medium-sized firms. If these three are consid-

TABLE 9.6   Selected Size Indicators for Firms with Seven to Ten Workers, by Sex

	Mean Amounts (Ksh) Firm Ownership	
	---	---
Item	Male	Female
Net income	920,837	473,872
Labor cost	157,075	87,211
Total capital	783,127	203,725
Total equipment	351,454	54,330
Inventory value	275,736	117,745

Notes: Sample size, n = 21 (8 men, 13 women); n weighted to population is 7. Differences in means are not statistically significant.
Source: Author's own survey, 1989–1990.

ered special cases, then little difference between men's and women's firms remains.

Women and Class

If men's and women's business performance is essentially the same, must we conclude that class has no relevance? Not necessarily. Class could explain differences in performance within the group of women entrepreneurs. The logic of the 1986 study suggests that middle-class women should outperform their poorer counterparts precisely because of their better access to resources necessary for business. We might reasonably expect both their rate of profit and their rate of capital accumulation to be higher. Yet, as Table 9.7 clearly shows, the forty-two middle-class women surveyed in the later study did not differ significantly from the other female entrepreneurs in these key performance measures.

TABLE 9.7   Rates of Profit and Capital Accumulation for Female Owners of Small Garment Firms by Class

	Class of Business Owner	
	---	---
Performance Measure	Middle Class	Other
Rate of profit	0.293	0.363
Rate of capital accumulation	0.777	0.819

Note: Differences in mean rates are not statistically significant.
Source: Author's own survey, 1989–1990.

Class and Firm Type

Nairobi's garment-producing firms vary not only in size but also in form. Closer examination of a group of middle-sized garment producers suggests that firms differ in their market relations, entrepreneurial networks, and operational problems (McCormick and Ongile 1993; McCormick and Kinyanjui 1994). The ability to deal successfully with certain problems—especially those related to resources—may depend on the entrepreneur's social class.

The typical tailor or dressmaker is quite unlike the mass-producing exporter in many respects. Informal observation of such differences led to an attempt to classify firms based on their differing relationships to input and product markets. The approach rests on theories of the firm that explain an enterprise's internal organization in terms of its market relations (Williamson 1975; Coase 1937; McGuinness 1991). Nairobi's garment industry has at least four distinct types of firms: custom tailors, contract workshops, minimanufacturers, and mass producers (McCormick and Kinyanjui 1994). The first and apparently largest group consists of *custom tailors*, who produce men's and women's garments to order. The owner of the business is often a tailor, who employs between two and five other skilled tailors. One could argue that such firms are not manufacturers at all. Some custom tailors mainly provide the labor and require the customer to supply the cloth and, sometimes, other inputs such as buttons, zippers, or lining. Others are fabric retailers who employ tailors as a service to their customers. The second category consists of *contract workshops*. Like custom tailors, these firms will make whatever a customer wants. Contract workshops, however, produce in quantity. A workshop may make an order of fifty uniforms for bank employees, provide choir robes for a local church, or outfit a complete wedding party. Sometimes the firm supplies the cloth, sometimes the customer does. The typical contract workshop uses a production process with little or no division of labor, though some owners consider cutting the cloth as a task important enough to be reserved for one person. Skilled tailors, often hired only for the duration of a particular contract, are expected to sew entire garments. The third group of firms, *minimanufacturers*, use a scaled-down version of mass-production technology. Some specialize in high-fashion garments that are marketed through specialty shops in town or in shopping centers in high-income neighborhoods. Most, however, produce at the low end of the price spectrum. Such firms generally concentrate on one or two products such as boys' school uniform shorts, women's petticoats, or men's trousers. They may use a combination of skilled and unskilled workers and often have some rudimentary division of labor. Garment manufacture may, for example, be divided into cutting, assembling, finishing, and pressing. The final group consists of *mass producers*, who manufacture

TABLE 9.8   Entrepreneur's Sex and Education by Firm Type

	Firms		Sex	
Firm Type	N	%	Male %	Female %
Custom tailor	13	33.7	41.2	58.5
Contract workshop	4	9.6	72.9	27.1
Minimanufacturer	22	54.6	20.8	79.2
Mass producer	1	2.1	100.0	0.0
Total	40	100.0	34.7	65.3

Notes: Cases are weighted to reflect entire population of firms in 4–49 employment range. The significance of the chi-square statistic for differences in sex by type of firm is .0926; the lambda statistic for dependence of sex on firm type is .2017.

Source: Author's own survey, 1993.

standardized goods using assembly-line production techniques. Mass producers' superior production facilities enable them to make good quality garments for the middle-income market.

Table 9.8 shows the gender breakdown of the various firm types. Women entrepreneurs are overrepresented in minimanufacturing enterprises, underrepresented in contract workshops, and totally absent from mass production. Custom tailoring is the most balanced, with 41.2 percent male entrepreneurs and 58.5 percent female. Further analysis of the two largest categories, custom tailors and minimanufacturers, suggests that the entrepreneur's social class affects a firm's prospects for growth. The relationship between class and growth is especially strong for minimanufacturers, the firm type with the highest proportion of female entrepreneurs. Minimanufacturers are generally less educated, have close ties to the rural areas, and are unlikely to have access to significant resources through their spouse or other relatives. Most operate from two large markets that offer them cheap space and benefits of proximity to other producers, but in other respects these firms are inadequate and unsuited to manufacturing. The minimanufacturers have found a market niche that enables them to make good use of their particular social networks. They sell their inexpensive products through wholesalers to consumers in small towns and market centers outside of Nairobi (McCormick and Kinyanjui 1994).

The data for minimanufacturers suggest a relationship between class and a firm's ability to grow (see Table 9.9). Firms run by middle-class entrepreneurs were much more likely to be growing or stable over the four-year period 1989–1993 than firms with lower-class owners. Nearly two-

TABLE 9.9 Minimanufacturers by Class, Sex, and Firm Growth

Class	Firms N	Shrinking Male Percentage	Shrinking Female Percentage	Growing or Stable Male Percentage	Growing or Stable Female Percentage
Not middle class	9	79.3	63.7	0.0	7.4
Middle class	12	20.7	36.3	100.0	92.6
Total	22	47.0	65.5	53.0	34.5

Note: The lambda statistic for dependence of the dichotomous variable *growing* on class is .404. The lambda statistic for dependence of *growing* on sex is .033.

Source: Author's own survey, 1993.

thirds of the firms with middle-class owners added workers or maintained their 1989 employment levels, whereas the vast majority (95.3 percent) of other minimanufacturers shrank. All (100 percent) of the male owners and nearly all (92.6 percent) of the female owners of growing or stable minimanufacturing firms were middle class. In contrast, most owners (79.3 percent of the men and 63.7 percent of the women) of shrinking firms were not middle class. Differences between men and women were not statistically significant.

Because minimanufacturers must buy raw materials without the benefit of customer deposits, they need either supplier credit or adequate working capital. Because they sell low-priced clothing in highly competitive markets, minimanufacturers have very low profit margins that make generating capital internally difficult. These enterprises also have the least access to credit of all the firm types (McCormick and Kinyanjui 1994). For such firms, the class position of the owner could mean the difference between growth and decline. A middle-class owner could invest personal resources to supplement working capital or use professional networks to secure needed credit. These owners' class position provides options that lower-class owners lack. Those without such class advantages may have to pass up orders when they cannot finance the supplies and, at some point, lay off workers to cut costs.

Conclusion

Many see small enterprise as a way out of poverty. Yet this analysis suggests that those who already have resources are most likely to succeed.

The disadvantages of class and gender combine to bar the poorest, least-educated women from any type of small-scale manufacturing. Women who manage to start a tailoring or dressmaking business are likely to be custom tailors or minimanufacturers. Few have contract workshops, and none have moved into mass production. Class appears related to performance for both male and female entrepreneurs. The relationship is especially strong in minimanufacturing, where most women are concentrated. Nearly all of the owners of growing or stable firms but only one-third of the owners of shrinking firms were middle class. It seems that lower-class entrepreneurs—both women and men—lack the means to take advantage of business opportunities leading to growth. Thus, instead of providing a means of upward social and economic mobility, participation in small enterprise may simply reinforce the existing class structure.

Notes

1. In early 1986, when this research was conducted, the Kenya shilling remained fairly steady at KSh 16 to US$1.

2. The unweighted sample included ten firms in which ownership consisted of both men and women. Because of the personal nature of many of the survey questions, these firms have generally been classified according to the sex of the owner who was interviewed. Table 9.10 shows the actual breakdown by sex.

3. The chi-square statistic for the cross-tabulation between sex and marital status was 9.06, with a significance of .01.

TABLE 9.10   Ownership of Nairobi Garment Manufacturing Firms

Firm Size	Unweighted Sample (N)			Weighted to Population (%)			
	M	F	M–F	M	F	M–F	Total
1 person	15	46	0	8.2	25.7	0.0	34.0
2–3 person	25	72	4	10.1	29.5	1.6	41.3
4–6 person	17	38	1	5.6	12.7	0.4	18.8
7–10 person	8	10	3	1.1	1.6	0.4	3.1
11–50 person	9	4	1	1.1	0.4	0.0	1.5
Over 50	14	0	1	1.4	0.0	0.0	1.4
Total	88	170	10	27.7	69.7	2.6	100.0

Source: Author's own survey, 1989.

References

Bujra, Janet M. 1979. "Proletarianization and the 'Informal Economy': A Case Study from Nairobi." *African Urban Studies* 3:47–66.

Coase, R. H. 1937. "The Nature of the Firm." *Economica* 4:386–405.

Cowen, Michael P., and Kabiru Kinyanjui. 1977. "Some Problems of Capital and Class in Kenya." Discussion paper, Institute for Development Studies, University of Nairobi.

Davison, Jean. 1988. "Who Owns What? Land Registration and Tensions in Gender Relations of Production in Kenya." In *Agriculture, Women, and Land: The African Experience*, ed. Jean Davison, 157–176. Boulder: Westview.

Folbre, Nancy. 1986. "Cleaning House: New Perspectives on Households and Economic Development." *Journal of Development Economics* 22:5–40.

Greenstreet, Miranda. 1981. "When Education Is Unequal." *IDS Bulletin* 12:14–18.

Kinyanjui, Kabiru. 1988. "Educational Opportunities for Girls at Secondary-School Level: The Need for a Curriculum to Enhance Women's Education." Institute for Development Studies, University of Nairobi. Photocopy.

Kitching, Gavin. 1980. *Class and Economic Change in Kenya: The Making of an African Petite Bourgeoisie, 1905–1970*. New Haven: Yale University Press.

Lewin, A. C. 1985. "The Dialectic of Dominance: Petty Production and Peripheral Capitalism." In *Planning for Small Enterprise in Third World Cities*, ed. Ray Bromley, 107–135. Oxford: Pergamon Press.

MacGaffey, Janet. 1988. "Evading Male Control: Women in the Second Economy in Zaire." In *Patriarchy and Class: African Women in the Home and the Workforce*, ed. Sharon B. Stichter and Jane L. Parpart, 161–176. Boulder: Westview.

McCormick, Dorothy. 1988. "Small Manufacturing Enterprise in Nairobi: Golden Opportunity or Dead End?" Ph.D. diss., Johns Hopkins University, Baltimore, Md.

———. 1989. "Garmentmaking in Nairobi: A Research Proposal." Working Paper no. 468, Institute for Development Studies, University of Nairobi.

———. 1992. "Gender, Participation, and Performance in Nairobi's Small-Scale Manufacturing Sector." Paper presented to the meeting of the International Network for Research and Action on the Role of Women in the Informal Sector, organized by the United Nations Educational, Scientific, and Cultural Organization (UNESCO), Bogor, Indonesia, 2–5 November 1992.

McCormick, Dorothy, and Mary Njeri Kinyanjui. 1994. "Networks, Markets, and Growth in Nairobi's Garment Industry." Draft research report on Barriers to Small-Firm Growth, International Centre for Economic Growth and Institute for Development Studies, Nairobi.

McCormick, Dorothy, and Grace Ongile. 1993. "Growth and Organisation of Production: Case Studies from Nairobi's Garment Industry." IDS Discussion Paper no. 294, Institute for Development Studies, University of Nairobi.

McGuinness, Tony. 1991. "Markets and Managerial Hierarchies." In *Markets, Hierarchies, and Networks: The Coordination of Social Life*, ed. Grahame Thompson et al., 66–81. London: Sage.

Nasimiyu, Ruth. 1985. "Women in the Colonial Economy of Bungoma: Role of Women in Agriculture, 1902–1960." *Journal of Eastern African Research and Development* 15:56–73, special issue on Women and Development in Africa.

Nelson, Nici. 1979. "How Women and Men Get By: The Sexual Division of Labor in the Informal Sector of a Nairobi Squatter Settlement." In *Casual Work and Poverty in Third World Cities*, ed. Ray Bromley and Chris Gerry, 283–302. New York: John Wiley and Sons.

Ritter, A.R.M. and R. Robicheau. 1988. "The Urban Small-Scale Enterprise Sector: Information from the 1986 Urban Labour Force Survey." Technical Paper 88-02, Long-Range Planning Unit of the Ministry of Planning and National Development, Nairobi, Kenya.

Robertson, Claire. 1986. "Women's Education and Class Formation in Africa." In *Women and Class in Africa*, ed. Claire Robertson and Iris Berger, 92–113. New York: Holmes and Meier.

Robertson, Claire C. 1984. *Sharing the Same Bowl: A Socioeconomic History of Women and Class in Accra, Ghana*. Bloomington: Indiana University Press.

———. 1988. "Invisible Workers: African Women and the Problem of the Self-Employed in Labour History." *Journal of Asian and African Studies* 23:180–198.

Roemer, John. 1982. *A General Theory of Exploitation and Class*. Cambridge: Harvard University Press.

———. 1986. "New Directions in the Marxian Theory of Exploitation and Class." In *Analytical Marxism*, ed. John Roemer, 81–113. Cambridge: Cambridge University Press.

Schatzberg, Michael G. 1980. *Politics and Class in Zaire: Bureaucracy, Business, and Beer in Lisala*. New York: Africana.

Sklar, Richard. 1979. "The Nature of Class Domination in Africa." *Journal of Modern African Studies* 17:531–552.

Smock, Audrey Chapman. 1981. "Women's Economic Roles." In *Papers on the Kenyan Economy*, ed. Tony Killick, 219–227. Nairobi: Heinemann Educational Books.

Stichter, Sharon B. 1988. "The Middle-Class Family in Kenya: Changes in Gender Relations." In *Patriarchy and Class: African Women in the Home and the Workforce*, ed. Sharon B. Stichter and Jane L. Parpart, 177–204. Boulder: Westview.

Williamson, O. E. 1975. *Markets and Hierarchies: Analysis and Antitrust Implications*. New York: Free Press.

Wright, Erik Olin. 1986. "What Is Middle About the Middle Class?" In *Analytical Marxism*, ed. John Roemer, 114–140. Cambridge: Cambridge University Press.

10 ᴂ

Beyond Simple Survival: Women Microentrepreneurs in Harare and Bulawayo, Zimbabwe

MARY JOHNSON OSIRIM

In academic and policy circles, discussion has been mounting in the 1980s and 1990s about the need for economic restructuring in both the West and the newly industrializing countries. With respect to the Third World, this has most often meant the establishment of austerity and structural adjustment programs (SAPs) by national governments at the behest of the multilateral lending community. In sub-Saharan Africa, the introduction of such policies in many nations has resulted in increased financial hardship for people at the bottom of the socioeconomic hierarchy (Onimode 1989; Gladwin 1991). Among those most adversely affected by the initiation of structural adjustment programs have been urban women who work in the informal economies of Third World nations and bear the brunt of escalating food prices and the removal of government subsidies for vital social services.

In the early 1990s in Harare and Bulawayo, Zimbabwe, market traders, crocheters, and self-employed seamstresses and hairdressers were among the many women microentrepreneurs to experience undue suffering as a result of the reductions in government spending, growth in unemployment and food expenditures, and the bans on some imports for production. Cutbacks in government spending were part of the justification for reducing official support for women's issues, and in the early 1990s women's affairs was moved from the Ministry of Community, Cooperative Development, and Women's Affairs to the Ministry of Political Affairs with an office at the headquarters of the major political party, ZANU-PF (Zimbabwe African National Union–Patriotic Front). This reflected a general slowdown in attempts to meet the needs of poor, self-employed women. In addition, although the postindependence government has made many efforts to advance the status of women in Zimbabwe, most women are still plagued by continued patriarchy in the public and private spheres.

Despite the difficulties imposed by the economy, the state, international capital, and the persistence of patriarchy, urban women microentrepreneurs in Zimbabwe continue to make substantial contributions to the maintenance of their families and the development of human capital. This chapter explores the contributions of self-employed women in the above-mentioned subsectors of the economy by examining why and how they establish and operate their businesses; the problems they have encountered as mothers, wives, and microentrepreneurs; and their aspirations for the future. How have these women navigated the urban landscape and managed to keep their enterprises afloat? Information on these issues was collected over several months in 1991, when I conducted intensive interviews with 55 women in Harare and Bulawayo who were self-employed as crocheters, hairdressers, seamstresses, and market traders. Policy recommendations are also offered in an effort to address those critical issues that limit not only the growth and viability of these businesses but also the likelihood of these businesswomen to realize their goals.

The Global Division of Labor and the Urban Informal Economy

Scholars in the sociology of development and feminist researchers on development have noted the increased specialization of production into specific poles of the North and the South during the past two and one-half decades. From the late 1960s to the 1980s, dependency and world-systems theorists postulated a growing international division into core and periphery regions, later adding the concept of the semiperiphery. However, these models are no longer adequate to illustrate the growing complexity in demarcation of production centers and markets around the globe and the international division of labor based on gender (Frank 1969; Cardoso and Faletto 1978; Evans 1979; and Wallerstein 1974). In the early

1980s, feminist scholars and development theorists correctly acknowledged the growth of an international capitalist system in which the labor force was increasingly stratified, not only according to region but by gender. In many areas of the South where transnational capital seeks cheap labor, young unmarried women are often a target of these employers (Young et al. 1984).

Although the Third World as a whole can no longer be viewed as solely a source of primary products, some areas of the South, such as most of sub-Saharan Africa, are encouraged to develop export-oriented economies that rely on trade in primary products. Throughout much of sub-Saharan Africa, including Zimbabwe, where Western governments and multilateral agencies are supporting efforts to "shrink the state" by removing it from the economy and by decreasing the number of state employees under SAPs, the sector of the economy that is perhaps growing most rapidly is the urban informal sector (Saito 1991). Under SAPs, when many formal sector employees are retrenched in attempts to cut government spending, women and men are increasingly forced to find income-generating activities to provide resources for the household. Whereas men can seek opportunities in the informal economy, most urban women, due to a history of patriarchy and socialization based on gender, have no other employment options besides work in the urban subsistence sector.

What is the informal economy and what are its major characteristics in sub-Saharan Africa today? The earliest and most widely recognized definition of the informal sector is derived from the International Labour Office's (ILO) Report on Kenya in 1972: "This sector can be characterized by its ease of entry, reliance on indigenous resources, family ownership of enterprises, small scale of operations, labor-intensive and adapted technology, skill acquired outside the formal school system, and unregulated and competitive markets" (ILO 1972).

In some of the earliest efforts to define the informal economy, formal and informal activities were viewed as dichotomous. Many theorists in this area have highlighted the efforts of urban microentrepreneurs to circumvent the regulations of the state to thereby avoid taxes, state-legislated minimum wages, and other laws (MacGaffey 1986; Portes et al. 1989).

Social scientists have more recently emphasized the interrelationship and interconnectedness of the formal and informal economies. Several authors have agreed that the informal economy is indeed growing in the North and the South, although in many cases, the characteristics associated with this sector differ (Portes et al 1989; Feldman 1991). Monetary exchanges and subcontracting arrangements do exist between the formal and informal sectors in areas of Latin America and in nations of the Pacific Rim, although in sub-Saharan Africa subcontracting arrangements are not prevalent. Those that regard the informal economy as petty commodity production recognize the interrelationship of this sector to the formal economy, but they stress the fact that relations in the former are typified by subordination and exploitation (LeBrun and Gerry 1975; Feldman 1991). Alejandro Portes, for example, admits that conditions for workers in informal sector firms can be very oppressive, but he also acknowledges that in the West many of these activities are dynamic and yield incomes for their entrepreneurs that surpass the earnings of their formal sector counterparts (Portes et al. 1989).

Feminist scholars and development researchers have more recently urged that the term "microenterprises" be substituted for "informal sector," precisely in order to remove the pejorative and hierarchical connotations from women's income-generating activities (Downing 1990; Horn 1991). In the South, women's businesses are most often concentrated in this sector. In fact, working in the so-called informal sector is the second-largest source of cash income for women after agriculture and, given the strength and organizational capacity of many women's groups associated with these enterprises, it is quite a misnomer to call such activities "informal." Feminist scholars of development have also cautioned that women's microenterprises should not be regarded as solely "survival" activities that are small, inefficient, and unprofitable, since some of these enterprises have grown, become dynamic, and contribute to human capital formation in regions that include the Caribbean and Africa (Downing 1991; Horn 1988, 1991; Sanday 1974).

In many societies, however, the microenterprise sector is stratified by gender. Women's firms are concentrated in the service-oriented, low-wage end of the sector, whereas men's enterprises are more likely to involve manufacturing and the sale and service of high-technology goods (Moyo et al. 1984; Downing 1991; Osirim 1992). In many cases, women's activities in this sector are still perceived to be an extension of their domestic duties; thus, such work is frequently not considered to be "real labor" and remains invisible. Many African women begin microenterprises as a result of patriarchal, gender-role socialization, which demarcates acceptable spheres of activity for women and men, and because they still experience structural blockage in access to education, training, business capital, and other support services (Osirim 1992). As a result of colonialism and persistent patriarchy, women who have received little or no formal education and have few marketable skills have little recourse but to begin microenterprises to assist in family maintenance.

Stratification on the basis of social class also shows in the types of businesses that women begin. Middle-class women who generally enjoy higher levels of educational attainment, positions in the formal sector, and greater access to capital through their spouses and family networks are more likely to begin enterprises that have greater initial capital requirements (McCormick, Chap. 9, this volume). Those who start hairdressing and sewing establishments are more likely to enjoy middle-class status, as opposed to their sisters in market trade, for example, who are more likely to be lower class. Women microentrepreneurs feel further pressure in a period of austerity and structural adjustment, as male relatives increasingly lose formal sector employment and women are relied upon to support the family financially.

Therefore, the international division of labor and resources based upon gender and region, as well as the establishment of SAPs, has its most deleterious effect on poor women in the South, who are disproportionately involved in urban microentrepreneurship and subsistence agriculture. Urban women microentrepreneurs in Zimbabwe have been some of the victims of this stratification in the global economy in the 1990s.

The State's Efforts to Enhance the Position of Women Microentrepreneurs

In the immediate postindependence period of the early 1980s, the Zimbabwean government was committed to enhancing the status of women and promoting national equality between women and men. Over the next decade, the state engaged in some efforts to directly advance the position of women's income-generating activities and took other actions designed to enhance the position of women in civil society. Such actions were in accordance with the aims of the liberation struggle, in which women actively participated (Seidman 1984; Weiss 1986; Batezat and Mwalo 1989; Stoneman and Cliffe 1989).

The first of the state's major efforts was the creation of the Ministry of Women's Affairs in 1981, which became the Ministry of Community Development in 1983 and later, the Ministry of Community, Cooperative Development, and Women's Affairs. Charged with many tasks ranging from providing women with access to social services to encouraging the development of appropriate technology for women, this ministry also promoted efforts to integrate the microenterprise sector into macroeconomic policies (Ministry of Community and Cooperative Development and Women's Affairs 1981). The potential for the growth and successful development of women's enterprises was further enhanced by the passage of laws that improved the formal legal status of women. No longer considered to be legal minors, women could enter into contracts and legally purchase land and apply for credit in their own names (Made and Whande 1989).[1]

The postindependence national government has established loan and training programs to advance the position of women microentrepreneurs. With the state as the major shareholder, ZIMBANK (Zimbabwe Bank) provides small loans of up to Z$6,000 with no collateral requirements to women entrepreneurs.[2] Training for women in small businesses and in microenterprises is provided by the bank, in collaboration with the Small Enterprises Development Corporation (SEDCO). To promote the development of cooperatives, the recently reorganized Ministry of Community and Cooperative Development (minus the Women's Affairs sector) provides loans of under Z$50,000 to women through the Community Development Fund, in conjunction with six short training courses. These classes are designed not only to give women engaged in these cooperatives accounting and entrepreneurship training but also to assist them in forming and maintaining a cohesive group within their cooperative. Once the cooperative has grown beyond the start-up phase into a small enterprise, loans are also available from this fund for amounts not exceeding Z$500,000. Women can apply for loans above this amount to SEDCO, which requires collateral and feasibility studies (Mabokwa 1991).

The city councils of Harare and Bulawayo have also been actively involved in assisting women microentrepreneurs. They have provided market stalls for produce vendors as well as sites and signboards for crocheters in these cities. Market traders in these two cities pay a rental fee to their local governments for their wooden stalls, the fee ranging from Z$10 to Z$14 per month; crocheters pay Z$15 to Z$23 per month for a small patch of land on bare ground. The vendors pay an additional Z$8 per month for security at the market, and the licensing fees paid to the city councils range from Z$11 to Z$14 per year. Even traders who work in makeshift stalls outside the established market pay approximately Z$10 per month for the rental space. In comparison, seamstresses and hairdressers who rent their shops from private owners pay rental fees ranging from Z$130 to Z$2,000 per month, with licensing fees paid to the government ranging from Z$20 to Z$115. The city governments have also encouraged the formation of cooperatives and have established training programs in textiles and handicrafts, as well as providing training in the nontraditional occupations of welding and carpentry for women.

Despite the assistance provided to women microentrepreneurs by the national and local governments, very few women in my study have benefited from most of these services, and some programs have fallen far short of what is needed. For the most part, urban microentrepreneurs were unaware of the loan and training programs provided by the government at all levels, even when their actual work sites were located directly in front of city hall. Those women who were the beneficiaries of the local government's training programs were most often younger women who had recently left school. With respect to training in nontraditional areas, approximately four to six women attended each of the workshops where training in welding and carpentry was given, whereas about thirty to forty men received instruction at each site. Although the city council furnished the crocheters with sites in Harare and Bulawayo, these locations were just plots of bare land with no stalls or other shelter from the elements; there were also no bathroom facilities. Similar conditions were faced by fruit and vegetable vendors who were unable to obtain a stall within the major market. At Manwele Market in Bulawayo, for instance, traders were working in makeshift quarters alongside the market, without toilet facilities or adequate protection from the rain.

Women working as vendors and crocheters under these conditions often reported that the government had promised to provide them with better facilities. With the economic decline and escalating unemployment in the late 1980s, coupled more recently with the pressure exerted by the multilateral lending community to adopt adjustment policies to stem the decline, urban women microentrepreneurs are unlikely to see a major improvement in their situation in the near future.

Methodology

In summer 1991, two research assistants and I began an intensive study of female microentrepreneurs in Harare and Bulawayo, Zimbabwe. These cities are the largest and second-largest in the country; at the time of the fieldwork, the estimated population of Harare was over 1 million and that of Bulawayo, about 600,000 (Stoneman and Cliffe 1989). Fifty-five respondents were selected (twenty-eight in Harare and twenty-seven in Bulawayo) in four subsectors, with each business employing no more than ten persons. The subsectors chosen were market trade, crocheting, sewing, and hairdressing, since these were areas with a high concentration of female microentrepreneurs.

After we had attempted unsuccessfully to obtain lists of such female-run businesses from the women's affairs office of ZANU-PF, we created lists of prospective participants with the help of informants and by walking up and down the major streets of these cities. We located hairdressing and sewing establishments, crocheting sites, and one major market in each city. Each major market was located within a high-density suburb; in Harare, Mbare Market was selected, and Manwele Market was chosen in Bulawayo.[3] As previously mentioned, crocheters worked on city council–provided land or in open spaces at or adjacent to shopping centers. Included among the crocheters studied were sites on Enterprise Road and at Avondale Shopping Center in Harare and in front of the city hall in Bulawayo.

Each participant was questioned from a prepared interview survey of over one hundred questions. The interview survey was divided into four parts: (1) personal attributes, (2) roles and responsibilities in the family, (3) operation of the enterprise, and (4) knowledge and use of support services, organizations, and informal networks in the maintenance of their firms. This study sought to discover the reasons these women began their enterprises, the problems and successes they had encountered, the impact of the economic decline and the SAPs upon their businesses, and their aspirations for the future. Because the survey produced similarities in responses across ethnic groups and cities, the data are analyzed in the following section according to occupational subsector.

Women's Microenterprises in Harare and Bulawayo

Although there are no accurate statistics on the numbers of Zimbabweans engaged in the microenterprise sector and on women's overall participation in this sector, earlier research in this area has demonstrated that women's roles are indeed significant (Gaidzanwa 1984; Muchena 1986; Horn 1988; Saito 1991). In 1978, 36 percent of all income-earning women were estimated to be involved in fruit and vegetable vending and handicrafts (Morgan 1984). The Zimbabwe Labor Force Survey of 1986–1987 estimated that over 64 percent of informal sector firms were owned by women (Saito 1991). My own fieldwork in Harare and Bulawayo in 1991 suggests that these figures might be underestimates of women's current participation, especially considering the state's retrenchment efforts and the need for increased income under structural adjustment.

Previous studies on the informal economy in Zimbabwe have confirmed the existence of a gender-based division of labor by sector. Women's microenterprises were focused on petty trading of foodstuffs and household goods and such agroprocessing activities as producing cooking oil from sunflower seeds, ground nuts, and cotton pits; producing honey, peanut butter, and jam; processing fruits and vegetables; and brewing beer (Gaidzanwa 1984; Muchena 1986). In one of the largest studies of small enterprises and microenterprises, which included over one thousand respondents, women were not employed in such manufacturing as metalworking, shoe repair, building, or upholstery work. They were found to dominate in enterprises relying on domestic skills such as hairdressing, clothes selling, knitting, crocheting, and preparing food for sale in tuck (snack) shops (Moyo et al. 1984; Muchena 1986; Saito 1990). Given women's documented roles as microentrepreneurs in trading, crocheting, hairdressing, and sewing and given the fact that these were significant activities for women in both cities, these subsectors were selected for investigation.

Market Traders

Of the twenty market vendors interviewed in both cities, one-half were Shona, the largest ethnic group in Zimbabwe. The next-largest group studied were the Ndebele, who constituted 20 percent of the sample (four women) and are most numerous in Matabeleland, the province that includes Bulawayo. The remaining 30 percent of the sample (six women) consisted of members of ethnic groups from South Africa, Malawi, and Zambia. Because of its proximity to South Africa, Bulawayo has become a major area of residence for many South Africans. More foreigners were present among market traders than in the other occupational subsectors, since trading has fewer barriers to entry than the other areas explored. There are lower capital and skill requirements involved in market vending, and formal education is not essential. Thus, this activity is one of the very few avenues open for income earning among lower-class women. In addition, there are greater opportunities for women from minority populations and foreign countries to become involved in produce vending in an area where members from their ethnic group also reside. Women tend to patronize vendors from their own ethnic group, and such vendors are also more likely to sell ingredients that are essential to their indigenous cuisine.[4] The fact that the Shona are the largest group among the traders is not surprising, given that the Shona make up about 70 to 75 percent of the population of Zimbabwe, followed by the Ndebele, whose population constitutes 16 to 19 percent of the total (Kurian 1987; Stoneman and Cliffe 1989).

The average age of the women in market trade was forty-two years, with 40 percent (eight women) of the sample currently married. Five women were divorced, and another five, widowed. The two remaining respondents had never married. The mean number of children among market traders was five.

The marital profiles of urban traders are similar to national and regional trends regarding the growth of female-headed households. The Southern African Development Coordination Conference (SADCC) has reported that 25 to 40 percent of all households among its member nations, including Zimbabwe, are headed by women and are disproportionately poor (Made and Whande 1989). These microentrepreneurs said that one of the reasons for the high number of divorces was the earlier urban

TABLE 10.1   Educational Attainment of Market Traders

Level of Education	Number of Respondents	Percentage
No formal schooling	2	10
Some primary	10	50
Completed primary	3	15
Completed primary and some secondary	1	5
Completed secondary	3	15
Completed secondary and teaching certificate	1	5
Total	20	100

Source: Author's own survey, 1991.

migration of their former husbands. In order to find work, black men under colonial rule frequently had to migrate to the cities for jobs. While there, some men would begin relationships with other women, later notifying their first wives that they were uninterested in continuing their previous union. The market traders said they would become aware of these other relationships, sometimes to their dismay, once they went to the cities to search for their husbands, which they would do particularly if they had not seen or heard from them in a long time. In many cases, these mothers then became the sole supporters of their children. For women with low levels of educational attainment and skills, market trade provides one of the few options open to them when they become increasingly responsible for the maintenance of their families.

What were the levels of education achieved by these respondents? As would be expected given the policies of the colonial government and patriarchy, most women had completed primary education or less. In the preindependence period, few black women had the opportunity to attend school; and those who did often lived on missions and completed four years of primary school at best (Seidman 1984; Summers 1991) (see Table 10.1).

One-half of the market traders had also received informal education through local women's clubs and organizations. None of these respondents had participated in the programs established by the Zimbabwean government to aid women microentrepreneurs, although one woman had participated in a government-sponsored agricultural extension program. Local women's clubs and the Zimbabwe Women's Bureau had provided

TABLE 10.2 Sources of Start-up Capital for Market Traders

Source of Capital	Number of Respondents	Percentage
Savings	9	45
Husband	5	25
Female relatives (including mother and sister)	3	15
Other male relatives (including father and brother)	3	15
Total	20	100

Source: Author's own survey, 1991.

these women with training in sewing, embroidery, and knitting, as well as teaching them skills in accounting, banking, math, and English that could help them to operate their businesses. These women were open and willing to participate in programs that provided basic skills but were unaware of the entrepreneur-oriented programs sponsored by the Ministry of Community and Cooperative Development and the city councils. As noted by Dorothy McCormick (Chap. 9, this volume), lower-class women have very limited access to resources, including information, that can assist them in business.

Market traders in this study had been in business for an average of seven years. These women, who sold a wide variety of vegetables and fruits and some types of nuts and grains, began their enterprises with an average of Z$50, obtained from their own savings or from their relatives.[5] After individual savings, spouses were the second major source of start-up capital for their firms. As indicated in Table 10.2, banks and established credit associations did not provide initial capital to these women.

Although the majority of these microentrepreneurs were able to obtain support from their families to establish their firms, extended families—particularly those at the margins—are likely to find it increasingly difficult to assist their relatives in the establishment of a business, given the current economic crisis, the growth in unemployment, and the adoption of SAPs.

Why did these women begin to trade? Despite the fact that when they were growing up most of these women aspired to enter teaching or nursing, they became market vendors because it was one of very few available options for them. Most of them did not have the benefit of a higher education that would allow them to enter one of the professions and had obligations to meet in supporting their children. Selling produce was one of the most accessible types of microenterprise for these women to begin, since the establishment costs are relatively low and the skills required are few. In addition, food is a necessity, and compared to vending some other products, they believed selling food would meet a demand of the local population. Thus, fruit and vegetable vending was a rational response to their situation. As one Manwele trader remarked: "I wanted money to put my children through school. With knitting, I only do it if someone places an order. Selling beans meets the daily needs of the local people. I will make more money doing the vegetable and bean business" (Masuku 1991). Many women also noted that trading provided a means of supplementing their family income. Other women became familiar with market trading in childhood, when they assisted their mothers or other female relatives, and some still had several relatives in this field.

With respect to contributions to employment generation and local and national development, these vendors did not provide paid employment. However, one trader did comment that her children assist her in the daily and weekly tasks of marketing, such as purchasing and transporting goods from the wholesalers to the market. Through the acquisition of profits from the business, however, these women are able to make important contributions to the support of their families. Although they did not have specific figures on the amount of profit they had generated over the years, all of the women reported that they had made a profit since they began their enterprises. These profits were reinvested in their businesses, saved in banks, used to buy household necessities and to educate their children, and were contributed to rotating credit associations known as rounds:

> I channel the profits to the round system or reinvest this or use it at home, buy some necessities for home. I give to my round Z$14 per day. These rounds are not organized based on where they [traders] are from. Both women and men can be in one round and people are members of one scattered throughout the market, selling different goods. (Kugarakunji 1991)

However, traders did note that their profits had been declining in the previous year, 1990. They remarked that the single greatest obstacle to success in their business was the government's removal of price controls under structural adjustment. Due to the problems in the national economy and the escalating unemployment, consumers have less money to spend, even for household necessities. In addition, the vendors have to pay more for their produce from the wholesalers and then attempt to pass some of these costs on to their customers. Since there are so many traders selling the same goods in the market, competition is intense, and customers seek out the lowest possible price for a commodity and in some cases avoid purchasing some products altogether. Furthermore, they commented that more men had begun selling fruits and vegetables in the market and produce stores, thus adding to the competition. Under the SAP, their numbers are likely to increase. As a result, vendors have been realizing smaller profits at the same time they are facing increasing demands from their families to provide support.

In addition to the rising costs charged by wholesalers, traders faced escalating transportation expenses after the removal of state subsidies. This was particularly traumatic for several Manwele Market traders, who, in an effort to increase their earnings, would leave their homes at approximately 4:00 A.M., pick up some commodities from the market, and begin to wait on long lines to catch a bus to downtown Bulawayo. Once there, they would attempt to illegally sell some fruits and vegetables and leave there before 7:30 A.M., the hour the police arrived. If caught, these women would be harassed and fined, their goods confiscated by the authorities. These goods would most likely not be returned to the vendors even upon payment of the fines.

Women who trade outdoors, directly adjacent to the markets, experience additional problems. They lack the protective roof of an established market and work either under makeshift roofing or without roofing at all. Thus, neither they nor their commodities are protected, and they face the increasing burden of escalating costs due to spoilage.

Under structural adjustment, these entrepreneurs not only experienced increasing problems in operating their businesses on a daily basis, but they faced more difficulties in their families and households. Women were still largely responsible for housework and child care, and in many cases, traders in Mbare and Manwele Markets were observed bringing their children with them to work. They certainly could not afford the charges of urban child care centers, which could easily amount to between Z$120 and Z$200 per month. (Free child care was available for some rural families before the SAP.) Although most of the married women in this sample described their relationships as stable, several women noted problems that have become more acute with the mounting economic difficulties. The most common difficulty discussed was the husband's financial neglect of the family, followed by his arguing, drunkenness, coming home late, and physical abuse.[6]

Despite these dilemmas, market traders' hopes for the future have not been daunted. In addition to their desire to provide education for their children, many of these businesswomen wanted to expand their enterprises by selling a greater variety of vegetables or by owning a shop where they could sell their products. A microentrepreneur from Mbare Market explained: "Yes, I look forward to possibly expanding this business. Then I would have to make an establishment elsewhere and have some of my kids get involved in this business. Right here in Mbare, I would like to have two stands in the market" (Bizure 1991). For others, diversification of their present activities was an important future goal: "[I] want to diversify—[get] knitting and sewing machines. [I would like to] establish links with influential people because of business and establish something better than the present situation" (Chera 1991).

Although these market traders were facing many obstacles caused by the current state of the economy, they approached the operation of their enterprises very seriously and generally regarded their success in business as a critical aspect of their self-identity.

Crocheters

Eighteen crocheters were interviewed in Harare and Bulawayo. As would be expected, the vast majority of crocheters, 83 percent, or fifteen women, in the sample were Shona, with the remaining 17 percent (three women) from the Ndebele group. When compared with the traders, the proportion of the crocheters who are Shona and Ndebele is more representative of the overall proportion in the national population.

Unlike the market vendors, the crocheters, who had a mean age of forty years, had a much higher rate of marriage, with the majority of those interviewed (over 70 percent in each city) involved in their first marriages at the time of the study. Eighty-three percent (fifteen) of the crocheters were married. One respondent was divorced, and two women had never married.

When compared with the market vendors, crocheters, who had an average of four children, were more than twice as likely to be currently married. Female-headed households were much less common among the crocheters than the traders and than current national statistics on this household type. One of the principal reasons for a higher rate of marriage among this sample is that many crocheters chose to work at one of the three major work sites studied here, Enterprise Road, because they were married to men who worked at the prison immediately adjacent to this site. Given the convenience of this location, the choice of occupation by these women was an especially rational one, considering the lack of opportunities for women in the labor market and the increasing costs of local transportation.

Crocheters were more likely to have completed at least primary school compared to women who worked in trade (see Table 10.3). Sixty-one percent (eleven) of the crocheters compared to 40 percent (eight) of the

TABLE 10.3   Educational Attainment Among Crocheters

Level of Education	Number of Respondents	Percentage
No formal education	1	6
Some primary	6	33
Finished primary	6	33
Finished primary and some secondary	5	28
Total	18	100

Source: Author's own survey, 1991.

traders had received at least primary-level education. Vendors, however, were more likely to have completed secondary school. Twenty percent (four) of the vendors had attained this level of education, whereas 28 percent (five) of the crocheters had some secondary training, though none had completed it. Nevertheless, the data generally indicate that microentrepreneurs in both of these sectors had usually received too little education to enable them to attain their aspirations for careers in areas such as nursing and teaching. The levels attained were in keeping with the situation for black Zimbabwean women on the whole, whose educational attainment level was restricted under colonialism.

Women in this study learned crocheting primarily from their mothers, other female relatives, and friends. One woman had gained these skills from a mission school she attended; another was taught in a woman's club. The majority of the respondents had female relatives who also worked as crocheters at the time of these interviews. Twenty-two percent (four) of the crocheters had received informal training in other fields, including typing, English, and math. Prior to running their current businesses, most crocheters had worked in retail sales or in market trade.

The crocheters' enterprises, which had been established for twelve years on average, were older than those of their counterparts in trade. Crocheters began their activities with about Z$168 on average, a larger amount than the vendors had invested, but their start-up capital most often came from the same sources—husbands and their savings—as is illustrated in Table 10.4. Like the traders, these women did not obtain any money to establish their firms from banks or other governmental or nongovernmental agencies that provide credit.

When asked why they began these businesses, crocheters responded that they needed the money to support their families, especially in cases

TABLE 10.4   Sources of Start-up Capital for Crocheters

Source of Capital	Number of Respondents[a]	Percentage[a]
Spouses	7	39
Respondents' savings	6	33
Other male relatives	3	17
Other female relatives	2	11
Children	1	6
Mother-in-law	1	6
Total	20	112

a. Numbers of respondents exceed the total in the sample and percentages exceed 100 because some participants had multiple sources of capital.
Source: Author's own survey, 1991.

where their husbands' income levels had dropped and the men were generally not providing enough to maintain their families. Further, women entered this area of microentrepreneurship because, as one Bulawayo crocheter remarked, "I have nothing to do and I can do this without school" (Chigonde 1991). These women also perceived crocheting, unlike some other activities, to be an occupation in which they would be able to earn cash immediately and provide other goods for their children: "[Through crocheting] you can find clothes for children. If you need money for bus fare, kids, etc., you can lower prices and sell faster to get money right away. When you sell something, [you] get cash, not credit" (Scholastic 1991).

Unlike traders, crocheters in Harare and Bulawayo do not work in market stalls. These women conduct their business on parcels of bare land in or near shopping centers or in open lots. Much of this land is provided for them by the city council and contains no protection and no toilet facilities. The only thing usually separating these women from the bare ground are the thin mats they bring to sit on. Several women mentioned that the city council had promised to improve these facilities; however, under the current conditions of structural adjustment, their needs are likely to remain unmet in the short term.

Crocheting is one of the few occupational subsectors in Zimbabwe in which subcontracting exists. About 60 percent (six) of the crocheters in Harare stated that they employ an average of two workers, who essentially work as subcontractors for these women. They are most often paid on a piecework basis, earning Z$20, for example, for a tablecloth. Two microentrepreneurs mentioned that they pay wages of Z$120 and Z$160, respectively. In addition to crocheting outdoors while waiting for customers, these women frequently work additional hours at home after they have completed their household tasks. Thus, some of their labor is household-based and remains invisible.

The crocheters in this study made a wide variety of goods, including table mats, doilies, bedspreads, sweaters, children's clothing, and chair covers. After establishing their businesses, nearly one-half of them had innovated by changing designs or the types of goods they produced. These respondents commented that they learned new patterns and introduced these new designs, especially once old patterns became common. They were attentive to changes in the market and attempted to gain an edge on their competition.

In fact, as has also been noted by Olivia Muchena (1986) in an earlier study, increasing competition is one of the major problems faced by these microentrepreneurs, in addition to the lack of adequate facilities. The market for crocheted goods is seasonal—the demand is highest in the Christmas season. Crocheters are very dependent on expatriate whites and tourists for their sales, and with recession in the West and difficult national economic conditions, more businesswomen are chasing fewer customers. This phenomenon is most evident at the Enterprise Road site in Harare, where crocheters run up to the cars of potential customers before they have even stopped. As these respondents commented: "[You] spend the whole day running, with women shouting at each other" (Fatma 1991); and, "There is no order; when a customer comes, everybody just runs" (Rudo 1991).

Prospects for expanding the market for crocheted goods appeared bleak at the time of this study. Although 11 percent (two) of the respondents interviewed had begun to establish export markets for their products and many other women expressed an interest in accomplishing this, support from the government to create these linkages is unlikely under the SAP. With the coming of majority rule in South Africa and the normalization of relations between the two countries, greater potential now exists for the increased export of crocheted goods to South Africa.

In addition, with the removal of price controls under the SAP, the price of cotton continues to increase, cutting into crocheters' potential profits. As a Bulawayo crocheter remarked: "The problem is that there are not that many foreigners buying the goods and the cotton is too expensive. . . . [In the past] there was more success but now, you buy cotton today and it is one price; you buy cotton tomorrow and the price has gone up" (Dhliwayo 1991).

While fewer crocheters (44 percent) reported earning profits compared to their counterparts in trade, they, like the vendors, did report that they were reinvesting in their firms, using their profits to buy cotton and to support their children.

In addition to their crocheting work, these women still bore the burden of full responsibility for housework. Although the majority of them described their relationships as stable, girlfriends and mistresses were mentioned as the major cause of domestic problems, primarily because of the money channeled away from the respondents' households to those of mistresses. One entrepreneur remarked that she began her business as a result of such suspicions and her concern over the impact this would have on her children's well-being: "[There were] problems because he wants to take another wife. He is never at home—that's why it is better to sell things to help the children. He doesn't tell me, but I've seen the other wife. I think they have a child—I heard somebody say it" (Mary 1991).

These women were committed to improving the lives of their children and had business-related goals geared toward accomplishing this. In addition to selling more goods to customers and becoming suppliers to shops, several women wanted to establish their own stores to sell their products. One woman wanted to fulfill a childhood desire of becoming a nurse or a teacher, and another hoped to establish a take-out business for indigenous foods. She saw a market niche for enterprises of this type with the increase in the urban population, since very few such businesses exist in Harare or Bulawayo.

Hairdressers and Seamstresses

As was the case in the other populations sampled, hairdressers and seamstresses were overwhelmingly Shona, accounting for 83 percent (twelve) of the seventeen women interviewed in this category. Two of these respondents each were Ndebele and Zambian; one was from South Africa. These microentrepreneurs were similar to the respondents in trade and crocheting, in that they had a mean age of forty-one years and an average of four children. The percentage of married respondents in this sample falls between the percentages noted for traders and crocheters. Sixty-five percent (eleven) were married; of the remaining respondents, two were divorced, and one, widowed.

Educational attainment among seamstresses and hairdressers generally exceeded those levels achieved by the vendors and crocheters, since all of the seamstresses and hairdressers had some formal education. Similar levels of completed secondary education were noted, however, among traders (20 percent) and seamstresses and hairdressers (see Table 10.5).

Although some market traders did complete secondary school, hairdressers and seamstresses were more likely to have had training in specialized fields and to have previously worked in the formal sector. The vast majority of this sample (82 percent) had received some training in hairdressing and sewing. Many of these women had apprenticeship train-

TABLE 10.5   Educational Attainment Among Hairdressers and Seamstresses

Level Completed	Number of Respondents	Percentage
Some primary	2	12
Completed primary	5	29
Some secondary	4	24
Some secondary and technical education	2	12
Completed secondary	2	12
Completed secondary and nursing training	2	12
Total	17	101

Note: The total percentage exceeds 100 because of rounding.
Source: Author's own survey, 1991.

ing at hair salons, and one had participated in an apprentice program at Bulawayo Technical College. Another hairdresser had completed courses in this field in the United Kingdom and had observed the operation of hair salons in the United States. Some seamstresses attended courses at sewing schools; one respondent had received private tutoring in sewing. This training significantly distinguished these respondents from the traders and crocheters, who had not received this level of instruction. Not only might specialized training in combination with secondary schooling assist women in practicing their craft, but such exposure can also provide women with connections that can result in greater access to information about possible business services.[7]

The hairdressers' and seamstresses' businesses were on average seven years old and had been started with an average of Z$5,866.50, much of which was used to purchase machines. Although the microentrepreneurs' savings were an important source of start-up capital in the previous samples, they were the major source of capital for seamstresses and hairdressers, as shown in Table 10.6.

Women in this population were more likely to have significant savings to invest in their establishments because they had occupied a wider range of more lucrative positions before becoming microentrepreneurs than had their peers in the other samples. Hairdressers and seamstresses were previously employed as nurses, teachers, receptionists, and sales clerks. The one woman who obtained part of her initial investment from a finance company had not only attained a relatively high level of education in comparison to respondents in the other samples (she had received some secondary education, had completed a technical program, and had fulfilled apprenticeship training in hairdressing), but she had also in-

TABLE 10.6 Start-up Capital Among Seamstresses and Hairdressers

Source of Capital	Number of Respondents[a]	Percentage[a]
Personal savings	14	82
Husbands	4	24
Female relatives	2	12
Other male relatives	2	12
Finance company	1	6
Total	23	136

a. Numbers of respondents exceed the total in the sample and the percentage exceeds 100 because some respondents had multiple sources of capital.
Source: Author's own survey, 1991.

vested Z\$11,000 of her own money and owned machines that could be used as collateral. This hairdresser later qualified for a credit line from ZIMBANK. Only one seamstress received any loans as operating capital for her business, receiving two loans from ZIMBANK. Like the hairdresser just mentioned, this seamstress had also received some secondary education and later earned a certificate in sewing and design. She discussed the difficulty of obtaining such loans as a microentrepreneur and the importance of personal connections: "[It] was very difficult to get these loans. When you go to the bank, [since] we are self-employed, you don't have trade reference, don't have insurance. They ask for these things—[you] have to ask a friend to put in a good word for you to say you can pay" (Winnie 1991).

The seamstresses specialized in making women's and children's clothing, although some also made men's attire; the hair salons were generally full service, providing everything from braiding to permanent hair relaxing. When questioned about why they began their businesses, these women were most likely to respond that they preferred to work for themselves and "be their own boss" and that these fields were of great interest to them. After all, most of these women had undertaken special training in these fields, and they further maintained that this provided them with a source of income independent of their husbands and enabled them to meet many of their needs:

> I established this because my husband spent most of his time in business and I had little to do. I discussed this and [realized] I could create employment for my niece who trained as a hairdresser and didn't do well in secondary school. I mostly wanted to do this to create employment. . . . I didn't want to rely on my husband. I started also because of the high taxes I was paying [for my knitting shop]. I had a hard time making ends meet. (Deena 1991)

These enterprises employed an average of three workers, whose salaries ranged from Z$100 to Z$350 per month. In a few salons, specialists who worked on commission could earn as much as Z$1,000 to Z$2,000 during the Christmas season, which was their peak sales period. The majority of these women had innovated by expanding their range of products and services, particularly through the use of imported fabrics and new hair products and by introducing styles that they had seen in magazines and through travel abroad.

Only one of the seventeen respondents in this sample reported that she had not earned any profits, although about 24 percent (four) of these women did not know how much profit they had earned. Several of these entrepreneurs also noted that profits had not grown steadily, particularly in the previous year, because of the economic problems in the larger society. In a period of unemployment and escalating prices, many Zimbabweans consider these services to be luxuries they can barely afford, and if they patronize these establishments at all, it is during the Christmas season. Hairdressers and seamstresses had also noticed that the number of customers had declined because of increased competition in these fields. One businesswoman observed: "There is a lot of competition. [There are] no jobs in Zimbabwe. They [other businesses] grab customers off the street and grab your workers. Prices increase every day. I go two, three days without customers but still have to pay bills as usual. If I increase prices, customers might stay away for a month" (Constance 1991).

Hairdressers experienced additional problems in their businesses because of the bans on importing certain goods, the costs of obtaining import licenses and paying customs duties, and the increase in the cost of such imports due to the massive currency devaluations under structural adjustment: "You can't import these products from abroad unless you have foreign currency or pay customs duty if someone sends it to you and it becomes unaffordable" (Deena 1991); another hairdresser commented, "[You] can't get a license to order imported hair creams because these are considered luxury items" (Elizabeth 1991).

One-half of the hairdressers and seamstresses, unlike the crocheters and traders, employed domestic workers who assisted them with their household responsibilities, including child care. More of the women in this sample reported problems in their relationships with their spouses than among the other groups. Several hairdressers and seamstresses cited marital infidelity as a major difficulty, but the reasons they gave for this differed from those of women in the other sectors. The microentrepreneurs in this sample were mainly concerned about the dishonesty and unfaithfulness embodied in infidelity, whereas the traders and crocheters had objected to the loss of financial resources. This might indicate their greater economic independence and the adoption of more Western ideals about marriage due to their higher levels of education. Another problem area observed early in marriage among this group was the husband's insecurity regarding his wife's ambition and independence. This was perhaps most problematic among this group since the hairdressers and seamstresses not only had more education and training but had previously held more lucrative positions that had enabled them to save and invest in their own firms with little reliance on their husbands.

Women in this group had many aspirations for the future. Their first priority was to secure their children's financial futures, which they believed they could accomplish by achieving their professional goals. Among these business goals were the following: to expand current operations to include a fitness center with a beauty salon or to combine dressmaking with hair care; to establish a factory to produce children's clothes; to combine the hair salon with a boutique and a factory to make hair products; to own a chain of salons in the city and to teach dressmaking. Traveling abroad to further their knowledge and skills in hairdressing was another desire for the future. In general, these women wanted to further their activities as entrepreneurs through business expansion and diversification.

In summary, microentrepreneurs in all four subsectors were making valuable contributions to the development of human capital, primarily through investments in their children. By providing employment, crocheters, seamstresses, and hairdressers were further assisting in national development. Crocheters, however, were in a more disadvantaged position in this regard, since fewer of them could provide paid employment and their prospects of doing so in the near future were dimmed by their inadequate facilities and declining sales. However, with the promotion of export markets for their goods, especially in South Africa, their situation is bound to improve, though this is not likely to happen immediately. Some market traders also had inadequate facilities in which to work and were further jeopardized by declines in sales and police harassment in their efforts to enhance their incomes. Their rotating credit associations, or "rounds," were vital in keeping their businesses afloat and in maintaining their families. Although seamstresses and hairdressers were also facing revenue losses because of structural adjustment and the government's austerity measures in general, they appeared to be in the strongest position to increase their contributions to development because of their higher educational attainment, prior work histories, and greater assets, which were likely to provide them with greater access to governmental and nongovernmental support services. Furthermore, because they could hire domestic help, they could devote more time to their enterprises than businesswomen in the other sectors. Although the results of this study suggest that the combination of these factors placed hairdressers and seamstresses in a "more advantaged" position for realizing their goals, women in all four categories were clearly involved in more than "survival" activities as microentrepreneurs. With an improvement in the economic environment, many of them would not only realize some of their professional goals, but they would enhance the prospects of urban and national development.

Policy Recommendations

To improve the working conditions of these microentrepreneurs and their contributions to future development, several changes are needed in urban policy. To begin with, city governments should make the provision of adequate facilities for crocheters and additional protected space within city markets for traders a priority. Under current conditions, crocheters operate outdoors, largely without any protective covering, and some vendors work under unstable, makeshift roofing; this results in lost work days and much spoilage and waste of products. The creation of new urban markets could house both traders and crocheters; in some cases, currently existing markets might be expanded, or protected space could be found in existing shopping centers for the crocheters. Microentrepreneurs in the crocheting sector depend on the resident white population and tourists for sales and thus would likely prefer work sites that are near the places often frequented by these potential clients. Such work areas need to include toilet facilities. Further, the traders need refrigeration to enable them to store perishable goods such as tomatoes and eggs. Nominal rents could be charged by city governments for the use of such space.

Both local and national governments also need to provide information and access to support services for women in microenterprises. As this study has shown, very few women benefited from any of the services provided by the state. Women in this project, and undoubtedly countless others, have no knowledge of the existence of many of the credit facilities and training programs that could assist them in their enterprises. Through the use of urban outreach workers, microentrepreneurs could receive information about existing programs. Further, the state could provide stipends for the businesswomen who attend classes and workshops to make up for lost work hours and sales.

With respect to the provision of training, the government should not only expand technical training courses but should also alter its orientation regarding who receives such instruction. Educational opportunities for training and retraining need to be established for women of all ages and not just for those who have recently left school. In particular, classes in nontraditional occupations, such as in carpentry and welding and in high-technology fields, should be made available to women across the age spectrum. Such instruction would likely result in many women beginning more profitable small enterprises and microenterprises using the skills they would thereby acquire, and they would ultimately increase their earnings.

To promote more long-term change in the position of women microentrepreneurs and to improve the status of women generally, socialization patterns in both the public and private sectors have to be transformed. The gender-based division of labor in the home and the workplace needs to be eliminated. Socialization practices that follow rigid gender prescriptions need to be replaced; the method and content of the instructions young women receive in the classroom should be empowering and should provide them with expanding options for employment and lifestyle choices that are not restricted by gender. It is not enough, however, for educators and students to change their thinking: Institutional practice is a critical component in the elimination of patriarchy. The state needs to more aggressively foster equality between women and men through promotional campaigns that not only inform the public about government programs but also advance a more egalitarian philosophy. In this regard, the state and its institutions should encourage the sharing of domestic responsibilities and try to increase the government commitment to providing affordable child care for those who can pay and free services for those who cannot. In some cases, perhaps on-site care facilities can be created. An on-site child care facility for market traders could be provided by the state based on plans for the reconstruction of Oba Market in Benin, Nigeria. This would benefit vendors in Harare and Bulawayo, Zimbabwe, who increasingly have to bring their children to work with them.

Such improvements in the lives of Zimbabwean women would require government expenditures that in the mid-1990s, given the economic difficulties, appear highly improbable, at the least. More macrolevel changes are required by the Zimbabwean state. Regional cooperation in production and trade needs to be strengthened among SADCC countries, so that member nations become more reliant on each other rather than depending on the international marketplace. Sub-Saharan African nations such as Zimbabwe need to emphasize national and regional development goals, as opposed to the goals of multilateral lending agencies and the international community that in the past have restricted their development and have increased their dependency. Rather than targeting southern nations for adjustment and austerity programs, the aim of economic restructuring efforts needs to shift to the international level, where financial markets and transnational corporations, among other organizations, should attempt, at the very least, to balance benefits between the Third

World and the West. Only such macrolevel changes in the international arena can ultimately improve the lives of poor women in the South over the long term.

Conclusion

The changes in the global division of labor and economic restructuring efforts throughout the South have made it increasingly important to understand the roles and operations of microenterprises, which constitute a significant sphere of income earning, particularly for women in sub-Saharan Africa. In urban Zimbabwe, women begin businesses in this sector because they view such activity as one of the only options available to them to support their families. The history of colonialism and patriarchy has limited their opportunities for education, training, and employment. In this study, mothers and other female relatives were largely responsible for training their daughters in the skills of market trade and crocheting, whereas established technical schools and apprenticeships were important sources of valuable skills for hairdressers and seamstresses.

Although the Zimbabwean state has attempted to promote equality between women and men and to enhance women's abilities as entrepreneurs, very few women in this study benefited from any of these programs. Those who did were mainly hairdressers and seamstresses, who, through their education and prior work experience, had made important contacts that often provided them with knowledge of and access to such services. Women in all four subsectors, however, have been adversely affected by the government's SAP, which has resulted in declining sales and increasing competition for women in all areas. Further hardship is borne by those poorer groups of urban microentrepreneurs, such as crocheters and traders, who often have inadequate facilities in which to work and are disproportionately burdened by increasing costs of food, transportation, and social services. Despite these current difficulties, the investments of these microentrepreneurs in their children and in their firms and their aspirations for the future clearly demonstrate that they are engaged in more than simple "survival" activities. Rather, they are advancing the future development of their nation.

Notes

This research was funded by grants from the National Science Foundation, the MacArthur Foundation, and the Bryn Mawr Africa Fund. I wish to thank Camille Carraher and Niambi Robinson for research assistance on this project. Many thanks also to the Carter G. Woodson Institute at the University of Virginia for its generous support.

1. Under customary law, however, women did not have their own land-use rights. Even today, most Zimbabwean women live in rural areas under the jurisdiction of customary law and are frequently not aware of their rights under civil law. Thus, many women might continue to face difficulties in their access to land. For further discussion of this issue, see Kazembe 1988.

2. At the time of this study, US$1=Z$2.30.

3. High-density suburbs are generally poor, black areas located further from the central city and lack the quality of housing and resources that exists in the low-density suburbs. Although blacks can certainly reside in low-density suburbs, these areas are still predominantly white and show little change in residential patterns since independence. In high-density areas such as Mzilikazi in the Bulawayo metropolitan area, examples of the barracks-like hostels where black men lived when they worked in the city are still evident as stark reminders of the racially based inequality that was legislated during the colonial period.

4. In comparative studies of market traders in southwestern Nigeria, I also observed that women tended to patronize vendors from their same group. In Tejuosho Market in Surulere, Lagos (a largely Yoruba area), for example, Ibo market women were noted to occupy stalls in the same section of the market and, among other items, sold produce that was used among the Ibo in food preparation.

5. In the early to mid-1980s, US$1=approximately Z$2.

6. At a recent curriculum development institute on "Gender, Justice and Development," in Amherst, Massachusetts, several speakers, most notably Peggy Antrobus, suggested that an association exists between the adoption of structural adjustment programs in the South and increasing violence against women.

7. In earlier research I conducted among small-scale entrepreneurs, the association between educational attainment and access to information about business support was very strong. For further discussion of this linkage, see Osirim 1990.

References

Batezat, Elinor, and Margaret Mwalo. 1989. *Women in Zimbabwe*. Harare: Southern Africa Political Economy Series (SAPES) Trust.

Bizure.* 1991. Interview by author with a trader in Mbare Market, Harare.

Cardoso, Fernando, and Enzo Faletto. 1978. *Dependency and Development in Latin America*. Berkeley and Los Angeles: University of California Press.

Chera.* 1991. Interview by author with a trader in Mbare Market, Harare.

Chigonde.* 1991. Interview by author with a crocheter, Bulawayo.

Constance.* 1991. Interview by author with a hairdresser, Bulawayo.

Deena.* 1991. Interview by author with a hairdresser, Harare.

Dhliwayo.* 1991. Interview by author with a crocheter, Bulawayo.

Downing, Jeanne. 1990. *GEMINI: Gender and the Growth and Dynamics of Microenterprises*. Prepared for the Growth and Equity Through Microenterprise, Investments, and Institutions (GEMINI). Washington, D.C.: Agency for International Development.

———. 1991. "The Growth and Dynamics of Women Entrepreneurs in Southern Africa." Paper presented at the annual meeting of the African Studies Association, St. Louis, Mo.

Elizabeth.* 1991. Interview by author with a hairdresser, Harare.

Evans, Peter. 1979. *Dependent Development: The Alliance of Multinational, State, and Local Capital in Brazil.* Princeton: Princeton University Press.

Fatma.* 1991. Interview by author with a crocheter, Harare.

Feldman, Shelley. 1991. "Still Invisible: Women in the Informal Sector," in *Women and International Development Annual,* vol. 2, ed. Rita S. Gallin and Anne Ferguson. Boulder: Westview.

Frank, Andre Gunder. 1969. *Latin America: Underdevelopment or Revolution.* New York and London: Monthly Review Press.

Gaidzanwa, R. B. 1984. "The Policy Implications of Women's Involvement in the Informal Sector in Zimbabwe." *MISS* 3, 3.

Gladwin, Christina, ed. 1991. *Structural Adjustment and African Women Farmers.* Gainesville: University of Florida Press.

Horn, Nancy. 1988. "The Culture, Urban Context and Economics of Women's Fresh Produce Marketing in Harare, Zimbabwe." Ph.D. diss., Michigan State University.

———. 1991. "Redefining Economic Productivity: Marketwomen and Food Provisioning in Harare, Zimbabwe." Paper presented at the annual meeting of the African Studies Association, St. Louis, Mo.

International Labour Office. 1972. *Employment, Incomes, and Equality: A Strategy for Increasing Productive Employment in Kenya.* Geneva: ILO.

Kazembe, Joyce. 1988. "The Women Issue." In *Zimbabwe: The Political Economy of Transition, 1980–1986,* ed. Ibbo Mandaza. Dakar: CODESRIA Books.

Kugarakunji.* 1991. Interview by author with a trader in Mbare Market, Harare.

Kurian, George. 1987. *The Encyclopedia of the Third World.* New York: Facts on File.

LeBrun, Oliver, and Chris Gerry. 1975. "Petty Producers and Capitalism." *Review of African Political Economy* 3:20–32.

Mabokwa, Dr. 1991. "The Role of Cooperative and Community Development in Women's Microentrepreneurship." Harare: Ministry of Community and Cooperative Development.

MacGaffey, Janet. 1986. "Women and Class Formation in a Dependent Economy: Kisangani Entrepreneurs." In *Women and Class in Africa,* ed. Claire Robertson and Iris Berger, 161–177. New York: Holmes and Meier.

Made, Patricia, and Nyorovai Whande. 1989. "Women in Southern Africa: A Note on the Zimbabwean 'Success Story.'" *Issue: A Journal of Opinion* 17, 2:26–28.

Mary.* 1991. Interview by author with a crocheter, Harare.

Masuku.* 1991. Interview by author with a trader in Manwele Market, Bulawayo.

Ministry of Community and Cooperative Development and Women's Affairs. 1981. "Policy Statement." Harare.

Molly.* 1991. Interview by author with a trader in Manwele Market, Bulawayo.

Morgan, Robin. 1984. *Sisterhood Is Global.* New York: Anchor.

Moyo, N. P., et al. 1984. *The Informal Sector in Zimbabwe—Its Potential for Employment Generation*. Harare: Ministry of Labor, Manpower Planning, and Social Welfare.

Muchena, Olivia. 1986. *Women's Employment Patterns, Discrimination and Promotion of Equality in Africa: The Case of Zimbabwe*. Jobs and Skills Program for Africa. Addis Ababa: ILO.

Nkomo.* 1991. Interview by author with a trader in Manwele Market, Bulawayo.

Onimode, Bade, ed. 1989. *The IMF, the World Bank, and the African Debt*. London: Zed.

Osirim, Mary J. 1990. "Characteristics of Entrepreneurship in Nigerian Industries That Started Small." Ph.D. diss., Harvard University.

———. 1992. "The State of Women in the Third World: The Informal Sector and Development in Africa and the Caribbean." *Social Development Issues* 14, 2/3: 74–87.

Portes, Alejandro, Manuel Castells, and Lauren A. Benton, eds. 1989. *The Informal Economy: Studies in Advanced and Less Developed Societies*. Baltimore: Johns Hopkins University Press.

Rudo.* 1991. Interview by author with a crocheter, Harare.

Saito, Katrine. 1991. "Women and Microenterprise Development in Zimbabwe: Constraints to Development." Paper presented at the annual meeting of the African Studies Association, St. Louis, Mo.

Sanday, Peggy. 1974. "Female Status in the Public Domain." In *Women, Culture and Society*, ed. Michelle Rosaldo and Louise Lamphere. Stanford: Stanford University Press.

Scholastic.* 1991. Interview by author with a crocheter, Harare.

Seidman, Gay. 1984. "Women in Zimbabwe: Post-Independence Struggles." *Feminist Studies* 10, 3:419–440.

Stoneman, Colin, and Lionel Cliffe. 1989. *Zimbabwe: Politics, Economics, and Society*. London: Pinter.

Summers, Carol. 1991. "Native Policy, Education and Development: Social Ideologies and Social Control in Southern Rhodesia, 1890–1934." Ph.D. diss, Johns Hopkins University.

Wallerstein, Immanuel. 1974. *The Modern World-System: Capitalist Agriculture and the Origins of the European World Economy in the Sixteenth Century*. New York: Academic Press.

Weiss, Ruth. 1986. *The Women of Zimbabwe*. London: Kesho.

Winnie.* 1991. Interview by author with a seamstress, Harare.

Young, Kate, Carol Wolkowitz, and Roslyn McCullagh, eds. 1984. *Of Marriage and the Market: Women's Subordination Internationally and Its Lessons*. London: Routledge and Kegan Paul.

---

* The respondents selected code names for use in this study.

11 ❧

Prostitution, a *Petit-métier* During Economic Crisis: A Road to Women's Liberation? The Case of Cameroon

PAULETTE BEAT SONGUE
Translated by Laura Mitchell

Periods of international economic crisis focus attention on money and the goods it can buy. How are these goods acquired, saved, or multiplied in times of hardship? Any response immediately raises questions of employment and occupation. In the context of African underdevelopment, in which the creation of new enterprises is often linked to the availability of capital, access to credit, and limited skilled labor, this question is problematic. The crux of the issue lies in the nature of the solutions that individuals find to resolve problems of unemployment, poverty, and subservience. These solutions are as observable at the macrosociological level of states as they are at the microsociological level of communities and individuals.

This study concerns the microsociological level and, in particular, examines women and prostitution. Women's liberation is used as an intellectual point of departure to point out that in situations of economic want, financial independence is often a precondition of liberation for women. Besides inherited wealth, financial independence presupposes the practice of a craft or profession. In this context, then, is prostitution a profession? Prostitution is increasingly widespread and is diffused among many social strata. Is it a solution specifically adopted by women to counter the effects of economic crisis, since women are especially hard hit by discrimination in the job market? As an income-generating profession, does prostitution contribute to the emancipation of women in relation to men? This chapter presents an attempt to answer these questions through an examination of prostitution in Cameroon, and it also touches on why prostitution is becoming more prevalent in Cameroonian society as a specific economic response to personal problems.

This study is structured in four parts. After a discussion of the terms "prostitution" and "profession," the first section proposes different conditions that push women to engage in this *petit-métier*,[1] among them a lack of professional qualifications and increasing familial responsibilities, particularly for unmarried women. In the second section, the nature and income from prostitution in an urban setting are discussed. The third section presents the argument that even if prostitution allows a woman to gain sexual liberation by managing her own body and provides sufficient income to allow her a certain amount of financial independence, it does not open an avenue for the liberation of women, who remain dominated by their clients' money. Finally, the study examines AIDS and prostitution.

Methodology

Three analytical methods have been used in this study:

1. Direct observation of prostitutes and their clients.
2. The examination of the results of two surveys conducted under the auspices of AIDS research, one in Yaoundé (Songue 1993) and the other in Yaoundé and Douala (Garcia et al. 1992). These surveys were based on questionnaires and open-ended discussions. The first survey polled 210 prostitutes and 90 clients; the second studied 262 prostitutes in Yaoundé and 236 in Douala.
3. Informal interviews with current and former prostitutes that were the sources for life histories. Some of the information in these histories is the result of observation and some comes from sustained contact with these prostitutes.

Definition of "Prostitution" and "Profession"

A "profession" can be defined as all work from which a person derives the means of existence. "Prostitution" can be defined as the act or practice of a man or woman consenting to have intimate sexual exchanges with one or several partners who pay for the exchange, with the primary objective of the purveyor being material remuneration.[2]

It is appropriate to add the definition of semiprostitution here, which applies to people who prostitute themselves while having another primary daily activity, whether remunerative or not. Thus, semiprostitution can apply to anyone who sometimes engages in prostitution—students, shopkeepers, household employees, office workers, barmaids, and even housewives, sometimes with children. Semiprostitution applies to men as well as women, although this chapter focuses only on the latter.

Prostitutes therefore derive all or part of their means of existence from their activity, which indeed makes prostitution a profession, by definition. Prostitution is a lucrative activity, whether engaged in as a breadwinning activity or to obtain supplementary income for the acquisition of luxury goods. However, prostitution is not conventionally thought of as a legitimate profession and carries the connotation of a marginal or illicit activity. I will not dwell on the moral considerations here but will rather concentrate on the fact that in the Cameroonian context, prostitution is not considered a distinct or traditional profession at the official level, and is not included formally in official lists of professions, nor is it covered by legislation on occupations.

Prostitution thus has illegitimate status and falls into the realm of activities created by individuals, given certain aptitudes and opportunities. It is categorized as a *petit-métier* within the informal sector.

As a *petit-métier*, prostitution provides a solution to the striking rate of unemployment in Africa, especially among women. In addition to assuming primary responsibility for raising the family, women are victims of innumerable forms of discrimination in education and employment. It becomes clear within this context of limited opportunity why prostitution is becoming increasingly valued as a *petit-métier* among women in Africa.

The Level of Education and Professional Qualifications of Women in Cameroon

The literacy rate among women in Cameroon is very low. Sexual discrimination in education further penalizes women. Five out of ten women (one-half the female population) do not know how to read or write. Of the 1,271,135 women who have been working for eleven years or more, only 393,315 know how to read or write in English or French, the two national languages.[3] This represents about 33.4 percent (one-third) of those economically active females working for eleven years or longer. The literacy rate is higher in urban areas, where 59.2 percent of women (146,790 of

TABLE 11.1   Level of Education in Cameroon (in percentages)

	All Women	Women Age 15 and Older	All Men
Illiterate	53.4	—	—
Have primary education	37.3	67.6	39.2
Have secondary education	8.9	31.3	44.9
Have higher education	0.3	1.1	14.6

Source: Demo 87: Deuxième recensement général de la population et de l'habitat du Cameroun (Yaoundé: Gouvernement Camerounais, 1990–1993).

247,880) who have worked eleven years or longer can read and write in English or French. But even in cities, four out of ten women cannot read or write in either of the two national languages. The statistics in Table 11.1 round out the description and provide details on the level of education.

These numbers indicate a low level of literacy and female education, even among those who are employed. This is not surprising, since sexual discrimination in education favors boys. Male children receive priority in education and are sent to school for longer periods because women are assumed to be destined for marriage, when they will be materially supported by their husbands. Alternatively, if a woman is economically productive, her income will go to her husband's family, since the patrilineal system predominates throughout almost all of Cameroon. Society counts much more on men to manage the parental or family finances, an expectation increasingly contradicted by reality since both the number and size of female-headed households are on the rise. The low levels of literacy and education among women dictate their representation in the workforce: Women often find themselves in the jobs that require the least demanding qualifications and education level.

Distribution of Economically Active Women According to Occupation

According to the classification adopted by the most recent census, women are represented in the occupations shown in Table 11.2.

TABLE 11.2   Economically Active Women

Type of Employment	Total Number	Percentage
Independent	766,576	60.3
Employer	1,375	0.1
Permanent salary	76,658	6.1
Temporary salary	8,247	0.7
Paid apprentice	1,302	0.1
Unpaid apprentice	8,421	0.7
Domestic worker	400,805	32.0
Total	1,271,135	100.0

Source: Demo 87: Deuxième recensement général de la population et de l'habitat du Cameroun (Yaoundé: Gouvernement Camerounais, 1990–1993).

The large percentage of independent workers among women (60.3 percent) is due to their working in a variety of *petit-métiers* in the informal sector. But these jobs, especially those in the commercial sector, often provide small incomes for women who work as produce sellers, dry goods retailers, hairdressers, public secretaries, and so on. In general, those with little capital have difficulty earning more than CFA Fr 30,000 per month.[4]

The low level of education among women destines them to occupy the lowest rungs of the occupational ladder, where they receive the lowest income. Of economically active women, 32 percent work providing household assistance in jobs that command the lowest official salaries. One in three working women is a domestic servant.

The average income of a domestic worker is between CFA Fr 20,000 and CFA Fr 30,000 per month, a sum lower than the official minimum wage of CFA Fr 33,000. Since the cost of renting the simplest of rooms in a poor neighborhood can reach CFA Fr 4,000 per month in the cities and since women are often responsible for the support of another family member who does not live with them, such as a parent, sibling, child, or cousin, it is apparent that many women have to seek alternate solutions to make ends meet. Prostitution is one of those solutions.

To round out the picture, note that the rate of unemployment is 29.4 percent in Yaoundé and 13.4 percent for women between the ages of fifteen and thirty-four. These figures indicate that one educated woman in ten is unemployed, but the number has undoubtedly increased greatly with the deepening of the economic crisis. A recent survey taken in 1991 of 262 prostitutes in Yaoundé and 236 prostitutes in Douala shows that in Yaoundé, 81.6 percent had received a primary education and 31.6 percent had gotten a high-school diploma (Garcia et al. 1992). In Douala, 48.9 percent had achieved a primary education, and 31.6 percent had finished high school. Thus, it seems that many girls interrupted their studies but became unemployed or held low-paying jobs, which confirms the tendency outlined above. They consequently engaged in prostitution. The average age of prostitutes in Yaoundé was 25.7 years old and in Douala, 30.9 years. Forty percent of the women in these groups were between the ages of twenty and twenty-nine years old.

In order to provide for family members dependent on them, these women frequently turned to prostitution as a *petit-métier,* an occupation that, for lower-class prostitutes, requires no official qualifications and poses no educational barriers to entry.

Family Responsibilities of Women in Cameroon

The question of family responsibilities is an important issue here. The pressure of family responsibilities is one of the explanatory factors in the choice of prostitution as a *petit-métier* among women. Whether single or married, most women have to support family members. Statistics show that unlike single women in the West, single women in Cameroon bear a discriminatory proportion of family responsibility compared to men. At the same time, they head more than one-half as many households as men.

The discussion that follows begins by considering women as heads of households in general before distinguishing between married and single householders. Almost all professional prostitutes and semiprostitutes are single.

In Cameroon, households headed by men are larger than those headed by women (5.50 members in male-headed households compared to 3.69 in female-headed households). This indicates, as shown in Table 11.3, that economically productive women have heavy family responsibilities.

The figures in Table 11.4 show the differences in the matrimonial status of women as heads of households. According to Table 11.4, married women and widows tend to have the largest households, averaging more than four members. However, single heads of households have three peo-

TABLE 11.3   Average Size of Households in Cameroon According to the Sex of the Household Head

Both sexes	5.17 members of household
Male	5.50 members of household
Female	3.69 members of household

Source: Demo 87: Deuxième recensement général de la population et de l'habitat du Cameroun (Yaoundé: Gouvernement Camerounais, 1990–1993).

TABLE 11.4   Average Size of Households Headed by Women

Marital Status	Household Size
All women	3.9
Single	3.0
Married	4.9
Widowed	4.3
Divorced or separated	3.2

Source: Demo 87: Deuxième recensement général de la population et de l'habitat du Cameroun (Yaoundé: Gouvernement Camerounais, 1990–1993).

ple to support who are living under their roof. It is these single women and women alone (especially widows) who are candidates (by choice or constraint) for prostitution, engaged in either full- or part-time.

As for prostitutes themselves, if the number of children is used as a reference point for family responsibility, the survey of 210 prostitutes in Yaoundé shows that 67.5 percent of them had at least one child and that 37.5 percent of them had two (Songue 1993). The prostitutes interviewed were single, and although the questionnaire did not specify whether the children lived with their mothers, the probability is high that the women had financial responsibility for the children. We can therefore conclude that the heavy burden of family responsibilities made these women's incomes insufficient and pushed them into prostitution as a part- or full-time *petit-métier*. At this point it is appropriate to examine the income generated from prostitution in order to assess whether this choice of solution is "worth the effort" compared to the income earned in other professions.

The Income of Prostitutes

Income from prostitution cannot be discussed without classifying types of urban prostitutes. This classification is based on the means of attracting business and the location where sex takes place. This will clarify the ranking of prostitutes' income, which is largely a function of the type of prostitution practiced.

The professional prostitute solicits either at her residence (for those who attract passing customers and wait for their clients in front of their dwellings) or in bars or nightclubs. There are also women who stroll on foot, mainly along certain well-lighted streets where prostitutes gather, generally in the center of town. Solicitation also takes place in restaurants and hotels, where one can find prostitutes sipping a drink or loitering near the reception desk. In addition to these various locations, semiprostitutes solicit their clients in the workplace, at sporting or cultural events, and at private and official receptions, or they solicit on the basis of acquaintanceship or through intermediaries such as taxi drivers, bartenders, and assistants to notable personalities. Solicitation by car or by telephone is more rare. The places where prostitutes go to solicit are chosen according to the type of clients who frequent those locations. The quality and the status of the client are the most determinant factors in the level of remuneration. The clients choose their places of leisure according to their social status and, consequently, in relation to the extent of their purchasing power.

Remuneration differs, for example, according to whether the prostitute is met in an upscale hotel or a neighborhood bar. Beyond that, the extent of remuneration is equally dependent on the location of the actual sexual activity. The remuneration is different depending on whether the activity takes place at home (be it meager or luxurious), in a high-class or low-class hotel, at the home of the client or of a third party, or in a vehicle. The pay scale also depends on the educational level of the prostitute, her standard of living, and the circumstances under which she picks up her client.

Prostitutes' Income Levels

At the bottom of the scale is the professional who attracts clients in passing and receives several a day at approximately CFA Fr 500 per encounter. The cost of a low-level prostitute rarely exceeds CFA Fr 1,000, and she usually has an average of two or three clients per working day. Then there are mid-level prostitutes who earn between CFA Fr 1,000 and CFA Fr 5,000 per encounter. High-caliber prostitutes earn between CFA Fr 5,000 and CFA Fr 20,000 per client and per encounter, although they rarely work without appointments as those in the lower levels do. At the top of the scale, elite prostitutes earn more than CFA Fr 20,000 per encounter. For these prostitutes, income is not always directly a function of the frequency of sexual relations with the client, as it is with lower-level prostitutes. Furthermore, remuneration may be monetary, but it may also be in the form of costly goods such as jewelry, vehicles, trips, or home furnishings.

The previously cited survey (Garcia et al. 1992), conducted in September 1992 among a sample of prostitutes in Yaoundé and Douala, indicates an average cost per encounter of CFA Fr 1,500 in Yaoundé and CFA Fr 1,000 in Douala. These figures include all categories of prostitutes together. The range of prices extends from CFA Fr 500 to CFA Fr 10,000 in

Yaoundé and from CFA Fr 500 to CFA Fr 5,000 in Douala. Fees for an entire night average CFA Fr 3,200 in Yaoundé and CFA Fr 2,700 in Douala.

By making a projection based on this survey and our own research observations, the monthly income of the prostitutes in the lowest category can be estimated at between CFA Fr 30,000 and CFA Fr 50,000, depending on the average frequency of encounters, taking into account both busy days and days off. The monthly income of mid-level prostitutes is between CFA Fr 50,000 and CFA Fr 60,000. High-caliber prostitutes earn between CFA Fr 60,000 and CFA Fr 100,000, and elite prostitutes can earn upwards of CFA Fr 100,000.

In comparison to women in official professions, a low-level prostitute earns more than a household employee, who is at the bottom of the salary scale and earns CFA Fr 20,000 to CFA Fr 30,000 a month. If she manages her activities well, a mid-level prostitute can earn as much as a person with a junior high–school education, whereas an elite-level prostitute can earn as much as a person with a high-school diploma.[5] The monthly salary of certain bureaucrats working in government ministries and holding the equivalent of a bachelor's degree is around CFA Fr 130,000. The monthly income of an elite prostitute can easily exceed that amount, and she usually works fewer hours each week than the forty hours normally associated with a salaried position. The relatively easy access to income and immediate payment (other workers have to wait until the end of the month), as well as the freedom of being self-employed and setting her own hours, are often advantages enough to push a woman into prostitution as a *petit-métier*.

Moreover, many of the prostitutes interviewed had been sexually active in normal romantic relationships before turning to prostitution. They transformed that "useful" relationship, adding a remunerative dimension. In cases like this, prostitution can link the agreeable with the useful, since the prostitute either chooses the client who pleases her (which is not the case for those who solicit) or in essence becomes a concubine. This is often the case for semiprostitutes, who chose their clients without suffering the constraints of survival of professional prostitutes.

Urban prostitution in Cameroon pays as much as some traditional jobs without requiring a forty-hour workweek. It has proven to be a safety net for women in times of crisis, permitting them, by selling themselves, to earn an income of various levels. The profession requires no specific qualifications and can be conducted as well by educated women as by those illiterate or unemployed. In this context, a woman finds herself advantaged in relation to men, since male prostitution is still rare in Cameroon, and in general, it is homosexual. This *petit-métier* thus discriminates negatively against men and can be considered a female response to the professional discrimination women face.

Three life histories serve to illustrate the argument that prostitution provides a considerable source of supplementary income. Of the three examples that follow, one woman is a professional and two are semiprofessionals who have "succeeded" in part-time prostitution.

> C. A. is thirty-four and single. She came to the city at age fourteen to continue her studies while helping one of her aunts with the housework. She came from a poor family in a village not far from Yaoundé. Her parents could no longer afford her schooling. Thus C. A. went to help her aunt, who lived with her children and no longer had a domestic servant in the home. In return, the aunt was to pay for C. A.'s clothing, medical bills, and educational expenses such as tuition, books, and supplies. C. A. ate with the other children and enjoyed household amenities such as electric lights and furniture. However, she went out less frequently than her cousins since she had such duties as cleaning, cooking, and washing the children. In time, C. A. began to have boyfriends in the neighborhood who were slightly older—being between twenty and twenty-five when she was sixteen. She had her first sexual relations with these boyfriends. She received occasional presents from them, usually pocket money. Eventually she began to look for boyfriends who could give her greater remuneration. She went out between 5:00 and 8:00 P.M. in the evening, but her aunt insisted on short outings. Some of her boyfriends were married men, friends of her aunt who, when the aunt was gone, arranged rendezvous with C. A. in town, either at their homes or in cheap hotels. With the profits from this semiprostitution, C. A. bought clothes or presents to bring to her family when she visited home.
>
> Finally, C. A. left school because she did not have the grades necessary to go on to high school and did not have the funds to pay for a private school. She moved from Yaoundé to Douala, where she was kept by one of her boyfriends, who also secured a job for her. While she worked, she continued in semiprostitution and was able to help her parents and brothers with money. She stopped these side activities when she became the mistress of a man who kept her as a virtual second wife, although she never officially married him. She stopped her semiprostitution at the age of twenty-six.
>
> C.H.E. is the daughter of a prostitute. She arrived in Yaoundé at eleven. Her mother lived in a semirural town in the countryside. Her father was a French expatriate, and she has a half sister whose father was also a French expatriate. C.H.E. came to the city to continue her studies and lived with one of her uncles. She lived with him for five years before renting a studio apartment with her sister. She began working as a prostitute while she was still in school. After school, she would passively pick up men, agreeing to go with clients who invited her for a drink or to go out in the evening. C.H.E. already knew, however, that expatriates paid the most, and she preferred them. She focused on expatriate teachers, social workers, and other *coopérant* workers [foreign workers, usually European or American] whom she met while walking home from school, in cafés and nightclubs, or through her cousins, who were also prostitutes.

Sexual relations took place either at the home of clients, in the homes of friends, or in hotels. She rarely used her own home, since her sister was there, but she occasionally received short visits there. The income from her semiprostitution grew, and she bought a moped to get to class before she dropped out of school. Later, she received a minibus as a parting gift from an expatriate client who returned to his own country. She used the van to set up a commercial transportation business between Yaoundé and a neighboring town. The bus had twelve seats and provided a stable source of income. She also continued seeing clients and graduated from intermediate-level to high-class prostitution. Income from her new clientele enabled her to buy a house and open a beauty salon. She finally established a household and had children with an expatriate. C.H.E.'s story illustrates the transformation from low-level to high-level prostitution.

But many daughters of prostitutes or girls who lived with a relative from whom they learned their trade are not as fortunate as C.H.E. and remain streetwalkers, continuing to solicit passers-by. This is the case with prostitutes who work the red-light areas in Yaoundé and Douala, who after five, ten, or more years of activity could not advance. Some prostitutes in these neighborhoods remain in business until they are forty-five or fifty years old. Sometimes, no longer having the strength or physical attractiveness to continue their activities, they return to their villages, where they are supported by their children or extended family.

X. T. is forty and the daughter of a retired bureaucrat. She had a typical education from elementary through high school. While a student, X. T. had more advantages than most Cameroonian students. Food, clothing, housing, and transportation were all above average. Her father drove her to school. They lived in government housing in a middle-class neighborhood. X. T. attended the most prestigious high school in the city, with children whose fathers were also bureaucrats, members of the government (including ministers), important businessmen, or European expatriates. At the age of fifteen or sixteen, she began to go to dances since she was a member of the cultural club at school. She made friends with the boyfriends of older girls, then with students at the university next to the high school. At that time university students received a government stipend equivalent to the salary of low-level bureaucrats. These students could therefore buy luxurious clothes, stereo equipment, and other consumer goods. Since she socialized daily with the children of rich families and well-subsidized university students, especially at dances, X. T. developed a taste for expensive clothes. She wanted to appear chic in the eyes of her girlfriends and to be preferred by the boys at dances. Since her father could not provide these luxuries, she gradually resorted to a form of occasional semiprostitution: She went out with older men who had high incomes. She met them while walking in the city. The men, usually in cars, would invite her for a drink or to come home with them. She also met men at social functions and through mutual acquaintances, as other prostitutes and semiprostitutes do, and she met the personal assistants of prominent men as well. Sexual relations took place at the homes of friends, in the homes of the clients, or in hotels. The income from this semiprostitution allowed X. T. to buy clothes her parents could not afford to buy her, and she could even afford to buy presents for her younger boyfriends. Her more affluent girlfriends were able to buy such things with the pocket money their parents gave them. X. T.'s income also allowed her to go to the movies and buy tickets to dances, among other extras.

X. T. continued this semiprostitution at the university, where she added foreigners to her clients. She met them through old clients, pimps, or other friends involved in similar activities. As a result, she was able to finance studies abroad after her degree. While away, she continued to work as a prostitute. After returning to Cameroon, she was able to acquire a legitimate business and a car and to pay for the education of a family member with her earnings. X. T. explained that a normal job in Cameroon would not have garnered her as much money as high-level prostitution had.

X. T.'s case demonstrates that prostitution often generates more money than traditional professions, particularly during a period of economic crisis when salaries plummet and unemployment rises. Given this economic potential, the next question is whether prostitution as a *petit-métier* contributes to the liberation of women and their financial emancipation from men.

Prostitution and the Liberation of Women

To what extent does prostitution as a *petit-métier* permit a woman to gain financial autonomy from men—from fathers, husbands, and brothers? Does prostitution reduce their control over her? Should this autonomy be described as liberation, since the woman has gained independence in managing both her body and her money?

Traditionally, the sexuality of a young girl or woman in Africa is jealously controlled by the social group she belongs to. This control is effected by her mother, father, and brothers and by all the elders directly concerned with the bridewealth her family will receive upon her marriage. For many, the loss of a young girl's virginity signifies the loss of bridewealth. Consequently, reproductive capacity is jealously protected, as are any other aspects of a girl's sexual relations. This control is exercised to avoid social disorder and often results in restrictions and prohibitions on young girls' behavior.

When a woman engages in prostitution, she frees the use of her body from the grip of society. She assumes sole management of her sexuality, since in theory, she decides with whom she will have intimate relations, as well as when and where they will occur. At this level, it is evident that she shakes off the traditional shackles imposed on her sexual activity: She freely enjoys her body. Considered from this perspective, prostitution contributes to the sexual liberation of women from men.

It is important, however, to put this assertion in perspective because the prostitute does not act alone. She cannot function without the client, who exchanges money for service. In reality, because the prostitute must obtain money from the client, she cannot apply aesthetic norms of choice. She is a commodity, thus she must submit herself to the desires of the consumer. This is reflected in her clothing, her overall appearance, and even in the sequence of sexual relations. In sum, if the prostitute enjoys the freedom to escape certain social norms, this freedom is nothing but a relative trope, since the man regains his authority and domination by imposing his standards on the situation (the prostitute must please *him*). This results in even more dependence on the client—this man whom she must please because he supplies her income, food, and clothing, as well as other primary and secondary needs (her extras or luxuries). Thus, a prostitute-money-client triangle characterizes this activity, in Cameroon, as elsewhere. Male control over females through the medium of money is basic to the transaction. Nonetheless, a prostitute does live on the money she makes: Behind every franc note she earns, there is a man who dominates her.

Moreover, the notion of freedom is tied to dignity. The liberation of women assumes that they can be independent of men and that they can attain this independence in a manner that permits them to acquire or affirm this dignity. Is it possible to speak realistically of dignity if a woman prostitutes that which is most dear in the material world: her own body, which is often said to be priceless? It can be said, of course, that the prostitute frees herself from misery and from poverty—and one cannot be dignified or free when bound in the slavery of poverty. But such speculation gives rise to a debate among feminists and philosophers that must remain unexplored here.

Conclusion: Prostitution, AIDS, and Women's Liberation in Cameroon

The extent to which prostitution emerges in Cameroonian society as a *petit-métier* during times of economic crisis has been outlined in this chapter. Women, still subject to discrimination in education and employment opportunities, compete at a disadvantage in the job market. Consequently, many of them turn to the sale of their bodies, which becomes their employment. This *petit-métier*, even if marginalized, is as remunerative as traditional employment and often requires less effort.

This chapter has also initiated a discussion of prostitution as an activity that contributes to the liberation of women from male constraints, in the sense that women acquire freedom of sexual activity and relative financial autonomy through its practice. This freedom, however, has been shown to be relative, since behind the prostitute's earnings stands a client, a man upon whom she depends for survival.

Participation in semiprostitution is spreading and merits greater attention in the political and economic frameworks of researchers. Prostitution affects more and more people in Cameroon, especially young girls; there are girls who are already prostitutes at thirteen. This phenomenon is causing social and economic transformation, and it has financial and legal implications as well. Moreover, there is the complication of AIDS, which is closely linked to prostitution. In Cameroon, where there is little intravenous drug use, HIV infection spreads, in order of decreasing importance, through sexual contact; blood contamination, either from dirty syringes or transfusions of untested blood; other sources of blood, such as mother-to-fetus infection, contaminated razor blades, and so on.

Since sexual contact is the primary means of transmission, emphasis has been placed on prevention among high-risk groups, especially prostitutes and soldiers. A survey of prostitutes revealed a 25 percent rate of HIV infection in Yaoundé and a 45 percent rate in Douala (Garcia et al. 1992). And these figures are certainly growing.

AIDS should therefore be considered when examining the link between women's liberation and prostitution. Although the profession may bring certain financial rewards, women find themselves once again discriminated against, since prostitutes are more likely than any other people in Cameroon to contract AIDS. The virus is more likely to travel from men to women than the reverse. A recent study shows that between 10 and 30 percent of women who had regular sexual contact with an HIV-positive partner contracted the virus, but only 5 to 15 percent of men with regular HIV exposure tested positive themselves (Panos Dossier 1990). Prostitutes, with their multiple partners, are thus particularly at risk.

Economically, a prostitute is dependent on her client for material survival, whether he is an occasional customer or a "sugar daddy." Consequently, she must submit to his sexual desires without always considering her risk of infection. Although prostitutes in Yaoundé and Douala are aware of the importance of using condoms, clients often refuse to cooperate. Men frequently propose a higher payment to keep a prostitute from insisting on a condom. They make offers attractive enough for many prostitutes to accept and thereby expose themselves to undue risk. When interviewed, low-level prostitutes often said that when a man refused to wear a condom, he might well double the standard rate for an encounter. At that price, they were inclined to accept the offer. Thus, unprotected sexual contact continues. Prostitutes are too economically dependent on their clients to exercise the option of insisting on safer sex.

Culturally, the initiative for sexual relations in Cameroonian society traditionally comes from men, whether among married couples or otherwise. Men decide when and under what circumstances sex takes place. It is unseemly for a woman to make advances. In sex, as in other domains such as conversation, finances, and choice of housing, men exercise authority over women. A prostitute is thus doubly dominated, both by culture and by the client's money.

In summary, the financial independence that prostitution can bring is only an illusion. If prostitution is to be considered a profession because it provides an income, it should also contribute to a woman's fulfillment and her liberation through the satisfaction of her needs. If these factors are included in the calculation, then prostitution remains only a *petit-métier*.

Notes

1. Translator's note: The term *petit-métier* has no direct English equivalent. The use of "odd job" comes closest and shares the connotation that the activity takes place in the informal sector of the economy, but it overlooks the sense of continuity and profession implied in *petit-métier*. Consequently, the use of the French term will be retained throughout this chapter.
2. This refers to sexual exchanges including not only copulation but also such acts as caresses, fellatio, the exposure of the prostitute's nudity to the client, and so on.
3. The demographic figures come from the most recent general census, taken in April 1987.
4. US$1 equals about CFA Fr 570.
5. Translator's note: "Junior high" and a "high-school diploma" are the U.S. equivalents of the French school system's *3e classe* and *baccalauréat*, respectively, the terms used in the original text.

References

Garcia, Dr. Calleja J. M., Dr. P. Ngoumou, A. Boupda, and V. O'Dell. 1992. "HIV Seroprevalence Study Among Commercial Sex Workers in Yaoundé and Douala." Yaoundé: Ministry of Health, AIDS Control Unit.
Panos Dossier. 1990. *Triple Jeopardy: Women and AIDS*. London: Panos Institute.
Songue, Paulette. 1993. *SIDA et prostitution au Cameroun*. Paris: L'Harmattan.

Part Five

City Streets:
Politics and Community

12

"I Am with You as Never Before": Women in Urban Protest Movements, Alexandra Township, South Africa, 1912–1945

JOHN NAURIGHT

Alexandra Township, located eight miles from central Johannesburg, has achieved almost mythical historical status in the minds of many black South Africans, its reputation perhaps eclipsed only by Sophiatown and District Six, both of which fell victim to apartheid bulldozers. As the "unhappy step-child of the Rand's sprawling industrial growth," Alexandra became almost synonymous with the resilience of resistance to apartheid (*Star*, 10 January 1947). Since the 1970s, many observers have noted that African National Congress (ANC) support appeared more solid in Alexandra than in any other township. Indeed, the township has a long history as a site of struggle for black political rights. During the 1930s and 1940s, black women and men fought to preserve the basic level of self-government granted to Alexandra as a freehold township in the first decade of the twentieth century.

In the period from 1933 to 1945, Alexandra residents were subjected to the increasingly harsh conditions of segregationist policies that firmly entrenched local white domination and black oppression along lines of race, class, and gender. This process also naturally fostered the concomitant growth of resistance, as residents perceived the potential of collective action. From 1938 to 1945, Alexandra was the site of protests against the white administration and its challenges to township self-government, its increases in bus fares and rents, and its threat of township removal and relocation. Each of these issues had dimensions particular to women. At times black women raised their concerns in conjunction with those voiced by the black male standholder elite (petit bourgeois landowners), but they also organized their own protests. Consequently, the nature of resistance reflected cleavages based on gender and class.

This chapter explores the complex dynamics of resistance to class exploitation and gender oppression by examining the roles played in this struggle by working women and the male township elite (although some women formed part of this elite layer in Alexandra). Specifically, attention focuses on the organic networks created by women. These networks evolved through commonalities like escaping police detection of beer brewing, attending church groups, and involvement in everyday collective experiences such as gathering water or buying food. Most women spent a large portion of their time in Alexandra, which allowed for the formation of tighter female networks than those formed by men. Mobilization of such networks enabled women to act in the forefront of protests, from initial action in 1918 through the 1940s bus boycotts. They exhibited a militancy that belies the accuracy of earlier explanations suggesting that they participated in spontaneous, unorganized uprisings or that local male leaders manipulated them. Through their actions, women tried to enforce a broad community solidarity that resisted white domination and intrusions by the state into local affairs. By contrast, the African and "Coloured"[1] property-owning male elite attempted to portray their particular class interests and ideology as the universal ideal of all township residents. Most property owners were unwilling to openly challenge state authority, preferring negotiation to mass meetings and protests. They constructed a sense of "respectability" on the basis of property ownership that often mitigated against an all-inclusive form of mass protest.

As a major center of apartheid resistance, Alexandra has drawn the attention of several scholars. Articles have appeared on the bus boycotts staged in the 1940s and in 1957 (Stadler 1981; Hirson 1989; Lodge 1983; Pirie 1983), a Ph.D. thesis has examined Alexandra from the time of its initial settlement in 1912 to 1948 (Nauright 1992), and other researchers have focused on the economic and political development of Alexandra from the beginning of the twentieth century to the 1980s (Tourakis 1981; Sarakinsky 1984).

Most accounts of Alexandra protest movements focus on the role of institutional leaders and draw attention away from the fact that working women enforced these movements. Although Alf Stadler states in "A Long Way to Walk" that the "importance of women in the [bus] boycotts can scarcely be exaggerated," he then proceeds to assert the dominance of men (1981:237). For Stadler, the boycotts of 1940 and 1942 "exemplif[ied] . . . the thousands of occasions on which black *men* have attempted to intervene in the direction of their lives, and . . . they constituted the forces which were indispensable in providing . . . larger movements with their momentum" (emphasis added) (1981:239). Thus, while Stadler acknowledges black men's agency, he fails to similarly recognize the role of black women.

Baruch Hirson's account of the bus boycotts in *Yours for the Union* (1989) acts as a partial corrective, since he acknowledges the prominence of the Women's Brigade in the protests. However, although Hirson asserts that "without the women there could have been no success in the bus boycotts," he is consistent with other accounts in concentrating on men's actions. Stadler and Hirson construct histories that praise the heroics of the male working class. Women exist, but only as a homogeneous group peripheral to the main action. This interpretation neglects evidence that shows that working-class black women formed the vanguard of protest in Alexandra, organizing and sustaining militancy at a grassroots level. Stadler and Hirson both indicate the special interests women had in the boycotts, but they fail to acknowledge that women and men acted as *gendered* beings. As such, we must reconceptualize the view of women's actions and their construction of the networks that mobilized resistance and sustained mass action.

The Making of Alexandra

In 1905, Herbert Boshoff Papenfus formed the Alexandra Township Company (ATC) with the intent of attracting white settlers to a new township located approximately nine miles from the center of Johannesburg. By 1912, however, no whites had purchased stands, and Papenfus was forced to revise his strategy. Papenfus, a member of Parliament at the time, applied for Alexandra's exemption from the Natives Land Act then under debate. He hoped to attract Africans and Coloureds who wanted to purchase land in an area free from white interference.[2]

As a private township, Alexandra was excluded from the provisions of the 1913 Land Act, and future regulations did not apply unless specifically extended by new legislation. As a result, the township remained exempt from most major segregation and influx-control measures until passage of the Better Administration of Designated Areas Act of 1964. Freedom from restrictions proved an attractive incentive for many blacks, particularly from the 1930s onward, when many Africans migrated to the urban areas in search of work in the rapidly expanding economy. Population statistics for Alexandra are scarce and inconsistent, but available estimates allow for a basic assessment of the township's rapid growth. Alexandra's population exploded from eight to ten thousand in 1932 to an estimated forty-five to fifty thousand by 1940 and reached eighty to one hundred thousand or more by the late 1940s, by which time it had become one of the most densely populated areas in South Africa (Nauright 1992:20–21).

White officials initially believed in the purported "civilizing" effect of property ownership. Indeed, Alexandra seemed the perfect place to establish a "respectable" propertied class of Africans. Since township residents could acquire freehold rights, many Africans and Coloureds purchased property and established businesses to try to accumulate capital. In 1943, Dr. A. B. Xuma, leader of the ANC and the medical officer for Alexandra, estimated that the township had 422 shops and 248 stores within its boundaries, although many of these were small operations such as fish-and-chip shops (Tourakis 1981:24). Property rights, along with business ownership, provided some Alexandra residents with the material basis for forming a township elite. In contrast to other predominantly working-class urban areas such as Brakpan (Sapire 1987), there was a substantial petit bourgeois "layer" in Alexandra with distinct interests and a worldview based on their class position and gendered identity.

Although women could own property in Alexandra, few acquired the capital necessary to purchase stands. Furthermore, there is little evidence that female standholders played a prominent role in the formal political affairs of the township elite. Women were not allowed to sit on the Alexandra Health Committee (AHC), the local governing body. From the beginnings of black settlement until the end of the 1930s, male household heads who held or owned property publicly dominated local ideology, politics, and business. Standholders initially portrayed themselves as "respectable" and "civilized" in hopes of obtaining more control over their own affairs and greater acceptance from white officials. Initially, respectability required some form of Christian beliefs (including ideas about gender roles), ownership of property, and a positive outlook toward whites. The male elite held regular meetings to discuss events in the township, and their wives and the few female standholders frequently organized socials. These events reinforced the unity of property owners as a distinct group. Standholders distanced themselves from tenants and weekend visitors and manipulated their ideological worldview in attempts to control events within Alexandra (Nauright 1992:44–81).

For the most part, members of the male elite were wary of mass action, preferring to position themselves in the eyes of the state as responsible representatives of residents. While resisting white attempts to limit their ability to accumulate, those in the township elite wanted to foster their connections with whites, hoping to increase their power in local government structures (Nauright 1992:61–69). Despite this, some standholders fought for the inclusion of residents in local politics and protest.

Although the standholders were not a homogeneous group, many of them created an identity rooted in their ownership of property and their business interests. They also established political organizations to further their particular class interests and maintain unity. However, a series of changes emerged in the 1930s that eroded the social and economic position of property owners and facilitated the transition to resistance through mass action. During the late 1920s and early 1930s, an increasing stream of people migrated to Rand (short for Witwatersrand) towns from the countryside. In addition, many blacks in urban areas were forced to relocate as a result of government removal programs. Alexandra attracted many of these displaced people because of its lack of municipal controls and the relatively easy access to work-seeker permits in the township. By the mid-1930s, most residents were not property owners but rather were tenants, creating a series of contradictions that challenged the hegemonic position of the elite. Standholders now encountered difficulties maintaining their political and social dominance in face of the larger number of residents. However, they also stood to profit from the increased income available from rents, a circumstance that often prevented total financial ruin for many property owners.

Despite the increase in the number of tenants, standholders faced increasing financial difficulties. Alfred Hoernlé, chair of the AHC from late 1941 until his death in 1943, observed that "European money-lenders" saw "a glorious chance of making a lucrative profit" by lending money to standholders so that they could build extensions for their houses (1943:10). An estimated 75 percent of standholders had to make regular payments on bonds, and as interest rates rose through the 1930s, standholders opted to raise rents for rooms that were often in terrible condition.[3] This phenomenon, which Hoernlé called "slum landlordism," drew fire from whites anxious to have Alexandra removed. Consistent with his ideas of liberal stewardship, Hoernlé defended the actions of male property owners in Alexandra, stating: "At worst, what the African standholders have done was to imitate many Europeans in doing what Europeans commonly regard as both legal and moral" (1943:22).

Standholders experienced economic and political marginalization. Some fought to maintain their former status by asking for increased state protection; others urged an all-inclusive movement of residents against state control, township removal, and rises in bus fares and rents. This was not an even and linear process, however, as elites often exhibited contradictory positions that resulted from the strong material and ideological ties that were part of their established and "respectable" status. Although many elite men were involved in formal protest leadership positions, it appears that women were the genuine vanguard of struggle. They organized and maintained militancy in Alexandra, whereas the male elite attempted to resolve conflict through administrative channels. The relationships formed among working women created different networks of mobilization for their work and for their protest activities than those of the male elite.

The Women of Alexandra

The erosion of precapitalist societies was a complicated process, one for which the timing and circumstances were often regionally specific. The Rand was the destination of thousands of men and women, and the process of urbanization had particular significance for young women, for whom migration "represented at least a partial escape from the expectations of the patriarchal system that prevailed" (Bozzoli 1991:81). Alexandra acted as a magnet for the influx of the women from rural areas and other urban centers cleared by government removal schemes. In *Women of Phokeng*, oral testimony reveals that women felt they were rarely forced to migrate to cities. For most, migration was "willingly undertaken" or came from "a sense of responsibility of kin." Significantly, migration to the townships was, for many women, a "matter of prestige or status" (Bozzoli 1991:92). Consider the typical case of Sophie Serokane, a woman from Phokeng in the northern Transvaal, who moved to Alexandra after originally deciding to go to Johannesburg:

> All of my friends were already working in Johannesburg. It was a prestige to work in Johannesburg by then. One had to try one's best to work there. Our friends used to tell us about all of the good things which were happening in Johannesburg. I also discovered that they were telling the truth when I was working there eventually. (Bozzoli 1991:92)

Although impoverishment was a crucial factor in the exodus from rural areas, many women actively sought to migrate as a means of controlling their own destiny.

Some women who moved to Alexandra came in search of their husbands, often finding them in new relationships. Women also were more vulnerable economically since their employment options were more limited than men's. Phil Bonner argues that these factors led many women to seek stability in new relationships with others in urban areas (1988). Material conditions may have mitigated against working women's freedom, but the lack of state restrictions in Alexandra allowed for a measure of female autonomy. Many male-female relationships were informal, allowing some women to leave abusive situations more easily than was possible in the rural areas.

Women often had to earn an income, as male wages were insufficient for family survival. Unlike most men, who worked in Johannesburg or its northern suburbs, working women had few economic options outside the township. Some women obtained employment in white northern suburb households as domestic laborers or washerwomen. However, most women stayed in Alexandra, minding children, tending whatever measure of crops could be grown on the small plots of land, and engaging in beer brewing. Participation in informal sector activities was significant because it allowed working women to spend time at home while earning extra income for their new households and families. Not only did this help to stabilize the tenuous existence of women themselves, but women's labor in the informal sector also served to secure the household as a productive unit.

Most working-class women in Alexandra appear to have brewed beer, an activity that took place in the yards. As an economic pursuit, beer brewing was a means to resist wage labor or to supplement an inadequate income. Only women brewed beer, which reflected the gendered nature of informal sector production. Beer brewing, traditional in rural areas, was also an integral part of African culture and religion (Krige 1932). With women entering the urban areas, the cultural and economic matrix of beer brewing was refashioned. In town, new relationships developed that "enmeshed the participants in relations of mutual assistance, and allowed an informal ethic of community solidarity to emerge" (Sapire 1987:375).

Beer brewing challenged the liberal Christian ideals of proper behavior, and there were women in Alexandra like Nthana Mokale who accepted these notions of "respectability," differentiating themselves from those women they labeled as "disreputable":

> We did not attend *stokvels* [savings clubs that included socializing and entertainment] and clubs. Only women who didn't mind to have their names degraded by being participants in such lowly gatherings attended these clubs. Drinking and being merry in this fashion wasn't our line. We were only interested in working and keeping our jobs, and not at things we didn't come out here for. (Bozzoli 1991:142)

Nevertheless, many working women ultimately merged Christian beliefs with the production of beer for sale, since the income thus derived was

often essential for economic survival. The contradictions between ideological ideals and material reality illustrate that African women did not
simply internalize Christian values but pursued their livelihood rather
than automatically accepting white-constructed moral constraints. Many
township Christian women regarded beer brewing as a respectable and
acceptable practice for Christians. Beer sales brought households much
larger amounts of money when compared to the low wages paid to washerwomen and domestic servants, who also encountered hard working
conditions. From the only precise evidence available, Ellen Hellmann
(1934:44–47) found that women's incomes from brewing were analogous
to the average wages earned by men. Belinda Bozzoli suggests that "of all
the informal activities," beer brewing "required the most robustly flexible
morality" (1991:141).

When the state attempted to halt the liquor trade from 1916 onward,
women developed sophisticated networks to avoid police detection.
Working women in Alexandra developed intelligence networks to protect them from police raids by making contacts with officers sympa-
thetic to their activities. As township resident Rosinah Setsome later
recounted:

> They used to raid us towards dawn. The black policemen did not arrest us.
> They told us when the white policemen would accompany them in their
> raids. Thus we knew when to expect them. . . . The black policemen did not
> bother us because they used to drink at my sister's place. These black police-
> men would normally pretend that they are searching. Thereafter they would
> come out and tell their counterparts that there was no liquor here. The liquor
> was however hidden in the wardrobe. . . . They knew that they would come
> back later to drink. (Bozzoli 1991:159–160)

Working-class women in Alexandra demonstrated a remarkable ability
to avoid detection through networks of cooperation. Because brewing involved confrontations with white notions of respectability, these relationships formed by women were a crucial part of resident oppositional
culture.

Women, Economic Hardship, Protest, and Politics, 1916–1933

Between 1912 and 1933, protest in Alexandra primarily took the form of
formal complaints to the AHC, to the township company, or to state officials, usually in the Native Affairs Department (NAD). Many residents
were aware of Alexandra's special status as a private township beyond
municipal control. In this period, state officials treated male standholders

with a certain respect, which allowed some mutual trust to emerge between NAD officials represented on the AHC and the local male elite. Police raids and the enforcement of restrictions on brewing and other activities eroded this trust. Residents did not agree with all regulations, but the prohibition on beer brewing caused the most complaints. In addition, economic hardship and competition from white and Asian traders located in or near Alexandra exacerbated tensions.

There is no evidence that Alexandra experienced a period of significant political radicalization after World War I. The protests are better explained by the rise in the cost of living, which severely affected Alexandra's residents. Bonner shows that the retail price index on the Rand rose dramatically in the second half of 1917 and continued to rise into 1921. This increase in the cost of living led to two years of militant agitation in some areas from 1918 to 1920 (Bonner 1982:273–274).

In February 1918, Alexandra women, with the support of a few men, organized a protest that led to an investigation by Herbert Sutton Cooke, sub-native commissioner of the Witwatersrand and assistant director of Native Labor. A rise in bus fares precipitated the women's complaints. The cost of bus transport was a historically contentious issue in Alexandra, given its distance from the city center of Johannesburg and the absence of a railway line. Fares especially affected many township women, as they had to carry laundry several miles on foot to the white suburbs if buses and taxis were too expensive. In early 1918, fares increased by one-third to one-half, rising from nine pence to one shilling for a one-way ticket and from one shilling to two shillings per round-trip. Shortly thereafter, officials announced without consultation a still higher fare of three shillings per round-trip.[4]

Alexandra Township Company Secretary Lilius Campbell, who ran or owned several businesses in the township until the 1930s, organized the bus service and set the fares. Her business activities were a source of contention for residents. Some residents opposed Campbell's involvement in any business within the township, as they wanted local control of all economic activity. Others were annoyed at the high costs of services and at Campbell's profiteering at their expense.

Furthermore, women protesting against higher bus fares also organized a boycott of Campbell's Alexandra store. By early 1918, the prices for items in the store had risen dramatically as well. The sharply increased cost of living compounded the township women's frustration, and Campbell was a natural target. They argued that Campbell had no right or title to conduct a business in the township, as the terms of deeds of purchase and sale explicitly stated that no "European" or "Asian" persons could own property or businesses. Women picketed the store to enforce their boycott.[5] Campbell and Native Affairs Department officials ne-

gotiated a settlement, and the result was an increase in the number of res-
ident-owned shops and greater dialogue between Campbell and residents in future years.

The demonstration led by township women was one of the few open
protests by Alexandra residents before the mid-1930s. As in the 1922 complaints against police night raids on liquor, many residents, primarily
women, directed their anger at whites invading their space (Nauright
1992:44–81). Standholders (and tenants) were hard pressed to maintain
"respectable" economic and social practices during the 1920s and 1930s, a
time of rising costs for consumer goods, higher costs of transport, and increasing building costs. Many were forced into the illicit liquor trade that
brought participants into direct confrontation with the police and state officials. Growth of the illicit liquor trade also prompted officials to argue
for intensification of state control over Alexandra.

Thus, the only significant public protest in Alexandra before the 1930s
was led by women. Women also played important roles in the bus boycotts of the early 1940s. They had created networks of communication
around beer brewing and spent more time in the township than most
men. Clearly, female participation in protests should not be dismissed as
"spontaneous" or unorganized reactions to immediate issues; rather, the
nature of women's organization and networks in African urban areas
needs closer examination.

A transformation of the social configuration in the townships emerged
during the mid-1930s. The number of migrants to Alexandra increased
dramatically, which rapidly changed the relations of production in
Alexandra. With the onset of World War II, prices rose rapidly, as did the
cost of fixed items such as rent and transportation, resulting in a general
deterioration of living conditions (Janisch 1940). Because women exercised control over the household economy, they were responsible for
making up for income shortfalls and had to reduce expenditures on such
"flexible" items as food and clothing. Economic tensions increased, and
the networks forged by working-class women became more and more
crucial to their own survival and to that of their families.

As Alexandra's population swelled and overcrowded conditions wors-
ened, the growth of violence accelerated. This led some women to leave
the township, but for others it fostered an environment conducive to the
growth of a militant political consciousness. The erosion of the male
elite's hegemonic position and the increase of female economic power
within the township created the conditions for working women to play a
critical role in mass resistance. In addition, frequent confrontations with
white authorities over beer brewing had generated a subversive culture
that, when coupled with material conditions, formed the basis for political opposition against the intrusions of the state. For example, consider

the experience of Naomi Setshedi, a woman involved in beer brewing in Alexandra:

> She enjoyed life in Alexandra in the earlier years, but gangsterism and later political and economic circumstances drove her to evolve a fairly militant political consciousness. She joined the bus boycotts, the potato boycott, and the women's antipass campaign, and in spite of experiences in jail and repression, remained loyal to the spirit of these causes in her later life. (Bozzoli 1991:24–25)

This opposition also had a practical political aspect, for brewers used the networks they had formed to protect themselves from the authorities and to mobilize for action. Women harnessed these networks to protest against many things, perhaps the most prominent of which were increases in bus fares and the dictates of white state officials.

Women and Resistance in Alexandra, 1939–1946

In Alexandra, resistance to increases in government control and bus fares took place under the overarching context of the threat of township removal. Some white residents living in suburbs to the north of Alexandra formed the North Eastern Districts Protection League (NEDPL) in 1938. They lobbied the Johannesburg City Council, urging that body to support the abolition of Alexandra Township "for the betterment of the inhabitants themselves and the security of the community as a whole."[6] African township residents reacted strongly against any suggestion of relocation, as property owners stood to lose their freehold titles and most tenants did not want to live under a system of increased municipal control. In addition, residents who owned their own property had established a psychological sense of permanence and refused to join the growing exodus of Africans who were constantly facing relocation in many urban areas. One woman summed up the feelings of many Alexandra residents when she stated: "Where do the white people want us to go? When I lived in Doornfontein until 1929 we were told that we were a nuisance and we were badgered to such an extent that we decided to remove to Alexandra Township" (*Bantu World*, 1 April 1939). After this threat was made to the future existence of Alexandra, mass meetings became commonplace in the township's Number Two Square, which could accommodate several thousand people.

In early May 1939, over one thousand residents attended a meeting to protest against attempts to abolish the township. The Communist Party–linked Youth League of South Africa sponsored the meeting, but all the speakers were representatives of various Alexandra organizations.

The participants expressed their indignation at white agitation to remove the township and decided to send a deputation to meet the Johannesburg mayor, J. J. Page, and the Transvaal provincial administrator, General J. J. Pienaar, to discuss the matter (*Bantu World*, 6 May 1939).

Josie Palmer, a Communist Party activist and member of the Daughters of Africa (DOA), led the deputation, and she firmly reiterated the residents' refusal to move to municipal townships. Palmer suggested that the state ought to loan money to the AHC so that conditions could be improved. Her statement sparked a response from Daniel Koza, secretary of the Alexandra Joint Committee and later a founding member of the African Democratic Party, who argued that township residents had not had a meeting to organize strategies for responses to the calls for removal. Koza challenged the right of Palmer, a woman and not a local resident, to lead an Alexandra deputation (*Rand Daily Mail*, 15 May 1939). In light of the mass demonstrations in support of Palmer's demands, however, it is likely that Koza was also upset that the deputation consisted of tenants and not standholders (Hirson 1989:94–104). This incident highlighted the growing power struggle in Alexandra over the control of protest between conservative standholders and the movement toward a mass struggle composed of women and male tenants.

The protection of property was not the only issue on the protest agenda. During 1939, bus fares for travel between 8:00 A.M. Monday and one P.M. Saturdays increased from four pence to five pence and rose to six pence for weekend travel. Fares remained at these rates until August 1940.[7] For several months, township residents tried to get owners to lower the fares to four pence but were unsuccessful. In early August 1940, a partial boycott of buses was organized. E. P. Mart Zulu chaired the first bus boycott committee and took a strong stand against R. G. Baloyi and other bus owners. However, Mart Zulu tried to decree that there should be no public protest meetings. Years later, Modikwe Dikobe noted that standholders "were dead against a tenant taking part in any activities . . . [tenants] were even prohibited from holding meetings on the square" (Couzens 1979:99–100).

Groups of women picketed at the bus stops to enforce the boycott as they had done in earlier local boycotts. The prominence of women reflects their inability to pay higher fares and the strength of women's communication networks formed during brewing and washing in the river or in the yards. Working women spent more time in the township than male workers and could quickly mobilize resistance supporters through these communication networks. As the *Bantu World* noted on August 31, 1940: "The women of Alexandra Township are the Amazons. They've sent an ultimatum to the bus owners asking for reduction in the fare." Owners agreed to return to the four-pence fare on weekdays, which satisfied residents.[8]

The success of the short 1940 boycott must have bolstered the confidence of residents in their ability to force bus owners to adhere to their demands. It also strengthened confidence in the potential of large-scale protest. The streets of Alexandra were not quiet for long, as residents quickly focused their attention on the authoritarian conduct of AHC leader H. G. Falwasser. The immediate issue that aroused protest against Falwasser was his continuing failure to accept the appointment of one Mr. Frederick, a "Coloured" man, as a junior clerk for the AHC, despite AHC approval of his appointment at two meetings in March and May 1940.[9] Soon after, the Transvaal administration's proposal to reconstitute the AHC further angered residents. The new AHC would consist of three nominated white members to be appointed by the administrator, thus ending the role of local property owners on AHC administration. In August 1940, A. B. Xuma argued that the scheme would be a retrogressive step and would alienate residents and strain African support for the government during the crisis caused by World War II. Xuma asked that the administrator receive a deputation of black AHC members before deciding how to reform the committee. Finally, he politely warned the government that the "people are very much agitated over this matter."[10]

Less than three weeks after the successful bus boycott, residents held a mass meeting at Number Two Square in Alexandra on August 25, under the auspices of the Alexandra United (Front) Committee (AUFC). Many township organizations were involved in the formation of the AUFC, which aimed to channel protest against Falwasser and the proposed all-white AHC. An estimated eight thousand residents attended the mass meeting, at which it was resolved unanimously to demand Falwasser's immediate resignation.[11] The advertising for the meeting stated local grievances clearly:

> Residents of Alexandra! Our rights in the Township are being further threatened. Everyone knows that the Health Committee lawfully elected a Non-European clerk about five months ago. He has not as yet been allowed to take up his job. Furthermore, there is a move to set up a totally European Health Committee and Non-European Advisory Board. Now you all know that the Advisory Boards have NO say whatever. Are we then to be left at the mercy of a handful of Europeans who have not our interests at heart? NO![12]

In response to the AHC crisis, the government sent the Native Affairs Commission (NAC) to investigate the situation for two days in October 1940. Hundreds of residents carrying placards demanding representation on the AHC demonstrated outside the hall before the first NAC hearings. The gathering concluded with the singing of "Nkosi 'Sikelele Afrika," then six hundred residents packed the hall to listen to the evidence pre-sented.[13] Xuma testified to Falwasser's hostile attitude toward blacks, and A. Lynn Saffrey, an SAIRR (South African Institute of Race Relations) leader on the AHC, stated that there was no case for the abolition of resi-dent representation (*Rand Daily Mail*, 10 October 1940). In the end, the commission decided that there was no proof that black AHC members had been a failure and recommended that blacks form a majority on the AHC, provided there was a white chairman with veto powers.[14]

The provincial administration dismissed the recommendations of the NAC and proceeded with plans for an all-white committee. In addition, the findings of the NAC investigation were not published for several months after the October 1940 inquiry. Nothing had happened by May 1941, prompting public calls for the findings to be released, and another mass meeting brought a unanimous protest against the delay. People in Alexandra became convinced that the provincial administration was ig-noring the NAC's recommendations.[15] After repeated calls, General Pienaar, the Transvaal provincial administrator, agreed to meet with rep-resentatives of the Alexandra residents in June 1941. Dr. Xuma, now president-general of the ANC, headed the deputation. He stated the resi-dents' uniform opposition to Falwasser's reign, to the proposal for an all-white committee, and to an advisory board with no real power. Xuma's response indicates a split between male standholders and female and male tenants over the proposed course of protest. According to Xuma, the AHC

is only tolerated for the time being because there are law-abiding and patient people among the standholders of Alexandra Township who have con-stantly pleaded with that large section of ratepayers who suggested boy-cotting the committee and refusing to pay rates as a protest against "taxation without representation." Even more drastic action has been suggested against the committee. The task of restraining the masses taking the law into their own hands has fallen upon the shoulders of some of these men who are now before you. . . . Some of the women members are said to have stated that they would rather be shot than be compelled to be legislated for by a Committee in which they have no confidence. I am not inclined to take this statement as an irresponsible, vain threat.[16]

Thus, although many Alexandra residents opposed Falwasser, clearly the question of how to protest prompted different answers from male stand-holders and working-class women. The propertied male elite restrained the more militant tactics of women in favor of further negotiation within the structures of white political power.

Falwasser responded to Xuma by attacking the "native and coloured agitators"—he feared they could establish themselves on the AHC. Falwasser found it "absurd" to suggest that the AUFC had "restrained the masses," believing instead that they had encouraged protest against him.[17] This view underestimates the self-generated militancy of working women, which was directed toward rational goals. On August 18, 1941, over seventy women entered the offices of the Alexandra Health Committee and demanded that they be closed. According to the director of Native Labor, "the women then took up a truculent attitude" and the appearance of the police "had no effect in silencing or moving the women away." Because the demonstration followed a mass meeting of township residents the day before, the director stated, "There is no doubt in my mind that it was instigated by the men."[18] Once again, this interpretation did not grant women the ability to organize toward a common objective. Women protesting outside the offices of the AHC made three demands. The first, removal of Falwasser as the chair of the AHC, was a popular desire of many residents, whether male or female. The other two demands related to the cost and distribution of the new water system.[19] The growth of the township population and the expansion of the illicit liquor trade prompted washerwomen and beer brewers to raise demands particular to their situation. Thus, contrary to government opinion, women were quite capable of extending the issues put forward by the male standholder elite to reflect their own concerns.

Falwasser eventually succumbed to official concern over the level of local protest against him. The director of Native Labor noted that "nothing now will stay this hostility. The Natives are resolved that Mr. Falwasser must go. . . . The Provincial Authorities should realise that when popular movements by property owners take place, there is practically no difference between those of Natives from those of Europeans."[20] Falwasser tendered his resignation and well-known liberal leader Alfred Hoernlé took over as chair of the AHC, chosen for the post in an attempt to restore the credibility of the AHC among both residents and state officials. Hoernlé was a leader in the joint councils movement and a founding member and leader of the SAIRR. It is clear, however, that Hoernlé was out of touch with events in Alexandra and with the wishes of many groups of residents. For example, he did very little regarding the disputes over bus fares in October 1942. More disconcerting to residents, however, was his rather contradictory stance on the removal of Alexandra. In *The Future of Alexandra*, written shortly before his death in 1943, Hoernlé made a plea for the retention of Alexandra providing conditions could be improved. Hoernlé stated that removal would stimulate mass discontent not only for the fifty thousand people affected but also for Africans throughout the Union of South Africa. He placed the blame for poor living conditions, which he felt had been exaggerated, on both blacks and whites, noting that the authorities who had put little money into town-

ship improvements were willing to spend exorbitant amounts on removal. Despite his last-minute efforts, Hoernlé was unable to sway state
opinion about removal, and he lost support in Alexandra by attending
meetings in which possible removal of the township was discussed.

The cost of economic survival, especially the high cost of bus fares, continued to concern Alexandra residents. Many thought that transportation
would only be improved if the JCC (Johannesburg City Council) or a public utility company took over the operation of buses. The JCC, however,
claimed it could not afford to subsidize transportation, sparking protest
from residents who were aware of proposals to spend millions on Alexandra's removal.[21] It was in this context of increased tension over the future
of the township that a bus boycott began on August 3, 1943, after bus
owners obtained permission from the transportation board to raise the
fare to five pence again.

Passengers boarded the buses on the morning of August 3, but refused to pay the extra fare. Inspectors boarded the buses on the way to
town and forced people off the buses because they would not agree to
the fare increase. That evening, J. B. Marks, who had kept the books for
Baloyi's bus company for five years, addressed a mass meeting. Marks
stated that the owners were making "surplus profits" on the route to
Alexandra, and his call for justice for Africans met with mass approval
from the crowd, which unanimously rejected the increase (*Rand Daily
Mail*, 4 August 1943).

The next day, residents formed the Emergency Transport Action Committee (ETAC), a forum for conflict resolution. Leadership of the ETAC included prominent local and national activists such as Senator Hyram Basner, Johannesburg Socialists Lilian and Vincent Swart, and African
activists Paul Mosaka, Gaur Radebe, Self Mampura, A.E.P. Fisch, Lilian
Tshabalala (all founding members of the African Democratic Party),
Baloyi, and Marks (Hirson 1989:139). Tshabalala, founder of the Daughters of Africa women's organization, quickly formed the Women's
Brigade, which consisted of "formidable churchwomen and beer-brewers
who made themselves responsible for the township's solidarity and good
order—especially among the faint hearted or riotously disposed men."
The Women's Brigade prevented the boarding of buses in both the 1943
and 1944 boycotts, the latter running for seven weeks (Hirson 1989:139).
Significantly, the groups of women prominent in the Women's Brigade
were churchwomen, organized through women's prayer groups known
as *manyanos,* and beer brewers, who maintained sophisticated communication networks to avoid police spies and raids. Both groups of women
were organized within the township and most earned their incomes
there, unlike the large number of men who worked in Johannesburg and
the surrounding areas.

Vincent Swart raised over one hundred pounds to hire horses and carts as substitute transportation, and the Women's Brigade continued to monitor the buses (*Rand Daily Mail*, 5 August 1943). Indeed, the complex matrix of networks formed by women was extremely effective in maintaining a controlled solidarity among protesters, for there was no mention of disorder in the *Rand Daily Mail*'s coverage of the boycott. While women were on the streets picketing and enforcing the boycott, A. B. Xuma met with bus owners and the secretary for Native Affairs, D. L. Smit. The owners agreed to return to the four-pence fare, subject to shortening the ten-mile journey by three-fourths of a mile, locating the terminus at the top of the hill leading into Alexandra rather than in the center of the township. Although Xuma thought the offer did not go far enough, he agreed to submit the proposal to a meeting of residents (*Rand Daily Mail*, 7 August 1943). J. M. Brink insisted on an early meeting when the majority of male workers were away from Alexandra.[22] The crowd reacted against the proposal, noting that relocation of the terminal point would mean long walks in unlighted areas for many women and children, exposing them to serious danger (*Star*, 7 August 1943). Working women strongly opposed the settlement since they would have longer walks with washing, parcels, and children. Those who did washing for whites would have an arduous walk up the hill when returning washed clothes. Residents unanimously rejected the offer and decided to boycott the buses until fares returned to four pence on the old route (*Rand Daily Mail*, 7 August 1943; *Star*, 7 August 1943).

Two days later, over five thousand residents again rejected a state-supported compromise, an even worse offer in which Brink proposed that buses would stop one and one-half miles from the township, with a return to the old fares. Fully aware of Marks's assertion about busing profits, residents argued that owners' statements about losses did not carry any weight. The bus owners' refusal to allow examination of their books or to produce balance sheets reinforced the residents' views (*Rand Daily Mail*, 9 August 1943). Again they rejected Brink's offer unanimously.[23] Residents resolved to meet each morning at 6:00 A.M. at the bus terminus and march together to work (*Rand Daily Mail*, 9 August 1943).

Negotiations with government and bus officials slowed to a crawl, and at a mass meeting on Sunday, August 9, residents unanimously decided to march the ten miles to town the following morning. Between ten and twelve thousand people marched in a three-mile-long procession along Pretoria Road and Louis Botha Avenue to the Noord Street terminus in Johannesburg. *Inkukuleko* reported on August 14 that the march was the greatest demonstration Johannesburg had seen for many years. With resistance from blacks becoming increasingly militant and cries emanating from white residents of the northern suburbs about the "inflammable possibilities" of the situation, the government intervened, appointing a commission of inquiry to investigate matters. Pending the outcome, fares and services returned to their former levels (*Rand Daily Mail*, 11 and 12 August 1943). Residents hailed this as a victory for the people, since they had prevented the fare increase through mass action (*Inkukuleko*, 14 August 1943).

Both David Duncan (1990) and Stadler (1981) assert that fighting a rise in bus fares was in the interest of the Alexandra "community," but they fail to observe how residents were divided over the form of protests. During negotiations between the standholders and the government, in which black men talked to white men, the proposed solution rarely satisfied the particular demands of women. It is precisely this dichotomy between the formal leadership of male standholders and the active organization of women enforcing the boycott that points to local gender and class divisions.

Eddie Roux (1964:319–320) describes the 1943 boycott as a "spontaneous mass movement" that owed little or nothing to political leadership in the formal sense. It is clear, however, that the movement was not spontaneous, as the militancy of the boycott was carefully organized and sustained through the Women's Brigade under the leadership of Lilian Tshabalala. Although Tshabalala was an exception among women due to her personal history and the prominent position she achieved as leader of the Women's Brigade, her political life serves as a microcosm of the political experience of women in Alexandra, encapsulating the radicalization by events and the subsequent seizure of initiative to direct and maintain the larger protest movement.

Born in South Africa, Tshabalala was educated and trained in the United States. She lived in Hartford, Connecticut, for a period, working in American Board Mission black churches and social centers with Ruth Cowles, who later served as a nurse in Alexandra's health clinic.[24] Upon her return to South Africa, Tshabalala taught in Durban before founding the Daughters of Africa. As set out in its constitution, which was finalized in fall 1940, the primary aims of the DOA were:

> To organize African Women into a National Movement of the economic life and the creation and propagating the ideals of social, health, economic, educational and cultural activities; . . . [and] To watch, protect and safeguard the inherent rights and privileges of African Women and with that end in view to seek affiliation with any recognized political organisation on such terms and conditions as may harmonise with the ideals of the Association.[25]

Although the DOA had been active since the early 1930s, it began to attract larger numbers in the early 1940s, and meetings drew delegates of women's groups from Alexandra, Benoni, Orlando, Pretoria, and Sophiatown, among other places (*Bantu World*, 4 May 1940). In December 1940, the DOA held its first conference of local chapters, chaired by Josie Palmer. The presence of Madie B. Xuma and Elizabeth Baloyi, the wives of A. B. Xuma and R. G. Baloyi, respectively, suggests that the DOA attracted a following among the female elite, whereas the involvement of Josie Palmer (Wells 1983:269–307) clearly demonstrates that women from different class and political backgrounds were beginning to organize politically as women (*Umteteli Wa Bantu*, 4 January 1941).

According to *Bantu World*, Tshabalala "was the moving spirit behind the campaign" (27 September 1941). She was the organizing secretary of the DOA, and under her guidance, the organization established offices in Alexandra, holding regular meetings and receptions (*Bantu World*, 31 January 1942). The slogan of the DOA was "All service ranks the same with God"; religion played a central role in the overall message of the DOA. In 1941, the second annual conference of Transvaal DOA clubs and societies was addressed by many figures from organized religion and officials from the Native Affairs Department and the ANC. The conference also invited local *manyanos* to attend the Women's Forum and join the discussion on the theme "Community Ambition to Serve."[26] This religious component, however, should not be taken as an indication of passivity, for this message could be transformed into one of resistance. For example, the concluding lines of the "Daughters' Hymn" reads: "They unashamed in the gates, Shall speak unto their foes."[27]

Tshabalala viewed the DOA as an organization that would prepare working women to lead the movement to improve their lives in the townships. For example, consider her address to the Bantu Women's Federation in 1937:

> What is absolutely necessary is an onward move *but a movement that is an expression of the great mass of us and whose leadership shall earn akin to us, just ourselves and more vital*. In each and every community there are other women, each with her unaroused power or making an individual contribution. . . . it is the little things that create differences, but that in the big things of life we are all one and may each leading Daughter strive to touch and to know the great common woman's heart of us all. . . . *I am with you as never before*. (emphasis in original, *Bantu World*, 13 February 1937)

Events in Alexandra radicalized Tshabalala, and she became one of the founding members of the African Democratic Party (ADP), a small left-wing political grouping formed in 1943. Tshabalala placed great importance on protests and boycotts as tactics by which women could improve their living conditions. The DOA established a strong following in Alexandra and was crucial to the creation of networks of working women in the township. As such, these channels of communication, which have remained invisible in previous accounts, constituted the political base that Tshabalala mobilized to form the Women's Brigade.

The Bus Services Commission met from September 1943 to January 1944 and heard evidence on the ability of Africans to pay bus fares and on the profitability of bus services. Most evidence showed that Africans could not afford the increase proposed by owners and that the ability to pay the fare was considerably less for working women than it was for male workers in Alexandra. Bram Fischer, a member of the AHC, testified before the commission that since an average wage for men was twenty-five shillings per week, bus fares represented 17 percent of their income. With the proposed increase, that figure would rise to 21 percent (*Rand Daily Mail*, 14 September 1943). This percentage was usually higher for women, since they commonly earned less than men. Those women who did not use the buses to get to work also had cause to reject the fare increase because most had to shop in Johannesburg to avoid the higher prices and poor selection in Alexandra. Most washerwomen usually had to pay two fares at night as well; those who did laundry outside of Johannesburg purchased a ride into the city to ensure themselves a seat because of the immense overcrowding on the route to Alexandra. Indeed, the *Rand Daily Mail* estimated on March 24, 1944, that 1,500 to 1,800 people queued for the evening trip home, often having to wait more than two hours to board buses. This led to a request that the fare be set on a sliding scale by stages, thus reducing the amount working women would have to pay for two trips.[28] Since women were in charge of household budgets, they were the ones who had to reduce their expenses for food and clothing to make up for increases in transportation costs. Thus, women were particularly aggrieved by the proposed rise in bus fares.

Before the publication of the Bus Services Commission Report, the bus companies made yet another claim to raise fares to five pence per trip. As a result, the government passed an emergency regulation that allowed the increase as of November 15, 1944, but required employers to pay the extra fare for their workers. Although this subsidy helped many of the men who worked in Johannesburg, it did nothing for washerwomen, domestics, casual workers, visitors, or the unemployed. Residents opposed the scheme on this basis and also because it threatened Alexandra workers, whose employers, anxious to avoid paying increased labor costs, would replace them with workers living closer to town.[29]

Formed out of several groups, the Workers' Transport Action Committee (WTAC), headed by A.E.P. Fisch, initiated mass demonstrations to secure a return to the old fare (*Inkukuleko*, 11 November 1944). The WTAC consisted of representatives from the Alexandra Workers' Union, the ADP, the CPSA (Communist Party of South Africa), and the Women's Brigade (Hirson 1989:144). At a mass meeting on November 14, over six thousand residents decided to renew the boycott. The WTAC planned a mass march into town, but police informed them that processions and meetings of more than twenty people were banned as of the following morning. Despite the restrictions, some fifteen to twenty thousand residents walked or received rides in trucks to go to and from work for fifty days (*Inkukuleko*, 18 November and 9 December 1944). On November 20, a mass meeting resolved to hold a "sit-down strike" to prevent buses from entering the township. However, the police escorted buses in on the 20th and 21st, but no one boarded, so they withdrew. A cordon chiefly formed by women blocked the road into Alexandra to prevent the buses from entering but was abandoned in the face of police presence. Despite state coercion and police protection of buses, the boycott held firm as a result of the militancy of women, who refused to allow anyone to board buses. By November 21, the bus owners claimed that they had lost twelve thousand pounds in revenue during the boycott, and they began to press for a solution (*Star*, 21 November 1944).

No agreement had materialized by December 20, and the mood of residents hardened after the government banned all transport of residents by trucks. Prior to this, over sixty trucks had provided lifts for workers. Again, a substantial number of women formed a cordon across the road into the township to block buses from entering. Tshabalala pushed the WTAC to defy the ban on meetings of twenty or more people, but the majority of the WTAC, led by Basner, rejected this idea, prompting Tshabalala to leave the ADP (Hirson 1989:144).

A temporary compromise was reached in late December. A coupon system was to take effect for a three-month trial period, but residents were able to buy single tickets or books of six or twelve tickets that would be valid for service from Monday morning to 1:00 P.M. on Saturdays. After 1:00 P.M. on Saturdays, the fare would be six pence cash, and on Sundays and holidays, seven pence. Resident representatives agreed and put the proposal to a public meeting on January 1.[30] An estimated two to three thousand residents and all the members of the ETAC and the WTAC attended the meeting. After Basner outlined the proposals in detail, assuring residents that "the Council only needed time to arrange for the transfer of the buses," Radebe and Tshabalala advised residents to accept the proposals, as it would mean a clear victory.[31] Residents assented to the coupon scheme, and the bus service resumed on January 4, with the Women's Brigade ensuring that lines were orderly and that residents had their four-pence coupons (*Rand Daily Mail*, 5 January 1945).

Most residents welcomed the end of the boycott. Many were tired; all had had to cope with unusually heavy rains during the seven weeks of the boycott. Some had lost their jobs and many others had become ill. In addition, washerwomen had been unable to get their bundles home during the boycott, thus losing vital income, though they still played a crucial role in maintaining the boycott through the Women's Brigade. Despite some criticisms of the final settlement in 1945, residents won their major demand of the four-pence fare. The fares remained at the same rate until 1957, when residents again took to the streets in protest.

Conclusion

As the study of resistance in the period from 1918 to 1945 indicates, Alexandra was divided by gender and class. The massive influx of people brought about a transformation of the economy during the 1930s and 1940s. The fluid nature of the economic and social relations within the township shifted the nature of resistance to mass action; this chapter has presented the gender-specific composition of this shift. The collective economic and organizational power of women within the township increased, prompting them to play the leading role in sustaining militancy and enforcing bus boycotts, a fact that has remained hidden in previous accounts. The wave of protests from 1939 to 1945 suggests that the male leadership of these movements was often forced to move quickly to recognize the accelerating aspirations of women in the transition to mass struggle.

The actions of Alexandra women and of women in other urban locations require us to look more closely at the history of African urban struggles. Women often appear just below the surface in official accounts of protest, when they appear at all. Despite not being recognized by the state, women did not passively accept their position in urban African society but struggled to achieve better living conditions. We need to place women as historical actors in their rightful position as active agents in the fight for economic and social justice in urban Africa.

Notes

I wish to thank Bay Ryley and Todd McCallum for providing extensive comments and for their assistance in constructing this chapter from material in my Ph.D. dissertation.

1. An unfortunate aspect of racial segregation in South Africa was the statutory delineation of specific racial categories. In this chapter, "Africans" and "blacks" are used interchangeably for people of purely African descent. The South African government used a variety of terms, most considered too pejorative to retain. "Coloureds" were people of mixed race descent.

2. Central Archives Depot, Pretoria (CAD): GNLB 418 85/2, Alexandra Township Commission (Young Committee), Minutes of Evidence, Evidence of Herbert Papenfus, 10 April 1929, 44.

3. CAD: NTS 4236 80/313, pt. 4, "Petition of Alexandra Ratepayers to Senator Heaton-Nicholls, Chairman of the Native Affairs Commission of Enquiry into the Alexandra Health Committee," October 1940, 3.

4. CAD: NTS 4234 80/313, vol. 1, "Report from Sub-Native Commissioner, Pretoria, and Town Inspector, Native Affairs Department, Johannesburg to the Director of Native Labour," 16 February 1918, 1.

5. CAD: NTS 4234 80/313, vol. 1, "Report from Sub-Native Commissioner, Pretoria, and Town Inspector, Native Affairs Department, Johannesburg to the Director of Native Labour," 16 February 1918, 1.

6. Reprint from *Libertas*, August 1942, 1.

7. Union of South Africa, "Report of the Commission Appointed to Inquire into the Operation of Bus Services for Non-Europeans on the Witwatersrand and in the Districts of Pretoria and Vereeniging, 1944" (Pretoria, UG 1/1944), 2.

8. CAD: KJB 479 N9/8/3, Native Commissioner, Johannesburg, to Chairman, Road Transportation Board, 8 August 1940.

9. CAD: TPB 1138 TA 13/8933, Alexandra Coloured Association to the administrator of the Transvaal, 5 July 1940. The appointment of Frederick as a junior clerk was passed at the AHC meeting of 26 March 1940 when Falwasser was on leave. Upon his return, Falwasser refused to accept the appointment. A second resolution was passed by the committee in May that Falwasser again refused to follow; NTS 4236 80/313, pt. 4, D. L. Smit, secretary for Native Affairs, notes of interview with Major Cooke, acting director of Native Labor, H. G. Falwasser, chairman of the Alexandra Health Committee and Mr. Brink, Native Commissioner of Johannesburg, 8 June 1940.

10. CAD: NTS 4236 80/313 pt. 4, Xuma to Smit, 12 August 1940, 3.

11. CAD: TAB 1138 TA 13/8933, Alexandra United Front Committee to the Transvaal administrator, 25 August 1940.

12. CAD: TAB 1138 TA 13/8933, Alexandra United Front Committee flyer for a mass meeting at No. 2 Square, Alexandra Township, 25 August 1940.

13. CAD: NTS 4236 80/313, pt. 5, "Notes on the Meeting of the Native Affairs Commission Held at Alexandra Township," 9–10 October 1940, 1; *Star*, 10 October 1940.

14. Union of South Africa, "Report of the Native Affairs Commission, 1939–49" (U.G. No. 42, 41, 1941), 30, para. 15.

15. CAD: NTS 4236 80/313, pt. 5, Transvaal African Congress, "Resolutions Passed at the Meeting of the Transvaal African Congress, Held at Alexandra Township," 4 May 1941; Alexandra United [Front] Committee, "Resolutions of Mass Meeting, Alexandra Township," 18 May 1941.

16. University of the Witwatersrand, Church of the Province of South Africa Archives (CPSA): Xuma Papers, ABX 410614, "Substance of the Representation Made by Dr. A. B. Xuma as Leader of, and on Behalf of, a Deputation of Alexandra Township Standholders and Residents Which Was Received at the Old Government Buildings, Pretoria, by His Honour, The Administrator, General J. J. Pienaar Accompanied by H. F. Pentz, Esq., Provincial Secretary," 14 June 1941, 3–4.

17. CAD: NTS 4236 80/313, pt. 5, H. G. Falwasser to H. F. Pentz, Transvaal provincial secretary, 15 June 1941.

18. CAD: NTS 4236 80/313, pt. 5, director of Native Labor to the secretary for Native Affairs, 19 August 1941, re: Mass Protest by Women of Alexandra Township.

19. Ibid.

20. Ibid.

21. A good account of the situation is provided in CPSA: A 1117/2, "Fourth International Submission to the Bus Services Commission," 22 September 1943, 6–7.

22. CPSA: Ballinger Papers A 410/F1.2, Johannesburg Joint Council of Europeans and Africans, "Minutes of a Meeting of the Johannesburg Joint Council Held on Monday, 9 August 1943 at the Bantu Men's Social Centre, Johannesburg."

23. CPSA: Ballinger Papers A 410/F1.2, Johannesburg Joint Council of Europeans and Africans, "Minutes of a Meeting Held on 9 August 1943."

24. Houghton Library, Harvard: ABC 15.4, vol. 41, D. Riggs to Clara Bridgman.

25. CAD: KJB 402 N1/9/3, "Constitution of the Daughters of Africa."

26. CAD: KJB 411 N1/14/3, "Program of the Second Annual Conference of Transvaal Province Daughters of Africa Clubs and Societies."

27. Ibid.

28. CPSA: Xuma Papers, ABX 430711a, "Memorandum Representing the Residents of Alexandra Township," 7 November 1943.

29. CAD: NTS 9694 717/400, pt. 3, "Notes of a Meeting Held at the Office of the Minister of Native Affairs," 1 December 1944, 5.

30. CAD: NTS 9694 717/400, pt. 4, "Meeting Re: Alexandra Township Buses in Mayor's Parlour," 30 December 1944 and 31 December 1944; *Star*, 2 January 1945. JCC officials met with representatives of Alexandra residents on 31 December. The delegation included Senator Basner, Lilian and Vincent Swart, Gaur Radebe, Lilian Tshabalala, A.E.P. Fisch, Schreiner Baduza (later leader of the Alexandra squatter's movement), and Self Mampuru.

31. Hirson, *Yours for the Union*, 144; CAD: NTS 9694 717/400, pt. 4, "Notes on a Public Meeting at Alexandra Township on 1 January 1945 by J. M. Brink, Acting Native Commissioner of Johannesburg," 5.

References

Bonner, P. 1982. "The Transvaal Native Congress, 1917–1920: The Radicalisation of the Black Petty Bourgeoisie on the Rand." In *Industrialisation and Social Change in South Africa: African Class Formation, Culture, and Consciousness 1870–1930*, ed. S. Marks and R. Rathbone. London: Longman.

———. 1988. "Family, Crime and Political Consciousness on the East Rand." *Journal of Southern African Studies* 14, 3:393–420.

Bozzoli, B., with M. Nkotsoe. 1991. *Women of Phokeng: Consciousness, Life Strategy, and Migrancy in South Africa, 1900–1983*. Portsmouth, N.H.: Heinemann.

Couzens, T. 1979. "'Nobody's Baby': Modikwe Dikobe and Alexandra, 1942–1946." In *Labour, Townships, and Protest: Studies in the Social History of the Witwatersrand*, ed. B. Bozzoli. Johannesburg: Ravan.

Duncan, D. 1990. "Liberals and Local Administration in South Africa: Alfred Ho-
ernlé and the Alexandra Health Committee, 1933–1943." *International Journal of
African Historical Studies* 23, 3:475–493.
Hellmann, E. 1934. "The Importance of Beer Brewing in an Urban African Native
Yard." *Bantu Studies* 8:39–60.
Hirson, B. 1989. *Yours for the Union: Class and Community Struggles in South Africa,
1930–1947.* London: Zed.
Hoernlé, R.F.A. 1943. *The Future of Alexandra Township: An Open Letter to the Citi-
zens of Johannesburg by the Alexandra Health Committee.* Johannesburg: Alexandra
Health Committee.
Janisch, M. 1940. *A Report of African Income and Expenditure in 987 Families in Johan-
nesburg.* Johannesburg: Johannesburg Municipality.
Krige, E. J. 1932. "The Social Significance of Beer Among the Balobedu." *Bantu
Studies* 6:343–357.
Lodge, T. 1983. *Black Politics in South Africa Since 1945.* London: Longman.
Nauright, J. R. 1992. "'Black Island in a White Sea': Black and White in the Making
of Alexandra Township, South Africa, 1912–1948." Ph.D. diss., Queen's Univer-
sity, Kingston, Canada.
Pirie, G. H. 1983. "Urban Bus Boycott in Alexandra Township, 1957." *African Stud-
ies* 42, 1:67–77.
Roux, E. 1964. *Time Longer Than Rope: A History of the Black Man's Struggle for Free-
dom in South Africa.* Madison: University of Wisconsin Press.
Sapire, H. 1987. "The Stay-Away of the Brakpan Location." In *Class, Community,
and Conflict: South African Perspectives,* ed. B. Bozzoli. Johannesburg: Ravan.
Sarakinsky, M. 1984. *From "Freehold" to "Model" Township.* Johannesburg, n.p.
Stadler, A. 1981. "A Long Way to Walk: Bus Boycotts in Alexandra, 1940–1945." In
Working Papers in Southern African Studies, ed. P. Bonner. Johannesburg: Ravan.
Tourakis, P. N. 1981. "The 'Political Economy' of Alexandra Township, 1905–58."
B. A. thesis, University of Witwatersrand, South Africa.
Wells, J. 1983. "'The Day the Town Stood Still': Women in Resistance in Potchef-
stroom 1912–1930." In *Town and Countryside in the Transvaal: Capitalist Penetra-
tion and Popular Response,* ed. B. Bozzoli. Johannesburg: Ravan.

13

Urban Women's Movements and Political Liberalization in East Africa

AILI MARI TRIPP

Since the late 1980s, women from Mauritania to Mali, Guinea, Zaire, and Zambia have engaged in militant protest action, playing an important part in the movement for political liberalization. Urban women living near seats of power in capital cities have been especially visible in expressing their outrage over human rights abuses, economic decline, and government repression. For example, in 1992 in Uhuru Park at the center of Nairobi, Kenya, women found themselves in a violent confrontation with police when they went on a hunger strike in support of political prisoners. The image of women stripping themselves naked and heaping the most vehement of curses on the military police trying to break the strike was a powerful condemnation of government authorities, and it left an indelible impression on the populace.

At the same time, the possibility of political change has galvanized women's movements in many countries. Women's groups have pressed for a political agenda that addresses the concerns of women, sometimes supporting but also going beyond the demands of the existing political reform movements. Women activists see female participation as essential and integral to the reform process. As Dr. Maria Nzomo, chairperson of the Kenyan National Committee on the Status of Women, succinctly put it: "Democracy in Kenya will be unfinished if the gender question is not fully addressed. The gender question goes far beyond multiparty politics" (1993a).

Similarly, the women's movements in Uganda, Tanzania, and Kenya have shown that the movement toward political democratization cannot be equated with multipartyism. Democratization of the broader political order also involves democratizing relations within the home, which allows women greater freedom to participate in the public sphere. Nevertheless, the complex relationship between women's movements and the proponents of multipartyism presents a paradox that is perhaps more revealing of the limitations of the current multiparty movements than of women's lack of political engagement. The paradox is this: At a time when women are gaining greater public visibility by pressing their demands for female participation, leadership, and women's rights, they have also been reluctant to join the multiparty movement (Meena 1992). To the extent that women have engaged in these movements, it has been to challenge them in a number of ways: by demanding greater female leadership and stronger representation around women's issues; by condemning the politics of patronage and corruption that they fear will change little with multipartyism; by encouraging ethnic and religious unity where the opposition has been divided along such lines; and by going beyond the rhetoric of reform and taking concrete action to change everyday political, economic, and social practices by forming associations and networks that address the needs of the community.

This chapter explores the uneasy relationship between women's movements and the multiparty movements in Tanzania, Kenya, and Uganda, addressing why women's increased activism has not been easily incorporated into the reform movements. The gap is especially noticeable when women's groups, especially at the national level, are concerned with opening up spaces for greater political participation, guaranteeing human rights, enhancing government accountability, and institutionalizing political pluralism and political liberalization. But the problem goes beyond the exclusions of the reform movements themselves. Often, women's mobilization takes forms that elude conventional definitions of political activism. Therefore, their participation is not accounted for in the political reform process, resulting in the perception that the key actors and leaders of civil society are students, civil servants, unions, and churches, while the role of the women's movements goes unmentioned (Bratton and Van de Walle 1992; Lewis 1992:51).

It is useful to begin by providing some background on the context within which the women's associations and women's movements emerged and by discussing how past relations with the state have shaped the continuing exclusions that women face as they confront the new political parties. The chapter focuses on urban women because they have been most visibly involved in the political reform movement, especially at the national level. Because of the focus on the relationship of women's movements to the political reform movements, many important issues of difference within the women's movement due to class, age, urban-rural differences, and so on are not fully explored in this chapter.

The Rise of New Associational Forms

Women in Tanzania, Kenya, and Uganda engaged in many new forms of activism in the late 1980s and early 1990s, ranging from involvement in women's lobbying organizations at the national level to participating in groups to meet local income-generating, credit, or social service needs. They creatively formed new types of organizations to meet new needs, sometimes combining older models of organization with newer models of proceduralism.

The proliferation of organizations arose in response to several factors. Some organizations were founded because the state no longer curtailed their formation, so women took advantage of the new openings for nongovernmental associations. This openness was not always a result of deliberate policy design, but when it was, the government continued to try to maintain as much control as possible over the new institutions. The new space was largely a consequence of a weakened state that needed to rely on other institutions with resources in order to deflect demands that might otherwise have fallen on the state. Bilateral donors also began to favor nongovernmental organizations (NGOs) in the 1980s, resulting in a diversion of resource flows toward this sector and often away from similar government initiatives. This sometimes, though not always, had the effect of encouraging the growth of organizations that formed in pursuit of funding, then often collapsed when funds were not forthcoming. Yet another impetus for the expansion of associations was the economic crisis and its concomitant pressures on women to secure new sources of income and welfare relief through collective activities at the community level. Few organizations arose in response to any one of these factors; rather, they all contributed in a combination of ways to affect women's changing associational life in East Africa.

In the 1990s at the national level, significant numbers of urban women became involved for the first time in organizations concerned with implementing legal reform around issues of inheritance, marriage, maintenance and child custody, sexual harassment, rape, and citizenship rights. Other nongovernmental organizations, such as the

Uganda Women's Credit and Finance Trust and the Kenya Women Finance Trust in Kenya, were active in supporting women entrepreneurs by providing advice, technical assistance, and loans. Numerous networks of women's groups (e.g., the Tanzania Gender Networking Programme) emerged in the late 1980s and early 1990s to coordinate activities around legal reform and policies affecting women's education, health, economic concerns, and other issues. Women participated in the growing array of women's regional networks, ranging from research organizations to activist organizations focusing on women's rights, environmental issues, and legal reform (e.g., the East African Women's Conference, formed in 1993 to network among women's groups in Kenya, Tanzania, and Uganda).

At the local level, women formed savings clubs, community improvement groups, income-generating groups, and other small, multipurpose associations. These groups often combined key elements of older models of self-help organization with modern organizational practices that might include proceduralism, relying on a constitution, obtaining registration, relying on banks to organize a credit society, and creating offices like those of president, treasurer, or secretary that had not existed in earlier forms of organization. Many of these organizations had emerged in response to economic crisis, the negative impact of structural adjustment austerity measures, and the decline in state provisioning of social services. Their importance is sometimes overlooked in the broader discussion of political liberalization because they were geared toward meeting local needs and did not usually engage in political advocacy. Although some of them did make demands on local government for resources, most were part of a conscious and deliberate political strategy by women to transform their everyday life circumstances and communities, especially in situations where the state had little to offer in the way of services and where employment opportunities were negligible.

The Decline of Party-Affiliated Women's Organizations

The formal urban-based nongovernmental associations became prominent in both Uganda and Tanzania only after the mid-1980s, as was the case in many parts of Africa. Countries like Kenya, where this sector already had more visibility, experienced a greater proliferation of associations. But up until this time, the leading and largest women's associations were tied to the ruling party and to the state, which manipulated them to serve its interests. This means that one of the biggest changes in the women's movements in the 1980s was their increased autonomy from institutions of patronage and conventional political power in all three countries. This circumstance also helps explain why the explicit break with these institutions gave the women's movements a voice outside of party interests and for the first time gave them the potential to challenge not only the status quo but, in particular, the politics of sectarianism and patronage. Wanjiku Mukabi Kabira and Elizabeth Akinyi Nzioki show how women's groups in Kenya have become savvy to the way male politicians, through political patronage, use women's groups to buy votes and obtain funds and rely on them for entertainment purposes at public functions. They argue that soon women's groups will be more inclined to use their cooking, votes, money, and ability to dance to endorse their fellow women. They predict that "this might well be the beginning of the end of the apparently uneasy relationship between the women's groups and the male politicians," suggesting that in the case of Kenya those groups depending on favors from male politicians are being eroded (1993:27).

One of the strongest indicators of this kind of disaffection has been the noticeable decline of women's organizations that were tied to and often controlled and co-opted by a single ruling party.[1] This decline occurred at the same time that other forms of women's association were on the rise.

Tanzania

Up until the emergence of the independent associations in the mid-1980s in Tanzania, a large portion of women's associational activity was circumscribed by the Women's Union, Umoja wa Wanawake wa Tanzania (UWT), with some notable exceptions.[2] The UWT had its origins in the Women's Section of the ruling party Tanganyika African National Union (TANU). In 1962, the Women's Section was transformed into the UWT, which became a TANU affiliate in 1962. With the merger between TANU and the Afro Shirazi Party of Zanzibar in 1977, Chama cha Mapinduzi (CCM) became the single political party, and the UWT merged with the Afro Shirazi Women's Section. As an affiliate organization of CCM, the Women's Union has had little financial autonomy and its leadership has been controlled by the party. Involved in income-generation activities, cooperatives, handicrafts, animal husbandry, efforts to improve child and health care, and political education programs, its activities were not only controlled by the party but its plans had to coincide with the government's five-year development plans and the designs of ministries and parastatals (government-owned corporations) (Geiger 1982). As one leader of the Tanzania Association of Non-Governmental Organizations (TANGO) put it:

The UWT was initially a good thing because it went to the grassroots, but it failed to maintain the links. The wives of CCM leaders took up reins of power and diverted the UWT to suit the interests of the Party. . . . The UWT was only interested in mobilizing women for the CCM, rather than mobilizing women for their rights and for development. They should have tried to organize women around women's workload, women's legal rights and to enhance women's participation in politics. Why did the UWT not lobby for women members of parliament and enhance women leaders in government? (Sherbanu Kassim, interview by author, 14 February 1994)

There had been leaders within the UWT who had tried to delink the union from the CCM and transform it into an NGO, hoping to make it a more viable independent women's organization and to attract foreign funding. Nevertheless, the CCM leadership would not give them autonomy, fearing the party would lose the women's vote, since women account for 52 percent of the electorate. The CCM, however, had granted autonomy to two of its other mass organizations, the trade unions and the cooperatives.

Kenya

Kenya's leaders also continued to try to control the women's movement into the late 1980s, but with limited success. Independent women's groups have long charged that the largest women's association in Kenya, Maendeleo ya Wanawake (MYW), was being run by male politicians, who saw to it that their female relatives claimed key seats. This ensured that the organization would be politically moderate and would not present a challenge to the government. Any attempts by MYW to make political statements were condemned by the government (Staudt and Col 1991; Wipper 1975).

Although KANU's (Kenya African National Union) co-optation of MYW had been going on for a long time, in 1987 KANU officially took over this once independent organization. Since then, women's groups have become even more openly critical of the organization and its claims to represent Kenyan women. Interference reached the point where President Moi became personally involved in changing the rules of voter eligibility for the organization. Although there are those within the organization, especially among the rank and file, who would like to be more active in taking up women's rights, the association in general has been dominated by leaders who are more interested in keeping the organization nonpolitical and under the influence of the government (Nzomo 1988:152).

The MYW was reduced to what some called a "public relations wing for KANU." MYW touted itself as an organization reflecting the "tradi-

tional African set-up," in which women play a major advisory role behind the scenes. Commentators like Wachira Maina have responded to
such claims, saying that "the assumptions made by KANU Maendeleo ya
Wanawake in these statements are insulting to any self-respecting person.
What makes women peculiarly suited for playing major advisory roles
behind the scenes whilst men steal the show up front?" (Maina 1992:35).

Uganda

In Uganda, the patterns of autonomy and state control of the women's
movement varied somewhat from those in Tanzania and Kenya. General
Idi Amin established the National Council of Women by presidential de-
cree in 1978 to serve as an umbrella organization for independent NGOs.
However, independent organizations were largely curtailed during
Amin's time. Under Milton Obote's second regime (1980–1985), the National Council of Women was subject to the manipulations of the
Women's Wing of the ruling party, Uganda Peoples Congress (UPC)
(Tadria 1987:88). Many Ugandan women activists attended the 1985
United Nations Decade for Women meeting in Nairobi as individuals and
not as part of the official delegation led by President Obote's wife. They
returned inspired to revitalize women's organizations in Uganda and create autonomous new ones. The Nairobi conference coincided with a coup
that overthrew Obote, following which the National Council of Women
organized a peace march in Kampala, in part to assert its autonomy from
the UPC.

The coming to power of the National Resistance Movement (NRM)
government of Yoweri Museveni in 1986 allowed women greater latitude
to mobilize, and women's groups even pushed for the formation of a
Ministry of Women, which became a reality in 1988. Although women's
associations flourished under the NRM-led government, the NRM made
continued efforts to control the mobilization of women. The NRM established an eleventh directorate, the Directorate of Women's Affairs in the
NRM Secretariat, which is in charge of political mobilization (Boyd 1989).
Although short on resources and not very visible in the women's movement, the directorate maintained long-standing feuds with the Ministry
of Women and in particular with the National Council of Women, which
functioned as a parastatal until 1993. The directorate was allegedly responsible (although it never took the credit) for pressuring the Ministry of
Women to redraft and submit to the National Assembly (Parliament) a
National Women's Council statute repealing the 1978 act that had created
the National Council of Women. The directorate also forced the council to
change its name to the National Association of Women's Organizations of
Uganda (NAWOU) and become a nongovernmental organization, thus

eliminating its financial support from the ministry. The directorate was probably anxious to undermine, if not do away with, this organization, given its origins under the Amin regime and its more recent association with the UPC government of Obote. In its place, a new "National Women's Council" was to be formed, the new name being almost identical to the former National Council of Women. This appeared to be a deliberate effort to confuse local women's organizations. Ironically, the directorate itself is financially strapped and almost invisible in the current women's movement.

Even though most organizations, including NAWOU, supported the repeal of the 1978 bill and the creation of an independent NAWOU umbrella organization, officials at the Ministry of Women, NAWOU leaders, and other heads of women's organizations were critical of the way the directorate intervened to get the bill passed and force the council to change its name. Many were also skeptical about the capacity of the new women's councils to fulfill their mandate but were taking a wait-and-see attitude. The new National Women's Council was to be made up of women's councils at the village, parish, subcounty, county, and district levels under the direction of the Ministry of Women, which appoints the secretary. The NRM claimed that these councils would enable them to reach all women, since the independent women's organizations did not mobilize the majority of women. But the relative strength of the women's NGOs and the weakness of the directorate have made it difficult for the NRM to impose its own distinct agenda.

Conflicts Between Women's Organizations and Women's Ministries

The independent women's organizations have also faced tensions in their relations with ministries, in the case of Uganda, with the Ministry of Women in Development, and in Tanzania's case, with the Ministry of Community Development, Women's Affairs, and Children. These conflicts reveal another dimension of the rift between the ruling parties and the women's movements. In both countries, the conflicts were basically over the need to secure limited donor resources but took the form of personality conflicts and turf battles. Leaders of women's organizations in Tanzania, for example, often remarked that the ministry was not open and forthcoming about its activities and had in some cases delayed the registration of various organizations. They felt it was trying to compete with them rather than cooperate.

This competition between the women's movements, the ministries, and the ruling parties (or the NRM, in the case of Uganda) reflects the shifting center of gravity in the mobilization of women. By the 1990s, it had become clear that the momentum in Uganda, Tanzania, and Kenya had moved into the hands of the independent women's movement, although the shift had not gone unchallenged.

A Paradox of Political Liberalization

As in many other parts of Africa, the new women's movements in Uganda, Tanzania, and Kenya emerged not only independent of ruling party control but also autonomous of opposition political parties. This somewhat paradoxical situation needs some explanation, given the fact that the women's movement represents one of the social forces advocating political reform.

Individual activists in women's groups might support a particular opposition party, but the groups have generally maintained their independence of political parties, arguing for unity among the opposition parties, especially in cases where ethnic or religious differences were being used in a divisive way by politicians. This careful maneuvering was clearest in the Kenyan case. Kenyan women, for example, were among the first to take militant action in support of imprisoned political prisoners and opposition leaders when they went on a hunger strike at Freedom Corner in Uhuru Park on March 3, 1992, to protest the government repression. In spite of visibly supporting the male opposition, women leaders were still critical of all parties, especially KANU, for putting out manifestos and political platforms that paid lip service to women's leadership but in practice did little to support it. Both KANU and the opposition Democratic Party had promised to give women the majority of nominated positions, yet neither party followed through with this; KANU did not nominate a single woman, much to the dismay of women's groups.

In the 1992 parliamentary elections in Kenya, women claimed six seats out of one hundred eighty-eight, one representing KANU and the rest claiming opposition party seats for the Forum for the Restoration of Democracy (FORD)-Kenya (one), FORD-Asili (one), and the Democratic Party (three). The six members seated represent an increase from two in the previous parliament. Moreover, a larger number of the men who were elected were considered by women's groups to be "gender sensitive." Although these seats were counted as gains, women's groups were outraged when no women were appointed as cabinet ministers; of the sixty-nine assistant ministers appointed, only one was a woman. Women leaders described the appointments as "a slap in the face" in a country where there are large numbers of capable and internationally renowned women leaders and where 52 percent of the electorate is made up of women.

Women activists vowed to go back to the drawing boards to devise new strategies to confront this blatant disregard for women's abilities. As Maria Nzomo explained at a seminar following the elections: "It is however my view that we should not waste precious time bemoaning women's continued marginalisation. Instead, we must face up to the fact the Kenyan political machinery and society are still dominated by men, who are not willing to share power with women" (Nzomo 1993b:9). And, indeed, the National Committee on the Status of Women (NCSW)[3] returned to the drawing boards, meeting after the elections in February 1993 to discuss new strategies, which included enhancing internal democracy within the women's movement, strengthening the linkages between organizations to devise a more cohesive strategy (e.g., developing a coordinated response to rape), and strengthening the capacity of women's organizations. The NCSW discussed the feasibility of starting a women's party that would cut across class, race, ethnic, and gender divisions to address not only women's concerns but also issues of poverty, the environment, class exploitation, and other inequalities related to human rights violations. The conference sought to find ways to better link rural and urban women and to shift the center of gravity of the women's movement from the urban areas to the rural areas, where the real power of the women's movement was said to lie. NCSW members talked about ways to strengthen the leadership abilities of women and help initiate gender sensitization efforts through civic education in schools, NGO training programs, and media information dissemination. Other plans included networking with gender-sensitive male leaders, getting a women's desk in every ministry, lobbying the government to mainstream women's issues in every sector, lobbying to reform or repeal laws that discriminate against women, and promoting the enforcement of laws that support women (Nzomo 1993b; Nzomo and Kibwana 1993). These ambitious plans set by the newly politicized women's movement suggest that political parties in Kenya will not be able to ignore women's associations for much longer and may have to begin taking greater cognizance of their demands for leadership.

Since the early 1990s, Tanzania, too, has seen the growth of a vibrant women's movement that has been promoting women's leadership, women's rights, and greater participation of women in the country's political and economic life, among other issues. The October 1995 presidential and parliamentary elections brought unprecedented levels of involvement by women in electoral politics. For the first time, a woman, Rose Lugendo, sought (albeit unsuccessfully) the CCM nomination to run for the presidency. Nonpartisan organizations like the Tanzania National Women's Council (BAWATA) and the Tanzania Association of Non-Governmental Organizations carried out civic and voter education and encouraged women's participation in the electoral process. Newspapers gave extensive coverage to debates within women's organizations over women's role in the electoral process.

Even though all parties had 15 percent of their parliamentary seats reserved for women, the new parties barely addressed women's concerns during the campaign. The new parties included Chama cha Demokrasia na Maendeleo (CHADEMA), the National Convention for Construction and Reform (NCCR-Mageuzi), Union for Multiparty Democracy (UMD), and the Civic United Front (CUF). Not surprisingly, the Tanzania Gender Networking Programme was critical of the parties' lack of a clear stand on gender issues in their platforms and has placed this on their action agenda regarding political issues (TGNP 1993:97). As one woman activist put it: "I have attended many meetings of the new parties and I have failed to witness that their policies are addressing women's questions. I find them following the same path as the CCM, picking one woman and saying she is the one to take care of women's desk" (Sherbanu Kassim, interview by author, 14 February 1994).

Some fear that women will lose out in a multiparty parliament because of the heightened pressure to vote along party lines rather than along the lines of special interests. One CCM woman parliamentarian, Hulda Kibacha, explained that if she were confronted with a bill addressing a key women's concern that was brought to Parliament by another party and the CCM opposed it, she would be forced to vote with her party. This, she felt, had not been as big a problem under the one-party parliament, where all bills were introduced by members of the same party (Hon. Hulda Kibacha, interview by author, 15 February 1994).

In part, the distance between the two movements is a continuation of women's historic exclusion from formal politics in the colonial and postcolonial periods. Women's involvement in politics in general has been curtailed by discriminatory educational opportunities for women; limited economic opportunities and resources necessary to run for office; time constraints due to domestic responsibilities; religious and cultural proscriptions on women's involvement in public life; and lack of access to networks of bureaucrats, politicians, military leaders, and patrons who facilitate bids for political power (Mba 1989; Chazan 1989:189–192; Parpart 1988:216–218). When women have successfully run for office, they have often encountered open hostility from their male counterparts. The continuing exclusion of women in the multiparty context has convinced many women in Africa that the opposition movements and the emerging multiparty regimes represent a continuation of "politics as usual" in some fundamental ways. Although on the one hand, the situation has opened up possibilities for new political actors and new arenas of political expression, on the other hand, the old politics of exclusion continue when it comes to women. New opposition parties (or the old ones, as in the case of Uganda) have not generally incorporated women into their activities, neither giving them significant leadership opportunities nor addressing key concerns of women.

Women's Challenges to Opposition Political Parties

Promoting Women's Leadership

One of the most dramatic developments in many parts of Africa has been the concerted effort among women's groups to press for women's leadership in politics as well as in other arenas, including business, NGOs, and academia. The effort has come out of a realization that in order for women to accomplish their goals in advancing economic growth and social welfare, they need to be involved in the process of formulating those plans.

Some have argued that the past government/donor/NGO emphasis on "development" has often served to deflect women from their pursuit of the goal of expanding female political leadership and participating in the formulation and implementation of government policy. Women leaders have reacted strongly to the cynical way in which some male politicians have counterpoised women's involvement in "development" activities against their involvement in politics. For example, women's organizations in Kenya condemned the public statement of Nicholas Biwott, former minister for energy, who commended leaders of women's groups for leading women "towards implementing development projects and steering them clear of politics" (Maina 1992:36–37).

One indication of the new emphasis on women's political participation was the formation of a Union of East African Women Parliamentarians by women members of Parliament at a March 1996 meeting in Moshi, Tanzania. Another example of this changing agenda was evident at the 1993 Kampala preparatory meeting that brought together 120 leaders of women's organizations from Uganda, Tanzania, and Kenya to plan for the Africa-wide United Nations Women's Conference to be held in Dakar in 1994 and for the subsequent international conference in Beijing in 1995. Women delegates placed access to power as their top priority on the agenda in all three countries, when asked to rank their preferences to determine overall strategic goals in the region. The Ugandan delegation, for example, set a goal of achieving 50 percent of women in decisionmaking positions by 1998 and outlined a plan of action that included lobbying, networking among women, leadership training, increasing public awareness of the need for women's leadership, and the creation of pressure groups. They specifically identified key national women's groups that could facilitate this agenda, link groups together both nationally and regionally, and disseminate information about organizations and their activities. This is not a new strategy in Uganda, where women's groups like Action for Development (ACFODE) have actively lobbied for women's leadership since the late 1980s. The campaign to change university admissions policies to admit proportionately greater numbers of qualified women was one such effort spearheaded by ACFODE to create a larger pool of potential women leaders. Similarly, Tanzanian delegates to the Kampala conference identified the passage of an Equal Opportunity Act, coupled with a campaign for education for democracy at all levels, as programs with the potential to enhance women's access to power and decisionmaking positions.

Likewise, the Kenyan delegation to the Kampala meeting adopted a strategy to lobby for women leaders and carry out political education. They made plans to network at the grassroots, regional, and national levels with a view toward forming a political organization to press for women's leadership. They also planned to lobby for legal reform to change laws that discriminated against women, to educate women about their legal rights, to lobby for institutionalizing and implementing existing laws that protected women's rights, and to press for more slots for women in secondary school and institutions of higher education.

The agenda of the Kenyan delegation represented a continuation of ongoing lobbying efforts to place women in key positions of political power. Prior to the December 1992 elections in Kenya, two thousand delegates representing women's associations held the National Women's Convention in Nairobi to discuss and endorse "A Women's Agenda for a Democratic Kenya," an agenda that focused on strategies to bring women into political power.[4] The convention criticized not only the ruling Kenya African National Union but also the new political parties for the "lack of clear policies on women," as Joyce Umbima of Mothers in Action put it. Participants saw this as a critical time to seize initiative. Eddah Gachukia explained: "I remember once in the 1980s when women demanded a bigger representation in (Kenyan) parliament they were said to be out to hijack national leadership. But the time is now ripe. What we couldn't talk then for fear of being called names and fearing reprisals, we can now say without fear" (*International Press Service*, 9 March 1992). Another delegate, Maria Nzomo, pointed to the limitations of the current multiparty movement: "We are saying that multipartyism on its own is not enough. Women must now participate as policy makers in politics and public life in large enough numbers so that we can make an impact in changing our subordinate status" (*Kenya Sunday Nation*, 23 February 1992). As a result of the conference, over 250 women stood for civic and parliamentary seats, with the result that 45 women won civic positions and 6 women were elected to Parliament (Nzomo 1993b:1).

Democratizing the Home

The way in which women were calling for new leadership roles was in itself distinct. In their argument for greater female leadership, women's associations made explicit conceptual ties between what goes on in the public and private realms. For example, at the March NCSW meeting in Nairobi, one woman leader argued that because women are responsible for the security and stability of the family and community, "it can be understood that women are already ministers of culture in their own homes" and now they want to take charge of key portfolios (*International Press Service*, 9 March 1992).

Similarly, women's movements were also conceptualizing democratization as a bottom-up process, connecting notions of family democracy to national democracy issues, a link that has not generally been made in the multiparty movement or even by scholars analyzing the movement toward political liberalization. As Fides Chale, president of the Tanzania Gender Networking Programme, explained in an interview, "Democratization should be not only with parties, it should start at the grass roots, in the family and in the community. It will be easier to bring it up at the national level if we have democracy in everyday life. Then it won't be something new" (Fides Chale, interview by author, February 1994). At the East African Women's Conference in Kampala, democracy in the home was seen as an issue that was intricately linked to democracy at the national level: "Hence homes are considered miniature nations and undemocratic upbringing at the family level breeds undemocratic decisionmaking and practice at the national level," explained one participant. Conference participants argued for a strategy of advocating a democratic home to free women to participate at the public level. This meant that a woman's ownership of property, reproductive rights, and right to be heard and acknowledged, as well as her right to be herself, which leads to respect and equal partnership, were seen as the kinds of issues that needed to be addressed in order for democratization to occur at the national level. The participants criticized those who take refuge in arguments about "culture" in order to justify the status quo in the home. The following were all seen as necessary means to address the issue of democratizing the home: working toward legal and constitutional reform; using the media, education system, and grassroots training programs to promote new images of women and models for family relations; networking and forming support systems; and using the extended family (Proceedings, East African Women's Conference, Kampala, Uganda, 5–8 July 1993:13–14).

Politics of Inclusiveness and Coalescence

Women's groups are distinct from many other social forces in that they have frequently played a unifying role in countering divisiveness based on ethnic, religious, and other sectarian differences that have entered into the reform process. This has been possible for several reasons, the most obvious of which is the fact that women's interests and organizations cut across diverse identities. This means that in order to strengthen the movement it has been necessary to include as many actors as possible, irrespective of their ethnic or religious identity. Another reason is that many women's groups, especially at the local level, have coalesced in response to economic crisis around income-generating activities and the provision of community services, since much of the burden to support the household financially has fallen on women. Again, these are unifying interests that are not peculiar to any particular ascriptive group, especially in the urban context, where one is more likely to find people of diverse backgrounds.

In addition to commonalities induced by economic crisis and the decrease in government provision of social services, women find themselves confronting political exclusion—a problem they can only address collectively, irrespective of their ascriptive identities. Groups have struggled for greater inclusiveness of women in the political process both at the national and local levels, although the national struggles led by urban middle-class women have gained greater public recognition. In local communities where women are forced to leave their natal home completely when they marry, women are forced to associate with women in the community of their husband. In the urban setting, people of different backgrounds intermingle in neighborhoods, schools, at the workplace, in churches and mosques, in the market, and in other locales where the self-employed carry out business. This has also made it easier for women to form organizations with people of diverse origins and faiths. Clearly, none of these factors alone would account for this new proliferation of pluralistic organizations, but a combination of incentives has created new bases for women's mobilization. The impact of these new trends is most noticeable in national women's organizations, which, unlike other political organizations, have often placed the struggle against sectarianism as a key objective both internally and externally.

Uganda's recent political history has been marked by ethnic, religious, and regional conflicts, yet women's organizations at both the national and local levels have organized along pluralistic lines. I interviewed leaders and members of hundreds of women's groups in urban centers of Kampala, Kabale, Mbale, and Luwero in carrying out fieldwork on the political impact of women's organizations during 1993. Apart from a handful of religious organizations, I found virtually no women's organizations formed along ethnic or religious lines except where possibilities for such integration were negligible due to the numerical predominance of one religion or ethnic group. Moreover, women members frequently seemed to consciously reject the politics of "sectarianism," as they put it, and associated those organizational forms with the politics of the past and with party politics, which in Uganda has been divided along religious and ethnic lines. Some women had deliberately left organizations like the Protestant Mothers' Union and Catholic Women's Guild in order to work with diverse women in other forums because they found the membership of the older religious organizations too restrictive to meet their needs. Other religious organizations, like the Muslim Women's Association, found it necessary to expand the diversity of their leadership in order to sustain the organization. In the 1970s, the executive committee of this organization was made up almost entirely of Nubians, whereas in the 1990s it is composed of Batoro, Nubian, Banyoro, Banyankole, and Baganda women (Hajati Nantongo, vice president, Uganda Muslim Women's Association, interview by author, 27 March 1993).

Women's groups naturally confronted difficulties in forging broader gender identities. When internal financial and leadership problems emerged, ascriptive differences were sometimes hinted at quietly, although perhaps not openly, and the organizations found themselves struggling to rebuild unity. But even in these instances where ethnic tensions simmered below the surface, the overriding and public concern was over how to create a pluralistic organization.

In many instances, women's groups translated this concern for internal pluralism into a struggle for unity within the broader polity. In Kenya, following the 1992 presidential and parliamentary election, the opposition parties rejected the outcome of the election results because of flagrant violations of electoral process by the ruling party, KANU. Women's groups, for example, the National Committee on the Status of Women, the National Council of Women of Kenya, and FEMNET (African Women Development and Communications Network), held a press conference to call on the opposition to accept the results and continue the struggle for democratization in Parliament in the interests of tolerance and consultation. A FEMNET representative called on Kenyans to "reject any attempt to divide them along ethnic, religious, ideological, cultural or any other differences" (Kwayera 1993). In calling for an acceptance of the election results, the women leaders demanded that politically inspired ethnic clashes end, that political prisoners be freed, and that action be taken on the Ouko Commission Report (which implicated government officials in the murder of Kenya's former foreign minister), and they called for the restoration of public morality and the elimination of corruption at all levels.

Although the women leaders in Kenya made a plea for accepting the results in the interest of peace and to keep the opposition above reproach in showing its respect for the election outcomes, they recognized the many irregularities that characterized the electoral process. These included the harassment of opposition leaders, politically inspired ethnic clashes, zoning of districts by KANU, bribing of voters, illegal use of refugees as voters, and abuse of the civil service machinery and other government institutions. Moreover, they showed how these irregularities worked against women. In all political parties, women were discriminated against in the nomination exercise, and the majority of those who were nominated were last-resort choices (Kwayera 1993). But women also faced other challenges in the election process. The single most important limitation women faced was their lack of independent financial resources. Even though most contenders were supported by their husbands, others faced pressure from husbands and male relatives to withdraw from the race. Some women could not find the sponsorship they needed from political parties, which tended to regard women as a "last resort" when suitable male candidates were not forthcoming (Nzomo and Kibwana 1993:104–105).

The plea for unity was one of many attempts by the Kenyan women's movement during the election campaign to counter the ethnic divisions that had surfaced during the electoral campaigns. President Moi covertly attempted to foment ethnic tensions between Kalenjins and non-Kalenjins in western Kenya, to give the impression at home and abroad that multiparty politics would necessarily result in the ethnic conflict. The opposition itself was increasingly split along ethnic and regional lines: The Democratic Party tended to represent the northern Kikuyu; the FORD-Asili faction represented southern Kikuyu areas of Central Province, Nairobi, and the Rift Valley; and FORD-Kenya constituted a multitribal alliance, though increasingly based among the Luo in Nyanza Province (Barkan 1993:92).

World-renowned environmentalist and human rights activist Wangari Maathai, who has been a major force in the women's movement, spent much of her time leading up to the election with the Middle Ground Group, lobbying for unity within the opposition. She argued that it was political and economic insecurity that had led to an electoral outcome in which people voted along ethnic lines, as they believed that only leaders in their own communities could protect their interests. Maathai, herself a founding member of FORD, viewed ethnicity as a tool used by politicians and bitterly disagreed with those politicians who claim that Kenyans are polarized along "tribal" lines. According to Binaifer Nowrojee and Bronwen Manby (1993), when Maathai tried to expose government complicity in the attempt to foment ethnic clashes between the Kalenjin and non-Kalenjin in a photo exhibit at the Vienna World Conference on Human Rights in June 1993, the display was stolen by the government delegation to the conference.

Reinventing Tradition

One of the most interesting dimensions of the movements in East Africa is the way they are manipulating popular perceptions of women's so-called traditional role. For example, reinvention of tradition shows in the reference made earlier to Kenyan women being the ministers of culture in their homes and therefore deserving key political portfolios. Women are claiming leadership of culture and using this to advance their cause. At the East African Women's Conference, a delegate argued that "women are the custodians of culture, its promoters and perpetuators, so we should take up the responsibility of bringing up men who will not dominate us. So it is us who must first rise up above these shackles of bondage" (Proceedings, East African Women's Conference, Kampala, Uganda, 5–8 July 1993:9).

Nowhere is this conflict over meanings of tradition as sharp as in Muslim women's associations. Often, Muslim women are castigated by non-Muslims in Uganda, Tanzania, and Kenya as being backward and uneducated. Muslim women find that such misconceptions abound. Uganda's President Yoweri Museveni attended a graduation at an Islamic university and remarked in his speech that he was surprised to see so many Muslim women graduating. He said he thought Muslim women were not educated and only made *maandazi* (fried pastries). At the Women's Day celebrations in Kampala on March 8, 1993, Minister Balakikirya said he was surprised to see Muslim women participating in the celebrations. When I asked the head of the Uganda Muslim Women's Association how she responds to such remarks, she said, "We do not get annoyed with them. This rather gives us strength, energy to go ahead and prove our positions to them."

But recent developments have shown that Muslim women are assuming political leadership, as they did during the independence movements (Strobel 1976; Geiger 1987).[5] These new incursions into politics have not been easy. For example, Fatuma Bakari Jeneby, who ran for the Mvita parliamentary seat in Mombasa District as a Kenyan National Congress nominee, had to fend off Islamic detractors, who argued that by running she was violating the teachings of the Koran and the view that women cannot lead men. She argued in her defense: "Let them read the holy book afresh" and follow the example of the Mohammed's wife, who was a successful businesswoman. At the center of Jeneby's campaign was the theme that "women are and can be as competent as men," and she argued the need to bring the plight of Kenyan Islamic women to the forefront of the national political debate. As in many women's campaigns, Jeneby saw her campaign as more than an electoral competition, as an opportunity to share her experiences and insights with other Muslim women. In particular, she voiced her opinions on political liberation, explaining why they needed not only economic and social liberation, but also political liberation, since, as she put it, "Woman does not make it in business and in fact other aspects of life, without having some sort of insight into leadership," meaning political leadership (*Daily Nation*, 26 December 1992).

Jeneby's comments are reflective of a movement within Islamic communities in many parts of Africa, from Sudan to Eritrea and Nigeria, that draws on interpretations of the Koran and alternative traditions within Islam to promote women's rights and leadership. By calling for greater gender inclusiveness in politics, Islamic women have become some of the staunchest forces for democratization and a secular state in countries like Sudan (Ibrahim 1992; Abdulai 1993:48–50).

Similar dynamics are found in Uganda. The Uganda Muslim Women's Association, the largest Muslim women's association in the country, is made up mainly of small entrepreneurs, *matooke* (banana) dealers, and vegetable sellers. In the 1990s, the association has shifted its focus to engagement in political activities. In the past, it was mainly involved only in religious and economic activities for women, but it now encourages women to support women of all religious affiliations to run for local government positions and for Parliament. The association has lobbied within the Muslim community and within its leading body, the Supreme Council, to give women more leadership positions and is proud that the once all-male executive committee of the Supreme Council now includes two women among its twenty-four members (Hajati Nantongo, vice president, Uganda Muslim Women's Association, interview by author, 27 March 1993).

In Tanzania, likewise, one of the most influential women's rights organizations, Tanzania Media Women's Association (TAMWA), has a strong contingent of Muslim women in its leadership. Established in 1979, TAMWA was one of the first of the new national women's organizations, preceding most others by almost a decade. In 1988, the association started the first women's magazine, *Sauti ya Siti*. Although its leaders are mainly Muslim, in a country where Muslims make up roughly one-half of the population, they address issues that affect all women. TAMWA is involved in research and its dissemination through popular education on a wide range of issues, from inheritance laws to wife beating to how to start NGOs, control teenage pregnancy, and answer women's health needs (Tanzania Gender Networking Programme 1993:92). The association works with women of all religions and has a religiously diverse membership and leadership. Moreover, TAMWA has been active in building coalitions among women's groups, both in Tanzania and internationally.

All of these developments in Kenya, Tanzania, and Uganda affirm the strength and ability of Muslim women to redefine their role in the changing conditions and to act not just as participants in the new movements but also to perform as leaders.

The Impact of Multipartyism

The disillusionment of women's organizations with party politics at this time is not necessarily a rejection of "multipartyism," at least in the cases of Tanzania and Kenya. Leaders of women's organizations in Tanzania, for example, point out that they appreciate the freedom that multipartyism has afforded them: They feel they can express themselves more honestly and can take advantage of a freer media through which they can convey women's concerns. They also enjoy the fact that they can openly admit that they do not belong to *any* political party, including the CCM. In the past, civil servants, university lecturers, and people in other top positions were forced to join the CCM. With the separation of party and state in 1992, party membership was no longer a requirement, hence they could choose not to belong.

Others pointed out that there was more accountability in government as a result of multipartyism. For example, they felt poor women now had a better chance to obtain a loan from a government-funded institution than in the past, when such loans went only to the well-connected elite.[6]

Finally, multipartyism has helped women's organizations shed some of their fears of government intimidation and reprisal. For example, on November 25, 1992, TAMWA held a public tribunal where women testified not only about violence against women but also about how corruption in the legal system worked to women's disadvantage. The government objected because the tribunal suggested that the government was not functioning as it should, but TAMWA refused to back down and saw the exposure as a way to challenge the legal system to work better for women. Similarly, members of TAMWA had also been pressing for many years for improved and more serious coverage of women's issues in the radio and press. In the 1990s, they are taking up issues of sexual harassment, wife battering, rape, and teenage pregnancy—issues that only a decade before were considered too controversial to air or publish (Edda Sanga and Pili Mtambalike, interviews by author, 7 February 1994).

Conclusion

Although women of Uganda, Tanzania, and Kenya have taken advantage of new political spaces emerging in the context of political liberalization, their involvement in multiparty politics has been guarded at best. This is only partly related to women's historic exclusion from party politics and the public sphere. Women are critical of the reform movement for not incorporating women leaders and demands at a time when the women's movement is actively lobbying for greater influence. More important, they have challenged the new parties' continuation of the politics of exclusion that characterized the former single-party states, especially regarding women's leadership. In many instances the new opposition parties have had a less promising record than the old single parties, with respect to promoting women leaders and women's demands. Women's groups are also critical of political lines being drawn along ethnic, religious, and other such sectarian divisions, viewing this as simply a continuation of the old way of engaging in political behavior. These objections are voiced strongly in countries where the women's movement is consciously trying to unify women of diverse backgrounds and religious identities.

Although women have taken militant action to protest against repressive regimes, human rights violations, environmental destruction, and undesirable economic policies, most of women's activity at the local, regional, and national levels has been focused around concrete organization building. This approach has been chosen in order to deal with many issues critical to women: economic betterment; the provision of social services, legal reform, and legal aid; and public education on women's rights. In other words, women's goals have gone beyond protesting government policy or making demands for resources or concessions from the government. In attempting to deal with the everyday survival challenges they face, women have created associations and institutions that contain the beginnings of the kind of society they would like to construct: a polity that is more inclusive and participatory at all levels and that is organized along lines that are meaningful to people themselves at the grass roots.

One sees new attempts to create participatory, internally democratic, and accountable associations, but there are also attempts under way to network and connect associations in order to achieve specific legal, economic, and political goals. In confronting the multiparty trend in Kenya, for example, the women's movement has wrestled with how to make

political participation and leadership more inclusive along these lines
and along the gender dimension. The movement has sought to give
greater recognition to women's concrete initiatives and to associations
that are involved in transforming communities, enabling them to meet
day-to-day income-generating, welfare, and other needs. In doing this,
women have struggled to discover ways for women's associations to
strengthen ties across clan, ethnic, religious, class, urban-rural, and
other social divisions.

Notes

1. Examples of such affiliations in other parts of Africa include the Organization of Mozambican Women and the Front for the Liberation of Mozambique
(FRELIMO), the Angola Women's Organization and the Popular Movement for
the Liberation of Angola (MPLA), the Women's Wing and the All People's Congress in Sierra Leone, and the Women's League in Zambia, which was part of the
United National Independence Party (UNIP).

2. Exceptions would have included a few formal organizations, e.g., the
YWCA, and informal ones such as ritual initiation groups, dancing groups, and
farming groups.

3. The NCSW is a nonpartisan organization formed by 120 women representing
different NGOs and by professionals who have been coordinating activities to enhance women's participation and the shaping of the multiparty democratization
process.

4. The conference was organized by the National Committee on the Status of
Women; participants included Mothers in Action, the National Council of Women
of Kenya, the International Federation of Women Lawyers (FIDA), League of
Women Voters, the Greenbelt Movement, African Women Development and
Communications Network (FEMNET), Young Women's Christian Association,
and Anti-Rape Organization.

5. Muslim women in the late 1950s were involved through the Muslim
Women's Institute and Moslem Women's Cultural Association in a movement to
petition the colonial authorities to scrap legislation that did not allow coastal
women to vote. They argued against the voting policy on the grounds that it was
discriminatory because women in other parts of the country were allowed to vote.
Once this victory was won, they initiated campaigns to get women to vote (Strobel 1976:183–212). In Tanzania, Muslim women like Bibi Titi were leaders of the
independence movement from the outset, whereas others were socialized into political activities through dance groups and networks of beer brewers, food sellers,
and other self-employed women. Because they were organized as Muslim women
into such groups, they were considered "harmless" and easily eluded the suspicions of colonial authorities (Geiger 1987; Meena 1992).

6. In interviews with women activists, I heard countless stories about continuing abuse of governmental lending institutions that had funds earmarked for low-
income women.

References

Abdulai, Napoleon. 1993. "Interview: Dr. Fatima Babiker Mahmoud." *Africa World Review* (May-October):48–50.

Barkan, J. 1993. "Kenya: Lessons from a Flawed Election." *Journal of Democracy* 4, 3:85–99.

Boyd, Rosalind. 1989. "Empowerment of Women in Uganda: Real or Symbolic." *Review of African Political Economy* 45/46:106–117.

Bratton, Michael, and Nicolas Van de Walle. 1992. "Popular Protest and Political Reform in Africa." *Comparative Politics* 24, 4:419–442.

Chazan, N. 1989. "Gender Perspectives on African States." In *Women and the State in Africa,* ed. Jane L. Parpart and Kathleen A. Staudt, 185–201. Boulder: Lynne Rienner.

Geiger, Susan. 1982. "Umoja wa Wanawake wa Tanzania and the Needs of the Rural Poor." *African Studies Review* 25, 2/3:45–65.

———. 1987. "Women in Nationalist Struggle: TANU Activists in Dar es Salaam." *International Journal of African Historical Studies* 20, 1:1–26.

Ibrahim, Fatima. 1992. "Women, Islam and Sudan." *Focus on Africa* 3, 4:34.

Kabira, Wanjiku Mukabi, and Elizabeth Akinyi Nzioki. 1993. *Celebrating Women's Resistance: A Case Study of Women's Groups Movement in Kenya.* Nairobi: African Women's Perspective.

Kwayera, Mukalo wa. 1993. "Women to Press Forward." *Society,* 18 January.

Lewis, Peter M. 1992. "Political Transition and the Dilemma of Civil Society in Africa." *Journal of International Affairs* 46, 1:31–54.

Maina, Wachira. 1992. "Women Participation in Public Affairs in Kenya." *Nairobi Law Monthly* 40.

Mba, Nina. 1989. "Kaba and Khaki: Women and the Militarized State in Nigeria." In *Women and the State in Africa,* ed. Jane L. Parpart and Kathleen A. Staudt, 69–90. Boulder: Lynne Rienner.

Meena, Ruth. 1992. "Do Women Have an Agenda in the Struggle for Democracy in Southern Africa?" *Southern Africa Political and Economic Monthly* 5, 8:39–42.

Nowrojee, Binaifer, and Browen Manby. 1993. "Divide and Rule." *Africa Report* (September/October):32–34.

Nzomo, Maria. 1988. "Women, Democracy and Development in Africa." In *Democratic Theory and Practice in Africa,* ed. Walter O. Oyugi, E. S. Atieno Odhiambo, Michael Chege, and Afrifa K. Gitonga, 139–159. Portsmouth, N.H.: Heinemann.

———. 1993a. "Good Governance and Accountability." *Society* (September).

———. 1993b. "Political and Legal Empowerment of Women in Post-Election Kenya." In *Empowering Kenya Women,* ed. Maria Nzomo. Nairobi: National Committee on the Status of Women.

Nzomo, Maria, and Kivutha Kibwana, eds. 1993. *Women's Initiatives in Kenya's Democratization: Capacity Building and Participation in the December 1992 Multiparty General Elections.* Nairobi: National Committee on the Status of Women.

Parpart, Jane L. 1988. "Women and the State in Africa." In *The Precarious Balance: State and Society in Africa,* ed. Donald Rothchild and Naomi Chazan. Boulder: Westview.

Staudt, Kathleen, and Jeanne-Marie Col. 1991. "Diversity in East Africa: Cultural Pluralism, Public Policy, and the State." In *Women and International Development Annual,* ed. Rita S. Gallin and Anne Ferguson. Boulder: Westview.

Strobel, Margaret. 1976. "From Lelemama to Lobbying: Women's Associations in Mombasa." In *Women in Africa: Studies in Social and Economic Change,* ed. Nancy Hafkin and Edna Bay, 183–211. Stanford: Stanford University Press.

Tadria, Hilda. 1987. "Changes and Continuities in the Position of Women in Uganda." In *Beyond Crisis: Development Issues in Uganda,* ed. P. D. Wiebe and C. P. Dodge. Kampala: Makerere Institute of Social Research.

Tanzania Gender Networking Programme. 1993. *Gender Profile of Tanzania.* Dar es Salaam: Tanzania Gender Networking Programme.

Wipper, Audrey. 1975. "The Maendeleo ya Wanawake Movement: Some Paradoxes and Contradictions." *African Studies Review* 18, 3:99–120.

Selected References Related to Urban African Women

COMPILED BY KATHLEEN SHELDON

This list of publications is presented as a resource for those concerned with urban women in Africa. It is divided into four areas corresponding to the divisions in this volume. However, this is not a reference list for the chapters, as each chapter has its own reference list.

Migration and Urbanization

Adepoju, Aderanti. 1984. "Migration and Female Employment in Southwestern Nigeria." *African Urban Studies* 18:59–75.

Assogba, Laurent N. M. 1989. "Comportements demographiques de femmes migrantes à Lomé." In *L'insertion urbaine des migrants en Afrique*, ed. Philippe Antoine and Sidiki Coulibaly, 71–78. Paris: Editions l'ORSTOM.

Barnes, Teresa A. 1992. "The Fight for Control of African Women's Mobility in Colonial Zimbabwe, 1900–1939." *Signs* 17, 3:586–608.

Barnes, Terri, and Everjoyce Win. 1992. *To Live a Better Life: An Oral History of Women in the City of Harare: 1930–70.* Harare: Baobab Books.

Bjerén, Gunilla. 1985. *Migration to Shashemene: Ethnicity, Gender, and Occupation in Urban Ethiopia.* Uppsala: Scandinavian Institute of African Studies.

Bonner, Phil. 1990. "'Desirable or Undesirable Basotho Women?' Liquor, Prostitution and the Migration of Basotho Women to the Rand, 1920–1945." In *Women and Gender in Southern Africa to 1945*, ed. Cherryl Walker, 221–250. Bloomington: Indiana University Press.

Brockerhoff, Martin, and Hongsook Eu. 1993. "Demographic and Socioeconomic Determinants of Female Rural to Urban Migration in Sub-Saharan Africa." *International Migration Review* 27, 3:557–577.

Cohen, Abner. 1969. "The Migratory Process: Prostitutes and Housewives." In *Custom and Politics in Urban Africa: A Study of Hausa Migrants in Yoruba Towns*, 51–70. Berkeley: University of California Press.

Deniel, Raymond. 1985. *Femmes des villes africaines*. Abidjan: Inadès.

Dickerman, Carol. 1984. "City Women and the Colonial Regime: Usumbura, 1939–1962." *African Urban Studies* 18:33–48.

Eales, Kathy. 1989. "Patriarchs, Passes and Privilege: Johannesburg's African Middle Classes and the Question of Night Passes for African Women, 1920–1931." In *Holding Their Ground: Class, Locality, and Culture in 19th and 20th Century South Africa*, ed. Philip Bonner, Isabel Hofmeyr, Deborah James, and Tom Lodge, 105–139. Johannesburg: Ravan.

Findley, Sally E. 1989. "Les migrations féminines dans les villes africaines: Une revue de leurs motivations et experiences." In *L'insertion urbaine des migrants en Afrique*, ed. Philippe Antoine and Sidiki Coulibaly, 55–70. Paris: Editions l'ORSTOM.

Geisler, Gisela, and Karen Tranberg Hansen. 1994. "Structural Adjustment, the Rural-Urban Interface and Gender Relations in Zambia." In *Women in the Age of Economic Transformation: Gender Impact of Reforms in Post-Socialist and Developing Countries*, ed. Nahid Aslanbeigui, Steven Pressman, and Gale Summerfield, 95–112. New York: Routledge.

Gugler, Josef. 1972. "Second Sex in Town." *Canadian Journal of African Studies* 6, 2:289–301.

———. 1989. "Women Stay on the Farm No More: Changing Patterns of Rural-Urban Migration in Sub-Saharan Africa." *Journal of Modern African Studies* 27, 2:347–352.

Gugler, Josef, and William G. Flanagan. 1978. *Urbanization and Social Change in West Africa*. Cambridge: Cambridge University Press.

Hamer, Alice. 1981. "Dioula Women and Migration: A Case Study." In *The Uprooted of the Western Sahel: Migrants' Quest for Cash in the Senegambia*, ed. Lucie Colvin, 183–203. New York: Praeger.

Hollos, Marida. 1991. "Migration, Education, and the Status of Women in Southern Nigeria." *American Anthropologist* 93, 4:852–870.

Hunt, Nancy Rose. 1990. "Domesticity and Colonialism in Belgian Africa: Usumbura's *Foyer Social*, 1946–1960." *Signs* 15, 3:447–474.

———. 1991. "Noise over Camouflaged Polygamy, Colonial Morality Taxation, and a Women-Naming Crisis in Belgian Africa." *Journal of African History* 32:471–494.

Little, Kenneth. 1973. *African Women in Towns: An Aspect of Africa's Social Revolution*. Cambridge: Cambridge University Press.

———. 1976. "Women in African Towns South of the Sahara: The Urbanization Dilemma." In *Women and World Development*, ed. Irene Tinker and Michèle Bo Bramsen, 78–87. Washington, D.C.: Overseas Development Council.

Loforte, Ana. 1987. "Migrantes e sua relação com o meio rural." *Trabalhos de arqueologia e antropologia* 4:55–69.

———. 1989. "A persistência dos valores 'tradicionais' nas comunidades urbanas e a etnicidade." *Trabalhos de arqueologia e antropologia* 6:21–27.

Lovett, Margot. 1989. "Gender Relations, Class Formation and the Colonial State in Africa." In *Women and the State in Africa*, ed. Jane L. Parpart and Kathleen A. Staudt, 23–46. Boulder: Lynne Rienner.

Mayer, Philip. 1961. "Girls and Women in Town." In *Townsmen or Tribesmen: Conservatism and the Process of Urbanization in a South African City*, 233–251. Cape Town: Oxford University Press.

Mbilinyi, Marjorie. 1989. "'This Is an Unforgettable Business': Colonial State Intervention in Urban Tanzania." In *Women and the State in Africa*, ed. Jane L. Parpart and Kathleen A. Staudt, 111–129. Boulder: Lynne Rienner.

Peil, Margaret. 1985. "Changing Structures: A Democratic [Demographic] Comparison." *Comparative Urban Research* 10, 2:76–91.

Peil, Margaret, with Pius O. Sada. 1984. *African Urban Society*. New York: John Wiley and Sons.

Peil, Margaret, Stephen K. Ekpenyong, and Olotunji Y. Oyeneye. 1988. "Going Home: Migration Careers of Southern Nigerians." *International Migration Review* 22, 4:563–585.

Pellow, Deborah. 1991. "From Accra to Kano: One Woman's Experience." In *Hausa Women in the Twentieth Century*, ed. Catherine Coles and Beverly Mack, 50–68. Madison: University of Wisconsin Press.

Pittin, Renée. 1984. "Migration of Women in Nigeria: The Hausa Case." *International Migration Review* 18, 4:1293–1314.

Schlyter, Ann. 1990. "Women in Harare: Gender Aspects of Urban-Rural Interaction." In *Small-Town Africa: Studies in Rural-Urban Interaction*, ed. Jonathan Baker, 182–191. Uppsala: Scandinavian Institute of African Studies.

Staudt, Kathleen. 1989. "The State and Gender in Colonial Africa." In *Women, the State, and Development*, ed. Sue Ellen M. Charlton, Jana Everett, and Kathleen Staudt. Albany: State University of New York Press.

Stichter, Sharon. 1990. "The Migration of Women in Colonial Central Africa: Some Notes Toward an Approach." In *Demography from Scanty Evidence: Central Africa in the Colonial Era*, ed. Bruce Fetter, 207–218. Boulder: Lynne Rienner.

Thadani, Veena. 1978–1979. "Women in Nairobi: The Paradox of Urban 'Progress.'" *African Urban Studies* 3 (new series):67–83.

Vaa, Mariken. 1990. "Paths to the City: Migration Histories of Poor Women in Bamako." In *Small-Town Africa: Studies in Rural-Urban Interaction*, ed. Jonathan Baker, 172–181. Uppsala: Scandinavian Institute of African Studies.

Vaa, Mariken, Sally E. Findley, and Assitan Diallo. 1989. "The Gift Economy: A Study of Women Migrants' Survival Strategies in a Low-Income Bamako Neighborhood." *Labour, Capital and Society* 22, 2:234–260.

van Westen, A.C.M., and M. C. Klute. 1986. "From Bamako, with Love: A Case Study of Migrants and Their Remittances." *Tijdschrift voor economische en sociale geografie* 77, 1:42–49.

Walker, Cherryl. 1990. "Gender and the Development of the Migrant Labour System c. 1850–1930: An Overview." In *Women and Gender in Southern Africa to 1945*, ed. Cherryl Walker, 168–196. London: James Currey.

Watts, Susan J. 1983. "Marriage Mobility, a Neglected Form of Long-Term Mobility: A Case Study from Ilorin, Nigeria." *International Migration Review* 17, 4:682–698.

Wells, Julia. 1982. "Passes and Bypasses: Freedom of Movement for African Women Under the Urban Areas Act of South Africa." In *African Women and the Law: Historical Perspectives*, ed. Margaret Jean Hay and Marcia Wright, 125–150. Boston: Boston University African Studies Center.

Courtyards: Marriage, Family, and Housing

Abu, Katharine. 1983. "The Separateness of Spouses: Conjugal Resources in an Ashanti Town." In *Female and Male in West Africa*, ed. Christine Oppong, 156–168. London: George Allen and Unwin.

Adrien-Rongier, Marie-France. 1981. "Les *Kodro* de Bangui: Un espace urbain 'oublié.'" *Cahiers d'études africaines* 21, 2–3:93–110.

Antoine, Philippe, and Jeanne Nanitelamio. 1989. "Statuts féminins et urbanisation en Afrique." *Politique africaine* 36:129–133.

———. 1990. "Nouveaux statuts féminins et urbanisation en Afrique." *Genus* 46, 3–4:17–30.

———. 1992. "More Single Women in African Cities: Pikine, Abidjan and Brazzaville." *Population. English Selection* 3:149–169.

Bernard, Guy. 1972. "Conjugalité et rôle de la femme à Kinshasa." *Canadian Journal of African Studies* 6, 2:261–274.

Brandel, Mia. 1958. "Urban Lobolo Attitudes: A Preliminary Report." *African Studies* 17, 1:34–51.

Callaway, Barbara J., and Katherine E. Kleeman. 1985. "Three Women of Kano: Modern Women and Traditional Life." *Africa Report* 30, 2:26–29.

Callaway, Helen. 1981. "Spatial Domains and Women's Mobility in Yorubaland, Nigeria." In *Women and Space: Ground Rules and Social Maps*, ed. Shirley Ardener, 168–203. London: Croom Helm.

Campbell, Catherine. 1990. "The Township Family and Women's Struggles." *Agenda* 6:1–22.

Clark, Mari H. 1984. "Woman-Headed Households and Poverty: Insights from Kenya." *Signs* 10, 2:338–354.

Coles, Catherine. 1983. *Urban Muslim Women and Social Change in Northern Nigeria.* Women in International Development Working Papers, no. 19. East Lansing: Michigan State University.

———. 1990. "The Older Woman in Hausa Society: Power and Authority in Urban Nigeria." In *The Cultural Context of Aging: Worldwide Perspectives*, ed. Jay Sokolovsky, 57–81. New York: Bergin and Garvey.

Comhaire-Sylvain, Suzanne. 1968. *Femmes de Kinshasa: Hier et aujourd'hui.* Paris: Mouton.

———. 1982. *Femmes de Lomé.* Bandundu, Zaire: Ceeba.

Cuentro, Stenio de Coura, and Dji Malla Gadji. 1990. "The Collection and Management of Household Garbage." In *The Poor Die Young: Housing and Health in Third World Cities*, ed. Sandy Cairncross, Jorge E. Hardoy, and David Satterthwaite, 169–188. London: Earthscan.

Ellovich, Risa S. 1980. "Dioula Women in Town: A View of Intraethnic Variation (Ivory Coast)." In *A World of Women: Anthropological Studies of Women in the Societies of the World*, ed. Erika Bourguignon, 87–103. New York: Praeger.

Etienne, Mona. 1979. "The Case for Social Maternity: Adoption of Children by Urban Baule Women." *Dialectical Anthropology* 4, 3:237–242.

———. 1983. "Gender Relations and Conjugality Among the Baule." In *Female and Male in West Africa*, ed. Christine Oppong, 303–319. London: George Allen and Unwin.

Faladé, Solange. 1960. "Women of Dakar and the Surrounding Urban Area." In *Women of Tropical Africa*, ed. Denise Paulme, 217–229. Berkeley and Los Angeles: University of California Press.

Gaitskell, Deborah. 1983. "Housewives, Maids or Mothers: Some Contradictions of Domesticity for Christian Women in Johannesburg, 1903–39." *Journal of African History* 24, 2:241–256.

Glaser, Clive. 1992. "The Mark of Zorro: Sexuality and Gender Relations in the Tsotsi Subculture on the Witwatersrand." *African Studies* 51, 1:47–67.

Hansen, Karen Tranberg. 1992. "Gender and Housing: The Case of Domestic Service in Lusaka, Zambia." *Africa* 62, 2:248–265.

Hellman, Ellen. 1974. "African Townswomen in the Process of Change." *South Africa International* 5, 1:14–22.

Karanja, Wambui Wa. 1983. "Conjugal Decision-Making: Some Data from Lagos." In *Female and Male in West Africa*, ed. Christine Oppong, 236–241. London: George Allen and Unwin.

Kleis, Gerald W., and Salisu A. Abdullahi. 1983. "Masculine Power and Gender Ambiguity in Urban Hausa Society." *African Urban Studies* 16:39–53.

Larsson, Anita. 1989. *Women Householders and Housing Strategies: The Case of Gaborone, Botswana*. Gävle: National Swedish Institute for Building Research.

———. 1993. "The Importance of Housing in the Lives of Women: The Case of Botswana." In *Shelter, Women, and Development: First and Third World Perspectives*, ed. Hemalata C. Dandekar. Ann Arbor, Mich.: George Wahr.

Le Guennec-Coppens, Françoise. 1983. *Femmes voilées de Lamu (Kenya): Variations culturelles et dynamiques sociales*. Paris: Editions Recherche sur les Civilisations.

Longmore, Laura. 1959. *The Dispossessed: A Study of the Sex-Life of Bantu Women in and Around Johannesburg*. London: Corgi.

Mack, Beverly B. 1992. "Harem Domesticity in Kano, Nigeria." In *African Encounters with Domesticity*, ed. Karen Tranberg Hansen, 75–97. New Brunswick, N.J.: Rutgers University Press.

Mann, Kristin. 1982. "Women's Rights in Law and Practice: Marriage and Dispute Settlement in Colonial Lagos." In *African Women and the Law: Historical Perspectives*, ed. Margaret Jean Hay and Marcia Wright, 151–171. Boston: Boston University African Studies Center.

———. 1983. "The Dangers of Dependence: Christian Marriage Among Elite Women in Lagos Colony, 1880–1915." *Journal of African History* 24:37–57.

———. 1985. *Marrying Well: Marriage, Status, and Social Change Among the Educated Elite in Colonial Lagos*. New York: Cambridge University Press.

———. 1991. "Women, Landed Property, and the Accumulation of Wealth in Early Colonial Lagos." *Signs* 16, 4:682–706.

Mirza, Sarah, and Margaret Strobel. 1989. *Three Swahili Women: Life Histories from Mombasa, Kenya*. Bloomington: Indiana University Press.

Moodie, Duncan, with Vivienne Ndatshe. 1992. "Town Women and Country Wives: Migrant Labour, Family Politics and Housing Preferences at Vaal Reefs Mine." *Labour, Capital and Society* 25, 1:116–132.

Moran, Mary H. 1992. "Civilized Servants: Child Fosterage and Training for Status Among the Glebo of Liberia." In *African Encounters with Domesticity*, ed. Karen Tranberg Hansen, 98–115. New Brunswick, N.J.: Rutgers University Press.

Muchena, Olivia N. 1980. *Women in Town: A Socio-economic Survey of African Women in Highfield Township, Salisbury*. Harare: University of Zimbabwe.

Munachonga, Monica. 1988. "Income Allocation and Marriage Options in Urban Zambia." In *A Home Divided: Women and Income in the Third World*, ed. Daisy Dwyer and Judith Bruce, 173–194. Stanford: Stanford University Press.

Nelson, Nici. 1978–1979. "Female-Centered Families: Changing Patterns of Marriage and Family Among Buzaa Brewers of Mathare Valley." *African Urban Studies* 3 (new series):85–103.

———. 1979. "'Women Must Help Each Other': The Operation of Personal Networks Among Buzaa Beer Brewers in Mathare Valley, Kenya." In *Women United, Women Divided: Comparative Studies of Ten Contemporary Cultures*, ed. Patricia Caplan and Janet M. Bujra, 77–98. Bloomington: Indiana University Press.

Niehaus, Isak A. 1988. "Domestic Dynamics and Wage Labour: A Case Study Among Urban Residents in Qwaqwa." *African Studies* 47, 2:121–143.

Nimpuno-Parente, Paula. 1987. "The Struggle for Shelter: Women in a Site and Service Project in Nairobi, Kenya." In *Women, Human Settlements, and Housing*, ed. Caroline O. N. Moser and Linda Peake, 70–87. London: Tavistock.

Ntege, Hilda. 1993. "Women and Urban Housing Crisis: Impact of Pulbic Policies and Practices in Uganda." *Economic and Political Weekly* 28, 44 (30 October):46–62.

Oppong, Christine. 1970. "Conjugal Power and Resources: An Urban African Example." *Journal of Marriage and the Family* 32, 4:676–680.

———. 1975. "A Study of Domestic Continuity and Change: Akan Senior Service Families in Accra." In *Changing Social Structures in Ghana*, ed. Jack Goody, 181–200. London: International Africa Institute.

Oruwari, Yomi. 1991. "The Changing Role of Women in Families and Their Housing Needs: A Case Study of Port Harcourt, Nigeria." *Environment and Urbanization* 3, 2:6–12.

Parpart, Jane L. 1988. "Sexuality and Power on the Zambian Copperbelt: 1926–1964." In *Patriarchy and Class: African Women in the Home and the Workforce*, ed. Sharon B. Stichter and Jane L. Parpart, 115–138. Boulder: Westview.

———. 1994. "'Where Is Your Mother?': Gender, Urban Marriage, and Colonial Discourse on the Zambian Copperbelt, 1924–1945." *International Journal of African Historical Studies* 27, 2:241–271.

Pine, Frances. 1982. "Family Structure and the Division of Labor: Female Roles in Urban Ghana." In *Introduction to the Sociology of "Developing Societies,"* ed. Hamza Alavi and Teodor Shanin, 387–405. London: Macmillan.

Pittin, Renée. 1983. "Houses of Women: A Focus on Alternative Life-Styles in Katsina City." In *Female and Male in West Africa*, ed. Christine Oppong, 291–302. London: George Allen and Unwin.

Preston-Whyte, Eleanor. 1981. "Women Migrants and Marriage." In *Essays on African Marriage in Southern Africa*, ed. Eileen Jensen Krige and John L. Comaroff, 158–173. Cape Town: Juta.

Preston-Whyte, Eleanor, and Maria Zondi. 1989. "To Control Their Own Reproduction: The Agenda of Black Teenage Mothers in Durban." *Agenda* 4:47–68.

Ridd, Rosemary. 1981. "Where Women Must Dominate: Response to Oppression in a South African Urban Community." In *Women and Space: Ground Rules and Social Maps*, ed. Shirley Ardener, 187–204. London: Croom Helm.

Sanjek, Roger. 1982. "The Organization of Households in Adabraka: Toward a Wider Comparative Perspective." *Comparative Studies in Society and History* 24, 1:57–103.

————. 1983. "Female and Male Domestic Cycles in Urban Africa: The Adabraka Case." In *Female and Male in West Africa*, ed. Christine Oppong, 330–343. London: George Allen and Unwin.

Sargent, Carolyn Fishel. 1989. *Maternity, Medicine, and Power: Reproductive Decisions in Urban Benin*. Berkeley and Los Angeles: University of California Press.

Saunders, Margaret O. 1980. "Women's Role in a Muslim Hausa Town (Mirria, Republic of Niger)." In *A World of Women: Anthropological Studies of Women in the Societies of the World*, ed. Erika Bourguignon, 57–86. New York: Praeger.

Schildkrout, Enid. 1978. "Age and Gender in Hausa Society: Socio-Economic Roles of Children in Urban Kano." In *Sex and Age as Principles of Social Differentiation*, ed. J. S. La Fontaine, 109–138. New York: Academic Press.

————. 1988. "Hajiya Husaina: Notes on the Life History of a Hausa Woman." In *Life Histories of African Women*, ed. Patricia Romero, 78–98. Atlantic Highland, N.J.: Ashfield.

Schoepf, Brooke Grundfest. 1988. "Women, AIDS, and Economic Crisis in Central Africa." *Canadian Journal of African Studies* 22, 3:625–644.

————. 1992. "Gender Relations and Development: Political Economy and Culture." In *Twenty-First Century Africa: Toward a New Vision of Self-Sustainable Development*, ed. Ann Seidman and Frederick Anang, 203–241. Trenton, N.J.: Africa World.

————. 1992. "Sex, Gender and Society in Zaire." In *Sexual Behaviour and Networking, Anthropological and Sociocultural Studies on the Transmission of HIV*, ed. Tim Dyson, 353–375. Liège: Editions de Rouaux-Ordina.

Schuster, Ilsa M. Glazer. 1979. *New Women of Lusaka*. Palo Alto, Calif.: Mayfield.

————. 1982. *Cycles of Dependence and Independence: Westernization and the African Heritage of Lusaka's Young Women*. Women in International Development Working Papers, no. 7. East Lansing: Michigan State University.

Shephard, Gill. 1987. "Rank, Gender, and Homosexuality: Mombasa as a Key to Understanding Sexual Options." In *The Cultural Construction of Sexuality*, ed. Pat Caplan, 240–270. London: Tavistock.

Sibisi, Harriet. 1977. "How African Women Cope with Migrant Labor in South Africa." *Signs* 3, 1:167–177.

Sithole-Fundire, Sylvia, Agnes Zhou, Anita Larsson, and Ann Schlyter, eds. 1995. *Gender Research on Urbanization, Planning, Housing, and Everyday Life.* Harare: Zimbabwe Women's Resource Centre and Network.

Stichter, Sharon B. 1988. "The Middle-Class Family in Kenya: Changes in Gender Relations." In *Patriarchy and Class: African Women in the Home and the Workforce,* ed. Sharon B. Stichter and Jane L. Parpart, 177–203. Boulder: Westview.

Trevitt, Lorna. 1973. "Attitudes and Customs in Childbirth Amongst Hausa Women in Zaria City." *Savanna* 2, 2:223–226.

Uyanga, Joseph. 1978. "Fertility Behavior in Crowded Urban Living." *African Urban Studies* 2 (new series):49–59.

van der Vliet, Virginia. 1991. "Traditional Husbands, Modern Wives? Constructing Marriages in a South African Township." In *Tradition and Transition in Southern Africa: Festschrift for Philip and Iona Mayer,* ed. A. D. Spiegel and P. A. McAllister, 219–241. Johannesburg: Witwatersrand University Press.

Verhaegen, Benoît. 1988. "La famille urbaine face à la polygamie et à la prostitution: Le cas de Kisangani au Zaïre." In *Processus d'urbanisation en Afrique,* vol. 2, ed. Catherine Coquery-Vidrovitch, 124–130. Paris: L'Harmattan.

Vidal, Claudine. 1977. "Guerre des sexes à Abidjan: Masculin, féminin, CFA." *Cahiers d'études africaines* 17, 1:121–153.

———. 1980. "Pour un portrait d'Abidjan avec dames." *Cahiers internationaux de sociologie* 69:305–312.

Wéry, René. 1987. "Women in Bamako: Activities and Relations." In *Sex Roles, Population, and Development in West Africa,* ed. Christine Oppong, 45–62. Portsmouth, N.H.: Heinemann.

Westwood, Sallie. 1974. "Fear Woman: Male Dominance, Female Transcendence; A Case Study of Ga Women in Jamestown, Accra, Ghana." *Cambridge Anthropology* 1, 3:39–50.

White, Caroline. 1991. "'Close to Home' in Johannesburg: Oppression in Township Households." *Agenda* 11:78–89.

Markets: Work and Survival

Adam, Michel. 1980. "Manioc, rente foncière et situation des femmes dans les environs de Brazzaville (République Populaire du Congo)." *Cahiers d'études africaines* 20, 1–2:5–48.

Akerele, Olubanke. 1979. *Women Workers in Ghana, Kenya, Zambia: A Comparative Analysis of Women's Employment in the Modern Wage Sector.* Addis Ababa: United Nations Economic Commission for Africa.

Bakwesegha, Christopher J. 1982. *Profiles of Urban Prostitution: A Case Study from Uganda.* Nairobi: Kenya Literature Bureau.

Bardouille, Raj. 1981. "The Sexual Division of Labour in the Urban Informal Sector: The Case of Some Townships in Lusaka." *African Social Research* 32:29–54.

Barrett, Hazel R., and Angela W. Browne. 1988. "Women's Horticulture in the Peri-Urban Zone, The Gambia." *Geography* 73, pt. 2, no. 319:158–160.

Barthel, Diane. 1975. "The Rise of a Female Professional Elite: The Case of Senegal." *African Studies Review* 18, 3:1–17.

Baylies, Carolyn, and Caroline Wright. 1993. "Female Labour in the Textile and Clothing Industry of Lesotho." *African Affairs* 92:577–591.

Berger, Iris. 1992. *Threads of Solidarity: Women in South African Industry, 1900–1980.* Bloomington: Indiana University Press.

Bonnardel, Régine. 1988. "Saint-Louis du Sénégal: Le règne des femmes dans les petites activités." In *Processus d'urbanisation en Afrique,* vol. 2, ed. Catherine Co-query-Vidrovitch, 150–168. Paris: Editions l'Harmattan.

Bryceson, Deborah Fahy. 1985. "Women's Proletarianization and the Family Wage in Tanzania." In *Women, Work, and Ideology in the Third World,* ed. Haleh Afshar, 128–152. New York: Tavistock.

Bujitu, Tshibanda Wamuela. 1979. *Femmes libres, femmes enchaînées: La prostitution au Zaire.* Lubumbashi: Editions Saint Paul.

Bujra, Janet. 1975. "Women 'Entrepreneurs' of Early Nairobi." *Canadian Journal of African Studies* 9, 2:213–234.

Chauncey, George. 1981. "The Locus of Reproduction: Women's Labour on the Zambian Copperbelt, 1927–1953." *Journal of African History* 7, 2:135–164.

Cheater, Angela P. 1974. "A Marginal Elite? African Registered Nurses in Durban, South Africa." *African Studies* 33, 3:143–158.

Chege, Rebecca. 1986. "Communal Food Production: The Mukuru-Kaiyaba Women's Group in Nairobi." *Canadian Woman Studies* 7, 1–2:76–77.

Clark, Gracia. 1991. "Colleagues and Customers in Unstable Market Conditions: Kumasi, Ghana." *Ethnology* 30, 1:31–48.

———. 1994. *Onions Are My Husband: Survival and Accumulation by West African Market Women.* Chicago: Chicago University Press.

Clignet, Remi. 1972. "Quelques remarques sur le rôle des femmes africaines en milieu urbain: Le cas du Cameroun." *Canadian Journal of African Studies* 6, 2:303–315.

Cock, Jacklyn. 1980. *Maids and Madams: A Study in the Politics of Exploitation.* Johannesburg: Ravan.

Cock, Jacklyn, Erica Emdon, and Barbara Klugman. 1984. *Child Care and the Working Mother: A Sociological Investigation of a Sample of Urban African Women.* Carnegie Conference Paper no. 115. Cape Town.

Cohen, Barney, and William J. House. 1993. "Women's Urban Labour Market Status in Developing Countries: How Well Do They Fare in Khartoum, Sudan?" *Journal of Development Studies* 29, 3:461–483.

Coles, Catherine. 1991. "Hausa Women's Work in a Declining Urban Economy: Kaduna, Nigeria, 1980–1985." In *Hausa Women in the Twentieth Century,* ed. Catherine Coles and Beverly Mack, 163–191. Madison: University of Wisconsin Press.

Date-Bah, Eugenia. 1978/1979. "Ghanaian Women in Academia: African Women in a New Occupational Role." *Ghana Journal of Sociology* 12, 1:44–71.

———. 1983. "Female and Male Factory Workers in Accra." In *Female and Male in West Africa,* ed. Christine Oppong, 266–274. London: George Allen and Unwin.

———. 1986. "Sex Segregation and Discrimination in Accra-Tema: Causes and Consequences." In *Sex Inequalities in Urban Employment in the Third World,* ed. Richard Anker and Catherine Hein, 235–276. New York: St. Martin's Press.

Dennis, Carolyne. 1991. "Constructing a 'Career' Under Conditions of Economic Crisis and Structural Adjustment: The Survival Strategies of Nigerian Women."

In *Women, Development, and Survival in the Third World*, ed. Haleh Afshar, 88–106. London: Longman.

———. 1991. "The Limits to Women's Independent Careers: Gender in the Formal and Informal Sectors in Nigeria." In *Male Bias in the Development Process*, ed. Diane Elson, 83–104. Manchester: Manchester University Press.

Di Domenico, Catherine M. 1983. "Male and Female Factory Workers in Ibadan." In *Female and Male in West Africa*, ed. Christine Oppong, 256–265. London: George Allen and Unwin.

Di Domenico, Catherine, Lee de Cola, and Jennifer Leishman. 1987. "Urban Yoruba Mothers: At Home and at Work." In *Sex Roles, Population, and Development in West Africa*, ed. Christine Oppong, 118–132. Portsmouth, N.H.: Heinemann.

Dinan, Carmel. 1977. "Pragmatists or Feminists? The Professional 'Single' Women in Accra, Ghana." *Cahiers d'études africaines* 17, 1:155–176.

———. 1983. "Sugar Daddies and Gold-Diggers: The White-Collar Single Women in Accra." In *Female and Male in West Africa*, ed. Christine Oppong, 344–366. London: George Allen and Unwin.

Dirasse, Laketch. 1978. *The Socio-economic Position of Women in Addis Ababa: The Case of Prostitution*. Ph.D. diss., Boston University.

Drakakis-Smith, David. 1984. "The Changing Economic Role of Women in the Urbanization Process: A Preliminary Report from Zimbabwe." *International Migration Review* 18, 4:1278–1292.

———. 1992. "Strategies for Meeting Basic Food Needs in Harare." In *The Rural-Urban Interface in Africa: Expansion and Adaptation*, ed. Jonathan Baker and Poul Ove Pederson, 258–283. Uppsala: Scandinavian Institute of African Studies.

Edwards, Iain. 1988. "Shebeen Queens: Illicit Liquor and the Social Structure of Drinking Dens in Cato Manor," *Agenda* 3:75–97.

Ekejiuba, Felicia. 1967. "Omu Okwei, the Merchant Queen of Ossomari: A Biographical Sketch." *Journal of the Historical Society of Nigeria* 3, 4:633–646.

El Bakri, Zeinab B., and El-Wathig M. Kameir. 1990. "Women's Participation in Economic, Social and Political Life in Sudanese Urban and Rural Communities: The Case of Saganna in Khartoum and Wad al-'Asha in the Gezira Area." In *Women in Arab Society: Work Patterns and Gender Relations in Egypt, Jordan, and Sudan*, ed. Seteney Shami, Lucine Taminian, Soheir A. Morsy, Zeinab B. El Bakri, and El-Wathig M. Kameir, 160–198. Providence, R.I.: Berg.

El Nagar, Samia El Hadi. 1988. "Changing Patterns of Participation of Women in Petty-Trading Activities in Khartoum." *Ahfad Journal* 5, 1:14–23.

Fadayomi, Theo Philus O. 1991. "Women in the Nigerian Labor Force." *International Journal of Sociology of the Family* 21:175–188.

Fapohunda, Eleanor R. 1978. "Characteristics of Women Workers in Lagos: Data for Reconsideration by Labour Market Theorists." *Labour and Society* 3, 2:158–171.

———. 1982. "The Child-Care Dilemma of Working Mothers in African Cities: The Case of Lagos, Nigeria." In *Women and Work in Africa*, ed. Edna G. Bay, 277–288. Boulder: Westview.

———. 1987. "Urban Women's Roles and Nigerian Government Development Strategies." In *Sex Roles, Population, and Development in West Africa*, ed. Christine Oppong, 203–212. Portsmouth, N.H.: Heinemann.

Freeman, Donald B. 1993. "Survival Strategy or Business Training Ground? The Significance of Urban Agriculture for the Advancement of Women in African Cities." *African Studies Review* 36, 3:1–22.

Frishman, Alan. 1991. "Hausa Women in the Urban Economy of Kano." In *Hausa Women in the Twentieth Century*, ed. Catherine Coles and Beverly Mack, 192–203. Madison: University of Wisconsin Press.

Gaitskell, Deborah, Judy Kimble, Moira Maconachie, and Elaine Unterhalter. 1984. "Class, Race and Gender: Domestic Workers in South Africa." *Review of African Political Economy* 27/28:86–108.

Gentili, Anna Maria. 1985. "Da Lourenço Marques a Maputo: La trasformazione delle aree agricole suburbane." *Africa* (Rome) 40, 2:183–219.

Hansen, Karen Tranberg. 1975. "Married Women and Work: Explorations from an Urban Case Study." *African Social Research* 20:777–799.

———. 1980. "The Urban Informal Sector as a Development Issue: Poor Women and Work in Lusaka, Zambia." *Urban Anthropology* 9, 2:199–226.

———. 1980. "When Sex Becomes a Critical Variable: Married Women and Extra-Domestic Work in Lusaka, Zambia." *African Social Research* 30:831–849.

———. 1982. "Planning Productive Work for Married Women in a Low-Income Settlement in Lusaka: The Case for a Small-Scale Handicrafts Industry." *African Social Research* 33:211–223.

———. 1984. "Negotiating Sex and Gender in Urban Zambia." *Journal of Southern African Studies* 10, 2:219–238.

———. 1987. "Urban Women and Work in Africa: A Zambian Case." *TransAfrica Forum* 4, 3:9–24.

———. 1989. "The Black Market and Women Traders in Lusaka, Zambia." In *Women and the State in Africa*, ed. Jane L. Parpart and Kathleen A. Staudt, 143–160. Boulder: Lynne Rienner.

———. 1989. *Distant Companions: Servants and Employers in Zambia, 1900–1985*. Ithaca: Cornell University Press.

———. 1990. "Body Politics: Sexuality, Gender, and Domestic Service in Zambia." *Journal of Women's History* 2, 1:120–142.

Harts-Broekhuis, E.J.A., and O. Verkoren. 1987. "Gender Differentiation Among Market-Traders in Central Mali," *Tijdschrift voor economische en sociale geografie* 78, 3:214–221.

Holm, Morgens. 1992. "Survival Strategies of Migrants to Makambako—an Intermediate Town in Tanzania." In *The Rural-Urban Interface in Africa: Expansion and Adaptation*, ed. Jonathan Baker and Poul Ove Pedersen, 238–257. Uppsala: Scandinavian Institute of African Studies.

Horn, Nancy. 1994. *Cultivating Customers: Market Women in Harare, Zimbabwe.* Boulder: Lynne Rienner.

House-Midamba, Bessie, ed. 1995. *African Market Women and Economic Power: The Role of Women in Economic Development.* Westport, Conn.: Greenwood Press.

International Labour Office. 1991. *The Urban Informal Sector in Africa in Retrospect and Prospect: An Annotated Bibliography.* Geneva: ILO.

Iyun, B. Folasade, and E. A. Oke. 1993. "The Impact of Contraceptive Use Among Urban Traders in Nigeria: Ibadan Traders and Modernization." In *Different Places, Different Voices: Gender and Development in Africa, Asia, and Latin America,* ed. Janet Henshall Momsen and Vivian Kinnaird, 63–73. London and New York: Routledge.

Johnson, Willene A. 1986. "Women and Self-Employment in Urban Tanzania." In *Slipping Through the Cracks: The Status of Black Women*, ed. Margaret C. Simms and Julianne Malveaux, 245–257. New Brunswick, N.J.: Transaction Books.

Jules-Rosette, Bennetta. 1977. "The Potters and the Painters: Art by and About Women in Urban Africa." *Studies in the Anthropology of Visual Communication* 4, 2:112–127.

————. 1982. "Women and Technological Change in the Urban Informal Economy: A Reconsideration of Entrepreneurial Behavior." *Resources for Feminist Research* 11, 1:37–42.

————. 1985. "Women and New Technologies in Comparative Perspective: Case Studies in Ivory Coast and Kenya." *African Urban Studies* 21:25–37.

————. 1985. "Women and Technological Change in the Informal Urban Economy: A Zambian Case Study." In *Women's Worlds: From the New Scholarship*, ed. Marilyn Safir, Martha T. Mednick, Dafne Israeli, and Jessie Bernard, 58–70. New York: Praeger.

————. 1985. "The Women Potters of Lusaka: Urban Migration and Socioeconomic Adjustment." In *African Migration and National Development*, ed. Beverly Lindsay, 82–112. University Park: Pennsylvania State University Press.

Kane, Francine. 1977. "Femmes prolétaires du Sénégal, à la ville at aux champs." *Cahiers d'études africaines* 17, 1:77–94.

Kanji, Nazneen, and Niki Jazdowska. 1993. "Structural Adjustment and Women in Zimbabwe." *Review of African Political Economy* 56:11–26.

Karanja, Wambui Wa. 1981. "Women and Work: A Study of Female and Male Attitudes in the Modern Sector of an African Metropolis." In *Women, Education, and Modernization of the Family in West Africa*, ed. Helen Ware, 42–66. Canberra: Australian National University.

Kerner, Donna O. 1988. "'Hard Work' and Informal Sector Trade in Tanzania." In *Traders Versus the State: Anthropological Approaches to Unofficial Economies*, ed. Gracia Clark, 41–56. Boulder: Westview.

Kuper, Hilda. 1965. "Nurses." In *An African Bourgeoisie: Race, Class, and Politics in South Africa*, by Leo Kuper, 216–233. New Haven: Yale University Press.

La Fontaine, J. S. 1974. "The Free Women of Kinshasa: Prostitution in a City in Zaire." In *Choice and Change: Essays in Honour of Lucy Mair*, ed. J. Davis, 89–113. London: Athlone.

Lacey, Linda. 1986. "Women in the Development Process: Occupational Mobility of Female Migrants in Cities in Nigeria." *Journal of Comparative Family Studies* 17, 1:1–18.

Lewis, Barbara. 1982. "Fertility and Employment: An Assessment of Role Incompatibility Among African Urban Women." In *Women and Work in Africa*, ed. Edna Bay, 249–276. Boulder: Westview.

Lewis, Barbara C. 1976. "The Limitations of Group Action Among Entrepreneurs: The Market Women of Abidjan, Ivory Coast." In *Women in Africa: Studies in Social and Economic Change*, ed. Nancy J. Hafkin and Edna G. Bay, 135–156. Stanford: Stanford University Press.

————. 1977. "Economic Activity and Marriage Among Ivoirian Urban Women." In *Sexual Stratification: A Cross-Cultural View*, ed. Alice Schlegel, 161–191. New York: Columbia University Press.

MacGaffey, Janet. 1988. "Evading Male Control: Women in the Second Economy in Zaire." In *Patriarchy and Class: African Women in the Home and the Workforce*, ed. Sharon B. Stichter and Jane L. Parpart, 161–176. Boulder: Westview.

Mack, Beverly B. 1990. "Service and Status: Slaves and Concubines in Kano, Nigeria." In *At Work in Homes: Household Workers in World Perspective*, ed. Roger Sanjek and Shellee Colen, 14–34. Washington, D.C.: American Anthropological Association.

Made, Patricia, and Birgitta Lagerström. 1985. *Zimbabwean Women in Industry*. Harare: Zimbabwe Publishing House.

Mainet, Guy. 1985. "Le rôle de la femme dans l'économie urbaine à Douala: Exemples du quartier Akwa et de la 'Zone Nylon.'" In *Femmes du Cameroun: Mères pacifiques, femmes rebelles*, ed. Jean-Claude Barbier, 369–383. Paris: Karthala-ORSTOM.

Malahleha, G. M. 1985. "Liquor Brewing: A Cottage Industry in Lesotho Shebeens." *Journal of Eastern African Research and Development* 15:45–55.

Mandeville, Elizabeth. 1979. "Poverty, Work and the Financing of Single Women in Kampala." *Africa* 49, 1:42–52.

Maxwell, Daniel, and Samuel Zziwa. 1992. *Urban Farming in Africa: The Case of Kampala, Uganda*. Nairobi: African Centre for Technology Studies.

May, Joan. 1979. *African Women in Urban Employment: Factors Influencing Their Employment in Zimbabwe*. Gwelo, Zimbabwe: Mambo Press.

McAdoo, Harriette, and Miriam Were. 1989. "Extended Family Involvement of Urban Kenyan Professional Women." In *Women in Africa and the African Diaspora*, ed. Rosalyn Terborg-Penn, Sharon Harley, and Andrea Benton Rushing, 133–164. Washington, D.C.: Howard University Press.

McCall, Daniel. 1961. "Trade and the Role of Wife in a Modern West African Town." In *Social Change in Modern Africa*, ed. Aidan Southall, 286–299. London: Oxford University Press.

Memon, Pyar Ali, and Diana Lee-Smith. 1993. "Urban Agriculture in Kenya." *Canadian Journal of African Studies* 27, 1:25–42.

Mitullah, Winnie. 1991. "Hawking as a Survival Strategy for the Urban Poor in Nairobi: The Case of Women." *Environment and Urbanization* 3, 2:13–22.

Muntemba, Dorothy. 1989. "The Impact of IMF–World Bank Programmes on Women and Children in Zambia." In *The IMF, the World Bank, and the African Debt*. Vol. 2, *The Social and Political Impact*, ed. Bade Onimode, 111–124. London: Zed.

Nelson, Nici. 1979. "How Women and Men Get By: The Sexual Division of Labour in the Informal Sector of a Nairobi Squatter Settlement." In *Casual Work and Poverty in Third World Cities*, ed. Ray Bromley and Chris Gerry, 283–302. New York: John Wiley and Sons.

————. 1987. "'Selling Her Kiosk': Kikuyu Notions of Sexuality and Sex for Sale in Mathare Valley, Kenya." In *The Cultural Construction of Sexuality*, ed. Pat Caplan, 217–239. London: Tavistock.

Obbo, Christine. 1975. "Women's Careers in Low Income Areas as Indicators of Country and Town Dynamics." In *Town and Country in Central and Eastern Africa*, ed. David Parkin, 288–293. London: International African Institute.
———. 1980. *African Women: Their Struggle for Economic Independence*. London: Zed.
Ogutu, M. A. 1985. "The Changing Role of Women in the Commercial History of Busia District in Kenya, 1900–1983." *Journal of Eastern African Research and Development* 15:74–90.
Okojie, Christiana E. E. 1984. "Female Migrants in the Urban Labour Market: Benin City, Nigeria." *Canadian Journal of African Studies* 18, 3:547–562.
Okpala, Amon O. 1989. "Female Employment and Family Size Among Urban Nigerian Women." *Journal of Developing Areas* 23, 3:439–456.
Osirim, Mary J. 1992. "Gender and Entrepreneurship: Issues of Capital and Technology in Nigerian Small Firms." In *Privatization and Investment in Sub-Saharan Africa*, ed. Rexford A. Ahene and Bernard S. Katz, 143–156. New York: Praeger.
Parpart, Jane L. 1986. "Class and Gender on the Copperbelt: Women in Northern Rhodesian Copper Mining Communities, 1926–1964." In *Women and Class in Africa*, ed. Claire Robertson and Iris Berger. New York: Holmes and Meier.
———. 1990. "Wage Earning Women and the Double Day: The Nigerian Case." In *Women, Employment, and the Family in the International Division of Labour*, ed. Sharon Stichter and Jane Parpart, 161–182. Hampshire, England: Macmillan.
Pearce, Tola Olu, Olugemi O. Kujore, and V. Aina Agboh-Bankole. 1988. "Generating an Income in the Urban Environment: The Experience of Street Food Vendors in Ile-Ife, Nigeria." *Africa* 58, 4:385–400.
Peil, Margaret. 1975. "Female Roles in West African Towns." In *Changing Social Structure in Ghana*, ed. Jack Goody, 73–90. London: International African Institute.
———. 1979. "Urban Women in the Labor Force." *Sociology of Work and Occupations* 6, 4:482–501.
Pellow, Deborah. 1977. *Women in Accra: Options for Autonomy*. Algonac, Mich.: Reference Publications.
Penvenne, Jeanne. 1986. *Making Our Own Way: Women Working in Lourenço Marques, 1900–1933*. African Studies Center Working Papers, no. 114. Boston: Boston University.
Pittin, Renée. 1984. "Gender and Class in a Nigerian Industrial Setting." *Review of African Political Economy* 31:71–81.
———. 1987. "Documentation of Women's Work in Nigeria: Problems and Solutions." In *Sex Roles, Population, and Development in West Africa*, ed. Christine Oppong, 25–44. Portsmouth, N.H.: Heinemann.
———. 1991. "Women, Work and Ideology in Nigeria." *Review of African Political Economy* 52:38–52.
Preston-Whyte, Eleanor. 1982. "Segregation and Interpersonal Relationships: A Case Study of Domestic Service in Durban." In *Living Under Apartheid: Aspects of Urbanization and Social Change in South Africa*, ed. David M. Smith, 164–182. London: George Allen and Unwin.
———. 1991. "Invisible Workers: Domestic Service and the Informal Economy." In *South Africa's Informal Economy*, ed. Eleanor Preston-Whyte and Christian Rogerson, 34–53. Cape Town: Oxford University Press.

Rakodi, Carol. 1985. "Self-Reliance or Survival? Food Production in African Cities, with Particular Reference to Zambia." *African Urban Studies* 21:53–63.

———. 1988. "Urban Agriculture: Research Questions and Zambian Evidence." *Journal of Modern African Studies* 26, 3:495–515.

Redding, Sean. 1992. "Beer Brewing in Umtata: Women, Migrant Labor, and Social Control in a Rural Town." In *Liquor and Labor in Southern Africa*, ed. Jonathan Crush and Charles Ambler, 235–251. Athens: Ohio University Press.

Remy, Dorothy. 1975. "Underdevelopment and the Experience of Women: A Nigerian Case Study." In *Toward an Anthropology of Women*, ed. Rayna R. Reiter, 358–371. New York: Monthly Review.

Robertson, Claire. 1974. "Economic Woman in Africa: Profit-Making Techniques of Accra Market Women." *Journal of Modern African Studies* 12, 4:657–664.

———. 1975/1976. "Ga Women and Change in Marketing Conditions in the Accra Area." *Rural Africana* 29:157–171.

———. 1976. "Change in the Organization of the Fish Trade in Twentieth-Century Accra." *African Urban Notes* 2, 2:43–58.

———. 1976. "Ga Women and Socioeconomic Change in Accra, Ghana." In *Women in Africa: Studies in Social and Economic Change*, ed. Nancy J. Hafkin and Edna G. Bay, 111–133. Stanford: Stanford University Press.

———. 1983. "The Death of Makola and Other Tragedies." *Canadian Journal of African Studies* 17, 3:469–495.

———. 1993. "Traders and Urban Struggle: Ideology and the Creation of a Militant Female Underclass in Nairobi, 1960–1990." *Journal of Women's History* 4, 3:9–42.

———. 1995. "Trade, Gender, and Poverty in the Nairobi Areas: Women's Strategies for Survival and Independence in the 1980s." In *Engendering Wealth and Well-Being: Empowerment for Global Change*, ed. Rae Lesser Blumberg, Cathy A. Rakowski, Irene Tinker, and Micheal Montéon, 65–87. Boulder: Westview.

Robertson, Claire C. 1984. *Sharing the Same Bowl: A Socioeconomic History of Women and Class in Accra, Ghana*. Bloomington: Indiana University Press.

———. 1984. "Women in the Urban Economy." In *African Women South of the Sahara*, ed. Margaret Jean Hay and Sharon Stichter, 33–50. London and New York: Longman.

Rogerson, Christian. 1991. "Home-based Enterprises of the Urban Poor: The Case of Spazas." In *South Africa's Informal Economy*, ed. Eleanor Preston-Whyte and Christian Rogerson, 336–344. Cape Town: Oxford University Press.

Sada, P. O., and M. L. McNulty. 1981. "The Market Traders in the City of Lagos." In *Urbanization Process and Problems in Nigeria*, ed. P. O. Sada and J. S. Oguntoyinbo, 63–79. Ibadan: Ibadan University Press.

Salih, Alawiya Osman M. 1986. "Women in Trade: Vendors in Khartoum Area Markets." *Ahfad Journal* 3, 2:37–40.

Sandee, Henry, and Hermine Weijland. 1988. "Dual Production and Marketing of Vegetables in Swaziland: A Case of Marginalization of Female Traders." In *Scenes of Change: Visions on Developments in Swaziland*, ed. Henk J. Tieleman, 150–162. Research Report no. 33. Leiden: African Studies Center.

Sanjek, Roger. 1990. "Maid Servants and Market Women's Apprentices in Adabraka." In *At Work in Homes: Household Workers in World Perspective*, ed.

Roger Sanjek and Shellee Colen, 35–62. Washington, D.C.: American Anthropological Association.

Sanjek, Roger, and Lani Morioka Sanjek. 1976. "Notes on Women and Work in
Adabraka." *African Urban Notes* 2, 2:1–25.

Schildkrout, Enid. 1979. "Women's Work and Children's Work: Variations Among
Moslems in Kano." In *Social Anthropology of Work*, ed. Sandra Wallman, 69–85.
London: Academic Press.

———. 1983. "Dependence and Autonomy: The Economic Activities of Secluded
Hausa Women in Kano." In *Female and Male in West Africa*, ed. Christine Oppong, 107–126. London: George Allen and Unwin.

Schilter, Christine. 1991. *L'agriculture urbaine à Lomé*. Paris: Karthala.

Schoepf, Brooke Grundfest, and Walu Engundu. 1991. "Women's Trade and Con-
tributions to Household Budgets in Kinshasa." In *The Real Economy of Zaire: The
Contribution of Smuggling and Other Unofficial Activities to National Wealth*, ed.
Janet MacGaffey, 124–151. Philadelphia: University of Pennsylvania Press.

Schuster, Ilsa. 1981. "Perspectives in Development: The Problem of Nurses and
Nursing in Zambia." In *African Women in the Development Process*, ed. Nici Nelson, 77–97. London: Frank Cass.

———. 1982. "Marginal Lives: Conflict and Contradiction in the Position of Female Traders in Lusaka, Zambia." In *Women and Work in Africa*, ed. Edna Bay,
105–126. Boulder: Westview.

Schuster, Ilsa M. Glazer. 1983. *Female White Collar Workers: A Case Study of Successful Development in Lusaka, Zambia*. Women in International Development Working Papers, no. 29. East Lansing: Michigan State University.

Schwarz, Alf. 1972. "Illusion d'une émancipation et alienation réelle de l'ouvrière
zairoise." *Canadian Journal of African Studies* 6, 2:183–212.

Sheldon, Kathleen. 1991. "A Report on a 'Delicate Problem' Concerning Female
Garment Workers in Beira, Mozambique." *Signs* 16, 3:575–586.

———. 1991. "Sewing Clothes and Sorting Cashew Nuts: Factories, Families, and
Women in Beira, Mozambique." *Women's Studies International Forum* 14, 1/2:27–35.

———. 1992. "*Creches, Titias*, and Mothers: Working Women and Child Care in
Mozambique." In *African Encounters with Domesticity*, ed. Karen Tranberg
Hansen. New Brunswick, N.J.: Rutgers University Press.

Shields, Nwanganga. 1980. *Women in the Urban Labor Markets of Africa: The Case of
Tanzania*. Staff Working Paper no. 380. Washington, D.C.: World Bank.

Simon, David. 1984. "Responding to Third World Urban Poverty: Women and
Men in the 'Informal' Sector in Windhoek, Namibia." In *Women's Role in Chang-
ing the Face of the Developing World*, ed. Janet Henshall Momsen and Janet
Townsend, 95–130. Durham, England: Institute of British Geographers.

Songue, Paulette. 1986. *Prostitution en Afrique: L'exemple de Yaoundé*. Paris: Editions
l'Harmattan.

Stichter, Sharon. 1986. *Women, Employment, and the Family in Nairobi: The Impact of
Capitalist Development in Kenya*. African Studies Center Working Papers, no.
121. Boston: Boston University.

Swantz, Marje-Liisa, and Deborah Fahy Bryceson. 1976. *Women Workers in Dar es
Salaam: 1973/74 Survey of Female Minimum Wage Earners and Self-Employed*. Dar
es Salaam: Bureau of Resource Assessment and Land Use Planning.

Tomaselli, Ruth Elizabeth. 1985. "On the Peripheries of the Defended Space: Hawkers in Johannesburg." In *The Struggle for Social and Economic Space: Urbanization in Twentieth Century South Africa*, ed. Richard Haines and Gina Buijs, 131–190. Durban: University of Durban Institute for Social and Economic Research.

Trager, Lillian. 1981. "Customers and Creditors: Variations in Economic Personalism in a Nigerian Marketing System." *Ethnology* 20, 2:133–146.

———. 1985. "From Yams to Beer in a Nigerian City: Expansion and Change in Informal Sector Trade Activity." In *Markets and Marketing*, ed. Stuart Plattner, 259–285. Lanham, Md.: University Press of America.

Tripp, Aili Mari. 1989. "Women and the Changing Urban Household Economy in Tanzania." *Journal of Modern African Studies* 27, 4:601–623.

———. 1993. "The Impact of Crisis and Economic Reform on Women in Urban Tanzania." In *Unequal Burden: Economic Crises, Persistent Poverty, and Women's Work*, ed. Lourdes Benería and Shelley Feldman, 159–180. Boulder: Westview.

Twumasi, Patrick A. 1979. "The Working Day of a Woman Trader: Is Trade an Easy Job?" *Journal of Management Studies* (Legon, Ghana) 2, 2 (2d series): 87–91.

Uyanga, Joseph. 1976. "Family Size and the Participation of Women in Labor Force: A Nigerian Case Study." *African Urban Notes* 2, 2:59–72.

Van der Vaeren-Aguessy, D. 1966. "Les femmes commerçantes au détail sur les marchés dakarois." In *The New Elites of Tropical Africa*, ed. P. C. Lloyd, 244–255. Oxford: Oxford University Press.

Vandersypen, Marijke. 1977. "Femmes libres de Kigali." *Cahiers d'études africaines* 17, 1:95–120.

Verhaegen, Benoît. 1990. *Femmes zairoises de Kisangani: Combats pour la survie*. Paris: L'Harmattan.

Wachtel, Eleanor. 1976. "Minding Her Own Business: Women Shopkeepers in Nakuru, Kenya." *African Urban Notes* 2, 2:27–42.

White, E. Frances. 1981. "Creole Women Traders in the Nineteenth Century." *International Journal of African Historical Studies* 14, 4:626–642.

White, Luise. 1980. *Women's Domestic Labor in Colonial Kenya: Prostitution in Nairobi, 1909–1950*. African Studies Center Working Papers, no. 30. Boston: Boston University.

———. 1983. "A Colonial State and an African Petty Bourgeoisie: Prostitution, Property, and Class Struggle in Nairobi, 1936–1940." In *Struggle for the City: Migrant Labor, Capital, and the State in Urban Africa*, ed. Frederick Cooper, 167–194. Beverly Hills, Calif.: Sage.

———. 1986. "Prostitution, Identity, and Class Consciousness in Nairobi During World War II." *Signs* 11, 2:255–273.

———. 1987. "Vice and Vagrants: Prostitution, Housing, and Casual Labor in Nairobi in the Mid-1930s." In *Labour, Law, and Crime: An Historical Perspective*, ed. Francis Snyder and Douglas Hay, 202–227. New York: Tavistock.

———. 1988. "Domestic Labor in a Colonial City: Prostitution in Nairobi, 1900–1950." In *Patriarchy and Class: African Women in the Home and the Workplace*, ed. Sharon B. Stichter and Jane L. Parpart, 139–160. Boulder: Westview.

———. 1990. *The Comforts of Home: Prostitution in Colonial Nairobi.* Chicago: University of Chicago Press.

Zack-Williams, A. B. 1985. "Female Urban Employment." In *Women in Nigeria Today*, ed. Women in Nigeria, 104–113. London: Zed.

City Streets: Politics and Community

Beik, Janet. 1991. "Women's Roles in the Contemporary Hausa Theater of Niger." In *Hausa Women in the Twentieth Century*, ed. Catherine Coles and Beverly Mack, 232–243. Madison: University of Wisconsin Press.

Bernstein, Hilda. 1975. *For Their Triumphs and for Their Tears: Conditions and Resistance of Women in Apartheid South Africa.* London: International Defence and Aid Fund.

Callaway, Barbara J. 1991. "The Role of Women in Kano City Politics." In *Hausa Women in the Twentieth Century*, ed. Catherine Coles and Beverly Mack, 145–159. Madison: University of Wisconsin Press.

Cole, Josette. 1987. *Crossroads: The Politics of Reform and Repression, 1976–1986.* Johannesburg: Ravan.

Constaninides, Pamela. 1979. "Women's Spirit Possession and Urban Adaptation in the Muslim Northern Sudan." In *Women United, Women Divided: Comparative Studies of Ten Contemporary Cultures*, ed. Patricia Caplan and Janet M. Bujra, 185–205. Bloomington: Indiana University Press.

Davies, Carole Boyce. 1993. "Epilogue: Representations of Urban Life in African Women's Literature." In *Women's Lives and Public Policy: The International Experience*, ed. Meredeth Turshen and Briavel Holcomb, 171–181. Westport, Conn.: Greenwood.

de Jongh, Michael. 1970. "The Ciskei Zenzele Women's Association—a Study in Selective Cultural Adaptation to Change." In *Culture Change in Contemporary Africa*, ed. Brian du Toit, 13–24. Gainesville: University of Florida Center for African Studies.

Dennis, Carolyne. 1987. "Women and the State in Nigeria: The Case of the Federal Military Government, 1984–5." In *Women, State, and Ideology: Studies from Africa and Asia*, ed. Haleh Afshar, 13–27. Albany: State University of New York.

Denzer, LaRay. 1987. "Women in Freetown Politics, 1914–61: A Preliminary Study." *Africa* 57, 4:439–455.

Eames, Elizabeth A. 1988. "Why the Women Went to War: Women and Wealth in Ondo Town, Southwestern Nigeria." In *Traders Versus the State: Anthropological Approaches to Unofficial Economies*, ed. Gracia Clark, 81–97. Boulder: Westview.

El-Nagar, Samia El-Hadi. 1980. "Zaar Practitioners and Their Assistants and Followers in Omdurman." In *Urbanization and Urban Life in the Sudan*, ed. Valdo Pons, 672–688. Hull, England: University of Hull, Department of Sociology and Social Anthropology.

Gaitskell, Deborah. 1979. "'Christian Compounds for Girls': Church Hostels for African Women in Johannesburg, 1907–1970." *Journal of Southern African Studies* 6, 1:44–69.

————. 1982. "'Wailing for Purity': Prayer Unions, African Mothers and Adolescent Daughters, 1912–1940." In *Industrialisation and Social Change in South Africa: African Class Formation, Culture, and Consciousness, 1870–1930*, ed. Shula Marks and Richard Rathbone, 338–357. London: Longman.

Geiger, Susan. 1987. "Women in Nationalist Struggle: TANU Activists in Dar es Salaam." *International Journal of African Historical Studies* 20, 1:1–26.

Gwagwa, Nolulamo N. 1991. "Women in Local Government: Towards a Future South Africa." *Environment and Urbanization* 3, 1:70–78.

Hackett, Rosalind I. J. 1985. "Sacred Paradoxes: Women and Religious Plurality in Nigeria." In *Women, Religion, and Social Change*, ed. Yvonne Yazbeck Haddad and Ellison Banks Findly, 247–271. Albany: State University of New York Press.

Imam, Ayesha M. 1991. "Ideology, the Mass Media, and Women: A Case Study from Radio Kaduna, Nigeria." In *Hausa Women in the Twentieth Century*, ed. Catherine Coles and Beverly Mack, 244–252. Madison: University of Wisconsin Press.

Jacobs, Susie M., and Tracey Howard. 1987. "Women in Zimbabwe: Stated Policy and State Action." In *Women, State, and Ideology: Studies from Africa and Asia*, ed. Haleh Afshar, 28–47. Albany: State University of New York Press.

Johnson, Cheryl. 1982. "Grass Roots Organizing: Women in Anticolonial Activity in Southwestern Nigeria." *African Studies Review* 25, 2–3:137–157.

Jules-Rosette, Bennetta. 1981. *Symbols of Change: Urban Transition in a Zambian Community*. Norwood, N.J.: Ablex.

Kappers, Sophieke. 1988. "Sitani—Let's Help Each Other: Women and Informal Savings-, Credit-, and Funeral-Organisations in Swaziland." In *Scenes of Change: Visions on Developments in Swaziland*, ed. Henk J. Tieleman, 163–190. Research Report no. 33. Leiden: African Studies Center.

Keirn, Susan Middleton. 1970. "Voluntary Associations Among Urban African Women." In *Culture Change in Contemporary Africa*, ed. Brian du Toit, 25–40. Gainesville: University of Florida Center for African Studies.

Little, Kenneth. 1972. "Voluntary Associations and Social Mobility Among West African Women." *Canadian Journal of African Studies* 6, 2:275–288.

————. 1980. *The Sociology of Urban Women's Image in African Literature*. Totowa, N.J.: Rowman and Littlefield.

Lyons, Harriet. 1990. "Nigerian Television and the Problems of Urban African Women." In *Culture and Development in Africa*, ed. Stephen H. Arnold and Andre Nitecki, 107–118. Trenton, N.J.: Africa World Press.

Middleton-Keirn, Susan. 1978. "Convivial Sisterhood: Spirit Mediumship and Client-Core Network Among Black South African Women." In *Women in Ritual and Symbolic Roles*, ed. Judith Hoch-Smith and Anita Spring, 191–205. New York: Plenum.

Modic, Kate. 1994. "Negotiating Power: A Study of the Ben Ka Di Women's Association in Bamako, Mali." *Africa Today* 41, 2:25–37.

Newbury, Catherine. 1984. "Ebutumwa Bw'Emiogo: The Tyranny of Cassava, a Women's Tax Revolt in Eastern Zaire." *Canadian Journal of African Studies* 18, 1:35–54.

Peil, Margaret. 1983. "Urban Contacts: A Comparison of Women and Men." In *Female and Male in West Africa*, ed. Christine Oppong, 275–282. London: George Allen and Unwin.

Rörich, Mary. 1989. "Shebeens, Slumyards and Sophiatown: Black Women, Music and Cultural Change in Urban South Africa c. 1920–1960." *World of Music* 31, 1:78–101.

Sargent, Carolyn. 1989. "Women's Roles and Women Healers in Contemporary Rural and Urban Benin." In *Women as Healers: Cross-Cultural Perspectives*, ed. Carol Shepard McClain, 204–218. New Brunswick, N.J.: Rutgers University Press.

Steady, Filomina. 1976. "Protestant Women's Associations in Freetown, Sierra Leone." In *Women in Africa: Studies in Social and Economic Change*, ed. Nancy J. Hafkin and Edna G. Bay. Stanford: Stanford University Press.

Strobel, Margaret. 1976. "From *Lelemama* to Lobbying: Women's Associations in Mombasa, Kenya." In *Women in Africa: Studies in Social and Economic Change*, ed. Nancy J. Hafkin and Edna G. Bay, 183–211. Stanford: Stanford University Press.

———. 1979. *Muslim Women in Mombasa, 1890–1975*. New Haven and London: Yale University Press.

Sylvester, Christine. 1991. "'Urban Women Cooperators,' 'Progress,' and 'African Feminism' in Zimbabwe." *Differences* 3, 1:39–62.

Tripp, Aili Mari. 1994. "Deindustrialisation and the Growth of Women's Economic Associations and Networks in Urban Tanzania." In *Dignity and Daily Bread: New Forms of Economic Organising Among Poor Women in the Third World and the First*, ed. Sheila Rowbotham and Swasti Mitter, 138–157. New York: Routledge.

Van Allen, Judith. 1976. "'Aba Riots' or Igbo 'Women's War'? Ideology, Stratification, and the Invisibility of Women." In *Women in Africa: Studies in Social and Economic Change*, ed. Nancy J. Hafkin and Edna G. Bay, 58–85. Stanford: Stanford University Press.

Wells, Julia. 1983. "'The Day the Town Stood Still': Women in Resistance in Potchefstrom, 1912–1930." In *Town and Countryside in the Transvaal: Capitalist Penetration and Popular Response*, ed. Belinda Bozzoli, 269–307. Johannesburg: Ravan.

Wells, Julia C. 1983. "Why Women Rebel: A Comparative Study of South African Women's Resistance in Bloemfontein (1913) and Johannesburg (1958)." *Journal of Southern African Studies* 10, 1:55–70.

Yacoob, May. 1983. "Ahmadiyya and Urbanization: Migrant Women in Abidjan." African Studies Center Working Papers, no. 75. Boston: Boston University.

———. 1987. "Ahmadiyya and Urbanization: Easing the Integration of Rural Women in Abidjan." In *Rural and Urban Islam in West Africa*, ed. Nehemia Levtzion and Humphrey J. Fisher, 119–134. Boulder: Lynne Rienner.

About the Book and Editor

Although women have long been active residents in African cities, explorations of their contributions have been marginal. This volume brings women into the center of the urban landscape, using case studies to illustrate their contributions to family, community, work, and political life.

The book begins with a rich introduction that discusses how women's work in trade and agriculture has been the foundation of African urbanization. The contributors then focus on patterns of migration and urbanization, with an emphasis on the personal and social issues that influence the decision to migrate from rural areas; women's employment in varied activities from selling crafts to managing small businesses; the sometimes unavoidable practice of prostitution when options are limited; the emergence of complex new family formations deriving from access to courts and the continued strength of polygyny; and women's participation in community and political activities. The volume includes material from all regions of sub-Saharan Africa and brings together scholars from all the social sciences.

Kathleen Sheldon is a visiting lecturer in history at the University of California at Los Angeles and a research scholar at the UCLA Center for the Study of Women.

About the Contributors

Philippe Antoine, a demographer, is director of research at the French Institute of Scientific Research for Development in Cooperation (ORSTOM) and has worked in Algeria and Côte d'Ivoire and most recently in Senegal in collaboration with the Institut Fondamental d'Afrique Noire (IFAN). He is now at the Centre d'Etudes sur la Population et le Développement (CEPED) in Paris. His most recent publications include *La ville à guichets fermé? Itinéraires, réseaux et insertion urbaine* (Dakar: IFAN, 1995) and *Les familles dakaroises face à la crise* (Dakar: IFAN, 1995).

Paulette Beat Songue completed a Ph.D. in sociology at the Université de Lille I, France. She is now in the sociology department of the Université de Yaoundé, Cameroon. She is author of *Prostitution en Afrique: L'exemple de Yaoundé* (Paris: L'Harmattan, 1986) and *SIDA et prostitution au Cameroun* (Paris: L'Harmattan, 1993).

Catherine M. Coles taught anthropology at Dartmouth College before earning a law degree from Boston College. She has written several articles on Hausa women in Nigeria and has coedited (with B. Mack) *Hausa Women in the Twentieth Century* (Madison: University of Wisconsin Press, 1991).

Miriam Grant, an assistant professor of geography at the University of Calgary, Canada, completed a Ph.D. in geography at Queen's University, Canada. She has presented a number of papers on housing issues in Zimbabwe.

Karen Tranberg Hansen is an associate professor of anthropology at Northwestern University. Since the early 1970s, she has conducted extensive research in Zambia on colonial culture, urban work, gender and household dynamics, and development questions. She is author of *Distant Companions: Servants and Employers in Zambia* (Ithaca: Cornell University Press, 1989) and is editor of *African Encounters with Domesticity* (New Brunswick, N.J.: Rutgers University Press, 1992).

Dorothy McCormick is a senior research fellow at the University of Nairobi's Institute for Development Studies. Her papers and publications on Kenyan industry and economics include *Risk and Firm Growth: The Dilemma of Nairobi's Small-Scale Manufacturers* (University of Nairobi, 1993).

Jeanne Nanitelamio, a psychologist, is currently a researcher in Dakar, Senegal, at IFAN. Among other works, she and Philippe Antoine have published "More Single Women in African Cities: Pikine, Abidjan, and Brazzaville," *Population English Selection* 3 (1991).

John Nauright is a lecturer in the Department of Human Movement Studies at the University of Queensland, Australia. He is the coeditor of *Rugby and National Identity* (London, 1995) and author of numerous articles on the history of gender and sport in South Africa and New Zealand.

Mary Johnson Osirim is an associate professor of sociology and director of the African Studies Consortium at Bryn Mawr College. She has published several articles on women in Nigeria and Zimbabwe, including "Gender and Entrepreneurship: Issues of Capital and Technology in Nigerian Small Firms," in *Privatization and Investment in Sub-Saharan Africa*, ed. R. Ahene and B. Katz (New York: Praeger, 1992).

Sean Redding is an associate professor of history at Amherst College. Her articles on women and social history in South Africa include "Legal Minors and Social Children: Rural African Women and Taxation in the Transkei, South Africa," *African Studies Review* 36, 3 (1993).

Claire C. Robertson is an associate professor of history and women's studies at Ohio State University. In addition to publishing a number of articles on women in Ghana and Kenya, she is author of *Sharing the Same Bowl* (Bloomington: Indiana University Press, 1984) and has coedited (with M. Klein) *Women and Slavery in Africa* (Madison: University of Wisconsin Press) and (with I. Berger) *Women and Class in Africa* (New York: Holmes and Meier).

Brooke Grundfest Schoepf, an independent scholar and consultant, has published extensively on issues concerning women and health in Zaire, most recently focusing on AIDS. She has previously taught at the Tuskegee Institute in Alabama, the University of Connecticut, and the Université Nationale du Zaire. Recent articles include "Culture, Sex Research and AIDS Prevention in Africa," in *Culture and Sexual Risk: Anthropological Perspectives on AIDS*, ed. H. Brummelhuis and G. Herdt (New York: Gordon and Breach, 1994) and "AIDS, Gender and Economic Crisis in Central Africa," in *African Women: States of Crisis*, ed. G. Mikell (Los Angeles: University of California Press, 1994).

Aili Mari Tripp is an assistant professor in political science at the University of Wisconsin, Madison. Her publications on Tanzania, women, politics, and labor include "Local Organizations, Participation, and the State in Urban Tanzania," in *Governance in Africa*, ed. M. Bratton and G. Hyden (Boulder: Lynne Rienner, 1992).

Index

4865